MODERN HEBREW LITERATURE

Library of Jewish Studies

MODERN HEBREW LITERATURE

Edited, with introductions and notes, by

ROBERT ALTER

BEHRMAN HOUSE, INC. | PUBLISHERS | NEW YORK

ACKNOWLEDGMENTS

The author and publisher thank the following for permission to reprint:

The American Jewish Committee and *Commentary* for S. Y. Agnon, "The Lady and the Peddler," tr., Robert Alter, © 1966; for H. N. Bialik, "Revealment and Concealment in Language," tr., Jacob Sloan © 1950.

Doubleday and Company for A. B. Yehoshua, "Facing the Forests," tr., Miriam Arad, in *Three Days and a Child,* © 1970.

Institute for the Translation of Hebrew Literature for Yehuda Amichai, "The Times My Father Died," tr., Yosef Schacter, in *Hebrew Short Stories,* © 1965; for Asher Barash, "At Heaven's Gate," tr., Yosef Schacter, in *Hebrew Short Stories,* © 1965; for Y. H. Brenner, "The Way Out," tr., Yosef Schacter, in *Hebrew Short Stories,* © 1965; for S. Yizhar, "The Prisoner," tr., V. C. Rycus, © 1962.

Holt, Rinehart and Winston, Inc., for Haim Hazaz, "Rahamim," tr., I. M. Lask, in *The Jewish Caravan,* © 1935.

The Jewish Publication Society of America for Ahad Ha-am, "Imitation and Assimilation," tr., Leon Simon, in *Selected Essays,* © 1912; for H. N. Bialik, "The Short Friday," tr., I. M. Lask, in *Aftergrowth,* © 1939; for M. Z. Feierberg, "In the Evening," tr., Hillel Halkin, in *Whither? and Other Stories,* © 1972.

Amos Oz for "Before His Time," tr., Gavriel Moses, © 1965.

Schocken Books Inc., for S. Y. Agnon, "Agunot," tr., Baruch Hochman, in *Twenty-One Stories,* © 1970; for S. Y. Agnon, "At the Outset of the Day," tr., David S. Segal, in *Twenty-One Stories,* © 1970; for S. Y. Agnon, "Forevermore," tr., Joel Blocker, [revised for this volume by Robert Alter], in *Israeli Stories,* ed., Joel Blocker, © 1962; for Haim Hazaz, "The Sermon," tr., Ben Halpern, in *Israeli Stories,* ed., Joel Blocker, © 1962.

Zionist Organization, Youth and Hechalutz Department, for Mendele Mocher Sforim, "Shem and Japheth on the Train," tr., Walter Lever, © 1952.

Library of Congress Cataloging in Publication Data

Main entry under title:

Modern Hebrew literature.

(Library of Jewish studies)
Bibliography: p.
CONTENTS: Mendele Mocher Sforim. Shem and Japheth
on the train.—Peretz, Y. L. Scenes from Limbo.—
Feierberg, M. Z. In the evening. [etc.]
    1. Short stories, Hebrew—Translations into English.
2. Short stories, English—Translations from Hebrew.
I. Alter, Robert.
PZ1.M7193   [PJ5059.E8]   892.4'3'01   75-9928
ISBN 0-87441-218-8

For
Gabriel Zvi

CONTENTS

PREFACE

SINCE THIS ANTHOLOGY constitutes a small selection from a large and varied body of literature, a few words are in order about the principles of selection. To begin with, poetry is excluded, mainly because the element of falsification in any translation is multiplied many times in the translation of poetry, and the problems of translating Hebrew poetry are particularly forbidding. The major Hebrew poets of the earlier twentieth century, to the extent that they have been translated at all, are available in English in versions that are, at best, unfortunate. Some of the more recent poets—most notably Yehuda Amichai and Dan Pagis—have fared much better in English translation, but that still leaves three previous generations rather badly represented. *The Modern Hebrew Poem Itself,* edited by Burnshaw, Carmi, and Spicehandler, is an interesting experiment in presenting the poems with literal prose translations and running explications, and it might usefully be consulted in conjunction with the present anthology, but its method of presentation makes it a little difficult to experience the poems fluently as poetry.

The exclusion of poetry here is bound to give a somewhat misleading general picture of modern Hebrew literature because many of its finest achievements are in verse. Thus, a major figure like the poet Saul Tchernichovsky is unrepresented in the anthology, and H. N. Bialik appears as a writer of prose, though his greatest accomplishment is of course his poetry. And even within the limits of prose, the anthology could not include all the important currents of Hebrew literature since the Enlightenment. A good many stories had to be eliminated from consideration simply because of their length, or because their subject matter or specific allusions would make them inaccessible without a cumbersome apparatus of notes and explanations. The selection, attempting to follow a central line of historical development within modern Hebrew literature, also does not do justice to the varieties of Hebrew fiction more concerned with strictly private experience. Finally, the choices for the anthology are intended to reflect one peculiarity of modern Hebrew literature —that there are a very few Hebrew writers who stand above the rest, with Bialik and Agnon generally undisputed as the two major creative figures. For this reason it seemed sensible to give greater weight to more important writers, representing Agnon with four stories that might suggest something of his range, and offering two important prose pieces by Bialik that are interesting in themselves and provide very different intimations of the poet in the writer of prose. The authors have been arranged in approximate chronological order, in the hope this might help readers to puzzle out patterns of continuity, recurrence, and change in a body of literature that stretches from the Russia of the tsars to the Israel of our own time.

Something should be said about the translations since they constitute a special problem. With three exceptions, I have used already existing translations, which was, of course, another limiting factor in the selections. All of the translations, however, have been carefully compared with the originals, and this means that in some cases substantial revisions had to be made. A few of the changes were to eliminate glaring infelicities or outright errors in English usage; most were to correct plain misconstruals of the Hebrew. Hebrew unfortunately resembles Russian in being a language for which it is always hard to find reliable translators. Many of the translations included here appear only in periodicals or in books long out of print; but even for those selections available in other volumes still in print in this country, the present versions have been modified—in a few instances extensively—to remove the more egregious betrayals of the original. In these circumstances, one owes a special debt of gratitude to the rare translator from the Hebrew who is both stylistically gifted and precise. Special mention should be made of Hillel Halkin's sensitive rendering of Feierberg, Jacob Sloan's adept version of Bialik's difficult expository prose, and Baruch Hochman's tour de force in creating an English equivalent for Agnon's archaized Hebrew. All points of ellipsis and parentheses in the texts of the selections are the authors'. The explanatory footnotes are the editor's except where the initials of the translator or author are given at the end of the note.

Obviously, any anthology of this sort cannot be much more than a taste of the unfamiliar. If the collection succeeds, at least some readers may feel enough curiosity to want to read more. Complete books—novels, collections of stories, poems, or essays—by most of the writers included are now available in English, and a list of suggested readings, with bibliographical data, appears at the end of this volume. It is hard to think of another field of modern Jewish cultural activity that provides, as does Hebrew literature, such a luminous mirror both of the creative élan and of the deep perplexities of Jews trying to define some relationship to an age-old heritage in a radically unfamiliar new world. It is hoped that the present volume, both texts and critical prefaces, will serve as an introduction to that double-faceted reflective power of Hebrew literature since the Enlightenment.

Typing costs and clerical assistance for this volume were paid for by a grant-in-aid from the Committee on Research of the University of California at Berkeley.

MODERN HEBREW LITERATURE

INTRODUCTION

THE HISTORY of modern Hebrew literature makes it in some ways the most peculiar of modern literatures. By all rights, it hardly should have been able to come into being in the first place. Once in existence, it should hardly have been able to maintain itself for a century and a half on European soil among a group of Jews who did not use Hebrew as a spoken language. Finally, no reasonable observer would have predicted that such a literature, subsisting in the meager hand-to-mouth way it did from one small center of Hebrew cultural activity to the next, could have ended by producing works of real genius in both poetry and prose.

The beginnings of modern Hebrew literature can be traced back to the latter part of the eighteenth century in Prussia, to the circles in Koenigsberg and Berlin associated with the prominent German Jewish Enlightenment philosopher, Moses Mendelssohn. Now, Hebrew, though it had not been the spoken language of the Jewish people since late in the biblical period, had continued as very much a living tongue in a variety of uses throughout the Middle Ages. Communal records were kept in Hebrew; correspondence, both business and private, was often maintained in Hebrew; chronicles, meditative and devotional works, guidebooks of morality, were regularly written in Hebrew; and the great philosophic works of

1

the Islamic period, originally written in Judeo-Arabic, generally enjoyed currency among European Jews in Hebrew translation. Hebrew writing, however, that could be called belletristic in any modern sense was infrequent through this long Diaspora experience. The bulk of the poetry that was composed was liturgical, or at any rate devotional, the poet usually writing on behalf of the community of believers with no sense of an individual "I" recreating its distinctive experience in poetry.

There was, to be sure, one remarkable exception to this general pattern: the flowering of Hebrew literature, in emulation of Arabic models, that took place in the Iberian peninsula beginning toward the end of the tenth century. Rich secular poetry and some forms of secular fiction were written in Hebrew in Spain and Provence from the eleventh to the fourteenth centuries; the Spanish tradition was continued, chiefly in Italy, through the Renaissance down into the eighteenth century. Nevertheless, the new, fundamentally secular, Hebrew literature that began in Enlightenment Germany was different because of its strong sense of itself as a purposeful *movement*. For the first time, the act of putting Hebrew to literary use became what we today would call ideological—that is, part of a general program for changing the social, cultural, even political conditions of a large group of people. When Immanuel of Rome in the fourteenth century wrote bawdy poems in Hebrew, archly turning biblical meanings inside out, he was participating as a Hebraist in a mode of contemporary Italian culture with no real sense of conflict between his identities as Italian and Jew. When Naphtali Hirz Weisel in late eighteenth-century Germany writes an epic on the life of Moses in emulation of Klopstock, the act is programmatic, seeking to convert Jewish culture into a reasonable facsimile of enlightened high-bourgeois German culture; and thus the poet, instead of playing freely with a European form as did Immanuel, gives us a poetic protagonist who is a didactically insistent embodiment of the values of reason, enlightened pragmatism, and decorum.

As it gradually became possible during the later eighteenth century for Jews in Western Europe to leave the walled-off life of the ghetto and enter into modern European society, some Jewish intellectuals, associated with the merchant and managerial classes, adopted Hebrew as the means of creating a new kind of Jewish culture that might take its place with the cultures of other peoples in a progressive international society of enlightened men. (The progressive cosmopolitanism of the European Enlightenment touched these Jews deeply.) In their eyes, Yiddish could not serve this purpose because it was a low "jargon," associated with their remembrances of the ghetto—and, one might add, linked with their own self-rejection. To adopt German exclusively, on the other hand, would have meant the renunciation of Jewish cultural distinctiveness —of all the historical memories, associations, and emphases of feeling, that a people stores in its own language. When an eighteenth century German Jew, then, decided to write a poem on spring, an essay on educational reform, a satirical sketch, in Hebrew rather than in his native Yiddish or his acquired German, he was strenuously affirming a new relationship as a Jew both to modern culture and to the Jewish past, and through this he was proposing a model for others. The Hebrew term itself chosen for "Enlightenment," *Haskalah*, suggests both a state of being and an active causative effect on others: a *maskil*, or proponent of Haskalah, is, according to grammatical context, a person who understands or one who induces understanding in others. This early sense of national purpose, it should be noted, and this effort of cultural self-definition, continue in radically transformed ways to play an important role in Hebrew writing down to many Israeli contemporaries, as the readings in this volume will indicate.

Wherever assimilation became widespread, Hebrew literature quickly disappeared, for the obvious reason that with assimilation the audience of readers who knew Hebrew through the traditional Jewish educational system rapidly dwindled, then vanished. *Ha-Measef*, the first journal of the Haskalah, founded in Koenigsberg as a monthly in 1783, declined into an annual in the 1790s, and by 1797 it had only 120 subscribers. By the 1830s, the main center of Hebrew literary activity had moved eastward from Germany to Galicia (the eastern end of the old Austro-Hungarian Empire) where Jewish population was more concentrated and traditional life stronger. A generation or two later, though significant Hebrew writing continued in Galicia, the most important centers had moved still further eastward to Poland and Russia.

This new Hebrew literature was by no means a mass movement. Typically, it would focus in some large town—Vienna, Lemberg, Warsaw, Vilna, Odessa—where emancipated Hebrew intellectuals (in general, former *yeshiva* students, self-made refugees from the small Jewish villages) would gather to put out a Hebrew newspaper or literary magazine and spread the good word of "Enlightenment" to their fellow Jews. *Ha-Measef,* the path-blazing Prussian-based journal, gasped its last in 1829 after years of intermittent publication. Meanwhile, a new Hebrew periodical had been launched in Vienna, *Bikkurei Ha-Ittim* (1820–1831), to be followed there in the next generation by *Kerem Hemed* (1833–1856). The two Galician journals tended to have more of a scholarly-historical emphasis than did *Ha-Measef,* but the general effect of a didactic miscellany was never lost, even as a whole series of more sophisticated periodicals in the course of time were established in the cities under tsarist rule where there were Jewish centers, culminating in *Ha-Shiloah* of Odessa in the late nineteenth and early twentieth century. These publications at best would have a circulation of a few thousand, sometimes of no more than a few hundred, and since the Orthodox community vehemently opposed the new secular writing, the journals were often read secretly in the provinces as a kind of underground literature. One must add that most of what was written during the Hebrew Enlightenment was characterized far more by earnestness than by originality or accomplished literary art. The poetry often seems composed mainly to prove that it is possible to write poems in Hebrew, or to demonstrate that there is something intrinsically poetic or "sublime" in the language of the Hebrew of the Bible. Altogether, a sterile infatuation with the Hebrew language in and of itself plagues Haskalah writing to the end. The essays, generally directed to topical questions concerning Jewish education and culture and the reform of Jewish society, are more of historical than of literary interest. The fiction, often a satirical exposure of the oppressiveness or rigidity of the old rabbinic authorities, is generally awkward in style and narrative method, and primitive in characterization.

Nevertheless, the literature survived, continuing to inspire loyalty in its readers and to have enormous personal meaning for them, perhaps because of the sheer fact, that whatever its faults, it was, after all, a developing modern literature in Hebrew. There were a few instances of interesting individual talent through the middle years of the nineteenth century, but Hebrew literature attained real maturity only after the Haskalah period, which Hebrew literary historians conventionally end around 1881. There was, for reasons that are not hard to imagine, a curious time lag in the mental world of the Haskalah. Its proponents still cherished the values of Frederick the Great, Voltaire, and Lessing at a point when cosmopolitanism and calm reason were forgotten dreams in European history and a fiercely assertive new nationalism was making itself felt everywhere. A full generation after the main wave of European Romanticism, some Haskalah writers do begin to produce idylls and to celebrate, decorously, the passionate aspects of life, but the more powerful themes—both in a literary and a political sense—of European Romanticism (like the engagement with the irrational and the occult, and the affirmation of organic national community) remain quite beyond the maskilim.

It took some historical shock waves impacting directly on European Jewry to change this whole orientation. By 1881 anti-Semitism in the West was established as a supposedly scientific doctrine and was already being translated into official edicts of restriction and banishment in Bismarck's new Germany. Mendele's story, "Shem and Japheth on the Train," included in this volume, vividly reflects this situation. In 1881 Alexander II was assassinated; the succession to the throne of Alexander III led to a new order of repressive reaction in Russia, with Jews among the principal victims. Jews were forced out of the smaller towns in the Pale of Settlement; with transparent government collusion, they were exposed to waves of murderous pogroms. "A third will die," as Pobedonostsev, one of Alexander's most infamous ministers, grimly put it, "a third will convert, and a third will leave." In these harsh circumstances, the cosmopolitan assumptions of the Haskalah were obviously no longer tenable, and they were replaced by a new quest for connection with the Jewish people by Hebrew writers. For some, this took the form of an incipient political nationalism, a sort of proto-Zionism. (Zionism as a political movement did not begin until the very last years of the century.) For some, it meant a return to the folk, an interest in its ways and traditions, a sympathy for its plight which did not, however, exclude satire. Now, this bond with the people, which some Hebrew literary historians regard as a form of late Romanticism, was obviously no guarantee of artistic quality; but at least writers were freed from the internal contradition of the Haskalah, where men of literary bent wrote in the classical language of a people from whom they were often profoundly alienated, a people many of them were seeking, perhaps unwittingly, to transcend.

In the 1880s the fiction of Mendele Mocher Sforim established a new high of imaginative complexity and artistic command for Hebrew prose. Beginning in the 1890s, H. N. Bialik's poetry, and soon after, that of Saul Tchernichovsky, gave Hebrew verse a breadth and depth and subtlety of expressiveness that deserve comparison with the best of modern poetry in other languages. After the 1890s there was a rich variety of original work in both poetry and prose on a fairly advanced level of literary sophistication. As in any literature, writing that was shallow or strained or imitative continued in abundance, but in view of the tiny group of potential writers and readers upon which Hebrew literature had to draw, it is remarkable—and to this day for Israel it is still remarkable—how much of quality was produced.

This anthology begins with the coming of age of modern Hebrew literature in the 1880s, and begins with a major writer of the Odessa renaissance, where the last and greatest of the European centers of Hebrew culture flourished until the Russian Revolution. It should not be surprising that it took the new literature over a century to mature. At first it had no independent tradition, no set of conventions, no established methods of its own, so it could only imitate European models, and often ones that did not suit it very well, or that were poorly understood. The fundamental problem of language was for a long time overwhelming: an ancient or medieval Hebrew had to be adapted to modern literary needs, made to reflect the inner and outer world of people who did not even use it as a spoken tongue. It was not only a matter of developing a new lexicon for modern things—having Hebrew words for "locomotive" and "factory" and "pharmacy"—but a new lexicon for feelings and motives, even in certain respects a new syntax to express newly assimilated patterns of conceptualizing. Finally, Haskalah literature was often seriously limited by its ideological character. Imaginative literature with a point to prove—or an axe to grind—often ends up being shaped by a narrow, shrilly insistent imagination, more concerned with laying down a program than evoking a complex world. As the Israeli critic Dov Sadan put it, the Haskalah writer, indignant over the ultra-Orthodox Jew who wore a filthy kaftan instead of decent modern European dress, was in no position to describe that Jew in loving detail, as a novelist should, down to the last spot of grease on the kaftan. A touching, but artisically crippling, quality of earnest naiveté persists in Haskalah fiction to the last: all would end well if only Jews would learn European languages, acquire decently productive professions, observe the laws of decorum and hygiene—in short, follow the path of the good *goy* who is the positive hero of a good many Haskalah stories.

In the 1880s, this whole situation began to change fundamentally. After a century of literary activity, Hebrew writers had at least made a start in developing their own viable traditions, and in learning how to assimilate their European literary models. More important, for the reasons we have seen, the old militancy toward the immediate Jewish past relaxed considerably, so that it was easier for a Hebrew writer to do work that was not so insistently ideological. Now it became possible to balance programmatic criticism with intimate insight and affection in rendering the world of East-European Jewry, and no one illustrates the artistic advantages of this new inner freedom more strikingly than Mendele. Perhaps most important, however, is the sudden forward leap of individual genius, which could not have been predicted and cannot be accounted for merely in terms of broad historical causes. It seems almost as though Mendele waved a magic wand and made modern Hebrew prose possible.

Prose style had been one of the most problematic technical features of Haskalah writing. Though in fact there are many available styles to choose from in the three millennia of development which the Hebrew language has undergone, one may speak, broadly, of two basic kinds of Hebrew: biblical Hebrew, which has a relatively small, indigenously Semitic lexicon and is mainly paratactic in syntax; and rabbinic Hebrew, which reflects an enormous lexical influx from Greek, Latin, even Persian, and which is basically hypotactic, with its own distinctive modifications of classical Hebrew grammar and morphology. Philosophical and scholarly prose of the Haskalah did often adopt an uneven mélange of rabbinical Hebrew and later prose models. For prose fiction, on the other hand, the biblical style, with very few exceptions, was felt to be obligatory, as it was in poetry, because the language of the Bible seemed loftier, more decorous, had more cultural prestige, than those forms of Hebrew which were associated with rabbinic discourse and the pre-modern, sequestered existence of the Diaspora. Biblical Hebrew, however, was a terribly cumbersome and inadequate medium for fiction, lacking the requisite resources of vocabulary, tightly restricted by the structures of its syntax in the organization of ideas, in the presentation of data about character and situation.

As late as the last generation of the Haskalah, in the Hebrew fiction of the 1860s, the characters hobble around on shaky stilts nailed together from the scraps and splinters of biblical verses—the language in which their world and their speech are conveyed. In Mendele's work of the 1880s and 1890s, the characters suddenly are made to move and talk with the lifelike fluidity of real people. Fusing the Hebrew of the Bible, the Mishnah, the Midrash, the rabbinic commentaries, and a wealth of other sources, Mendele is able to give us, for example, a man descending from a sleigh, entering a house, peeling off layers of winter clothing, then lighting his pipe, with all the convincing vividness of a Dickens, a Gogol, a Balzac. Bialik's poetry, in an analogous way, suddenly illuminates layer after layer of past association in the Hebrew words it uses, all brought to bear on the expressive needs of the present, even as the language remains predominantly biblical, in sharp contrast to Haskalah poetry, which was so often a lifeless mosaic of biblical phrases. In a less spectacular way, the disciplined clarity of language in Ahad Ha-am's essays helps establish a new kind of expository prose, adapting Hebrew to modern requirements of analytic generalization.

While these decisive advances in style were being made, new qualities of innerness, emotional subtlety, introspective self-confrontation, began to manifest themselves in both poetry and prose. The cultural time lag of which I have written began to narrow noticeably. Hebrew became more a medium of intensely personal expression at the same time that it was often used, now in a non-ideological, unprogrammatic way, to probe the bewildering predicament of tradition-bound Jewry thrust into a modern world where it could not feel at home. Thus the didactic concerns of the Haskalah became existential concerns, these writers only being more acutely aware than writers in firmly established national groups of the collective contexts for individual existence. The new complexity of consciousness among Hebrew writers also gradually led to experiments with literary form. Hebrew poetry would remain formally traditionalist until the 1920s, but by the first decade of the twentieth century one Hebrew writer in Russia, Uri Nissan Gnessin, was already experimenting with a mode of interior monologue, and in Palestine the Galician-born Shmuel Yosef Agnon, at the beginning of his long career, was already reaching toward new possibilities of symbolism, expressionist fantasy, and structuring through motif.

For Hebrew writers in Russia, the most interesting recent achievements of Russian literature now began to be imaginatively assimilable; the same was true of recent German literature for writers in the Austro-Hungarian cultural sphere.

Although not all European Hebrew writers of the twentieth century have been Zionists, when the first awakenings of the idea of a return to Zion stirred Russian Jewry in the 1880s, the new movement understandably had particularly strong support among the Hebraists: from an "as-if" Hebrew reality of fiction and poetry—the notion is Dov Sadan's—the writers, with the din of spreading pogroms in their ears, started to think of creating a Hebrew reality in fact, with a real geographical location. As the new Zionist settlement in Palestine began to grow during the first decade of the twentieth century, some of the young men aspiring to be Hebrew writers emigrated to Palestine very early in their careers. Among the figures included in this volume, Brenner left Russia in his mid-twenties, Agnon and Barash arrived in Palestine from Galicia at an even younger age. In any case, World War I and the Russian Revolution effectively destroyed the Hebrew literary movement in Europe. Most of the important writers in the Odessa center and elsewhere in Russia managed to get out of the country by the early 1920s. (Within a few years after the revolution, Hebrew was declared a "counter-revolutionary" language in the Soviet Union, and the few brave souls who persisted in writing Hebrew, at one point or another generally found themselves in an interrogation chamber of the secret police, or in a labor camp.) Some of the Russian Hebrew writers lingered for a while in France or Germany, but after World War I the center of Hebrew literary activity decisively shifted to Palestine. There was a contemporaneous attempt among East-European Hebraists who had emigrated to the United States to transplant Hebrew literature to America, but despite some interesting individual works, the experiment failed, largely because the Russian situation of cultural and linguistic pluralism did not obtain in the U.S. As for the writers in Palestine during this formative period, most of them were European by birth and education, and though many labored to adapt themselves to the new cultural reality and the new natural landscape, their relation to the Hebrew language and their sense of reality remained in many respects those of the European generations before them.

In the 1940s, before and during the emergence of the new

Jewish state, the first full generation of native Israeli writers became active—the first generation that learned Hebrew naturally as a spoken language and not through the intense study of traditional Hebrew texts. Prose writing now sought to incorporate the new colloquial language in a variety of ways, though, as the literary critic Gershon Shaked has convincingly demonstrated, the writers of this generation also strained after heavily rhetorical literary effects, perhaps compensating for a sense of unsureness about the new Hebrew with which they were working. They knew traditional Hebrew sources imperfectly, and occasionally made the mistake of imitating them badly. Unlike their European-born predecessors, they also were not completely at home in any language beside Hebrew, and so here, too, their imitation of literary models (for the most part, now, English and American) tended to be faulty. In any case, the very fact that Hebrew writers now drew upon a bona fide vernacular meant the normalization of a literature that previously had developed under entirely peculiar conditions. It also meant, in some respects, a painful need to make a fresh beginning after almost two centuries of modern Hebrew literary activity, some of it on an impressively high level. But Hebrew literature in Israel has not yet become altogether normalized, partly because Israel's historical predicament is far from normal, partly because the Hebrew past—both the immediate one in Europe and the literary heritage that goes back to the Bible—continues to have a powerful hold on the imagination of many Hebrew writers, however much they direct their attention to the contemporary realities of the kibbutz, the struggle with the Arabs, the quality of life in the new and the changing Israeli cities. It is instructive that younger Israeli writers have recently evinced growing interest in some of the early twentieth-century, European-born Hebrew writers like Y. H. Brenner, M. Y. Berdichevski, and Gnessin, in addition to the imposing model of Agnon.

For reasons which may be clear even from this rapid historical sketch, Hebrew literature has been rather more explicitly concerned with problems of Jewish identity and the fate or future of the Jewish people than, say, American literature has been concerned with American identity and American destiny (though the ultimate difference may be only in explicitness, not in degree). In one important respect, literature written in Hebrew offers a uniquely valuable key to the difficulties of being a Jew in the modern world. Its medium is the language of Jewish tradition, the language in which the values and ideals and imperatives of classical Judaism were crystallized. Though this is less true of Israeli Hebrew as it draws on the new colloquial patterns of the revived language, surprising continuities with the past persist even there, particularly in poetry but sometimes in prose as well. The literary forms, however, that Hebrew literature adopts are of course modern and Western. The social and historical realities with which it works are distinctly part of the post-traditional world we all live in, whatever loyalties we may aspire to maintain to an older tradition.

The act of writing in Hebrew, then, often seems to be an attempt to bridge—or to measure—the gap between the old and the new, between the world of Jewish tradition and the realm of upheaval and confusion that the modern era so often seems to be. Ahad Ha-am's "Imitation and Assimilation" is an attempt to create such a bridge, while Mendele's "Shem and Japheth on the Train," by contrast, defines the gap through irony, and Peretz's "Scenes from Limbo" does something similar through a more direct social panorama. Hazaz's "The Sermon" is a public declaration of divorce of the new from the old, while Feierberg's "In the Evening," Agnon's "The Lady and the Peddler," and Amichai's "The Times My Father Died," all, in very different ways, record the pain or terror of separation from the older world with its secure values. The stories in the volume by Brenner and Yizhar make us confront the agonizing difficulties of carrying out traditional ethical ideals in a brutally harsh new historical setting; A. B. Yehoshua's "Facing the Forests" goes a step further by showing how a malaise of troubled national conscience can flow into the enactment of suicidal fantasy. At least one of the stories here, Agnon's "At the Outset of the Day," proves in the end to be the affirmation of a deep imaginative connection with the vanished world of the European Jewish past, though the affirmation must be made through the obliquities and ambiguities of a dreamlike narrative mode.

At first thought, this overarching concern with Jewish historical destiny may seem to limit the scope of Hebrew literature, diminishing its universality. Some reflection, however, may suggest that the idea of a "universal man" is merely an abstraction, that men always have to live in particular societies, struggling to realize themselves as individuals and as groups with the materials of a particular culture. These literary experiments in self-definition, then, these various broodings over the puzzle of Jewishness in the modern age, are at least implicity connected with the larger question of what it means to be a man, or to live a genuinely human life, at this troubled point in history.

It is, of course, quite possible to be concerned with Jewish national self-interest in a narrow, parochial way; but the writers represented in this volume, whatever their limitations, do not set up any opposition between being a Jew and being a man—at its worst moments, that was a dichotomy that dogged the psychology of the Haskalah. Imagining the Jew in his concrete historical difficulties implies for them a full imagination of mankind, and of individual human life; and this complex subject they set in distinctive perspective by bringing to bear on it the special literary resources of Hebrew—ancient, medieval, and modern.

SHEM AND JAPHETH
ON THE TRAIN

MENDELE MOCHER SFORIM

INTRODUCTION

MENDELE MOCHER SFORIM *("Mendele the Bookseller," penname for S. Y. Abramowitz, 1836–1917), enjoys the distinction of being the father of both the Hebrew and the Yiddish novel. He began writing in Hebrew in the 1860s in the stiff biblical style then in literary use, but found the language too artificial, and his audience too limited, so switched to Yiddish. During the next twenty years he made himself the first modern master of Yiddish fiction. Then, as a mature artist moving back to Hebrew, he was able to give that language life and suppleness by calling on all its varied resources accumulated through centuries of development. In his stories and novels about the miserably poor Jews of the little villages in the Russian Pale of Settlement, Mendele mingles irony, playful humor, satiric sharpness, and affection in an elusive combination about which critics are still debating. He was the first Hebrew writer to achieve a fully convincing detailed fictional representation of the familiar social world of nineteenth-century Russian Jewry, always emphasizing its abysmal material conditions.*

The immediate historical setting for "Shem and Japheth on the Train" is Bismarck's chancellorship (1871–1890) in the newly created German imperial state which became the principal European focus for two closely related historical phenomena—modern nationalism and modern anti-Semitism. With the new German stress on an "organic" national community that was supposed to maintain a homogeneous national culture, even loyal native German Jews were held in profound suspicion. Resident-aliens, like the Polish Jew and the Christian Pole of the story, were actually expelled by Bismarckian decrees in 1880. It was against this background that age-old Gentile hostility toward Jews took a new form: a purportedly scientific theory of the relations between races and the inherent characteristics of the different races that went under the name of anti-Semitism.

Reb Moshe and Panie (Polish for Mr.) Przecszwinczicki are thus called Shem (or Sem) and Japheth in allusion to the biblical names adopted by the new racist theory. The title specifically involves a verse from Genesis (9:27): "God shall enlarge Japheth and he shall dwell in the tents of Shem." Japheth was taken by Jewish tradition as the ancestor of the Greeks, and by extension, of the Europeans or Christians, while Shem was understood to be the progenitor of the Hebrews. According to the ahistorical interpretation of this verse found in the Midrash, the "tents of Shem" were the studyhouse where the ancestor of the Jewish people devoted himself to the Law, and Japheth's "dwelling" in them meant his becoming the disciple of Shem, learning from him the intricacies of the Torah. That, of course, is the ironic plot of this story, in which the Jew is named Reb Moshe, or Mr. Moses, the giver of the Law. The Law he teaches to his disciple, however, is only the canny strategems of survival that must be used by a permanent refugee.

The irony of situation is powerfully reinforced by the irony of style, and in this regard it is important to keep in mind the nature of the persona of the bookpeddler that Abramowitz uses here, as elsewhere in his fiction. In a story about rapid and painful historical change, the bookselling narrator—and one must remember, he sells prayerbooks and religious calendars, not, Heaven forbid, novels and poetry—belongs to the old world, thinks in its terms, writes in its pious Hebrew. By his very inability to comprehend the sweep of modern history, the narrator both throws a comic light on it and points up its effects on a Jewish world that cannot change with it. Thus, in answer to Reb Moshe's remark, "It seems you do not know what age we are living in," he makes a confident calculation, beginning with Creation, from the traditional Jewish calendar, but that calendar has no place in it for personalities like Bismarck—

whom Mendele takes to be a doctor—and movements like anti-Semitism.

The persona Mendele adopts a kind of language perfectly appropriate to him, but, unfortunately, very little of its special quality can be conveyed in translation. Mendele uses a Hebrew brilliantly compounded from the Bible, the Talmud, the Midrash, the prayerbook, and other traditional texts, and much of the appeal of his fiction is in the way he adroitly juggles all these sources, and magically transforms them. Sometimes it is for effects of sheer comic play. Thus, the "guard" at the beginning of the story appears much more elaborately in the Hebrew as ha-memuneh al ha-tekiot lemasa et ha-agalot—*literally, "he who is appointed over the* shofar *blasts for the departure of the wagons." This ornate phrase is a willful anachronism that makes the train conductor blowing his whistle look like an ancient trumpeter in the biblical wilderness calling the tribes of Israel to move their camp. Many of the ironic usages of traditional phrases have a more satirical point, adopting the language of a divine revelation fraught with meaning to depict a "fallen" reality where meanings are prosaic, grubby, trivial. Thus, a seemingly indifferent formulation like "no bird flies, no ox lows" recalls the midrashic description of the stillness that seized the world before the giving of the Torah on Sinai, but, here, the end of the series is merely a slumping back in the seat to enjoy a timely sweat. (As elsewhere in Mendele, the pleasures of the average Jew, the high "privileges of the Seed of Abraham," are grossly physical and mundane.) Or again, God in Deuteronomy "opens his goodly treasure, the heavens," while here Chaim opens "the goodly treasures of his knapsack." What happens then, as one Israeli critic has described it, is that the original sacred text is "short-circuited," giving the reader a jolt of new perception.*

The repeated ironic gap between language and its object of reference is heightened by the very situation of the train ride, for the train itself is an alien mode of transportation for Mendele (who in his other stories travels about in a leisurely fashion on a one-horse wagon). The lament over the change to the train from the coach recalls similar passages in Dickens (e.g., the transition from the leisurely world of Pickwick Papers *to the ferocious industrial rush of* Dombey and Son*). In the context of this story, however, that lament carries the specific suggestion that Mendele, the old-style Jew with his prayerbooks and calendars, is out of his medium, hurtled* *forward by a vehicle of historical change he cannot comprehend. The characters exist in a different order from that of the fiction to which we as Western readers are generally accustomed. Mendele goes out of his way not to individualize his characters too much. He wants Reb Moshe and his family to stand for the poor Jewish family in general and in this generalizing way to bring home to the reader the plight of the whole Jewish people at a particular point in history. Similarly, Japheth is a generalized representative type of a whole class of Gentiles.*

Through this generalizing technique, focused in the allusion of the title, Mendele is able to bring a broad historical perspective to the phenomenon of modern anti-Semitism. There is a serious point in Reb Moshe's ironic thrust: "The Germans, who perform miracles of science, have turned the clock back a thousand generations, so that all of us at this day are living in the time of the Flood." A few lines down, the phrase, "the earth is filled with violence," is a direct quotation from the Noah story. One must keep in mind that the biblical generation of the Flood remains in Jewish tradition the great model of universal depravity; it is the generation that created a world so enmired in moral degeneration that its only cure was cataclysmic destruction.

Things seem to be falling apart historically, but Mendele, finally both optimistic moralist and unregenerate sentimentalist, can affirm—against the ravages of this new historical order—the universal solidarity of the empathetic victim: Bible-quoting Jew teaches Gospel-quoting Christian the wiles necessary for survival in a world where nationalist ideologies try to define the powerless and the alien out of existence.

SHEM AND JAPHETH ON THE TRAIN   (1890)
MENDELE MOCHER SFORIM

I

THERE, in haste and confusion, our brethren press on, with bundles
of every size and shape in their hands and on their shoulders;
women too, encumbered with pillows and bolsters and wailing
infants; all jostling one another as they perilously hoist themselves
up the ladder to the third-class compartments, where a fresh
battle will be fought for places in the congested train. And I,
Mendele the Bookseller, burdened with my goods and chattels, join
manfully in the fray: I climb, stoop, and jostle my way through as
one of the crowd. Yet, while we Jews hustle and work ourselves into
a state of frenzied irritability, lest, Heaven forbid, someone should
get ahead of us in the crush, and while we gaze beseechingly upon
the railway employees, as if the fact that we are traveling at all indicates an unrequited act of grace on their part—all this while, the
Gentile passengers are strolling up and down the hallway in front
of the station with their luggage and waiting until the bell rings for
a second or even a third time, when they will mount the train at
leisure, and each proceed to his appointed place.

After the hubbub outside, there is a renewed scramble for seats.
Some lucky ones find places straightaway; others trail up and down

in a fruitless quest. A stout, loquacious female is thrust forward, pushing baskets and bags ahead of her. She trips over them and falls headlong. Lying there, she looks for all the world like a goose bought in the market before Passover, after it has been taken home and the strap untied from its legs. It collapses on the floor with its tail and wings outspread, gazing up in terror, and gasping for air. Now, another woman appears in the doorway, clutching her bedding and bits of old clothes, shrilly urging her children to bustle along behind. This is the woman it has pleased the Lord to designate as my traveling companion, together with her husband and her numerous offspring: it is in their compartment that I shall sit, wedged in with the maximum of discomfort between bundles of household goods and bedding that mount up on either side.

All this business of a railway journey is new to me. Never in my life have I experienced it, and I am surprised at everything I see. My place is so cramped that I am unable to stir, but can only sit cooped up and perspiring. Formerly, when I used to travel by coach through all the lands of Jewry, I did not mind being hemmed in by bundles of my own books and—needless to say—it was a special joy to perspire. (Everyone knows this who has chanced to be on the road in the month of Tammuz, when the blessed Lord puts forth such insufferable heat at noon that no bird flies, no ox lows to his fellow in the stall, the forest does not stir, the very leaves on the trees cease their whispering: then, when the world is hushed and mute, one slumps back in the carriage seat and enjoys, as I have done, the most timely sweating of all.) But now it is quite otherwise: perspiration brings no solace, and the constriction only saps my strength. I begin to think that for my sins my innate Jewish character has somehow been transformed, so that I am no longer able to appreciate these same two privileges of the Seed of Abraham.

But the treatment the railway officials accord to the passengers, and the passengers to one another, together with the experiences I have just undergone, combine to persuade me that the change is not in my own disposition, but in this strange mode of travel. For a coach journey in former times was quite unlike today's journeys by train. Then a man was his own master and free to choose for himself. Even if the travelers were crowded in, two facing two with one extra for makeweight, so that their legs were jammed together like herrings in a barrel—well, they could always get out and take a walk, there was nothing to stop them, and they had the world at their feet.

Indeed, this very fact that they had a free choice would mitigate their discomfort, so that their afflictions became, as it were, the trials of love. But in the train there is no feeling of independence. One is like a prisoner, without a moment's respite from durance vile. And that, of course, is why this perspiring is so unpleasant: for an imposed sweat is altogether unlike the majestic sweating of a free man. Consider, moreover, that the passengers in a coach are set apart from the common populace; they make up a little colony, a corporate entity of their own. Time flows on for them, evening and morning, one day . . . a second day . . . a third. . . . There is world enough and time to meditate on all things, to satisfy every desire in the course of their travels. The sky is a tent over their heads, the earth spreads its bounty before them, they watch the glorious pageant of God's creation, they rejoice in its variety—yes, and if sometimes the coach is upset, this is not so bad either: for the earth like a kindly mother merely receives her children back into her lap. But in contrast the railway train is like a whole city in motion, with its multitude and its uproar, its population split into classes and sects, who carry with them their hatred and envy, their bickerings and rivalries and petty deals. Such passengers may traverse the whole world without regard to the grandeur of nature, the beauty of mountains and plains, and all the handiwork of God . . . .

The guard blew his whistle and the train started. Our people were now able to relax. They began to take notice of one another, and to make their inquiries as to each man's trade, and his occupation, and whence he came, and whither he was heading; as is right and natural for our people. Strangers fraternized and addressed one another by their first names, as if they had been friends since childhood. And so Chaim opened the goodly treasures of his knapsack and produced a bottle of wine, drank from it and passed it on to Shmuel while Shmuel broke off a piece of his loaf for Chaim, offering it with some cucumber and onion from his bag, and so they feasted together. In the same spirit Shmerl slipped a sum of money to Anshel with the request that he be so good as to pass it on to an in-law whose business was in the town where Anshel would be staying; and Reuven gave documents and bills to Shimon for Levi the produce-dealer; and the whole compartment became a hucksters' mart. We of Israel are preoccupied with the problems of making a living; no wonder that the winds of petty commerce raged mightily. My own business instincts awoke too, and I bethought me of trying to sell some books. But I was obliged to abandon this project. My belongings were submerged in a great wave of other people's possessions, and it would have been impossible to salvage them save by very strenuous effort; in fact, cooped up as I was, this was altogether beyond my power. So I continued to sit in idleness perched on the edge of the seat, contemplating without relish the passengers who shared my compartment.

An unattractive-looking woman with a bleak nose faced me, propped up on a large pillow, from which feathers were constantly escaping and floating out into the world. Her eyes were timid, her lips dry and compressed, and her whole countenance shriveled like a baked apple. Since her arrival she had not had a moment's rest from her children, who pestered her continually with their questions and bickerings. The three smaller ones kept exchanging places and disturbing her as they bobbed up and down. In her lap a baby was drowsing now, after having wailed for some time; it snored in its sleep; a tear still stood on its cheek, which seemed utterly bloodless. And beside me sat her husband: a tall, spare man, his back somewhat bowed, with a lean neck, a long nose, and a stunted beard. Sorrow lurked in his eyes, and his lips carried the suggestion of a bitter smile. To the right of him his grown-up daughter sat in a kind of sad trance, with two small girls leaning against her.

I sinned in my heart, I must confess, for I resented these companions from the start of the journey. Their presence irked me, and I silently cursed my ill luck that had placed me in the same compartment with such odd and vexatious folk. But as I considered them more carefully I began to view them in a new light. Their dress, their appearance, their wan expression, testified to extreme poverty and roused my pity. The mother's intermittent sighs moved me; and even more, the excessively humble attempts of the father and children to avoid getting in my way. But what touched me most deeply was the sight of the infant, who had fallen asleep out of sheer weakness, after pouring out his woes on his mother's lap. All this led me to paint in my fancy a grim enough picture of the life of that poor family. My imagination drew me into further speculations as to the many families among our people in a similar plight, who bear in silence their poverty and distress. I was sunk in these reflections when one of the children began to plead with his mother for something to eat. To soothe him she answered:

"See, Yankele, it's still daylight: now isn't the time for food; you must wait a bit longer!"

"Hush, Yankele," added his father, crooking his lips into a smile, "Bismarck made rules against eating."

"Is your child ill, then?" I asked the father in a gentle, sympathetic tone for I felt a strong urge now to enter into speech with him.

"Ill? God forbid! He's perfectly sound in wind and limb. I wish I had the weight in gold of the food he can put down at any time of the day!"

"Then who is this Bismarck of yours, who makes rules to keep a healthy boy from eating?" I was all ready for a heated polemic against this man.

"Don't you know who Bismarck is? I'm astonished!"

"And what if I don't? He's some doctor, to be sure; and in Kisalon, my hometown, let me tell you, there are hundreds of smart doctors and bloodletters of his type. We have a common saying, that no man, if he followed the doctor's orders, would live out his year."

I laughed across at this man and his daughters, and they smiled back tolerantly. Taking this as a mark of their approval, and an encouragement to further eloquence, I laughed again in my complacency, and was about to reveal further depths of wisdom and discernment in a series of anecdotes about the physicians of my town, when the ticket inspector, accompanied by other railway employees, entered our compartment, and the conversation came to a halt.

After these had departed without incident, and such folk as had made themselves scarce during the visit had popped up again (in the usual way) from under the benches, the pillows and other paraphernalia were heaped up once more. Suddenly a strange individual appeared from beneath the seat opposite me. He was bareheaded and dressed in outlandish Gentile fashion, with ragged trousers and a Polish cape that fastened with brass hooks across the chest and fell short to the knees. His face was chalk-white, his cheeks sunken, and his moustache formed thin fringes whose ends dropped like lizards' tails from the sides of his mouth. As he stood up on his feet he belched, yawned and stretched himself, like a man who has just come out of his sleep. All my companions, old and young, greeted him in the most friendly fashion, and he in turn gazed smilingly upon them. For my part I was quite amazed, and could not explain to myself the connection between this Pole and the poor family with whom I was traveling, so Jewish in every detail. Many conjectures came into my head, of which the most probable seemed to be that the stranger was that Bismarck of whom my neighbors had already spoken. But at once I found that I was mistaken, for the woman now addressed him by name, in a mixture of Polish and Yiddish:

"Why are you standing, Panie Przecszwinczicki? Sit down here in our Itsik's place, and Itsikl will go over and sit in with his father."

"Please don't put yourselves out for me, Chaya dear," answered the man with the seventeen-lettered name. "I can take Itsik on my knee. Reb Moshe, I see, has already too many children squeezed in with him on one seat." He spoke the same queer mixture of Polish and Yiddish.

"Did you sleep sweetly under the bench, Panie Japheth?" asked Reb Moshe with a smile of affection. "You see now, that I gave you good advice, and you followed my instructions perfectly! Lucky fellow! As for me, after the next stop it will be *my* turn to lie under the luggage."

"Take me on your knee too, Reb Japheth!" begged Yankele; and he went over and seated himself together with Itsikl, while the stranger affectionately clasped them both.

I gaped at Reb Moshe, quite unable to grasp the situation, but he seemed to read my thoughts, and turning to me said:

"This man you see before you is of pure Polish stock, and his birthplace is a little town in Poland."

"Why do you call him Japheth, then?"

"Because his real name, Przecsczwinczicki, is such a jawbreaker. And besides, the name Japheth fits him perfectly, and nowadays he well deserves it."

"Your explanation, I'm afraid, only confuses me the more. You are like those exegetes who twist their texts to make them the more cryptic to the ordinary man. Tell me your story, please; but let it be a connected account, and not cut up in bits and snippets."

"Not cut up! I am a tailor by trade, and the tailor's way is to stitch the pieces of his cloth together with a needle. But when he has to deal with words, he cuts up the seams of the narrative, patches on digressions, and tears his story into remnants. All the same, I shall try, so far as I am able, to do as you ask . . . . But I have forgotten my manners. Let me say first, in common politeness, *Sholom Aleichem,* my dear sir, and may I have the pleasure of knowing your name?"

Reb Moshe greeted me, after the fashion of our people, by rising a little from his seat, and I returned his greeting (doing my best to budge myself likewise) and informed him of my name and occupation.

II

Moshe the Tailor was by nature one of those "happy paupers" of whom we have many in our midst. Poverty, it seems, is unable to break their spirit; and its train of afflictions does not lead them to rail, like melancholiacs, at the ways of the world. The notion is fixed in their minds that they have received their deserts, and that it is their inexorable lot to pass their years in squalor and privation: therefore it is not for them to desire, or even to depict in their fancy, those pleasures of life which were created for their more fortunate superiors. They bow their heads submissively before storms, and when they recount their troubles, they spice the story with a touch of humor, and seem to deride even themselves.

"I take it," Reb Moshe began, "that you are not contemplating any marriage negotiations so there is no need for me to trace my pedigree back to Father Abraham, or to relate the entire history of my life since the day I was born. It is enough to say that my story is a familiar one, and repeats the experience of our race. So I shall pass over many things which may be taken for granted and avoid all needless ornamentation.

"I was born in Lithuania. As a young man I migrated to Prussia, where for many years I supported myself and my wife, who is also a Lithuanian, together with our children, by the work of my trade. All this time I and my family were Jews. I plied my needle and we ate our bread without fear. True it is that the title 'Jew' brought me no great honors, and did not raise me to the rank of princes and peers. Yet it was not exactly held to be a crime, and did not prevent me from earning a living of sorts . . . ."

"What is all this?" I cried in dismay. "Do you mean that now you are *not* a Jew?"

"I am a Jew no longer, for there are no Jews left anymore," answered the tailor with a smile. "It seems you do not know what age we are living in."

"How can I fail to know? Look, here is my calendar, which I have had printed at my own initiative and cost. Today is Wednesday, this week's portion of the Law is about Korah, it is the year five thousand six hundred and forty—by the full reckoning." I recounted the number of years and days back to the creation of the world in a high voice and all in one breath. And taking out one of the little calendars I carry in my breast pocket, I flourished it in front of Reb Moshe, implying by this that I could sell him a copy.

"But the Germans think otherwise," said Reb Moshe quietly. "The Germans, who perform miracles of science, have turned the clock back a thousand generations, so that all of us at this day are living in the time of the Flood. Nowadays they call the Jew "Shem," and the Gentile "Japheth." With the return of Shem and Japheth the customs of that far-off age have returned too, and the earth is filled with violence. The non-Semites are hostile toward the Semites; they discover imaginary wrongs, and in particular—do you know what?—in the matter of eating and drinking! For in this the Semites behave like other human beings, and such conduct is regarded as tantamount to treason and theft. Others find fault with the sons of Shem because they reproduce their kind—if you will pardon the phrase—like other men. At first these reactionaries were derided by their neighbors, and held to be madmen, but the madder they became, the more followers they found, until this lunacy struck root in the minds of people and rulers alike, and seemed to be a right and proper attitude. As the animosity spread, many hardships befell us daily, until their great Count Bismarck arose and decreed the expulsion of all the sons of Shem who were not of German nationality. And so thousands of unfortunate people were deprived of their living and turned into a helpless rabble. As for my dear Yankele," he ended with a bitter smile, "this stubborn child refuses to obey the decrees of his rulers. He is hungry, so he will cry for bread. He has a stomach and wants to fill it—the wicked rebel!"

"So now you have come from Prussia?" I asked.

"It is nine months since we left Prussia, just as it is nine months since this child of our old age was born," he replied, pointing to the baby asleep in his mother's lap. "When the police came to expel us, my wife Chaya was brought to bed of our Leiserke here. They informed me that I was required to leave the state at once. I told them that my wife was in childbirth, and I begged them to grant us three months' stay until she had recovered and the summer season had come round. But the police gave me visible proofs—using the strong arm of the law, not to mention its fists—that the exigency of driving

Jews across the frontier is so great that it takes precedence over care for human life, and that even to be naked and barefoot in the rain, to be dangerously ill or on the point of death, does not exempt one from this decree. When I saw that my plea was rejected and they had the law on their side, I took my staff in my hand, slung my knapsack over my shoulder, and we all went forth, on a cold day of falling snow. Thus we left the town I had lived in from the time of my youth until now when I am in the years of decline. The police escorted us with a guard of honor for we Israelites are, after all, the sons of kings!

"And so," he went on, "Reb Moshe the Tailor and his family went on their travels, from town to town, through all the lands of the Exile. Our clothes wore out, we were left without money or possessions, there was not a coin in our pockets save what came to us in the way of charity from our own people. But unfortunately our Jewish poor, who wander in search of bread, are all too numerous. They come from all points of the compass, from Prussia and Yemen, from Persia and Morocco, and throng the gates of the charitable, so that there are not enough alms to go round, and the local poor must have priority over strangers. Thus we wandered long, I and my dependents, exhausting ourselves in the search for a resting place but finding none. And at this time I have come from Galicia."

Profoundly affected by this story, I sat staring at the floor and could think of no word to reply. But as I sighed to myself at the fate of our homeless people, the infant Leiserke awoke from sleep, and raised his voice in loud lament. For me, his weeping made up a dirge on the misfortunes he had brought forth with him from the womb, on the poverty that preceded his birth, and on the world from which he had been exiled even before his eyes had beheld it. His wails mounted into a crescendo of accusation, directed against this world that had embittered his life from the hour when he first saw daylight, and had deprived him even of the allotted period of rest in his mother's body that is the natural right of all creatures. His mother rocked and caressed him, beguiling him with false promises of sweets and all manner of good things in time to come, but he complained the more loudly, as if to prevail over her blandishments, crying, so it seemed to me: *Woe is my lot that you have borne me, O my mother, to see toil and sorrow, and to waste away my days in the vain hope of promises and pledges!* His father, too, in his ironic way, sought to console the child. "Put your finger in your mouth and suck it," he said. "It is not for Jews to complain, my dear Leiserke, nor to make their voices heard, even if their bellies are empty and their flesh grieves them. If they do, a great bear will come and gather them into his sack." But the little Jew, Leiserke, only grew more indignant; he kicked out angrily, waved his fists and glared wrathfully at his father, as if to reply: *Wretched beggar and sycophant that you are, father of mine! Why did you beget a luckless soul like me, with as many sorrows as the hours of my life—with as many doors for you and me to knock on in our exile as there are hairs to my head!* Thus Reb Moshe and the infant Leiserke answered one another, while the mother sighed, the daughters grieved, and I pondered bitterly until the Pole stood up and took the child in his arms. He caressed him, dandled him, and Leiserke at last grew quiet.

With mounting curiosity, I turned to Reb Moshe:

"Tell me please, who is this Pole, and what have you to do with one another?"

"He is an old disciple of mine—not in the tailor's art, for he is a cobbler by trade—but in the art of being a Jew. Have a little patience," he added, noting my surprise, "for I will explain everything.

"This Polish cobbler and I lived for many years in the same town in Prussia. Each of us practiced his trade, and we were at peace with one another. On holidays we used to drink together in the tavern, and ask each other's advice about our problems and those of our fellow workers. In times of need we would help each other, in a brotherly way. True, we used to have our disagreements now and then, as people do, and especially would we dispute about matters of religion. He would take sides for his own faith, I for mine, and each of us would quote chapter and verse for his opinions. He would never allow me to say a word against pigs—naturally, I find them abominable—but he would act as devil's advocate, praising these animals and telling me how good they were to eat. I, for my part, would spit in disgust and retort that they were such ugly, nauseating brutes, that nothing could make them any better, not even the butcher's knife. That is how we used to carry on with each other, but always the argument would end with a 'Well, let's leave it at that,' and we would part as friends.

"He told me once that he thought the Jewish way of cooking fish and making puddings was better than theirs. He also thought that our Jewish girls were prettier and more attractive than those of his own people. And he said quite emphatically, that as far as he was concerned, he saw nothing wrong with the Jews being given a small share of the next world for themselves to which I answered, just as generously, that I would not put any obstacle in the way of Gentiles eating pork, if they wanted to, and was ready on my side to rail off a corner of the lower paradise for good *goyim*. In fact, since we were both in a mood for concessions, I went so far as to say that I would let them have all *this* world as well—on condition only that they set apart a small share of it for us. So we stayed on good terms, and drank a toast to our friendship, he filling his glass and crossing himself over his heart, and I filling mine and saying the blessing for ale —while we both put the drink down in one draught.

"So it was in those days. But when they brought back the times of the Flood, and chaos returned to the world, human nature changed also. Friends became estranged, and my old comrade's bearing toward me was not as it had been. If he chanced to see me in the marketplace, he would behave like a stranger, neither greeting me nor returning my greeting to him. He no longer drank with me in the tavern, but each of us would choose his own corner. The time came when I saw him there with a set of men who were abusing the Jews in loud voices with the object of baiting me. I let them rage on as if I had heard nothing and when they realized that I was ignoring them and treating them like the stupid cattle that they were, their anger blazed up. They began aiming personal remarks in my direction, they insulted me in their drinking songs, at last they laid hands on me and shouted at me to clear out. At this point the innkeeper came up and with cunning excuses to save his face, expelled me without too much loss of dignity. So I went out, sick at heart.

"This experience was mental torture for days after, and in my bitterness I would dispute with God. 'God of heaven,' I would say, 'Thou who hast chosen us from all peoples, and cherished us, why have I and Thy people Israel come to this degradation and shame? If such is the portion of those whom Thou lovest, would then that Thou hadst *not* loved us, and hadst *not* desired us above all other nations. It is said, indeed, that the Creator, blessed be He, will reward all mankind according to their deserts. But I find no comfort in this. For what profit is it to me, Moshe the Tailor—the son of Thy people—whose days are brief and full of sorrow—whose soul is trodden down like dust under the feet of the impious—if, at some date in the far-off future, Thou wilt keep faith with my sons' sons and work their salvation? And what if, at the end of days, the descendants of the impious receive the punishment that their fore-fathers deserved? Then neither the oppressors nor the oppressed will have received their due. The former will not have been punished, nor the latter rewarded, and what purpose is served by settling accounts, when neither debtor nor creditor remain alive?' Yes, indeed I sinned greatly in these thoughts, and even at the time I feared them, for they were nothing but the promptings of evil, and blasphemy and defiance against the heavens. But all my efforts to suppress them were useless, for they rose up of their own accord, against my conscious will.

"Once I was walking in one of the streets of our town, very low in spirits, for hardships were accumulating, and for lack of customers my livelihood was dwindling away—when suddenly I saw my old companion coming toward me. His head was in the air, his moustache was waxed proudly, and there was a look of scorn on his face. By some impulse, as if the devil had prompted me, I stood in his way, and humbly greeted him, as if nothing had happened.

" 'Nowadays there is no getting away from these nuisances!' he replied provocatively, meaning to insult both me and my people at the same time.

" 'Panie Przecsczwinczicki!' I said imploringly. 'What harm do you find in me, that you have become a stranger?'

" 'What creature is this?' he cried angrily, and averted his glance. I realized from this curt reply what hatred he nursed in his heart, to the point where he could turn his eyes away from his fellow-man and refuse to acknowledge a friend. Nevertheless I made yet another attempt.

" 'Don't you recognize me, your true old friend and comrade? Again I ask you, what harm have I done? How have I sinned?'

" 'You are tainted with the sin of your nation for they are always robbing and plundering people!'

" 'Whom have I robbed? And whom have I oppressed? Don't you know full well that I have no property, and no money, and if you were to search my house from floor to ceiling, what would you find, but a few threadbare bits of bedding, a table, and two or three rickety chairs that still, by some miracle, stand on their legs? You should know better than anyone how poorly I live; how the potatoes cooked by my wife Chaya, God bless her, are the only dish to be seen on my table, and that is as much as I have got from all my labor. Do I have to tell you that I am a workingman, and toil away at my trade by day and night?'

" 'I know that well enough!' he answered scornfully. 'That's exactly the point—that you toil at your trade by day and night! It's your work that takes work away from us. So all your labor is to cause other people loss.'

" 'My trade and yours are completely different,' I said in self-justification. 'I work with a needle and you with an awl, and nobody else has lost anything on my account, either, for I am, thank God, a first-class tailor—you yourself have paid me all sorts of compliments about the trousers I made you. The chief thing is that I don't put up my charges like others in the trade. Now look here,' I said with a friendly smile, 'stop being foolish. Come to my place and we'll have potatoes and fried onions again, as my wife Chaya knows how to cook them . . . . I see that your trousers are torn. They've done you good service for something like three years . . . . And the shoes I'm wearing are down at heel and fairly ask to be mended. Can't you see that we need one another? But if we helped each other, then I would patch your trousers, and you would repair my shoes, so each would be the gainer.'

"Like a man whose objections have all been met, my companion stood silent and bewildered. I could see from his face that he was inwardly considering what to do next, and judging that this was the right moment to win him over, I went on:

" 'Yes indeed, Panie . . . you are not as simple as you look, and in your heart, I'm sure, you think other than what you say aloud. You have been playing the fool too long, brother. Now tomorrow happens to be Friday, so what about your coming over for the Sabbath evening, and enjoying some good fish with us?'

" 'You wouldn't touch my pork, would you? So you can keep your rotten fish!' he retorted, flushing in anger.

" 'So it's the pork you want to pick a quarrel about!' I cried, perceiving what was at the root of his fanatical hatred. 'Just because I won't defile myself with what is forbidden me by my faith, you are ready to persecute me and destroy me! Well, well, I shall only say that I can't understand you, for you are acting like a lunatic. Tell me the truth, Panie: Are you quite sound in body and mind?'

"My companion's only response to this question was to thrust out his hard fist—and in a flash he had slipped away out of sight.

"From that time on I did not see him again. But from what I

heard, he was one of the rioters in the city of Stettin, when they burned the synagogue there, and he took part in that exploit."

III

While Reb Moshe was telling his story, his grown-up daughter would sigh from time to time and tremble convulsively. Suddenly her face turned white. She got up from her seat and went to the door of the compartment for air. Her mother followed her, with tears in her eyes, while the father's face clouded over and he became silent. Sensing after a while that some explanation was called for, he leaned forward and whispered to me. It appeared that his eldest daughter, named Breindl, was betrothed to an admirable young man who was a carpenter's apprentice in the Prussian town where they used to live. This young man loved her dearly, and she returned his love with all her heart. Accordingly Reb Moshe in his capacity as father had promised a dowry of two hundred silver marks, to be paid in cash before the nuptials to his future son-in-law, Zelig. The young man would thus have the means to fit up a workshop with the tools of his trade. The date of the wedding was provisionally fixed for such time as his apprenticeship would come to an end and he would qualify for a diploma from his master. Anxiously these lovers waited for the arrival of their wedding day, and only three months lay between them and their happiness, when the decree of banishment was promulgated. According to its provisions, Reb Moshe and the members of his household went into exile, and the lovers were parted.

"This is the worst burden I have to bear," the father concluded sadly. "My feelings for my daughter are such that I would give my life for her happiness. What a calamity it is, Reb Mendele, that I must watch her grieving day and night for her lover! The whole world has grown dark for her."

So now I understood why this girl had sighed and trembled while Reb Moshe was recounting their experiences; and I could have wept, myself, in sheer compassion.

The train stopped at a small station on the way. The Pole took up the jugs that were under the seat, and raced off to draw water from the pump. He quickly returned, and passed the jug round, first to Breindl, then to Leiserke, and then to the rest of the children, so that they all were able to refresh themselves. I felt a strong impulse to thank him for this, and was all the more desirous of an explanation to the whole enigma. How came this man to attach himself to Reb Moshe and his family, after all that had passed between them?

Almost as soon as the train began to move again, the tailor made a gesture dismissing, as it were, the sorrows of his mind, and went on again with his story, telling it in his usual ironic fashion.

"It was once upon a time, in Galicia. I was wandering by night in the street of a small town there when I came upon a tavern, a dim tumble-down place whose lamp did not serve to light up the ends of the room. As I entered I glimpsed the shapes of men scuffling in a dark corner, and heard the voices of a man and a woman yelling curses and abuse. The person they were insulting lay on the floor, begging for mercy and crying: 'Have pity on me! You are human beings too! Hunger and thirst drove me to it, and that's why I ate your bread and drank your wine, though I haven't a penny in my pocket.' But his enemies kept up their abuse, and threatened to tear the clothes from his back and the cap off his head by way of compensation. I perceived that this cruel pair were the innkeeper and his wife, and that all their rage was because a man had not the money to pay for his meal. Familiar, as a Jew, with every aspect of poverty and hunger, I sympathized with this poor wretch and came forward to rescue him. I entreated the keepers of the tavern to show mercy, speaking fair words and quoting the Bible, which declares that he who commits a crime for the sake of bread has acted under duress and should be dealt with leniently. When this produced no result, I paid them the price of the meal out of my own pocket. They were then silent and slunk away.

"The poor man I had saved was just beginning to thank me feverently, when, coming from the dark corner into the full light of the lamp, we caught sight of one another's face, and each of us started back in dismay. I recognized this humble wretch as—who do you think—Przecsczwinczicki!

"As tailors do, I looked first at his clothes, and found them torn and ragged. His shoes were worn through; the cap on his head was creased like a rag, and scarcely improved his appearance. As for his body, it was shrunken to mere skin and bones, while his face had the livid, unnaturally bloated look of starvation. For some moments we stood speechless. At last, moved by pity for my old companion in his misery, I found words.

" 'What has become of you, Panie Przecsczwinczicki?' I asked. 'How do you come to be in such a state?'

"He hung his head, and slowly the answer came, in a still, small voice:

" 'They've issued the same decrees for us Poles as they did for you Jews. So now I have to wander about like you, and beg for my bread.'

" 'I really am sorry for you,' I said, shaking my head at his plight.

" 'How can you possibly be sorry for me?' he answered bitterly. 'Why don't you show how much you hate me? You, especially, after I've treated you like dirt, and plagued you all for nothing!'

" 'Exile atones for sin,' I quoted. 'God will not remember our past iniquities.'

" 'But I cannot forget my own for it's my fate to stand now in your shoes, I have learned what lies the well-fed tell about the hungry, and the citizens of a country about aliens, and the strong about the weak . . . . It has been a lesson to me, what happened here in this tavern. Oh, if only those pampered fools could have the same experience, they might learn some sense, and then there'd be less trouble in the world. Well, you may forgive me if you wish, but I only feel the more ashamed of myself.'

" 'Be that as it may, you *are* forgiven,' I said to him. 'Say no more about it, for you are not the only one to have done wrong, brother. Many have sinned like you—in every generation. And now, let us sit down together and drink to our old friendship.'

"We made a good evening of it there, and talked our hearts out. It was like the old times we used to have together back in Prussia. We called to mind those days, when we lived in peace and followed our own trades, and then we told one another of all the hardships we had been through since we were driven out of that land. I let him know the troubles that were on my mind, and he told me of his. He had been wandering about for a long time and could not make a living among strangers. There was no work, and no one to give him a helping hand—for such was the competition in every trade nowadays that each man had only time to think of himself. And so this ex-cobbler had spent all his small savings on the road, and sold his few belongings to buy food, and now had nothing left but the clothes he sat in. It was three days since he had spent the last coin he had, and his position was desperate.

"I cheered him up with glass after glass for it is written, 'the laborer is worthy of his hire,' or, as I read the text, 'a man in trouble deserves a drink.' And the drink lit him up so that he flung his arm around me lovingly, and we forgot all about the old quarrel and were very happy together, till in the end the innkeeper came round to tell us that it was long past bedtime.

"It was a fine, clear night, and the full moon shone in all its beauty. The marketplace was deserted, the whole town slept, and we walked on in silence, each man thinking his own thoughts. Not a sound could be heard except the tramp of our own footsteps and the occasional barking of dogs in the distance. When we reached the crossroads, and it was time to part from my friend, I took his hand— to find it was trembling and cold as ice.

" 'My lodgings are up this lane,' I said to him. 'Which way do you go?'

" 'Wherever my feet take me,' he answered with a sigh.

" 'But have you no place to stay the night?'

It appeared not. "Birds, it is written, have their nest, and foxes their holes—but I, the Son of Man, have nowhere to lay my head."

" 'Are there no wealthy folk among you?' I asked him. 'Does nobody help the poor?'

" 'Our idea of charity is different, and our wealthy folk are different too. A man may be poor and a stranger, but if he is able-bodied, then no one is sorry for him. The houses of the rich are not open to all comers, and there are porters to keep the poor away from the courtyards.'

" 'Listen,' I said to my friend. 'Life in exile—this precious gift from God's store—belongs only to the Jews, His chosen people. It is ours alone, for no other nation or race in the world has the strength to take it and to bear its weight. And since you, my friend, seem to have won a share in this gift, there is no remedy for you but Judaism.'

" 'What!' he cried in terror. 'Are you telling me that I must become a Jew?'

" 'No, you fool! The God of the Hebrews is in no hurry to acquire more souls: He is content with the Jews he already has. In fact, he is sufficiently burdened with His own Jewish paupers, whom He has to care for and sustain by miracles each day and hour. No, I am not trying to convert you. Stay a Christian as you have always been, and keep your religion in your own way, but there is one thing you must do. You must come to master the Jewish art of living, and cleave to that, if you are to preserve yourself and carry the yoke of exile. At first this will be hard for you, but in the course of time you will learn through suffering—for pain begets endurance. Do you believe that the Jews from the beginning of their history were such as I am today? You are wrong, friend! For long ages they went through every kind of affliction and retribution. They tried out many ways of life until they became as they are now. It is exile that has given them special characteristics that mark them off from all other peoples, has taught them special contrivances to gain a living, and has set a special stamp upon their charity, too, from the point of view of both giver and receiver. *Who is like Thy people Israel, a unique nation in the world!* which is skilled in ways of procuring its needs; which must, by the very nature of its being, maintain itself in the teeth of all oppressive laws and decrees that seek to prevent this. What nation in the world has such strange customs as we? Our paupers constantly return to the same doors; they *demand* alms, as if they are collecting a debt that is due to them. And our wealthy benefactors do not scrutinize each case. They give, again and again, freely to all comers, even if these are healthy and able-bodied. Not only this, but of their own accord they invite these paupers as guests to their table, on weekdays, not to mention Sabbaths and festivals, so that the poor are as members of the household. Such is the law of the Exile, with all its six hundred and thirteen prohibitions and exactions. Yes, we know how to keep this law; and we have the strength of rocks to bear the burden of it, and to endure it, and to live by it.' "

"You have spoken the truth, Reb Moshe," I said in reply. "How many qualities of body and soul are peculiar to us Jews, solely as the result of our dispersion among the nations and our precarious position in the world! Indeed, these very qualities have given us the strength to bear up, to satisfy our needs, and to survive in the Exile. The story goes back to ancient times. Our economic history is one long record of miracles—from the harsh fare of our forty years' wandering in the wilderness to the bread of affliction in our present exile—wherefore every son of Israel reads in his morning prayers the portion of the law relating to the manna, which is appropriate to all occasions and has its permanent spiritual significance. But let us come back to your own story. Proceed, Reb Moshe, for I am eager to hear more."

"There is very little left to tell. After I had spoken, my friend, the Pole, stared hard at me, and said:

" 'See now, you say to me: learn to master the Jewish way of living. But you have not told me what I must do. You have talked such a lot, Panie Moshe, but I can't understand a single word of it all.'

" 'Don't let that trouble you. I shall teach you the rules—the things a man must do if he is to live in the Exile, and which if he neglects, he will certainly perish. From now on you are adopted into my family, and will come with us along the way until we find some resting place. Be brave, my son, to take upon you the afflictions of the Jews, and be faithful to my teaching!'

"From the hour my friend joined us and came under my wing, I have educated him in the ways of poverty, and given him good counsel to ward off evil and to share our kind of life. I have taught him to be content with but little food and drink, to withstand the clamor of the belly, and to punish it at times by fasting. I have revealed to him the mysteries of the art of begging, and have taught him how to bow his head before calamities, as well as how to prevail over obstacles and hindrance in obtaining, by all manner of devices, his essential needs. All these things I have taught him, and, I thank God for it, my labor has not been in vain. At the beginning it was hard for this disciple of mine to face up to such trials, and it seemed preferable to die a speedy death than to draw out his life amid the sufferings and misfortunes of our strange people. But little by little he grew accustomed to them, and made great strides in his studies, until he attained the proficiency standard in penury and endurance, in humility and submission, in mortification of the body and the soul. He became like a real Jew, and is now fully adapted to exile, and trained to welcome its strokes and afflictions.

"Happy man!" concluded Reb Moshe with a contented smile. "And happy too am I, his teacher, that I am privileged to see this!"

I looked across at the Pole, and observed him playing cheerfully with the infant Leiserke. He was entertaining him with a series of imitations of animal and bird calls: now he crowed like a cock, now mooed like a cow, neighed like a horse, croaked like a frog, or growled like a bear—and all this as quietly and unobtrusively as possible, lest he disturb the other passengers. The children romped round him merrily, Yankele on one side, Itsikl on the other. Even the unfortunate maiden Breindl forgot her beloved Zelig sufficiently to smile, and her mother, perceiving it, for the moment seemed transformed into a happy matron. As for Moshe, he delighted in the whole spectacle, and beaming with pleasure, cried:

"Rejoice, children of mine, for I have lived to see Japheth in the tents of Shem! May you prosper, Panie Japheth, and acquit yourself well in your studies, for your own good as well as for the good of your master, who has taught you to be of such service. So may you flourish and go from strength to strength!"

I had many more questions to put to Reb Moshe, but there was no time left to ask them for now the train had stopped at a main junction, where I had to take leave of him and cross to another line.

As I left the compartment carrying my luggage, I saw the Pole standing outside and whispering to one of the train employees in a most humble and ingratiating manner, while he pressed a coin into his hand. I understood at once what this mystery signified, and what the disciple of Reb Moshe was requesting. . . . And raising my eyes aloft, with a sigh that came from the depths of my heart, I said:

"Lord of the universe! Grant us but a few more such disciples— and Shem and Japheth will be brothers—and peace will come to Israel!"

Translated by Walter Lever

SCENES FROM LIMBO

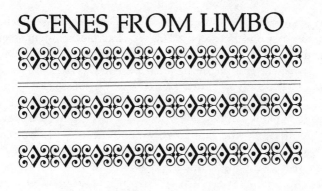

Y. L. PERETZ

INTRODUCTION

LIKE MENDELE, *Yitzhak Leib Peretz (1852–1915) was noteworthy for occupying simultaneously a commanding place in two literatures, Hebrew and Yiddish, though from the 1890s on the greater part of his energy was devoted to Yiddish, and he finally looms much larger as a writer of Yiddish than of Hebrew fiction. Almost all the Peretz stories that have become familiar to English readers were translated from the Yiddish (the present story, done especially for this volume, is a rare exception), and even the stories by Peretz studied in the Israeli schools are largely Hebrew translations of Yiddish originals.*

Peretz, however, never abandoned the work in Hebrew that had been part of his earliest experiments as a writer. Hebrew, even if it was not actually the vernacular, he announced in an 1891 essay, was like the hoops holding together the staves of the national barrel. There were, on the other hand, compelling ideological reasons for his greater commitment to Yiddish: a dedicated socialist and a non-Zionist, he felt the urgency of getting through to the working masses of the Jewish people in their own language. His activities in Warsaw as a publicist, lawyer, functionary of the Jewish community, were in fact devoted to the people and to the cause of Jewish socialism, and his writing was perfectly of a piece with his life.

Peretz is probably best known for his artistically recreated folk-tales and his fictional free variations on Hasidic motifs. (In fact, this urban, secular Jew was personally quite removed from Hasidism and from the milieus of old-fashioned piety.) He also did valuable work, however, as a social portraitist, an aspect of his fiction vividly illustrated by "Scenes from Limbo." Peretz's representation of Jewish life in a small provincial Polish town toward the end of the last century diverges from the influential model of Mendele in not emphasizing the grotesque. There are no crammed catalogues of grubby and comic details, no fantastic play in the language with incongruous imagery and bizarre allusions, no surrounding of characters and events with the constantly obtrusive presence of a narrator—all of which, after Mendele, became virtual conventions for the portrayal of shtetl life in both Hebrew and Yiddish literature. The narrator of "Scenes from Limbo," to be sure, does step forward twice to address the reader directly while the characters wait, but this would seem to be more than anything else a kind of vestigial mannerism on the part of an author steeped in the previous tradition of Yiddish and Hebrew fiction. By and large, the characters, who surely have their grotesque aspects, are allowed to present themselves, which means that dramatic dialogue, or narration by various of the characters, takes up most of the story. Authorial presence is relatively minimized, the last word literally left to one of the characters. As a result, the social panorama of Jewish provincial life tends to be clearer, more coherent, less subject to the techniques of comic and fantastic distortion, than it is in other Hebrew and Yiddish writers of this period.

Like so much Hebrew fiction written in the aftermath of the Haskalah, this story evokes a society in the pain and confusion of far-reaching historical changes which it can scarcely comprehend. The "real" rabbi of the community has been shunted to one side as part of the tsarist government's scheme of imposing "official" rabbis (rabbanim mitaam) with modern European education, who presumably could assist in the general program of russification of the Jews. (Poland, it should be remembered, was under Russian rule at this time.) Peretz, the modernizer, in fact sympathizes with the government-appointed rabbi of the story, who is regarded as an abominable scoundrel and a fool by the studyhouse crowd, while the rabbi's "enlightened" son, who has gone off to Warsaw, is an obscene heretic to these traditionalists.

The special satiric sharpness of the story stems from its perception of folly and self-seeking in all the social spheres of the Jewish town. The studyhouse hangers-on are ne'er-do-wells, reactionaries, petty gossipers, and money-hungry to boot. But the nouveau riche Jewish merchants, with their aspirations to European culture, are pretentious and self-deceived, qualities that appear in another guise, still more pathetically, in the children to whom they have given a modern education. The supposed proponent of Enlightenment in the story, the rabbi's son, turns out to be an arch-cynic, more corrupted by his modernity than are the obscurantists by their pettifogging provincialism. The four young literary intellectuals of the town may be portrayed with a modicum of sympathy, but they are after all naive and ineffectual figures, satirically exposed in the mock-lyric prose with which they are introduced, and in another five years one might easily imagine these callow young men, after a plunge into the corrosive bath of worldly experience, soured into the cynicism of the rabbi's son.

The two characters exempted from Peretz's satirical vision are the rabbi and his friend the watchmaker, and the two of them produce at the end what is a regrettably long moment of sentimental softness in an otherwise brilliantly sharp perception of Jewish life in the throes of modernization. The conclusion of the story is surely an artistic flaw, though one that graphically illustrates Peretz's particular location in literary and cultural history. Any Jewish writer as engaged as Peretz was bound to carry on some of the explicit didacticism of the older Haskalah literature, and that is what makes itself felt with such clarity at the end here. The sad and touching thing is the obvious gap between description and diagnosis. In the social portraiture, we are given vivid representations of a culture in the dismaying disarray of radical transition; in the diagnosis at the end, the author, through his protagonists, mounts the rostrum as a moralist and asks us to believe that all these ills issue from the fact that Jews, traditionalists and modernists alike, have neglected moral instruction in the upbringing of their children. The conclusion is suffused with didactic earnestness, but the high comedy that constitutes the body of the story does more than teach: it illuminates.

SCENES FROM LIMBO (1896)
Y. L. PERETZ

THE GEM ARRIVES

THE RUMOR that the heretic, the son of the government-appointed rabbi, had returned, took wing, and flew from house to house, from shop to shop, until it alighted in the studyhouse, raising a great ruckus between afternoon and evening prayers.

Everyone knew the "Gem" as a downright troublemaker for all Jews, a person given to dissoluteness, and so they were all astonished at this sudden change of heart—that he should have returned home to live, even temporarily, in this small town. Many conjectured that there was more here than met the eye. Who knows, it was even possible that he was traveling as a representative of the Lovers of Zion, to make speeches for the new settlers in Palestine and to take food out of the mouths of our religious leaders. . . . And who knows if he wasn't coming to open a secular school, or a reformed *heder*,[1] which was even worse than a secular school? Who could tell?

But just when everyone was imagining mortal danger in this arrival, Yokhanan the Schoolmaster—or, as he was called in town, the Stubborn Ox—denied the whole business, claiming it was pure fabrication. Stuff and nonsense! he argued. Our Gem, who had

---

1. Traditional Hebrew school.

been his pupil, was sitting in Warsaw, strolling through the parks
and public gardens, skirt-chasing and writing news reports from the
four corners of the earth—for who could tell him what he might
not do? The Stubborn Ox insisted, "He has not come, and he
definitely will not come. I know him. As Proverbs says, 'By his deeds
shall the lad be known.' "

Yekhiel the Matchmaker stared down the schoolmaster as
though he intended to attack him. "You stubborn-headed Stubborn
Ox," he shouted angrily. "I tell you he has come, and that's as
clear as daylight."

"Clear as daylight just before evening prayers!" the Stubborn
Ox rejoined.

"Idiot! He has come!"

"Where's your proof? Who told you?"

"Who told me? Haven't you heard, Stubborn Ox, that Mikhailko
told me, Mikhailko. Do you know Mikhailko? Mikhailko himself
brought him, I mean, with his horses from the station. Do you hear?"

"And where did you see Mikhailko?" the schoolmaster coun-
tered.

"Where, you ask me, where? And where could I have seen
Mikhailko if not at Yekhiel the Matchmaker's tavern. If you are
a man of understanding, just go to Yekhiel's and you'll see him with
your own eyes."

"But—a matchmaker and a second-hand witness!"

"Forget about the Stubborn Ox!" several people entreated the
matchmaker. "Tell us what Mikhailko said."

The matchmaker, having won out, was exultant: "What more
do I have to tell you? I've already said the main thing. Mikhailko
swore to me, it's five years now that he's made the trip twice a
day to the station to bring back passengers, but this is the very
first time he's brought back a disfigured Jew like this one."

The schoolmaster leaped up as though he had been bitten by
a mule: "It's a lie, a lie. After all, he was my pupil. I say to you,
gentlemen, that the boy was handsome, and my wife will agree.
Now the lie is out!"

"Idiot," the matchmaker answered and spat in the direction
of the schoolmaster. "That's all past history, and now Mikhailko
says he is absolutely disfigured. A complete *goy!* His earlocks are
entirely chopped off, his beard is shaven, and on his head, according
to Mikhailko, he wears a big hat, black and pressed like a lady's

shoe. Mikhailko swore that he spat at him, just as I spat now at the Stubborn Ox."

The schoolmaster, ignoring the matchmaker's anger, persisted: "If the boy is so changed, how could Mikhailko have recognized him? Mikhailko must have seen some German and got mixed up."

The matchmaker retorted almost in disgust: "Mikhailko got mixed up! Idiot, Mikhailko never makes a mistake, he's known for his sharp eye."

At that very moment, the door clattered open and Yossil the Bastard burst into the room shouting, "I saw him, I saw him."

In an instant the debaters and listeners crowded round Yossil the Bastard to hear what he had to say, but he was panting heavily from running, and until he gets his wind and is able to speak, I have the time to assure you that our Yossil was conceived and born in holy wedlock but that he was a "diligent" sort, this lad (a lad with a wife and five daughters)—"fire won't burn him nor water drown him!", "he's both a fiery flame and unstill water!" All matters of material support Yossil left to his wife the shopkeeper, while he was the animating spirit in the wheels of the community. He had a hawkeye to see everything done secretly and in the inner-most privacy, an ear like a funnel to catch the confidential whispers of the deepest night . . . besides which Yossil had a honeyed tongue to tell the tale as it should be told, and swift hands to provide un-answerable demonstration for whatever his tongue pronounced. If an itinerant preacher came to town, Yossil was the first to stop up his mouth with a rotten apple. If the eruv[2] fell, Yossil ran through the streets announcing it on the Sabbath day before prayers, stopping the householders in their tracks, prayershawls in hand, like dumb statues in the open square. If a government inspector came to examine trade permits, Yossil was the one who had knowledge of his every whereabouts, and before you knew it he was on the synagogue roof warning people with a rooster's call. Who was it arranged an official marriage ceremony between Shmaryahu the Drifter and Yekhezkel the Ascetic? Yossil!

But Yossil has now caught his breath, and he reports: "So, I've seen him in the flesh. This is how it was. I, too, saw Mikhailko and I said to myself—Is it possible? Can the Gem come into our midst without a reception from Yossil the Bastard?"

"I should say not," his audience encouraged him.

2. A symbolic fence drawn around the town with cord nailed to posts. Within this perimeter, carrying on the Sabbath, otherwise prohibited, became permissible.

"No sooner said than done. So off I go to the German's house. But the government rabbi wasn't born yesterday either. He comes out to greet me in the sitting room while the Gem is hidden within, in the next room.

"*Ai-yai-yai*," many of the studyhouse crowd expressed their astonishment.

"But Yossil the Bastard won't take no for an answer. As our Sages said, 'he who is performing a divine precept is enjoined. . .' "

" 'To finish!' " the schoolmaster chimed in.

"And I had made up my mind to speak with this German of ours till the light of day, to speak, to taunt, to provoke him, if need be, to curse him and pull his beard, until that good-for-nothing would rush in to his father's aid."

"Water won't burn him!" mumbled one of the listeners in hasty confusion. "And fire won't drown him," another tumbled after the first.

"Meanwhile, he humbly asks me: 'What can I do for you, Reb Yossil?' The damned scoundrel addresses me with fine language! In everybody's book I'm Yossil the Bastard, and he calls me Reb Yossil! Tit for tat, I will call you 'rabbi'! So I answer him innocently: 'I've come to you to request a special talisman.'

" 'What kind of a talisman?'

" 'For a child.'

" 'For you, Reb Yossil?' he asks with a friendly smile, extending his hand, which I let dangle while I answer coolly: 'There's time enough for that, my wife hasn't yet given birth.'

" 'Then why do you need a talisman?' the old fool wonders.

" 'But she has a big belly!' I tell him.

"The old sinner sees I'm making a fool out of him, twists his face around, and, laughing, too, he asks: 'So what's all the fuss about?'

" 'What's all the fuss?' I answer, my blood beginning to boil. 'Do you think I too am a rabbi with bed and board all free and clear? Do you think I too shear the newborns, the newlyweds, and the dearly departed to stuff my own gullet? I have to earn my bread by the sweat of my brow.' His face, let me tell you, turned the color of sour mustard. And I say to him: 'Yes, "Rabbi", I have to make a trip to the Count's to buy a timber tract. I'll have to stay there a week or more, and I want to leave the talisman with my wife, Heaven protect her.'

"He all the while restraining himself with all his might, and trying to force a laugh again. 'But Reb Yossil,' he says, 'you yourself are versed in the Law. How can I give you a talisman when there is a double doubt involved?'

" 'What double doubt?'

" 'First, that she may not give birth.'

" 'Is this some sort of joke?' I ask bitterly. 'Didn't I tell you she has a bulging belly?'

" 'Second, if she does give birth, it may be to mere wind.'

"Now I was the one who couldn't restrain myself. This filthy old man says my wife will give birth to mere wind. 'May a withering wind seize your father's father!' I tell him and I also raise my hand, but at that moment the door opens and there is the good-for-nothing in the doorway. Just what I wanted, so I've run here to tell you and now I'm off to sick Reb Yisrael to tell him."

"Blessed be the Lord!" the prayer leader's voice rang out with the call to prayer, and the worshipers scattered to their places, except for Yekhiel the Matchmaker and Yokhanan the Schoolmaster, who as Hasidim did not join this prayer quorum and so withdrew to the area behind the stove where they continued to talk.

"And what do you say now, Stubborn Ox?" asked the matchmaker.

"What do I say now? Now I say that if I were in the Countess's place, I would not have allowed the Gem to enter the city. I can tell you, he will turn this town upside down!"

The matchmaker sighed. "No doubt about it. A sinner like him!"

"He will of course hold public meetings, make speeches . . . But what's to be done?"

"And whose fault is it? It's the rabbi's fault. From the day the rabbi came we have become like Sodom, even like unto Gomorrah. The real rabbi is afraid to open his mouth, doesn't dare protest. . . . The householders are concerned only with their own profits, every one of them."

"Do you know, Yokhanan?" the matchmaker interrupted. "Yesterday I saw something new at the house of Raphael Kotzker. Just imagine, a huge box half as high as a man, wide on one side and narrow on the other, a really lovely box. I ask: What's this? And they tell me: A musical instrument, Reb Raphael's daughter plays this instrument!"

"And I," says the schoolmaster, "two days ago I was at Shimon's house, the one that used to be a shoemaker, and I called the son to his studies, for I tutor there, but he refused to come because they were having a ceremonial feast."

"A ceremonial feast at the shoemaker's? Were they celebrating because someone had completed a round of study of the Talmud?"

"God forbid! His big sister was eighteen years old, and her birthday is a family holiday, a regular Jewish holiday. Can you understand a thing like that?"

But the matchmaker was already lost in calculations. Then suddenly he snapped to attention. "My dear friend, Reb Yokhanan," he asked hastily, "did I say anything at all against the rabbi's son, or against his father?"

"You? It seems to me you called the son a sinner."

"It's a lie, a lie!" the matchmaker denied.

"Now I remember very well. You also said 'good-for-nothing'."

"Also 'good-for-nothing'?" repeated the matchmaker fearfully.

"And also 'mongrel'."

" 'Mongrel?' Oh, no, no! Reb Yokhanan, my friend, swear to me that you will reveal to no one what I have said."

"Why? What's happened to you? Have you found a match for him?"

"Yes, yes, I admit."

"Hurry, hurry. Clean out this contamination from our city."

"I can't, Reb Yokhanan, I can't. It's the hand of God. Yesterday Raphael's wife complained to me that there's no properly cultivated young man for her daughter. Just this morning she cursed me up and down because I could not provide for her house, and now this evening a cultivated young man comes to town."

At that point Yokhanan was stirred to open anger. "What are you saying? Do you mean to leave this source of infection in our midst?"

"What can I do, Reb Yokhanan, it's God's hand. Passover will soon be here, and a Jew needs to earn a living. Why, this is personal Providence!"

"A Jew needs to earn a living . . . true, true," the Stubborn Ox murmured reflectively on his part. Then he added, "So be it. I won't say a word, but what percentage will you give me? After all, I'm practically a member of the household there."

A GATHERING OF INTELLECTUALS

Dusk. On the sand by the river three boys are stretched out.

I am a simple storyteller, and I shall conceal nothing from you, so let me tell you at once, that the little one is Blond Shmuel, with the golden hair and the fine skin, who is full of feeling and freckles. The tall skinny one lying in the middle, with the deep black eyes that are always moist, with the chalk-white melancholy countenance, is Michael the Poet, who sings of the four seasons and of Israel and its redemption. The third one, whose ears are like a donkey's, whose nose is like an eagle's, whose eyes are like a deer's darting back and forth, and whose swift hands are like a windmill—he is Tongue-Tied Gabriel, called that ironically for his special gift of piling question upon question, particularly on the subject of the disgraceful state of education among Jews.

But I forget the main point: Blond Shmuel plans to be a writer.

The three friends have gathered and are waiting for a fourth, Aharon the son of Shimon (the one who used to be a tailor).

If Aharon were only with them, we could see in one view the four wheels of the wagon of Enlightenment in limbo city. They are all secret adherents of the Enlightenment: that is to say, after midnight in the rainy season, in the studyhouse, and on summer evenings, under the starry skies, when the mist spirals up from the damp meadows and moves out to cover the town stretched along the edge of the forest.

And the forest murmurs and whispers gravely from afar, as though it, too, were solving lofty questions . . . between the tangled growth of trees flows the pure river, its waters welling tranquilly, silently, while up above the silvery mist glides, its coral borders following the sun in stately progress to the sea . . . the sun on its part ignores the adherents of Enlightenment, pays them no heed. It makes its way quietly, bathing in crimson splendor and pouring streams of beaten gold down on the mountain and on the flock of sheep on the banks. A fresh evening breeze plays with the whispers of the forest and the murmur of the flowing water, with the sound of the grave questions that the enlightened young men were preparing to propose to the rabbi's son, who had come from Warsaw and set them all into a fine state of pleasant commotion.

They had already decided to go and welcome him, even if the whole town went beserk because of it . . . but why hadn't Aharon come?

"He never keeps his word!" Blond Shmuel complained.

"I'm sure he couldn't make it," the Poet defended him. "And why should you make such a fuss?"

"Why should I make a fuss? You would too if you were as hungry as I am! I haven't had a bite of food since this morning, and he was supposed to bring bread and cheese."

"Glutton!" Tongue-Tied Gabriel called out, while the Poet added, "In my right-hand pocket wrapped in paper are apple seeds I collected Saturday. Put your hand in and you'll find them."

The Blond follows his advice while the Tongue-Tied One goes through all sorts of questions till he comes to the tenth question— the issue of the people in Argentina now complaining.

"Absolute nonsense!" insisted the Poet. "We have no connection with Argentina. Hasn't the Baron Hirsch read Eisenstadt's Hebrew article which clearly demonstrates that the Argentine colonization scheme will never work?"

"But the Baron has already purchased the land!"

"If that's the case," the Poet went on, "he's thrown his money out the window. Why did he make such a decision all on his own? Why didn't he consult the literary world?"

"But, any way you look at it," the Blond said after eating the seeds, "our brothers are settling there and we have to help them."

"You're right about that," answered the Poet.

"Afterward, one can deal with the question of literature, I mean, the question of nature and the imagination, for even if our blond friend inclines to the imagination and divorces himself from nature, we still have to hear what they say about this in Warsaw!"

"That's all right with me," said the Blond. "I won't swerve from my own path even if every chief-cook-and-bottle-washer in the world decides to contradict me, but it would be nice to hear from the Poet himself that imagination is finer than nature and superior to it."

"In poetry," responded the Poet, "but not in prose."

"And I say, even more so in prose. For in poetry, sound can make up for the deficiencies of imagination. As for me, if I can't

ride on an angel's back, I will not soar, and if I don't soar, I will
flop on my face. But enough questions. Aharon isn't coming and
I am very hungry—those seeds were only oil to the fire. I'm afraid
that an unworthy thought may be occurring to me, that the material
and economic question takes precedence over all others . . ."

"But Aharon will come!" the Tongue-Tied One tried to re-
assure his ravenous companion.

"And I do not believe it," said the Blond. "And let me tell
you this besides—if it is Aharon's fate to be the first of us to marry,
he will not keep his word, he will not fulfill the pledge we all made!
One of two things will happen—either he'll back out of the match
and run away, or he'll obey his parents and take a wife but he
won't turn over the dowry to the benefit of the group. Can't you see?"

"No, but we can hear," his friends answered. And in fact they
could make out footsteps—it was Aharon leaping over the hillocks
of the meadow. In a moment he stood before them.

"Bread and cheese!" called the Blond.

"I didn't bring any. When we get back to town I'll give you
change to buy something. But I have brought the strangest and most
wonderful news."

"What happened? What happened? Tell us!"

"Yekhiel the Matchmaker is proposing a match between
Raphael Kotzker's daughter and the rabbi's son!"

"Are you serious?"

"I swear! My mother told me!"

BIRDS OF A FEATHER

In the city tower is a clock: its columns are stone, its sinews, wagon
rope; its members, iron and copper. But the giant is lazy, and from
time to time it goes slack and moves heavily. Then suddenly it
loses its voice, and it stops.

The clock tower is the only one of its kind in town, and the
only, lonely one of his kind is Nahum the Watchmaker, its constant
physician who knows how to treat its complaints, to cure it again
and again, and to set it right once more. Nahum is in his seventies

and his hair is white, but he holds himself erect, and when he raises his heavy eyebrows, a steady light illuminates his face, a tranquil, confident light. Nahum is devoted to the clock. He says: one day he and I will both stop working—and he knows what he is talking about—without Nahum the clock will stop, and if the clock stops the one bond connecting Nahum with life will be severed, for who or what else is there for him here?

It is ten years since he came all alone to the town, and he lives all alone till this day. At first he was pestered with questions: "Where is a fellow like you from?" "Where is your wife, my good man?" "What's your story?" And so forth. But he would answer with another question: "Do you have a clock to repair?" If not, he would turn himself around and move on.

So he had very little to say. He made himself scarce in the townsmen's homes; he did not go around looking for jobs. When someone came to him and showed him a broken watch, he looked it over, then set a fee without yielding a penny from the amount he announced. He never did work on credit, and if one of the prosperous householders insulted him because of it while taking the repaired timepiece from him, he paid no attention but went on with his work, and when the customer had finished his tirade, he would answer quietly, "all that is neither money nor the equivalent of money."

When he first came to town he was a target of opprobrium. The women were afraid of his "evil eye", for, they claimed, "that's why his brows are so heavy, to hide his evil eye."

The artisans resented his pride because he had nothing to do with them. The studyhouse worshipers viewed him with scorn and disdain. He was neither a tailor nor a leather-worker, yet he went out of the studyhouse right after the service without so much as looking into a copy of *Ein Yaakov*,[3] and the householders considered him a wild man.

With the passage of time, however, people got used to him, to his silence and his deliberate movements, and they came to ignore him.

Now before the son of the government-appointed rabbi came back, the rabbi, too, was lonely and neglected in the town. His wife had died some time before and he remained in a mourner's

3. A popular collection of rabbinic legends in Yiddish translation.

deep melancholy. He was short, thin, an excitable man. His movements were rapid and impetuous, but his eyes revealed a gloomy, exhausted spirit. Nevertheless, there were still fiery sparks in this pile of ashes. Sometimes his eyes would kindle. From his lips would flow a burning incandescent stream, then, all at once, the flame would go out. His eyes would lose their luster, his lips turn pale, and the old man would seem to shrink and become still smaller.

But this lonely person, instead of a clock, had a library from the '60s, and that was the solace of his existence.

Once the sleeping town was roused from its slumber, and the drifters, the shopkeepers, the women, and the young boys pointed up at the railing around the clock in the middle of the tower— where the rabbi and the watchmaker could be seen standing together, and afterward coming down the stairs together. On the bottom step they parted with a handshake—a thing for all to puzzle over.

The enigma deepened when it became known that the watchmaker, on his daily trip to visit his patient in the tower, stops at the rabbi's house to wish him well. It is said that he rarely crosses the threshold. For the most part, he stands in the doorway, says "good morning" to the rabbi, listens for the response—"and a good year to you"—then turns around and retraces his steps.

§‹›§

THE WAY IT'S SUPPOSED TO BE

The rabbi's son, despite the testimony of his former teacher, did not have beautiful eyes, his eyes were dull and tired; at the age of twenty-four, he had already lost the sap of youth, and there was a small bald spot on his head. But he was also not disfigured as Mikhailko had pretended, or as the matchmaker had reported in the wagon-driver's name. Perhaps his eyes were dull and tired from too much work, and his forehead was encroaching on his scalp from too much thinking—who knows? But when he came dressed in a suit and white collar to visit Raphael Kotzker's daughter, he was splendidly attired, and that is how he looked to her, too.

The meeting that was arranged in advance in all its minute

details by the cultivated young lady, had been accepted by her
mother (who because of an optic disorder had been over the border
to Lemberg and had seen there proper "Germans" and even Jewish
army officers). The meeting was supported without reservation by
Raphael, who realized that if a treacherous inclination had led him
to give his daughter a modern education, he now had to drain the
cup to the dregs, to introduce "the distinguished author" to his
"beloved wife, Madame . . .," to his "accomplished daughter,
Mademoiselle . . .," then to sit a few minutes conversing in a clear,
broadminded manner, and afterward—to follow his wife out of
the room, when she gave the sign, to leave the young people alone
to talk to their hearts' content.

Neither hide nor hair of the matchmaker was to be seen, for
it was forbidden to appear publicly with the matchmaker, but
Raphael was attending to things as though driven by a demon,
every moment wiping the sweat from his forehead with a red
handkerchief. Yet his trembling eyelids bore witness to the fact
that his heart was not tranquil, and at the last moment he was
stirred with a spirit of rebellion against the *Shulhan Arukh* [4] of the
Enlightenment, and as he went out after his wife to the next room
he did not close the door all the way . . . and thus he put an attentive ear to the open crack, his wife standing behind him, clinging to
his coattails for fear he might burst into the room and "ruin the
business."

The rabbi's son needs only a single moment to pass silent
judgment on the woman who was intended to be his bride: Her
dress hangs from her like a sack, her eyes are large, black, and pretty,
but she flutters her eyelids tastelessly . . . her nose isn't too long.
Well, for six thousand rubles . . . .

And in a pleasant voice, he says out loud:

"The sky's a bit cloudy."

"Cloudy," answers Raphael's daughter indistinctly, with a little
sigh that also had been prepared well in advance.

There is a short silence. The rabbi's son picks up the book
that is lying on the table—the poetry of Schiller.

"And you, Mademoiselle, do you like Schiller?"

"Do I like him?" she asks with a heavy sigh. "Do I like him!

4. An elaborately detailed codification of Talmudic law considered strictly
binding by Orthodox Jewry.

And who else would I like here? Schiller is the one consolation of my life, my sole and solitary joy . . ."

"Her voice," thinks the rabbi's son, "is like that of a bird, and she speaks well . . . if it weren't for that fluttering of the eyes."

"I like him very, very much!" she concludes, tipping her head back a little and fluttering her eyelids toward the ceiling.

"At least that's one flutter at the appropriate moment," thinks the rabbi's son, "but why is her mother coarse and fat while she is all skin and bones?"

And behind the door Raphael rages: "Who does she like, damn her? Who does she like? Who is this Schiller?"

While his wife, hanging on to his coattails with all her might, breathing heavily from fear and excitement, tries to calm him: "Idiot, Schiller is a book and not a person. The book lying on the table is Schiller."

"Then why is she talking nonsense?"

"Be quiet, idiot, that's the way it's supposed to be. After all, I was the one who went to Lemberg, not you!"

"And I am absolutely amazed," says the rabbi's son audibly, "that you, Mademoiselle, you, a truly cultivated young woman—"

A delicate blush appears on the young woman's face, "But, Sir . . ."

"No, Mademoiselle, I am not a man to make empty compliments . . . how can you live here in this world of primitives and obscurantists?"

Behind the door Raphael rages: "What is he saying, the dog?" To which his wife responds: "Wild man, that's the way it's supposed to be. Didn't I tell you that's how it's supposed to be?"

The rabbi's son looks around him and continues to be amazed: "Schiller and unstained wooden furniture! Schiller and an unvarnished floor! Schiller," he adds turning to the girl, "and a city the size of your palm, with houses like nutshells."

"And I," she answers with a sigh, "have spent all twenty of my years here. Twenty years! If only I had a friend, a companion with a sensitive heart like mine—that's how I imagine the line from Schiller: 'For two happy lovers one shepherd's hut is enough.' "

"A shepherd's hut, yes, but not in a benighted city on a dung-heap! Schiller speaks of a shepherd's hut . . . a pitched tent . . . a

forest . . . a pasture . . . a flock of sheep in the pasture . . . a
brook . . . a garden . . ."

"Why, you, Sir, are a poet," the young woman cries out joyfully.

"No, Mademoiselle," the rabbi's son answers with gracious
modesty. "If I were inspired with poetry, you would be its source!
For your eyes alone are poetry, sublime poetry . . ."

And carried away by the sweep of his own language, he adds,
"I can imagine you there in the great world, in Warsaw."

The girl's chest swells with joy and pleasure—but suddenly the
door is noisily flung open and Raphael appears on the threshold.
His face is livid, his eyes burning coals.

"Young man!" he shouts in a voice not his own.

The rabbi's son gets up calmly from where he sits and comes
over to Raphael.

"Young man," Raphael goes on, "I told the matchmaker from
the beginning, and I didn't mince words . . . from the beginning
I told him that I would not let my daughter go off to Warsaw. The
six thousand rubles you asked for, you crook, I'm prepared to give,
I'd give the shirt off my back, but the one thing I will not do is
let my daughter go off to Warsaw."

"But Sir," the rabbi's son answers in a whisper, "I realize what
you're saying. I will fulfill every single article that we agreed on."

"Then why did you say what you said?"

"Why did I say that?" the rabbi's son answers with an engaging
smile. "Don't you understand yet, Sir? That's the way these meetings
work, that's how it's supposed to be . . ."

At that moment Raphael's wife summons the last of her
strength and pulls him backward, as he cries out: "Go ahead and
talk, but remember that I am listening."

The rabbi's son returns laughing to the girl, who stands motionless by the window like a marble column, pale, but eyes flashing.
. . . They had betrayed her, utterly betrayed her! The meeting was
finished, it was absolutely worthless!

But at that moment the rabbi's son finds himself liking her
very much. A warm surge of blood suddenly fills his heart which
pounds very hard . . . drawing near, he seizes both her hands.

"Forgive me, Mademoiselle," he says in a voice trembling with
compassion. "Forgive me for my sake and for the sake . . . of my
love for you."

The marble column trembles. A fine, delicate tinge of crimson slowly appears in her cheeks; her eyelids tremble and in her lashes there are twin tears, twin pearls.

"Mademoiselle!" cries the rabbi's son with great feeling and trepidation, "Mademoiselle, allow me, as a sign that I have found favor, to wipe away the precious tears from your dovelike eyes. Let me drink of thy tears, for the heart within me is warm, I am consumed by an inner fire."

And slowly the girl leans her head on his shoulder . . .

Once more the door opens. Into the room bursts Raphael. His wife, still clinging to his coattails, drags after him.

"*Mazel tov, mazel tov!*" Raphael thunders in a great voice.

"Wild! A wild man!" his wife exclaims in anger and consternation, while he replies emphatically:

"Quiet, idiot. I say—that's the way it's supposed to be."

WHOSE FAULT IS IT?

The watchmaker pursued his work by the window, and the rabbi paced up and down the room complaining to him about his bitter lot. His face was pinched and troubled, his voice like that of a crying child: one moment it was choked with sorrow and the next it was like an angry shout.

"Do you realize," he turned to the watchmaker, gripping his shoulder, "why the boy returned? He came back to claim his mother's legacy from me. He didn't ask a thing about her illness or her last moments, but he conducted a thorough investigation of every last dress, kerchief, and pair of shoes . . . when the young literary intellectuals came to present questions to him, he had one answer for them: Everything is vanity of vanities! Then he asked them to tell him if there were any good-looking girls in town."

"He seems to be a connoisseur," the watchmaker guessed.

"And he also showed them a poem with three different titles: Love of Zion, City of Moses, To My Beloved. The poem was full of love and panegyrics, and he told them that he had sent one copy with the title Love of Zion to the well-known philanthropist, another copy with the title To My Beloved—to some girl on her birthday. Do you hear?"

"I am not deaf."

"When I asked him if he liked Raphael's daughter, he held up six fingers, in other words, six thousand rubles! And when I asked him whether the money might have been earned through usury, he answered me, 'so much the better, a sinner will be parted from his ill-gotten gains'!"

The rabbi stood once more by the watchmaker and, gripping his shoulder, demanded: "Tell me, whose fault is it?"

The watchmaker laid down his little hammer, took the jeweler's glass out of his eye, then said, "Wait, and then you can ask. I myself would like to tell you something, a thing that really happened, and then we can both ask. But sit down, and don't interrupt me."

The rabbi, obeying him, sat, and the watchmaker began his story:

"I had an acquaintance, an artisan, a worker in . . . but what difference does it make whether he happened to work with wood, stone, or leather? This man was an enlightened person, quite well-read, and he also enjoyed the fruits of his own labor, so he lived a gratifying, pleasant life. Things were good for him, for his beloved wife, to whom he was devoted, for his three small children, for his workers, and the poor were not turned away empty-handed from his door . . . then suddenly everything was overturned. The beloved wife died. The children were orphaned . . . the father could not take his own life even though existence had become a loathesome burden to him . . . afterward the youngest son contracted diphtheria, choked, and died. Then the oldest caught the disease and he, too, died, so only a little girl remained. She was so beautiful that she amazed whoever saw her, and she delighted everyone. She was her father's great consolation.

"In all the troubles, when his wife and two sons died, the man lost his little wealth, his workers left him, and he had to ply his trade alone, but he was not altogether downcast—by the sweat of his brow he earned his own keep and that of his little daughter . . . the girl grew, and as she grew she became still more beautiful and intelligent; her voice was as sweet as music, her eyes bright as evening stars, flowers bloomed in her cheeks like the light of dawn . . . a thousand times each day her father raised his eyes from his work to look at her, and late at night he would sit by her bed, basking in her presence.

"The girl grew up, and the father deprived himself in order to send her to school, to give her piano lessons, and so a long time passed—a good time, a time of quiet, tranquility, and pleasure until . . . until the pitcher was shattered."

The rabbi looked up at his friend, drawing back in surprise. The watchmaker's face had turned almost green and his eyes glared strangely.

"Did she die, too?" the rabbi asked fearfully.

"No," answered the watchmaker bitterly, "she's still alive, but her father has no idea where she is. He left the place where he used to live and became a wanderer."

"Poor fellow. You're a poor fellow!" the rabbi exclaimed compassionately. But at that moment an uproar from outside could be heard and, mingled with the hubbub, were the footsteps of men running, asking, talking, screaming, and cursing.

"It's a fire," the rabbi said anxiously, sticking his head out through the open window. When he pulled his head back into the room, the watchmaker had already returned to himself. The strange glare had gone from his eyes, and he had managed to resume his habitual appearance of quiet and calm.

"Did you hear?" said the rabbi, "the son of Yerukham the Schoolmaster has been sent to jail."

"I've heard. I happen to know him. He's my next-door neighbor. No doubt Yerukham is also now standing and asking: Whose fault is it?"

"And whose fault is it?" the rabbi pursued.

"Ours," answered the watchmaker. "We who have built castles in the air, without foundations. You and I stuffed our children with Enlightenment and modern knowledge, geography, biology, botany, music. And Yerukham, who wanted his son to become a great rabbinical scholar, stuffed him with the commentaries to the Talmud . . . but the heart, morality, the foundations of human character, we all neglected. If only we had worried about the moral upbringing of the young, Reb Yerukham's son would now be a great rabbi, indifferent to monetary concerns, my daughter would be a loving child, a modest wife, a good, educated mother, and your son would be a true proponent of Enlightenment, a writer serving the public interest faithfully. But since we built on sand, the wind has swept away the whole structure of our hopes . . . for my daughter beauty and charm have become a snare, your son turns his knowledge into a shovel to dig worms with, and Yerukham's son has learned through his sharp Talmudic casuistry merely how to cheat people. Yes, the fault is ours."

Translated by Robert Alter

IN THE EVENING

M. Z. FEIERBERG

INTRODUCTION

DEAD OF TUBERCULOSIS *before his twenty-fifth birthday, M. Z. Feierberg (1874–1899) never had the opportunity to develop fully the
talent so strikingly evident in his short stories and in his brief
novel,* Whither? *Nevertheless, the degree of maturity as a writer that
he attained in so short a career is astonishing. His fiction, with its
gloomy scenes, its love of the fabulous and dreams, and its sensitive
reconstruction of early childhood, gives Hebrew literature a new
quality of innerness. The anguish of lost faith and the sense of
being cast out of the shelter of tradition into a large and threatening
world make Feierberg very much the spokesman for his generation
of Russian Hebrew writers. This was a generation caught between
two worlds—the old Jewish one that was too cramping and a modern
European one where they did not belong—and no one captured this
sense of inner division so finely as Feierberg. For Mendele and
Peretz, the clash of the two worlds was a social question, a moral
one: for Feierberg it is a spiritual and psychological question. One
might note of "In the Evening" that the story within a story is
about a young Jew who is quite literally torn between two worlds,
and it is worth observing that the Gentile world, as the means of
getting hold of him, seduces him with alluring music away from
the stern, God-fearing world of his Jewish father.*

Although the story conveys a convincing sense of what it must have felt like as a small boy to attend a traditional heder in a small Jewish town in Russia, the vision of reality rendered here is a very personal one—it is what catches the eye and moves the feelings of a particular kind of sensibility. An important index of the child-narrator's sensibility (and Feierberg's as well) is the fact, that of the whole day in heder, only the moments of late afternoon and evening are reported. In a cold, damp, grim, muddy world, indirect and flickering sources of light allow the child to see only indistinct, wavering forms, more ghostlike than substantial—"figures in sil-houette, houses like sepulchers"; "all I could make out from the window were the shadows passing slowly through the mist." This evening world of shadows is, of course, scary to the child, but it also attracts him by its very spookiness: he loves to stand by the window (a sheltered place) and look out at the shadows, just as he loves to hear the spooky stories—an extension of the world of shadows—that the boys tell one another.

In the gloomy light, distinctions blur between shadow and substance; tales and "real" facts tend to intermingle; and in the tales told, natural and supernatural are also intertwined. It is not sur-prising that there should be multiple connections of motif and theme between the frame and the inner story told by the mother. Especially significant is a major imagistic connection between the two parts of "In the Evening": the recurrent image of a small flame flickering in a vast darkness that threatens to engulf it. At the beginning, we are made aware of "the flame of the Eternal Light burning dimly again in the dark, shadowy building," with the boys drawing into a narrow circle to protect themselves from the imagined hosts of demons, just as the boy at the climax of the mother's tale will draw a circle to protect himself from the surrounding demons in the great shadowy forest. Hofni, struggling home through the evening dark with a feeble lantern lighting his way, is very distinctly an adumbration of the boy alone in the forest: "My lantern lit only a few square feet around me, making the darkness seem even thicker. I, Hofni, made my way in the dead of night through the perilous world, which was teeming with ghosts, demons, phantoms, sorcerers, and gypsies." At the end of the story, as the frame closes on the mother's tale, the motif of lights dimming in ominous darkness is repeated once more: "The oil was gone from the lamp . . . patches of darkness spread over the room."

Hebrew fiction before Feierberg had little imaginative sense of childhood, but the kind of child's vision that Feierberg evoked in his stories is often troubling in its very sensitivity. Hofni here is obviously eager to be a "big kid," to be studying Bible at last, yet the story communicates a strong sense that moving toward the adult world means moving toward a realm of stern discipline and obligations. The rabbi's image is almost frightening, "his face contorted and a terrible wrath in his eyes . . .furious with the Will of God for having created such a horrible, contentious world." Altogether, the adult male figures in the story tend to be harsh and threatening (Hofni's own father is away at the fair), while it is the mother who is gentle and affectionate, a warm shelter in the cold and blustering world.

Hofni has a mother but no visible father in the story. Reb Yosef's son, on the other hand, is torn between his Jewish natural father and his violently adoptive Gentile father. His story, one would assume, is told from the Jewish point of view, but, in fact, neither of his fathers seems much of a bargain. The Gentile father is a sorcerer, a demonic figure, and if his music—by implication, his mastery of realms of aesthetic and sensual pleasure—makes the heart melt with desire, the pleasures he promises are surely of a sinister nature. He instructs his adopted son in a course of self-rejection (which is, of course, what "assimilation" means): "'Then are a Jew and a devil the same?' 'Exactly the same, son.'" The Jewish father, on the other hand, appears to the child in a dream as a hideous, threatening figure, pulling the boy's hair and scratching him till he bleeds: "'You're a Jew and I'm your father—rise and follow me, or else I'll kill you right now.'" A few lines later, Reb Yosef appears as an angelic creature with "voice as soft and sweet as a lute"—to the village rabbi, not to the boy.

The apparition of this murderously menacing father who insists on strict adherence to the Law has its obvious Freudian implications, especially when it occurs in a tale told to a child by a mother who provides affection and refuge. "In the Evening" is, in fact, a classic narrative study in the psychology of Jewish guilt. Precisely for this reason, the note of irresolution on which it concludes is quite appropriate. The story breaks off, and the mother promises Hofni a happy ending, but the protagonist of the tale is left dangling and impotent, his martyred father exhorting him and promising dire consequences while the demonic wind carries the child off.

IN THE EVENING (1897)
M. Z. FEIERBERG

"BRING A CANDLE back with you," the rabbi told me as I started home
during lunch hour, "because as of tonight"—it was already autumn,
the Sunday of the third Torah reading in the Book of Genesis—"all
the boys studying Bible will come in the evening as well. From now
on each boy in the Bible class will have to bring a candle every
week to light his place at the table. And you'll have to bring
lanterns too, to light your way home at night."

Tonight I would begin to study in the evening, I thought as
I walked home for lunch. What marvelous news! As soon as I
reached home I would tell my mother that I was now grown-up.
And I would tell my sisters Breyndl and Sarka that I was too old
to play with them and their toys any more. How splendid it felt to
be grown-up! Just a year ago, I remembered, I had still been considered a baby. "Hofni's too little," all the boys had said then, "he
won't be studying evenings." And the rabbi's assistant had had to
carry me home on his shoulders and tell my mother: "Hofni's still
a little boy and can't wade through the mud by himself." "Too
little," "too little"—I was forever hearing the words. How terribly
I wanted to be big, to study Bible and spend evenings in the heder.
My mother wanted me to grow up too. "How long will this go on?"
I once heard her ask the rabbi. "The years fly by like shadows—is

he to be allowed to grow up wild like a shepherd or a swineherd?"
The rabbi answered, "Hofni's still too little, and isn't ready to
study Bible yet." Whereas now . . . now I would be studying it,
and in the evening too. How splendid, how marvelous it felt!

I returned to the heder.

The mud in the streets seemed neck-high. Beneath an overcast
sky, the wind whipped thin drops of rain that beat furiously against
the passersby, who walked bent beneath the weight of their torn,
ragged cloaks, which were soaked through with rain and grime.
Boots struggled to break free of the stubborn slush. An excruciating
curtain of gloom, the shadow of deep anxiety, lay over each despairing face, though the one thing all felt was neither joy nor sorrow
but the single-minded desire to get through the mud as quickly as
possible to the safety of some low, damp, dark home.

I, Hofni, loved to stand at such times on a bench by the
window of the heder and look out; I loved to watch the spray and
the pockmarks that formed on the surface of the puddles when the
rain spattered down on them; I loved to look at the doleful faces
of the people as they fought their best with the flagstones and
planks of wood that had been strewn about to make footpaths,
colliding with each other when they met, grappling and losing their
balance until one or both of them fell. Mire and muck, figures in
silhouette, houses like sepulchers, wet stone, bits of broken glass,
snow and rain mixed together . . . all were engraved on my heart
with a grim and terrible hand. I stood stock still and stared straight
ahead. There was nothing that I wanted, nothing that I felt, nothing
else that mattered in the whole world . . .

Dusk. The traffic in the street quickened slightly. Little children
were escorted home from the heder. Men set out for the afternoon-
and-evening prayer. Women went to buy kerosene and other provisions. Here and there a shopkeeper started for home, her keys

and bundles in one hand and a bucket of smoldering coals in the other. A dense fog filled the air. It was getting darker. All I could make out from the window were the shadows passing slowly through the mist. The rabbi had gone off to pray. The rabbi's wife was out buying kerosene and chatting with her friends. The rabbi's assistants were taking the little children home. The darkness outside had thickened into a terrible gloom. The shadows vanished. I turned from the window and faced the room, which was dark and hushed. The boys stood in a circle and huddled closely together. My flesh crept, my hair stood on end. I was afraid to remain by the window alone and I joined the circle of boys.

One of them stood in the center and told in a low, woebegone voice of a youth who had awakened in the middle of the night to find that he had been sleeping in the Great Synagogue. The flame of the Eternal Light burning above the lectern threw the building into dim relief. Suddenly the synagogue was filled with a great radiance and a loud commotion could be heard in the distance. It came nearer and nearer . . . Lord God of Hosts! The building was filling up with ghosts from end-to-end . . . they stood in white shrouds and swayed back and forth in prayer . . . they stepped up to the Holy Ark, took out the Torah scrolls, and the reader called out: "Let a priest come forth for the first blessing!"—and up to the Torah came a dead man wrapped in his prayershawl and recited the blessing. "Let a Levite come forth for the second blessing!" called the reader, and a second ghost stepped up to the Torah. "Let a worshiper come forth for the third blessing!" called the reader. "Let a worshiper come forth for the fourth blessing!" And after all seven blessings had been said: "Let the groom Zerach, the son of Reb Gronim, come forth for the *maftir!*" [1] The young man lay on the bench like a log, too petrified to stir or even blink. Whereupon the reader called out again: "Let the groom Zerach, the son of Reb Gronim, come forth for the maftir!" The young man hid his face in his hands but the voice called out once more: "Let the groom Zerach, the son of Reb Gronim, come forth for the maftir!" He fainted dead away . . . two ghosts were standing over him . . . they carried him to the lectern and stood him up in front of the Torah. "Say the blessing over the Torah!" thundered the ghost reader. He said the blessing and the ghost read the final portion.

1. Last person called to the Torah, who then chants a portion from the Prophets.

Then Zerach himself read the portion from the Prophets together with all the ghosts and recited the blessings at the end while the dead men cried "Amen!" The service was still in progress when the sexton of the Great Synagogue arrived to prepare for a midnight vigil. He rapped three times on the door—and immediately the great light went out and the ghosts disappeared, leaving the flame of the Eternal Light burning dimly again in the dark, shadowy building. The sexton found the youth in a swoon on the floor, from which he recovered long enough to tell what had happened—and then died.

The teller was done with his tale. The other boys stood with their mouths wide open, ready to listen endlessly on and on. In our fright, we had narrowed the circle even more. We held on to each other and pressed tightly together, prepared to defend one another against the ghost or the demon who might come to carry one of us off.

But there were more stories still to come. No sooner had one boy begun to tell about "the twelve thieves" than another interrupted him with "the king of the demons." The inventions multiplied, each of us seeking to outdo his neighbor with one that he knew . . . when suddenly, the rabbi's wife appeared and lit the lamp. The room was flooded with light and we stood rubbing our eyes in the sudden glare. Our fears and fantasies took flight, our tall tales and thoughts were forgotten. For a moment we stood immobile, struck dumb as golems without mind or will. The rabbi and his assistants returned to the heder. A new din arose. The boys broke up and spread all over the room, some quarreling or conversing, others feasting on a crust of bread spread with a bit of herring, butter, cheese, chicken fat, or some other leftover from lunch.

The rabbi took his seat at the head of the table flanked by his two assistants, a leather-thonged switch placed before him. The children sat around the table on benches. The rabbi's voice mingled with the voices of his assistants and his young pupils. The noise was terrific. The switch lashed out, striking a child who burst into tears. But it did not return to the table. The rabbi's hand stayed outspread, his face contorted and a terrible wrath in his eyes. He was furious with the children, with his assistants, with his wife, with the table, with the switch, with the Will of God for having created such a horrible, contentious world. In practically no time two

children were crying, three children, four children, five . . . the
rabbi dealt out blows, shouted and taught us the Bible on one side
of the table, while his assistants did the same on the other. The
third reading from the Book of Genesis flowed forth in a frightful
lament, each word dripping with misery and the dread fear of God:
"Get thee from thy land, and from thy kindred, and from thy
father's house, to the land that I will show thee." How terrible to
have to get up now! It was fearfully dark outside. Rain, snow, and
slush. The air was cold and damp. The fierce wind would slice
through the holes of one's coat. At home were a mother and sisters,
perhaps potatoes were baking there too—but even the rabbi and
his switch seemed a pleasanter prospect than to have to venture
outside by oneself.

One group of boys was dismissed by the rabbi and withdrew
to the end of the bench while another took its place in front. There
were more beatings and blows, loud shouts and cries, and the
sorrowful, sob-watered chant: "Get thee from thy land, and from
thy kindred, and from thy father's house, to the land that I will
show thee." The tumult began to die down. The rabbi was exhausted. His assistants belched and yawned. Several of the children
were already nodding, their heads on their arms. The rabbi's wife
sat by the stove darning a sock. The entire heder was filled with a
toilsome, wearisome, enervating apathy. The one thing that we
desperately wanted was to be allowed to go home at once. The
desire grew stronger and stronger. It was all anyone thought about.
We counted the minutes and scrutinized the rabbi's face to decipher
from its grimaces whether or not he meant to let us go soon. All
at once he rose from the table with his assistants. There was a
sudden scramble. The children jostled each other behind the table,
battling to be first off the bench, eyes sparkling brightly with
exuberance. Were it not for our fear of the rabbi, we would have
danced deliriously in the aisles. Our young hearts felt a burst of
wistful, mutual love and we looked at each other with affection.
All day long we had been cooped up together under the rabbi's
horrible gaze, while now that it was averted and we were free at
last, we had to bid one another good-bye and go each our own
way . . .

The assistants helped the children to button their coats, wrapped
thick scarves around their throats, straightened their caps, brushed
back their earlocks, and sent them off in groups by the streets on

which they lived. The rabbi cast a glance at us as he leaned against the table, but his magical power was broken. He could stand there as long as he pleased with his eyes hard upon us—the spell was gone from them and a dreadful fatigue had taken its place. His drawn face, which he now turned toward his wife, announced that in a moment he would scratch himself, front and back, and mumble drowsily: "Tsipa, let me have my dinner. I'm tired. I need to sleep."

We lit our lanterns and rushed noisily outside, bursting with youthful energy that demanded an outlet after its imprisonment throughout the long day. Our boyish hearts craved a moment of life. Forgotten were the heder with its sorcerers and demons, the rabbi with his cries of "bandits!" and "goyim!", his warnings of hellfire and the Angel of Death. For a minute each of us scampered gaily off by himself. It was terribly dark and the cold cut through to the bone. A wettish stuff, indistinguishable in the night air as either rain or snow, struck wickedly at our faces and frozen ears and trickled now and then down our necks, from where it slithered to our chests and down again. Our feet fought desperately to keep their footing . . . but what did any of it matter when we were beside ourselves with joy? We chattered merrily, pushing each other in fun from the pathway into the mud and quarreling with spirited good humor.

Our ranks began to thin. Every few minutes another boy left the column with a loud cheer and disappeared into his home. The merriment died down. Our laughter trailed away. I was left by myself in the street. The wind wailed through the awful black stillness. Faint rays of light crept through the low windows to cast a mournful glance at the dead street. My lantern lit only a few square feet around me, making the darkness seem even thicker. I, Hofni, made my way in the dead of night through the perilous world, which was teeming with ghosts, demons, phantoms, sorcerers and gypsies . . . I was all alone . . . but I would be brave! I marched with giant steps . . . on I strode, utterly at the mercy of whoever might come along . . . one more narrow street . . . five more houses . . . four . . . three . . . ahead was my father's house . . . a light shone in the window! How good to be indoors where there were no ghosts to fear, no cold, no mud, no slippery paths— in a second I would be there! In I burst with a triumphant whoop, my lantern in one hand while I shut the door behind me with the other, heartily shouting "good evening!", feeling every inch the grown man. My mother was sewing on a stool by the warm stove, mending her linen. A kerosene lamp burned dimly on the table in front of her. By the stool near the table hung a wicker crib, which she rocked back and forth with her foot by the rope which held it. She was putting my little brother Sandrel to sleep. My eldest sister, Breyndl, sat beside her on a wooden bench and practiced darning socks, while my youngest sister, Sarka, lay dozing on her lap. The beds were already made. There wasn't a sound in the room. My mother looked happy to see me. She didn't say a word, but I could tell by her face that she had been waiting for me impatiently. She threw me a sharp, probing glance as I came through the door.

"Are you all right, Hofni? What did you learn today in the heder, son? But Hofni, you must be hungry, aren't you?"

"Yes, mama, I'm starving."

"Here, let me give you a slice of bread with chicken fat."

"But, mama, I don't like chicken fat."

"Then have your bread with some pears."

"I don't want pears."

"Is it food fit for a king that you're asking for then, or is it the troubles of my soul?" And she added angrily: "That's what I get for spoiling you! Do you really think you're still an only child? There's Sandrel too, may he live, and Breyndl and Sarka also."

"But, mama, if you'll tell me a nice story I'll eat my bread with chicken fat."

My sister Breyndl looked at my mother with big eyes, as though begging her to agree. With a laugh both yielding and vexed, my mother said:

"Well then, I'll tell you a story about an unlucky boy, so that you'll know how fortunate you are to have a rabbi and a heder, and a father and a mother, and chicken fat and pears. Because this poor boy . . ."

"Mama," I interrupted her, "where's papa?"

"Your papa?" she asked with a sigh. "Your papa has gone to the fair . . . and on a rainy night like this! But perhaps he'll earn something there."

"But, mama," I said after a moment's silence, "tell us. Tell us the story!"

My mother put down her linens and bent to look at my sleeping brother Sandrel. Then she pressed my sister Sarka to her breast and began:

"Long, long ago, when my grandmother's father was still a tiny little boy, and his parents lived in a village that belonged to a rich Polish landowner—so I heard from my grandmother when I myself was a little girl no bigger than you, Breyndl, and she was an old, old woman—there lived in the same village another Jew whose name was Reb Yosef. He was a very pious and a very learned man, and he collected the landowner's taxes, though he himself was very, very poor. The landowner was fond of him and used to call for him often to sing Sabbath hymns and melodies from our holy days—the rich Christians too, Hofni my darling, like our melodies—and sometimes, when the landowner was feeling merry with drink, he would ask Reb Yosef to dance for him. In return, he didn't press him for the tax money he owed. And so many, many years went by and Reb Yosef lived in peace and quiet. His wife—I can't remember her name—was a good-natured, hospitable, God-fearing woman. It was she who ran the tavern that they kept, while Reb Yosef spent most of his time shut up in his room, where he busied himself in study and in prayer. Even the Christians in the village knew that 'Yoske' was a holy man of God and they honored him greatly for it. Now one day Reb Leib Sorehs, who was a disciple of the Baal Shem Tov, may his memory be blessed, happened to pass through the village and asked to spend the night at Reb Yosef's house. Reb Yosef and his wife had no idea that he was a holy man of God, but they gave him dinner and a place to sleep just as they did any guest. When morning came, Reb Leib Sorehs rose from his bed, prayed, and made ready to depart. 'I can't let you go,' Reb Yosef's wife said to him, 'until you've stayed and lunched with us first.' She insisted—and he stayed. After the meal, he reached for his satchel and his walking stick and said turning to Reb Yosef and his wife: 'It's clear from what I've seen that you're God-fearing folk and that the good Lord's blessing is over this house. But tell me, good people, if there's anything you lack and any wish that I might ask for you. Perhaps the Lord will grant my request.' 'God be praised, we want for nothing,' Reb Yosef answered. 'We earn our living, meager and troublesome though it be, and we certainly don't wish for wealth. Why should we wish for it when we'd never know how to spend it? But there is one thing that we're missing'—Reb Yosef sighed as he spoke—'and that's a son to study Torah and grow wise. Daughters we have, thank the Lord, but what good are they to me? Come with me, dear guest, and I'll show you a bookcase full of books. Who will read them when I'm gone?' 'In that case, Reb Yosef,' said Reb Leib, 'when the year comes round again, your wife will be cradling a son in her arms. The lad's soul will be a great one, great in Torah and in holiness, but Samael will set his eye on him, so that holiness will wrestle with the *klipa'* " [2]—(we children already knew all these words, because my mother had told us such stories many a time)—" 'and the struggle will be very, very bitter. Take heed then that you guard the boy well and keep him from anything unclean.' As soon as he finished speaking these words, he quickly opened the door and vanished away.

"Nine months passed and a boy was born to Reb Yosef, as handsome as an Angel of God. When the landowner heard the news, he sent for Reb Yosef and said to him: 'Listen here, Moshke'—that's what the landowner called him—'I hear, you poor man, that you've gotten yourself a son. What can you possibly want with a son, Moshke? Isn't it enough that you've brought so many daughters screaming into this world to grow up without a penny to their name? You might care to remember, Moshke, that you haven't paid me any taxes for the past eight years, which I've been kind enough to overlook. And what will this son of yours be? A Moshke like yourself! He'll wear your miserable clothes, and speak your miserable tongue, and sing your miserable songs in front of a landowner like myself. What kind of life will that be? Poverty and degradation, penury and deprivation, just like your own. Now I, Moshke, out of the goodness of my heart, feel compassion for the lad—who they tell me is a handsome child too—and I don't wish him to grow up an accursed, disgusting Jew. Give him over to me, Moshke, and let me raise him. I swear to you, he'll have the best of everything. I'm a lonely, childless man, and whatever riches God has granted me will be his too.'

" 'But your grace!' said Reb Yosef in a fright. 'You know that I'm a Jew . . .'

" 'To hell with your Jewishness, you scum! A miserable Jew doesn't want a Polish nobleman to bring up his child! I'm giving you eight days to pay me my back taxes from the past eight years, and if you don't bring me the money, I'll have you and your wife and your children thrown into the pit in my yard. Do I make myself clear, Moshke?'

2. Literally, "husk." In Kabbalistic lore, the principle of impurity or evil imprisoning holiness.

"Now this landowner was a great and terrible sorcerer, so that when Reb Yosef told his wife what he had threatened, she said to him: 'Listen to me, husband. I've been told that the Baal Shem Tov, who is a man of God and can work miracles, is staying in a town not far from here. Go to him and ask him to give you a charm to protect the child against sorcery.' So Reb Yosef set out for the Baal Shem, and as soon as he entered the house where the Baal Shem was staying, he saw the old man whose blessing had brought him a son. Reb Yosef recognized him, but the old man pretended not to know him, until the Baal Shem called out: 'Leib! Why are you pretending? Let the world know that your powers are great in heaven and on earth! Go with this man and help him, be quick and don't fear. Take my stick with you too, but don't let go of it for a moment—remember that I've warned you. And take eight men along with you, so that you'll have a *minyan* for prayer. On the eve of the child's circumcision you're to stay up all night studying the Mishnah and reading in the Zohar, and you're to close all the doors and plug all the holes in the windows and the chimney. If anyone knocks on the door, you're not to open it. If anyone calls you, you mustn't answer. Even if he calls in my name, you mustn't reply. Remember, I've warned you!'

"The night arrived. The minyan assembled in the mother's room. Reb Leib Sorehs pronounced spells and incantations and drew a circle around the mother's bed with the Baal Shem's walking stick. He whispered holy names over it and said, turning to those present: 'You had better know now that the battle we must fight tonight will be very hard and grueling. Samael has summoned his forces because he wants to steal the child's soul; the landowner is Samael's offspring; he wants to take the child and raise him to be a goy, to hand him over to the klipa, God forbid. So, brothers, be strong! Stay awake through the night studying the Mishnah and reading in the Zohar and don't take your eyes off your books for a second. You'll see and hear many things tonight, but you needn't be afraid. This stick'—and he raised it for all to see—'belongs to the Baal Shem, and it will drive away all goblins, wizards, and devils. So in the name of the Lord God of Israel, and of our master Israel ben Havah the Baal Shem Tov, don't be afraid! The Lord will fight for you, and ye shall hold your peace!'

"The words were scarcely out of his mouth when there came a loud knock on the door: 'Open up! In the name of the landowner,

open up!' But no one opened. 'Open up! I'm the landowner's
servant! He'll make you pay for it dearly, you miserable Jews, if
you don't open the door!' But no one opened. Silence. An hour
went by and there was a knock on the door again. 'Open up!
Moshke, open the door! It's I, the landowner. Moshke, don't you
know who I am? Open up! I'll have you flogged with a wet birch
rod tomorrow if you don't open up! Moshke! Moshke, I have something to tell you. Open the door! I'll have you thrown out tomorrow
for good if you don't open up!' But no one opened. Another hour
went by and a great commotion could be heard far away. The noise
was of a large crowd of men loudly approaching the house. Someone
knocked rowdily on the door: 'Yoske, open the door, we want some
brandy!' But no one opened. 'Yoske! What's the matter with you,
Yoske, why don't you open the door? We need a drink. Give us
some brandy or we'll break the door down! Yoske, open up! Enjoy
yourself all you want with your Jew friends that you brought from
town, but give us our brandy. Give us brandy, Yoske, or we'll bash
down the walls of your house until there isn't a stone left in place.'
They banged furiously on the door until it seemed certain to break;
they ripped the shutters from the windows and hurled rocks through
them; the house groaned out loud as though it were about to collapse on them all—but still no one opened . . .

   "Yet another hour passed and the distant sound of music could
be heard. Ah, what a wonderful melody! It tugged hard at their legs
to run greet the musicians. All their senses felt drugged: their
hearts pounded, their eyes grew moist, their legs began to move of
their own accord; the blood pulsed sweetly yet strangely through
their veins in time to the music. The melody came nearer. They
sought to stay in their seats and read on in the Zohar, but the music
kept calling them away. They mustered all their strength to stay
put, but the music kept calling . . . their vision dimmed, thousands
of dots swam helter-skelter before them . . . their eyelids craved
sleep and their drowsy minds, rest—but their hearts leaped within
them for life—soon they would splinter into pieces from so much
desire . . . the sound came still closer. The music seemed to be
directly behind the windows and door. Now it was sad and their
eyes filled with tears as they read in the Zohar; now it grew merry
again, and they laughed as they read with sheer joy while their feet
danced in place. The instruments called them. Their hearts were
filled with a pleasant yearning. If only they could step out for a

second and see the marvelous musicians—but it was forbidden. Reb Leib stood leaning on the walking-stick with all his might, his lips moving soundlessly through charms and incantations. The music stopped . . . suddenly there was a knock on the door: 'Open in the name of Rabbi Israel Baal Shem!' 'Coming!' called out one of the minyan. Reb Leib shuddered and made a face . . . but it was already too late: a black cat sprang into the house, ran to the bed, snatched the child from its mother, and disappeared. 'Samael has triumphed!' Reb Leib exclaimed and fell unconscious to the floor.

"The next morning Reb Yosef came to the manor house and asked the servants to be admitted to see the landowner.

" 'The landowner's orders are to flog you fifty strokes with a wet birch rod,' the servants said.

" 'But in God's name,' Reb Yosef protested, 'what crime have I committed? Let him give me back my son and flog me eighty strokes! I beg you, for the love of God, let me see the landowner.'

" 'Beat him without mercy!' came the landowner's voice from within the house.

"Reb Yosef died the next day and his family was banished from the village.

"The boy grew up in the landowner's house. He was a striking, fair-eyed lad, bright and attentive, and the landowner loved him dearly. He taught him all seven sciences and was amazed at how quickly he learned.

" 'Father!' the boy asked one day. 'Tell me, what is a *zhid?*'

" 'A zhid is an evil spirit, a devil, an imp.'

" 'Then why do all the boys in the manor yard calle me a zhid?'

" 'I wouldn't know,' said the landowner, biting his lips in anger.

"From that day on he wasn't called zhid any more.

" 'Father!' he asked another time. 'I saw you talking today to a miserable-looking, stooped man, and you said to him, 'Moshke, you dog.' And as he was leaving the boys called him zhid and threw rocks at him. Is he really a devil? Then why aren't you afraid of him?'

" 'No, my son, he's a Jew, a member of that miserable, damned race on which the curse of God rests eternally.'

" 'Then are a Jew and a devil the same?'

" 'Exactly the same, son.'

" 'Father!' the boy asked yet another time when he was twelve

years old. 'Am I really a zhid? Today one of the boys in the yard
said to me: "Peter, you may as well know you're a zhid. My father
told me last night that your father was a zhid and that his name
was Yoske. My father said that your father was a good, honest man,
and that he never got drunk or beat his wife, but that he prayed
all day long to the God of the zhids." Is it true, father, that I'm
really a zhid?'

"No, son, it's a lie!' the landowner answered, distraught.

"But before the boy's thirteenth birthday he dreamt a dream
in which a white-haired old man was standing over him. His face
was all bruised and looked poor and ill-favored like a sick zhid's.
'I'm your father,' the bowed old man exclaimed. 'The landowner
snatched you from your mother's lap, and me, your father, he killed.
But you're a Jew and you must live like a Jew . . . in a few days'
time you'll be thirteen years old, and a Jewish boy of thirteen is
commanded to perform God's will and to devote himself to His
holy Torah. Come, rise, my son, and follow me.'

"The boy shuddered and cried out in his sleep—and awoke.

"'What made you cry last night?' the landowner asked him
when he arose the next morning.

"'I had a terrible dream, father!' answered the boy with tears
in his eyes.

"'What was it, son? Tell me about it. Dreams musn't be taken
seriously.'

"'Oh, father, I'm afraid even to tell you . . . it's so awful . . .
in my dream a flayed, beaten zhid came up to me, and he said he
was my father, and that I was a Jew, and he said that I must follow
him. Ah, father, is it really true that I'm a zhid? The boys in the
yard say I'm one, too.'

"'They're lying,' said the landowner, 'and your dream doesn't
mean a thing.' But it was clear that he was frantic.

"'Oh, father!' said the boy the next morning. 'Last night the
Jew beat me terribly. He pulled my hair and scratched me with
his nails until I bled. If only you could have seen how awful he
looked with his bloodshot eyes and his wrinkled brow, which
seemed so full of worry and affliction . . . if only you could have
heard how dreadful he sounded when he said to me: "You're a Jew
and I'm your father—rise and follow me, or else I'll kill you right
now!" . . . if only . . . oh, father, father, father!'

"And on the third morning, when he awoke from his sleep, he

found himself lying naked in one of the streets of the village on the threshhold of the synagogue.

"That night the rabbi of the village dreamt that he saw a white-haired old man with an angel's face and a voice as soft and sweet as a lute, in which he implored him: 'Rabbi, tomorrow morning, on the threshhold of the synagogue, the sextons will find a naked, handsome, fair-eyed boy. The boy is my son. The landowner made off with him by black magic, murdered me, and banished my wife and children from the village. Tomorrow the boy will be thirteen years old, yet he doesn't know a word of Yiddish or a letter of the Hebrew alphabet. I beg you, be a father to him. Teach him God's Torah and the way of His commandments. And know too that his is a great soul, but that Samael lies always in wait for it, so that you must wage the Lord's battle to keep the fiend from carrying it off through your gates.'

"The rabbi took the boy into his home.

"By the end of the first day the boy had learned the letters of the alphabet. By the second, he knew the vowels too. By the third, he could read in the prayerbook. By the fourth, he was able to pray. By the fifth, he began to study Bible. The rabbi loved him like a father and the rabbi's wife raised him as though he were her own. Whatever he did, he did well, and all were amazed at his prowess in Torah.

" 'My boy!' the rabbi said to him one morning, 'You were born to be a great rabbi and scholar in Israel, and I can no longer be your teacher. Here, take this letter of recommendation to Amsterdam, where you'll study in the Great Yeshiva. But always remember your dead father, and remember me too, and the God of Israel, Who is One. Never forget, my boy, that Satan lies in wait for your soul. Both your father and I have fought mightily to save it, but now it is God's will that you leave me, for it's time you were put to the test. Here, take this amulet, and take my walking stick too, which I shall give you. Whenever you lie down to sleep, make a circle around you with this stick, and don't dare leave it until sunup. And hold this amulet in your hand until you rise. Remember, I've warned you! Now be of good cheer.'

"Then the rabbi fell upon the boy and wept, and the boy wept too, and the rabbi's wife, too, wept where she stood.

"The boy shouldered his pack—and set out.

"And so the young lad, who had been raised in satins and

silks, whose every step had been guarded like the apple of their eye by valets, tutors, governesses, menservants and maidservants, now made his way on foot with a pack on his back. The way was a long one. He had to pass towns and villages, rivers and forests, in order to reach the Great Yeshiva in Amsterdam. But pass them he must, and he did. His path took him through a great forest. Huge oak trees towered by each side of the road. The way seemed endless, the forest endlessly deep. The sun began to set. His feet were weary from walking. He stopped to recite the afternoon prayer while darkness covered the earth, and then he recited the evening prayer too. After he had prayed, he took a crust of bread from his pack and sat down to eat. But there was no water with which to wash his hands. How could he eat without washing? He felt terribly tired and weak. His eyes began to close on their own. He said the *Shema* and drew a circle around where he lay. Then, clutching the amulet in his hand, he placed the pack beneath his head and fell asleep.

"He had hardly shut his eyes when a great noise woke him. When he opened them, he spied a pack of wolves racing through the forest and heading straight for him. The wolves' eyes glittered like fire and their horrible, sharp fangs were bared in their gaping mouths. The pack came nearer and nearer . . . it reached the limits of the circle . . . it pressed against them, but the pack couldn't break through. The harder the wolves tried, the harder they were thrown back, so that they leapt insanely with fury. But they couldn't cross the circle. The wolves vanished . . . and out of the forest rushed a wild boar. It charged as far as the circle and halted, because it, too, couldn't advance any further. Then the boar vanished, and all of a sudden the most wonderful music came forth from the depths of the forest. It wafted on the wings of the unsullied wind which was then blowing softly through the forest. The wind which blows all the way from the Garden of Eden at the stroke of midnight when the Gates of Paradise swing open for the Thirty-Six Just Souls who come every night to study Torah with the Seven Shepherds.

"He felt that the wonderful musicians were calling to him . . . he remembered the landowner and his fiddle . . . yes, the landowner was a marvelous fiddler, and he had taught the boy to fiddle too. How he had loved his little fiddle! He wanted to step out of the circle, but he forced himself not to. His heart melted like water within him from desire . . . his hands shook, the amulet slipped

from his grasp . . . it fell to the ground, and against his will, he
was dragged from the circle and carried off on the wings of the
wind, up and away toward the sound of the music. He flew over
oceans and rivers, fields and forests, while the musicians played
before him. They seemed just a handbreadth away, but he couldn't
catch up with them. Here was his native village . . . here was the
landowner's manor . . . he was standing in front of the door . . .
it opened, and—and a powerful, large hand seized him, pulling him
back. There was a furious struggle. One force pulled him mightily
into the landowner's house, while another pulled him back just as
mightily. 'I'm your father,' called a figure like that he had seen in
his dreams. 'I'm Yosef, your father, and you're my son. Don't you
recognize me? I'm your father, and you're my son. You're a Jew,
you mustn't enter the house! Here you'll become a goy, a creature
of appetite, a drunk! Don't follow the music of the fiddle. The
music is the service of a strange god and the fiddler is Asmodai,
Satan himself. Son, go to Amsterdam, to the yeshiva. There you'll
study Torah, the Law of the Living God! Look at me, son. My
flesh is tattered and flayed, the cruel landowner flogged me. If you
become a landowner, you'll be cruel too. Son, go to Amsterdam and
study Torah! Don't listen to the music of the fiddle . . . here, take
this amulet which you lost in the forest. Go back, my son, go back.'
And once again he was carried off on the wings of the . . ."

My little brother Sandrel suddenly awoke from his sleep and
began to cry. My mother broke her story and bent down to quiet
him, then laid my sister Sarka on her bed. My sister Breyndl was
drowsing while sitting up—a stocking in one hand and her ball of
yarn and darning needle in the other. Her eyes were shut and her
head bobbed up and down, tossing her pretty curls to and fro. The
oil was nearly gone from the lamp, whose light grew steadily dim-
mer. Patches of darkness spread over the room. The blackened
ceiling cast its shadow halfway down the walls. A terrible melancholy filled the house. Something hung in the air and I didn't know
what—whether it was good or evil, holy or unclean, but I did know
that whatever it was, it was dreadful. Yes, the house was dreadful,
the heder was dreadful, the rabbi was dreadful, the synagogue was
dreadful, the world was dreadful, and life was dreadful . . . and in
this dreadful life we had to battle every minute with dreadful
powers that lay constantly in wait for us. We had to battle with the
goyim, with imps disguised as chimneysweeps, with the unclean

spiders who brought the fire with which to burn down the Temple of our Lord, with exile, with demons, with the Evil Urge. Sometimes the Evil Urge might even tempt a Jew to look at a woman or to eat unclean meat . . . ah, how dreadful it was! The Evil Urge was so strong! How hard it was to have to lead such a dreadful, sinful life! The tears came to my eyes. My mother looked at me and said:

"Hofni, tomorrow I'll tell you the rest. Now say the Shema [3] and kiss the *mezuzah* [4] and go to sleep because there's no oil left in the lamp and this is no time for telling stories."

"But, mama, what happened to the boy in the end?"

"I'll tell you the rest tomorrow."

"But did he stay with the landowner?"

"No, it's still a long story. I'll tell you the rest tomorrow. The boy stayed a good Jew, and you too, Hofni, must be a good Jew like your forefathers."

Full of emotion, I said the Shema and kissed the mezuzah. When I lay down in bed I continued to think fondly of the brave boy, who strove with Samael and prevailed, until my eyes shut and I slept.

Translated by Hillel Halkin

---

3. "Hear O Israel" the bedtime prayer.
4. A small case nailed to the doorpost containing passages from Deuteronomy written on parchment. The *mezuzah* was popularly believed to ward off demons.

IMITATION
AND ASSIMILATION

AHAD HA-AM

INTRODUCTION

AHAD HA-AM *("One of the People," pen name of Asher Ginzburg, 1856–1927) was the most influential of modern Hebrew essayists in Europe. His importance is both literary and ideological. His lucid, balanced Hebrew created a new model for modern Hebrew prose. His "cultural Zionism," stressing that the return to Zion must be part of a general renaissance of Jewish culture and values, had a profound effect on the thinking of many of the founding fathers of the modern Jewish community in Palestine. Though he spent the last two decades of his life in London, and then in Tel Aviv, his most important literary activity was in the Hebrew literary center at Odessa, especially in the 1890s and the first years of the twentieth century. He was involved there in editing—most notably, of the prestigious Hebrew journal, Ha-Shiloah—and in publishing as well as in the writing of his reflective essays on Zionism, Jewish culture, and related matters.*

Ahad Ha-am and those around him were engaged in what they viewed as a challenging and perilous experiment in sustaining the life of the Jewish people under radically different circumstances— not as an enclosed religious community but as a new kind of national entity that would participate fully in modern Western culture while incorporating both religious and secularist factions, with a

*geographical center for some of its members, though others would
continue to be scattered around the globe. Against this background,
it was of the greatest importance to determine what it was that made
national groups hold together and that enabled them to maintain a
distinctive cultural life. This essay, then, which might at first seem
to be a series of general reflections on a question of social theory, in
fact had the utmost practical relevance for its audience.*

*Ahad Ha-am's enormous influence stemmed partly from his
talents as a popularizer of leading European intellectual currents
among his Hebrew readers (most of them self-educated men, former
yeshiva students and the like), and the argument of this essay reflects
both the strengths and the weaknesses of his approach. The essay
betrays a somewhat facile reliance on a notion of historical meliorism
inherited from the European Enlightenment and from the optimistic
currents of nineteenth-century thought. It draws upon Bentham and
the British Utilitarians in a rather mechanical way. It assumes that
every society strives to "approach the perfection of its form," an
ultimately Platonic idea which Ahad Ha-am appears to have translated into the realm of historical causation with little attention to
its demonstrability.*

*Similarly, the analogy drawn between the way a hypothetical
small community comes into being by imitating a central individual,
to the way a people with millions of members, scattered over the
globe, speaking many languages, and living in highly variegated
circumstances, is supposed to achieve unity by imitating a "local
center," leaves something to be desired. Unfortunately, this sort of
armchair anthropology and armchair history is all too frequent in
Ahad Ha-am's writings, though perhaps the very appearance of
simple plausibility in such reasoning was what made Ahad Ha-am
attractive to his first audience of autodidact Hebraists.*

*Nevertheless, if Ahad Ha-am is limited by his transitional state
between two intellectual cultures, seeming to understand the modern
one more than he often did in fact, he was also able to capitalize on
his own ambiguous position with valuable insights.*

*As a secularist who had grown up in a religious background,
Ahad Ha-am had a keen sense of how a whole dominant segment of
Judaism in recent centuries became the powerless captive of its own
past. He cites the Talmudic statement, "If our predecessors were as
men, then we are but as asses," as the summary of the relationship
of an entire culture to its past. He is, then, dedicated to promoting*

a new forward-looking orientation. Yet he insists on the necessity of the self-effacing imitation of the past as a source of stability in any society, and his perception of the need to balance change with continuity has abiding relevance, as modern Jewry continues to struggle with this tension of opposites. Whatever the faults in Ahad Ha-am's general social theory, he had a firm sense of pride and self-respect as the member of a vulnerable minority group, and an excellent understanding of the moral and psychological perils of the marginal existence lived by minority-group members.

His analysis of the kind of self-abasement a minority undergoes in aping the majority culture out of a sense of its own inferiority carries great conviction; and the conclusion he draws from this understanding about the mechanism of assimilation is a probing one: "It is not imitation as such that leads to assimilation. The real cause is the original self-effacement, which leads to assimilation through the medium of imitation."

There is a core of compelling truth in the concomitant argument that competitive assimilation is the key to the persistence of the Jews through all the centuries of their dispersal. One may wonder whether the concept of a "spiritual center" in the Land of Israel can ever have the historical efficacy that Ahad Ha-am imagined, whether the commitment of historical Jewry to spiritual rather than physical power was as clearcut as he liked to think, but it is hard to gainsay the "genius for imitation" that he attributes to the Jews, with the large historical implications such a genius carries with it. It is instructive that one of the most forceful general interpretations of Jewish history, that of Yehezkel Kaufmann in Gola ve-Nekhar *("Diaspora and Alien Lands"), includes a devastating critique of Ahad Ha-am yet forges into one of its basic principles an idea of competitive assimilation.*

IMITATION AND ASSIMILATION (1893)
AHAD HA-AM

WE USE THE TERM imitation, generally in a depreciatory sense, to indicate that which a man says, does, thinks, or feels—not out of his own inner life, as an inevitable consequence of his spiritual condition and his relation to the external world—but by virtue of his ingrained tendency to make himself like others, and to be this or that because others are this or that.

If we accept the doctrine that moral good is good in itself, and evil is evil in itself, and that we distinguish between the two not by syllogisms, but by a particular moral sense implanted in our being, then we are certainly justified in regarding imitation as a moral shortcoming. The moral sense does not approve this habit of the ape. But if we agree with another school of thought,[1] that the distinction between good and evil rests on a balancing of gains and losses from the point of view of the happiness and development of human society, then we may doubt whether the judgment of the moral sense in this case is just. There may be a certain amount of exaggeration and one-sidedness in the doctrine of the French thinker

---

1. The British social philosophy known as Utilitarianism, founded by Jeremy Bentham (1748–1832). It held that the main goal of any social ethic should be "the greatest possible good for the greatest possible number."

Tarde,[2] who holds that all history is but the fruit of imitation, acting in accordance with certain laws. But as to the essential point, a cursory examination of history is sufficient to convince us that this not entirely praiseworthy habit is in truth one of the foundations of society, without which its birth and development would have been impossible. For consider: had men been by nature not inclined in any way to follow one another, had each one thought his thoughts, and done his deeds, out of his own inner world alone, without yielding obedience to the force of any other personality, could they have attained, by common consent, to such social possessions as established laws and customs, and common ideas about religion and morality, possessions which are, indeed, in their general aspect, natural results of general causes, but which, regarded in detail, depend wholly on causes of a particular and individual character? Above all, how could language have been created and developed in any society, if no man had imitated his neighbor, but each had waited until he reached the spiritual condition in which he would be impelled to call each thing by the particular name by which his neighbor called it? Without language, no knowledge: and so man would never have risen above the beast.

But even imitation would not have been enough to secure the spreading of these common possessions among all the individual members of society, if each individual had imitated all the rest in an equal degree. In that case the number of the objects of imitation would have been equal to that of the imitators; each man would have chosen one object of imitation out of many, according to his "spiritual condition"; and so the same difficulty would confront us again. If society is to be molded into one single form, there must be some center toward which all the forces of imitation are attracted, directly or indirectly, and which thus becomes the single or the chief object of universal imitation.

Such a center was, indeed, found in every society in the earliest stages of its development, and especially in that primitive period in which the human spirit was struggling to emerge from the depths of beasthood and attain to a human and social form of life. At that low stage (in which some savage tribes remain to this day), when man

2. Gabriel de Tarde (1843–1904), who developed a general social theory distinguishing between inventive and imitative persons, and whose *Laws of Imitation* (1890), published only three years before this essay, would seem to be behind much of Ahad Ha-am's theorizing here.

was constantly threatened by dangers from all sides, he set an exaggerated value on brute force, and revered the stronger as an angel of heaven. Every family or tribe looked with reverence on its head and protector, "the prince of God in its midst." The individuality of each man, with all its particular characteristics and qualities, was completely suppressed before the majestic dignity of this their ideal. Thus he became the center toward which the imitative instinct of all his fellow-tribesmen directed itself automatically; and it is no wonder if, not of design or set purpose, but merely through the effacement of the lower personality before the higher, his words and his actions and his habits became the common possession of the whole tribe.

This common possession was handed down as an inheritance from father to son; and in each succeeding generation there was another "prince of God," who was faithful to tradition, but also amplified it where it no longer satisfied the needs of a more developed life; and so his addition became, through imitation, common property. Thus, by an easy process, certain fixed habits of life became general in that particular society, until, in time, its individual members were like so many reproductions of a single type.

There is no nation or society, not even the most modern, that did not originally pass through this or a similar stage: the stage of becoming, or growth, in which scattered elements are welded together into a single social body around certain central figures, by means of self-effacing imitation. But in more modern times, when the human spirit has progressed somewhat, there is this difference: the cause of self-effacement, and thus of imitation and of the welding process, is not necessarily a purely physical force, but may equally well be some great force of a spiritual character.

Imitation of this kind, however, which has for its central object some living, active individual, inevitably grows rarer and rarer from one generation to another. Each new generation inherits from its predecessors the results of imitation up to that time—that is, the things that have become common property. As these things increase in number, so does the society approach the perfection of its form until, at last, that form is complete and rounded on all sides—and the best men of the living generation have no opportunity of adding anything essential. From that time onward, therefore, the central object of imitation lies wholly in the past, in those "mighty men of renown" who in their day impressed their own image on the form of society. Just as the results of imitation during all the generations of growth have been combined into a single form of life, so, too, those who made that form in those earlier generations are now combined under the name of ancestors or predecessors into a single abstract being, which is the central object of imitation. Before this model the men of later generations, great and small alike, efface their own individuality. They gaze on this with reverence and say, "If our predecessors were as men, then are we but as asses" (Shabbat 112b).

At the same time, the imitation of one man by another within the living generation does not cease, but is confined to unimportant details. It lacks a single common center, and, as a rule, arises from quite a different cause. That self-effacement, which is the result of reverent awe, no longer finds a suitable object in the present, which lives entirely on the past. The impulse to imitation of the living, by the living, is now given by competition, the roots of which lie in jealousy and self-love. There are many who succeed even then in attracting the attention of society, and rising above their fellows, through some new discovery in matters of detail, whether theoretical or practical. Their success impels others to follow in their footsteps, not by way of self-effacement, but, on the contrary, out of jealousy for their own individuality, and a desire to rise to the same level as others.

This kind of imitation differs from the other in its character as well as in its cause. At the stage that we have called self-effacement the imitator wishes to copy the spirit or personality of the model, as it is manifested in his actions. Therefore he imitates these actions in every detail—faithful to the impress stamped upon them by the personality by which he is attracted. But at the stage of competition, the whole desire of the imitator is to reveal *his own* spirit or personality in those ways in which the model revealed *his*. He therefore endeavors to change the original impress, according as his personality or his position differs from that of his model.

This kind of imitation, also, is of benefit to society. The self-effacing imitation of the past secures stability and solidity; the competitive imitation of one individual by another makes for progress—not by means of noisy and sudden revolutions—but by means of continual small additions, which have in time a cumulative effect, and carry society beyond the limits laid down by the predecessors.

But imitation is not always confined to the sphere of a single society. Progress gradually brings different societies into closer intimacy and fuller acquaintance with one another, and then imitation widens its scope, and becomes intersocial or international.

The character of this imitation will be determined by the character of the communities that are brought into contact. If they are more or less equal in strength and on much the same level of culture, then there will immediately be "competitive imitation" on both sides. Either will learn from the other new ways of expressing its spirit, and will strive to surpass the other in those ways. But it will be different if one of the two societies concerned is so much smaller and weaker than the other in physical or spiritual strength as to feel its own lack of vitality and individuality when brought face-to-face with the superior community. In that case the result will be a self-effacing imitation on the part of the weaker, arising not from a desire to express its own spirit, but from respect and submission. This imitation will be complete and slavish. It will not stop at those qualities which have impelled the weaker community to efface its own individuality, and in which the imitated community really excels. It will extend also to those qualities which, in the superior community itself, are only the result of subservience to the distant past, and which, accordingly, would never have forced themselves, of their own strength, on any community which had not *itself* inherited that past.

No community can sink to such a position as this without danger to its very existence. The new subservience to a foreign community gradually replaces the old subservience to its own past, and the center to which the forces of imitation are directed shifts more and more from the latter to the former. The national or communal self-consciousness loses its foundation, and gradually fades away, until at last the community reaches an unnatural condition, which is neither life nor death. "The soul is burnt out, yet the body remains" (Sanhedrin, 52a). Then the individual members find a way of escape from this death-in-life by complete assimilation with the foreign community.

When the cause of this self-effacement is physical or material strength, and the weaker community cannot hope to strengthen itself on the material side, then, indeed, there is nothing for it but assimilation. It was in this way that the smaller nations of ancient times disappeared when their territories were conquered by more powerful nations. The strong arm—the highest ideal of those days—always brought about the self-effacement of the conquered nation before the conqueror. After long years of slavery and humiliation, with no possibility of self-help, the survivors lost their reverence for their own past, and one by one left the fold to become swallowed up in the stronger enemy.

But such is not the usual development when the self-effacement is due to some great spiritual force. An external, material force is clearly discernible in its effects, and it is impossible for the weaker community to belittle its importance, or to stem the tide of its progress. But the advent of a foreign *spiritual* force is not so obvious. Means can be found by which its importance can be made to appear less, and its progress can be hindered, among a people to which it is foreign. When, therefore, a community finds its individuality endangered by an alien spiritual force, and men begin to imitate the foreign mode of life in which that force is embodied, there will always be a party of zealots, striving to belittle the external force in the estimation of their own people, and to cut off their people entirely from all contact with foreign life, so that it may have no attraction for them. These zealots generally succeed at first in staying the progress of the external force, and thus prevent imitation.

But this prevention is not a complete cure. The community remains always in danger. It may be that the conditions of life will break down the barriers erected by force, and then contact will lead to self-effacement, self-effacement to imitation, and imitation to assimilation. Nay, more. The very separation sometimes has the opposite effect to that which is intended. There are many who catch glimpses of the foreign life from afar, and admire it without being able to approach, until at last they leap over the barrier once for all, and escape to the enemy's camp.

As a result of this experiment in restriction, the leaders of the community generally learn—and it is fortunate for them and for the community if they learn in time—that it is not imitation as such that leads to assimilation. The real cause is the original self-effacement, which leads to assimilation through the medium of imitation. Their task, therefore, is not to check imitation, but to abolish self-effacement. This abolition, too, must be effected by means of imitation— but of the competitive kind. That is, they must appropriate for their community that spiritual force which is the cause of the self-effacement, so that the community will no longer look with distant awe on the foreign life in which that force is embodied. On the contrary, it will turn that force to its own uses, in order, as we said, "to reveal *its own* spirit or personality in those ways in which the model revealed *his.*" When once the community is started on this path of imitation, self-love will make it believe in its own strength, and value the imitative actions peculiar to itself more than those developed by its model. The further imitation proceeds on these lines, the more it reveals the spirit of the imitators, and the less it remains faithful to the original type. Thus the self-consciousness of the imitating community becomes ever stronger, and the danger of assimilation disappears.

Examples of this kind of imitation are found both in ancient and in modern history. Such was the relation of the Romans to Greek culture, such the relation of the Russians to the culture of Western Europe. Both began with self-effacement before a foreign spiritual force, and therefore with slavish imitation of a foreign kind of life—in thought, speech, action. Zealots like Cato, who tried to shut out the stream of imitation altogether, succeeded only partially and temporarily. Patriots of clearer vision began subsequently to lead imitation along the road of competition, of striving to embody the spiritual force (the cause of self-effacement) in the particular type of life of their own people. The result was that the self-effacement ceased, and the imitation produced a strengthening of national self-consciousness.

This will explain why the Jewish people has persisted in Exile, and has not become lost among the nations, in spite of its inveterate tendency to imitation.

As early as the time of the Prophets, our ancestors learned to despise physical strength, and to honor only the power of the spirit. For this reason, they never allowed their own individuality to be effaced because of the superior physical strength of the persecutor. It was only in the face of some great *spiritual* force in the life of a foreign people that they could sink their own individuality and give themselves up entirely to that life. Knowing this, their leaders endeavored to cut them off entirely from the spiritual life of other nations, and not to allow the smallest opening for imitation. This policy of separation, apart from the fact that it caused many to leap over the barrier once for all, could not, in view of the position of our people among the nations, be carried out consistently. When the era of contact set in, and continued unbroken, there were con-

stant proofs that the apprehensions of the zealots had been ground-
less, and their efforts at restriction unnecessary.

The Jews have not merely a tendency to imitation, but a genius
for it. Whatever they imitate, they imitate well. Before long they
succeed in appropriating for themselves the foreign spiritual force
to which they have become subservient. Then their teachers show
them how to use this force for their own ends, in order to reveal
their own spirit, and so the self-effacement ceases, and the imitation
—turned into the channel of competition—gives added strength to
the Hebrew self-consciousness.

Long before the Hellenists in Palestine tried to substitute Greek
culture for Judaism, the Jews in Egypt had come into close contact
with the Greeks—with their life, their spirit, and their philosophy—
yet we do not find among them any pronounced movement toward
assimilation. On the contrary, they employed their Greek knowledge
as an instrument for revealing the essential spirit of Judaism, for
showing the world its beauty, and vindicating it against the proud
philosophy of Greece. That is to say, starting from an imitation
which had its source in self-effacement before an alien spiritual force,
they succeeded, by means of that imitation, in making the force their
own, and in passing from self-effacement to competition.

If those Elders, who translated the Bible into Greek for the
benefit of the Egyptian Jews,[3] had also translated Plato into Hebrew
for the benefit of the Jews in Palestine, in order to make the spiritual
power of the Greeks a possession of our people on its own land and
in its own language, then, we may well believe, the same process
(the transition from self-effacement to competition) would have taken
place in Palestine also—but in a still higher degree, and with consequences yet more important for the development of the inner spirit
of Judaism. As a result there would have been no "traitorous enemies
of the covenant" [4] among our people, and perhaps there would have
been no need of the Maccabees and all the spiritual history which
had its ultimate cause in that period. Perhaps—who knows?—the
whole history of the human race would have taken a totally different
course.

3. The first translation of the Hebrew Bible, known as the Septuagint, was done
in Alexandria between 250 B.C.E. and 100 B.C.E. According to the traditional
legend, it was done by seventy sages, the "Elders" referred to here.
4. The Hellenizing Jews in Maccabean times who adopted Greek ways and
Greek religion.

But the Elders did not translate Plato into Hebrew. It was only at a much later date, in the period of Arabic culture,[5] that the Greek spirit became a possession of our people in their own language—but not on their own land. And yet even then, though on foreign soil, self-effacement soon gave place to competition, and this form of imitation had the most astonishing results. Language, literature, and religion, all renewed themselves; each helped to reveal the inner spirit of Judaism through the medium of the new spiritual possession. To such an extent did this new spirit become identified with Hebrew individuality that the thinkers of the period could not believe that it was foreign to them, and that Israel could ever have existed without it. They could not rest satisfied until they found an ancient legend to the effect that Socrates and Plato learned their philosophy from the Prophets, and that the whole of Greek philosophy was stolen from Jewish books which perished in the destruction of the Temple.

Since that time our history has again divided itself into two periods—a long period of complete separation, and a short period of complete self-effacement.[6] But once more we are nearing the conviction that safety lies in neither of these ways, but in a third, which is midway between them: that is, the perfection of the national individuality by means of competitive imitation.

Signs of this conviction are to be found not alone in the most recent years, since the day when nationalism became the watchword of a party in Israel, but also much earlier. We find them on the theoretical side in the production of a literature, in European languages, dealing with the spirit of Judaism and its value; on the practical side, in a movement toward the reform of the externals of Judaism. This practical movement is, indeed, held by many, including some of the reformers themselves, to be a long step toward assimilation. But they are wrong. When self-effacement has pro-

5. The reference is mainly to the so-called Golden Age of Hebrew culture in Spain (eleventh to fourteenth centuries) during which poetry, philosophy, philology, legal studies, flourished, producing such great creative figures as Maimonides, Judah Halevi, Solomon ibn Gabirol, Samuel ha-Nagid, Moses ibn Ezra, and Abraham ibn Ezra.
6. Ahad Ha-am is referring first to the period from the late Middle Ages to the French Revolution or thereabouts, a period of isolation and intense persecution for Jews, of growing pietism and legal rigidity in their religious life, of relative stagnation in cultural creativity. The second, shorter period encompasses the "adventure" of assimilation, the collective flight from Jewishness that began among Western Jews in the late eighteenth century.

ceeded so far that those who practice it no longer feel any inner bond uniting them with their own past, and really wish to emancipate the community by means of complete assimilation with a foreign body, then they no longer feel even the necessity of raising their inheritance to that degree of perfection which, according to their ideas, it demands.

On the contrary, they tend rather to leave it alone and allow it to perish of itself. Until that day comes, they imitate the customs of their ancestors to an extent determined by accident. It is a sort of artificial, momentary self-effacement, as though it were not they themselves who acted so, but the spirit of their ancestors that had entered into them at that moment, and acted as it had been accustomed to act of old.

Geiger [7] expresses the opinion that a writer who writes in Hebrew at the present day does not express his own inner spirit, but lives for the duration in another world, the world of the Talmud and the Rabbis, and adopts their mode of thinking. This is true of most of our Western scholars, as is evident from their style, because in their case the link between their ancestral language and their own being is broken. But with the Hebrew writers of Eastern Europe and Palestine, for whom Hebrew is still a part of their being, the case is just the reverse. When they write, the necessity of writing Hebrew springs from their innermost selves; they therefore strive to improve the language and bring it to a perfection that will enable them to express their thoughts in it with freedom, just as their ancestors did.

When, therefore, we find Geiger and his school giving their whole lives and all their powers to the reform of another part of their inheritance, according to their own ideas; when we find them content to accept the language as it is, but not content to accept the religion as it is; we have here decisive proof that it is on the religious side that their Hebrew individuality still lives. That individuality is not dead in them, but only stunted; and their real and true desire, whether or not they admit this to themselves and to others, is just this: "To reveal *their own* spirit or personality in those ways in which their model reveals *his.*"

7. Abraham Geiger (1810–1874), one of the important figures in the German renaissance of Jewish historical scholarship known as *Wissenschaft des Judentums* ("Science of Judaism"), and an outstanding spokesman for religious reform among German Jews.

Assimilation, then, is not a danger that the Jewish people must dread for the future. What it has to fear is being split up into fragments. The manner in which the Jews work for the perfection of their individuality depends everywhere on the character of that foreign spiritual force which is at work in their surroundings, and which arouses them to what we have called competitive imitation. One cannot but fear, therefore, that their efforts may be dissipated in various directions—according as the spiritual force varies in different countries—so, that in the end, Israel will be no longer one people, but a number of separate tribes, as at the beginning of its history.

Such an apprehension may derive support from experience. The Jews of Eastern Europe, for example, received their first lessons in Western culture from the Jews of Germany. Thus their central object of imitation, before which they sank their own individuality, was not the foreign spiritual force at work in their surroundings, but that which they saw at work among their own people in Germany. They therefore imitated the German Jews slavishly, without regard to differences of place and condition, as though they also had been perfect Germans in every respect. But, in time, when the Jews of Eastern Europe had made Enlightenment their own to a certain extent, and became conscious of their newly won strength, they passed from the stage of self-effacement to that of competition in relation to the Jews of Germany. They began to depart from their prototype, influenced by the different character of the spiritual force in the countries in which they lived. Similarly, the Jews of France are even now a model for imitation to the Jews in the East; but even in their case this state of things is only temporary, and will disappear when the Eastern Jews become conscious of their new strength. Thus, the more any section of our people adds to its spiritual strength, the more completely it becomes emancipated from the influence of that other section which it formerly imitated, and so the danger of being split into fragments grows ever more serious.

But there is one escape—and one only—from this danger. Just as in the stage of growth the members of the community were welded into a single whole—despite their different individual characteristics, through the agency of one central individual—so also in the stage of dissipation, the different sections of the people can be welded together—in spite of their different local characteristics, through the agency of a local center, which will possess a strong attraction for all of them, not because of some accidental or temporary relation, but by virtue of its own right. Such a center will claim a certain allegiance from each scattered section of the people. Each section will develop its own individuality along lines determined by imitation of its own surroundings, but all will find in this center a purifying fire and a connecting link at once.

In the childhood of the Jewish people, when it was split into separate tribes, the military prowess of David and the wise statesmanship of Solomon succeeded in creating for it a center such as this, "whither the tribes went up, the tribes of the Lord." But today, in its old age, neither strength nor wisdom nor even wealth will avail to create such a center anew. And so all those who desire to see the nation reunited will be compelled, in spite of themselves, to bow before historical necessity, and to turn eastward, to the land which was our center and our pattern in ancient days.

Translated by Leon Simon

THE SHORT FRIDAY

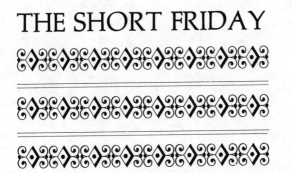

H. N. BIALIK

INTRODUCTION

H. N. BIALIK *(1873–1934) is still almost universally regarded as the greatest of modern Hebrew poets. His extraordinarily rich language, which seems to fuse creatively three thousands years of Jewish experience, raised Hebrew to a level of complexity and maturity it had not reached since the great Hebrew poets of medieval Spain. His poems provide a profound record of the spiritual crisis of modernity for Jews born in the world of pious tradition. He also wrote some extraordinary pieces of short fiction, many of them with a satirical realism directly influenced by Mendele. For a variety of reasons, Bialik wrote very little poetry in the last twenty years of his life, but, in compensation, he concentrated more than he had earlier on prose writing, and some of his essays on language, Jewish culture, and Hebrew literature have become classics of modern Hebrew thought. Bialik's peak years as a poet were spent in Odessa. Shortly after the Russian Revolution and the ensuing civil war, he managed to get out of Russia, and he spent the last decade of his life in Palestine.*

The plot of "The Short Friday" is a parody-reversal of familiar tales of wonder-rabbis caught in the woods before Sabbath, where coaches are miraculously flown home through the air to preserve the saintly men from desecrating the Sabbath. In order to get a sense of the story's intended impact, one should keep in mind the full force of the Sabbath for the traditional Jewish community, which would view with horror—even physical horror—the slighest infringement of any of the multitudinous Sabbath laws. There is, in a curious way, a certain analogy between the ending of this story and that of "The Emperor's New Clothes." For a rabbi to be seen riding on the Sabbath before the eyes of the community would be no less shocking than for an emperor to march naked in full view of his subjects.

It is clear that the presence of the narrator, with his comic manipulation of language and his ironic management of perspective, is indispensable to the total effect of the story. He could be described as an "as-if pious" narrator: "pious" because throughout he uses the language of tradition to be found in the mouths of the devout; "as-if" not only because he is the artful invention of a sophisticated modern writer, but because he clearly maneuvers his pious rhetoric for comic effect. Sometimes the effect is sheer burlesque, as when Reb Lippe opens his door at the beginning of Section II and "a pillar of vapor, bearing a Gentile in its midst, entered the house." This is descriptively accurate (it is a cold Russian winter day), while the "pillar of vapor" recalls, with delightful incongruity, the pillar of cloud that went before the Israelites in Exodus. As an instance where the "as-if pious" language introduces a more complex irony, one might consider the paragraph near the end of Section III ("At length, with the aid of Him . . ."). The drunken rabbi is lifted up, as a good Jew should say, "with the aid of Him who giveth the weary strength" (a quotation from Psalms). But of course we understand at once that it is really the "little extra aid from the guests" that does the trick. The narrator respectfully speaks of his two characters as "fine creatures," though both are dead drunk and the rabbi is seen here as a "bulging, bulky body." The narrator, again like a good Jew, says "pardon the proximity" (lehavdil) when he mentions the rabbi and the Gentile coachman in the same breath, but the real effect is to lump the two together in the same drunken cloddishness, as the story in general breaks down distinctions between separate realms, separate times. The two travelers leave Reb Getzi's house "in an auspicious and favorable hour," as any pious soul would wish, though the hour is in fact inauspicious and unfavorable.

The narrator, in the stylistic decorum he imposes on himself, is repeatedly careful to distinguish between Reb Lippe and Ivan.

The rabbi, indeed, is so far from entering into Ivan's world that "Ivan, Ai Vai" are offered as "the only three words of the language of the Gentiles" known to the rabbi! But Bialik again and again devises strategems for connecting the two men. Ivan sits in the kitchen at the brit, drinking glass after glass in parallel, as it were, with Reb Lippe. The description of the sleigh ride in the forest at the beginning of Section IV is a tour de force of ironically reversed distinctions. The first three paragraphs would seem to be arranged in descending order on the scale of creation—from Jew to Gentile to beast. The Jew falls into a "divine slumber"—but of course it is a drunken stupor, the narrator's irony at work again—while the coachman snores "like any swine." The horse, who at least stays awake, comes off best, though she imitates Reb Lippe in straying from the true road, forgetting, like a sinful human, the "promises of delights to come" and deciding on the "advisability of a penitent return" only when it is too late.

In a variety of ways, the rabbi at the inn, where the Sabbath becomes a weekday, is associated with a confusion of distinct realms. Half-asleep, half-awake, he mixes Torah with business, the world to come with rabbinical dues and communal imposts. On a physical level of confused distinctions, sweat intermingles with the rivulets of melting ice from his frozen beard. God in His heaven is said to be "engaged in His work" setting the cocks to crow and dividing between night and day, yet man mixes up the count of the succession of days. As Reb Lippe flees the inn with his absurd misunderstanding about what day of the week it is, he prays for an eternity of endless journeying—that is, not only an escape from his present situation, but a world of undifferentiated time, without weekday or Sabbath.

On its most obvious level, the story is a high-spirited satirical anecdote, and the technique and conception owe something to Mendele, though Bialik's anecdotalist does not participate in the action like the Bookseller, and the method of ironic indirection here may embody a covert sympathetic understanding for the target of the satire which one is not so likely to find in Mendele. In any case, the story is a translation into satiric farce of a serious problematic that continually preoccupied Bialik in his poetry and his essays: What happens to man and to meaning if the tradition-honored ordering of time and experience into separate realms of sacred and profane is broken down, if life can no longer be lived out as the

constant fulfillment of a set of divinely predetermined commandments? Disruption in the story is of course strictly comic, but Reb
Lippe's dream of endless journeying, his last sudden descent on the
Sabbath congregation like a grotesque epiphany from the weekday
world, intimate graver historical and theological dislocations.

THE SHORT FRIDAY (1925)
H. N. BIALIK

I

IF THOSE who are up and doing early on ordinary Fridays deserve praise, those who are up and doing early on the Short Friday deserve it far more. There is no excuse for laziness on the Short Friday at the turn of the year! Any sign of laziness whatsoever, and you may end up by desecrating the Sabbath, God forbid. Satan is always sure to be up to his devilish tricks just when the danger is greatest.

So it is in no way remarkable that the rabbi, Reb Lippe—long life to him—who was a gentle sort of Jew and timorous by nature, began to take steps against the Short Friday long before daylight. He treated himself with the greatest strictness. He feared and trembled exceedingly lest, God forbid, he might be even a little bit late, for then the entire order of his day would be spoiled.

Nor is there anything to scoff at in the order of Reb Lippe's day. Figure it out for yourself, and scrutinize the items closely. To begin with, there was the *Tikkun Hatzot,* or Midnight Prayers for Zion, consisting of both *Tikkun Rahel* and *Tikkun Leah.*[1]

---

1. It would take a long time to explain both of these in full, but very briefly, Rachel here represents the *Shekhinah* or Divine Presence in Exile, according to the words of the prophet Jeremiah who wrote, "A voice is heard in Ramah,

Then came Psalms arranged according to the days of the week; things to say and hors d'oeuvres before and after the prayers proper; the prayers proper; a few chapters of the Mishnah; a lesson in *Gemara;* two or three paragraphs of the Shulhan Arukh, which gives all the laws for the daily life of the Jew; and last, but not least, two readings of the actual text—and one of the Aramaic translation, of the Portion of the Week. All this was for the sake of the Lord. And now, how about himself? Food, that is to say. What was he to do, being, after all, flesh and blood! You have to eat, in spite of yourself sometimes . . .

A fresh series of tasks began after the noon hour. First the bath; then his nails had to be pared; then he prepared snuff for Sabbath; and the like. To which must be added his decisions, as called for, on questions of Jewish law and life, and on occasion a *Din Torah* or case to be heard and decided according to Jewish law. It is a known fact that quarrels are peculiarly frequent on Sabbath eves . . . And what with one thing and another, your day has gone! Before you turn this way and that, the sun's already setting.

So it is in no way surprising, as has been said, that Rabbi Lippe, rising valiant as a lion on the morning of the Short Friday, together with the morning star, hastened to wash his hands and set about his duties at once. Would that he might enter the day and leave it safe and sound! He trembled for fear lest a moment run to waste. From time to time his eyes rested on a venerable ancient, laden with limbs and years—the old grandfather clock which stood against the wall in front of him. He very much feared and dreaded, did Reb Lippe, that he might, God forbid, miss one of his daily duties, in which case he would begin his Sabbath without an easy mind, God forbid.

Yet the Sages have long since said that all things depend on luck. And neither wisdom nor understanding nor nimbleness are of avail, be it known, against luck . . .

Give ear therefore and hearken to this tale of woe.

lamentation and bitter weeping, Rachel weeping for her children, refusing to be comforted for her children who are not." Leah, on the other hand, represents the Shekhinah or Divine Presence which unites itself with each son of Israel through the study of the Torah. Clearly no trifle these; certainly not for Reb Lippe.   I. M. L.

II

Reb Lippe had finished all preliminaries of the early morning, as described above, and was just about to concentrate on the prayers proper, when suddenly his door creaked, and a pillar of vapor, bearing a Gentile in its midst, entered the house.

"Why should this fellow be at my door so early?" the rabbi wondered somewhat uneasily, shivering slightly and cowering at the wave of cold which had entered the house.

The Gentile set his whip against the doorpost, took off his gloves, thrust his hand into his bosom, groped about and finally withdrew from thence and handed to the rabbi a folded missive, crumpled and dirty all over. The rabbi read the missive through and shrugged his shoulders.

One of the devil's tricks! His heart had warned him! The wealthy Reb Getzi, the tax collector of the neighboring village, was inviting him to be present at a *brit*.[2] Whereas, ran the missive, whereas he, namely Reb Getzi, was on this day introducing his first grandson, the firstborn child of his firstborn daughter, into the Covenant of our Father Abraham, therefore, on account of the said reason, he honored him, namely the rabbi, long life to him, with the high office of *sandak* or godfather. It was therefore incumbent upon him, namely the rabbi, to give himself the trouble of coming down to the village; and to do so immediately. The sleigh stood waiting . . .

The worthy tax collector Reb Getzi, begging his pardon, was no great scribe, and no reader could course headlong through his letters. This time, however, he had taken wise precautions and had added three sufficient interpretations.

The first was a new currency note worth three rubles all nicely wrapped up; a "living and talking" bill which passed there and then from hand to hand; from the hand of the peasant to that of the rabbi, pardon the proximity.

The second was a sack of huge potatoes and beside it, trussed, a protesting goose, well fattened. The servant girl had removed this luscious brace from the sleigh, and they lay in the kitchen.

The third was even plainer and simpler. It was a fine, warm, broad, fur overcoat with felt overshoes which Reb Getzi had sent him in the hands of that Gentile, and which came from the winter

2. Circumcision ceremony.

store of garments of Reb Getzi's own worthy and honorable self, in order that the rabbi, long life to him, might wrap himself well and keep properly warm.

These three plain interpretations promptly cleared the eyes, as they say, of the rabbi, and his luminous intellect immediately compassed the entire affair.

"Tut, tut, what's to be done," he sighed. "Doubtless this is the will of the Holy and Blessed One; the Covenant of Circumcision, an injunction of that magnitude! But all the same, it's advisable to take counsel with the rebbetzin."

Reb Lippe entered the next room where the rebbetzin was, did whatever he had to do, stayed as long as he needed to stay, and came out clad in a white shirt and his Sabbath *zhupitza* (long coat), all ready to take the road. In the first room he now put on, over the zhupitza, the overcoat that had been sent him, tugged the yellow overshoes on his feet above his black boots, covered the skullcap on his head with his round furskin Sabbath *shtreimel*, girded his loins with the red belt of Ivan the Emissary; and so, magnificiently arrayed in these garments with their commingling of sacred and profane, Reb Lippe stopped and kissed the mezuzah on the doorpost. Then he departed from the house.

The sleigh which stood in front of the house was roomy and well bedded with hay and straw. Reb Lippe climbed in and settled himself comfortably, as though he were quite at home. The Gentile covered the rabbi's feet with straw and chaff and also got in. He whistled once, and the sleigh slid off across the snow.

III

The road was good and smooth and the mare was lively. Verily a contraction of the road, as described in legend . . .

Within an hour, and before day fully dawned, the rabbi had reached the village and the house of the celebrants.

The guests had already assembled. After drinking something warm they stood up and prayed with the quorum of ten according to all requirements of the Law. It turned out that a certain butcher, who had happened to come to the village to buy calves, had a pleasant voice and acted as the prayer-leader. His Hebrew, to be sure, was a trifle out of sorts. He could not quite make up his mind whether he wanted the winds to blow and rain to fall as in winter, or the dew to drop as in summer; but that was not serious. Finally they spat—as is fitting and seemly with the last prayer *Alenu,* in sign of dismissal of the emptiness and vanity worshiped by the peoples of the lands and the families of the earth. Satisfactorily done with prayer, the Order of the Circumcision commenced at an auspicious hour.

The baby in his diapers and swaddling clothes was brought in and passed from hand-to-hand. The uncle passed him to the father's uncle; the father's uncle to the brother's son; the brother's son to the father's father; the father's father to the mother's father; and so on and so forth till he finished up on the lap of the sandak, where that was done which had to be done. After it was over the passage began in reverse order. They lifted the tiny pink body, tied hand and foot, and wailing and shaking and quivering all over, and sent him back the way he had come: from the lap of the sandak to the arms of the father; from the arms of the father to the arms of the mother's father; from the arms of the mother's father to the arms of the father's father; and so on and so forth until the tiny mite was returned to the source of his being behind the walls, where he became a little quieter.

And now came the vital issue—namely the feast.

Reb Getzi the tax collector is a hospitable Jew, blessed by nature with a friendly eye and big heart even at ordinary times; and now that the Holy and Blessed One had permitted him to live to see a little grandson, firstborn son of his firstborn daughter, he was more hospitable than ever. So it stands to reason that the feast was worthy of a king. There was fish that brought to mind the biblical verse about the great whales. For meat they had a whole calf, a dozen geese, and three fattened swans, to say nothing of hors d'oeuvres such as stuffed crop, smooth, velvety stomachs, and breast and tongues and fried craws and other such trifles. And then for the pudding, the far-famed pudding with all its raisins!

Dismissing victuals, let us proceed to liquor. Reb Getzi, be it known, was an ordinary Jew without any particular pretensions and fancies. If he says brandy, it means brandy—that is brandy plain and simple, meaning not less than ninety-five percent spirit, and right old stuff at that! Meaning? Meaning brandy stored in his cellar for years and years and put away at the very beginning—at the very beginning, mark you—for the first grandson whenever he might see fit to arrive. By all means let the rabbi drink just one glass more,

this tiny glass—and Getzi stuffed into the rabbi's hand a fair-sized
tumbler. "Please, just this! Please drink, Rabbi! There's nothing to
be afraid of! Why, is this brandy? No, it's not brandy at all, it's
purest, smoothest olive oil, running smooth into the glass without the
slightest splash or sound. Real olive oil! As sure as my name is Getzi!
Please, Rabbi, long life to you, long life!"
Getzi the tax collector became tipsy. His fleshy, hairy face began
to flush, and shone like a polished samovar, while his eyes seemed to
roll in fat. From time to time he thrust a finger toward his heart,
prodded himself, and murmured: "Getzi, do you know what? You're
an old man from now on. You're a grandpa! D'you hear? Hee-hee-
hee, you're a grandpa. And what's happened to your old woman?
Why, she's a g-g-g-granny! Where are you, g-g-g-granny? Come along!
Grandpa wants to drink to your very g-good health! Come here,
come here, don't be ashamed, the rabbi will say amen . . . won't
you, R-r-rabbi?"
And at this point Reb Getzi took the rabbi by the shoulder,
gripped him with all his strength, and shook him like a sack of
potatoes, then suddenly began kissing him heartily. Joyful and
happy, he wept and laughed at the same time because of the honor,
hee-hee-hee, the honor which Reb Lippe, the Rabbi, long life to
him, had shown to him, namely to Getzi, by his life and head, the
honor. And but for him, the Rabbi, long life to him—hm, hm,
hm . . .
"Well, well, that will do! Long life to you," Reb Lippe soothed
the weeping Getzi, swallowing a sip very carefully from the glass.
"Long life to you! But why are you crying? There's no need to cry,
no need at all . . ."
Reb Getzi took heart and wiped the tears away with his sleeve.
"You've put it well, Rabbi, as sure as my name's Getzi! There's no
need to cry. No need. But long life, and again long life! And long
life above all things! That means—real life! A l-l-life with a decent
living . . . oh, oh, Rabbi," and here Reb Getzi began weeping
once more with redoubled fervor, "oh, oh, oh, how to manage to
make a li-v-i-ing!"
And Reb Lippe, who was gentle and softhearted by nature,
could not bear to watch the sorrow of the master of the house, and
did him the last true kindness of drinking another little drop with
him, and another little drop, and another little . . .

Meanwhile the day, the Short Friday of all days, began to decline. Reb Lippe, who had himself grown slightly fuddled, roused himself once and again, and tried to rise on his shaky feet in front of the table. "Ah, ah, ah," he complained, shaking his head, spreading out his hands, and stammering. "It's Sabbath eve! The short day . . ." But Reb Getzi would have none of this and would not listen—Reb Getzi grabbed both his hands and would not let go.

Meanwhile Ivan the Coachman was sitting at ease in the kitchen, likewise gladdening his heart with feasting. He felt particularly pleased that they had inducted the little one into the faith, and in his joy he tossed glass after glass down his throat: one, once and again, twice and again, thrice and again, and again and again . . .

In the middle of this, the clock struck three. Reb Lippe started up from his seat in great haste, but his legs were not in any such hurry. After he had risen and put on his two overcoats and more, namely his bearskin and sheepskin, had buckled on his red leather belt, and had thrust his legs into those two barrels (namely the heavy overshoes), his legs refused to pay the slightest attention to him. Instead of moving forward, Reb Lippe suddenly found his bulging self sitting down on a bench in the middle of the house. He tried to shift himself. "Eh-eh-eh," he panted. But it was no use. He did not move.

The "oil" that had entered Reb Lippe's bones apparently had done its work. But Reb Lippe did not regret this in the least. On the contrary, he felt very cheeful and good-humored, and while his body, with outspread hands and working fingers, was trying to shift itself willynilly from its place, his voice came chirruping from his throat like a bird, chirruping and cackling!

"Hee-hee-hee, Reb Getzi, my legs . . ."

"Hee-hee-hee!" laughed all the guests in turn. "The Rabbi!"

At length, with the aid of Him who giveth the weary strength, and a little extra aid from the guests, the bulging, bulky body began to move, and the two fine creatures, namely the rabbi, Reb Lippe long life to him, and Ivan the Coachman his companion, pardon the proximity, departed from the house in an auspicious and favorable hour; and aiding one another and leaning each on the other's shoulder, they climbed into the sleigh in perfect order.

So once again our rabbi sat at ease in the sleigh, his body wrapped up and his legs covered. And once again Ivan sat in the driver's seat. One long and cheerful whistle and the mare lifted her legs . . .

And here we reach the main part of the story.

IV

No sooner had the sleigh started and our rabbi wriggled deep into his covers, than he suddenly felt a pleasant warmth, sweet as honey, spreading throughout his limbs. The lids of his eyes were taken captive in the toils of slumber and his head began to nod. "Hee—hee—hee—the oil!" the rabbi silently laughed to himself, feeling, as it were, grains of sand in his eyes—"pure olive oil!" And the moment the sleigh had crossed the little bridge beyond the village, there fell upon the rabbi a divine slumber—and he slept.

At the same time Ivan the Gentile was sitting on his seat having a little chat with his mare, just a friendly chat out of the goodness of his heart, promising her, when the time should be ripe, all sorts of fine things for the future, provided, that is, that she would pick her way and not depart from the straight path. While yet he held converse with her thus, behold! the whip and reins slipped from his hands, his head under its round sheepskin hat sank into the bosom of his overcoat, and within a moment, there he was, snoring for all the world like any swine.

As for the mare, the moment she sensed herself at liberty, she straightway forgot all the wise counsel of her owner and his promises of delights to come; when she reached the crossroads she stopped and hesitated for a moment as though considering whether to take this way or that. Then she suddenly tugged at the sleigh with all her strength and by way of compromise turned neither here nor there but directly between and out into open country.

Meanwhile clouds gathered, and day began to turn to darkness while the mare was on her way. Snow fell plentifully; it was coarse and moist, mixing up the whole world and hiding the traces of the roads. Presently the mare, it would appear, began to doubt whether she had done wisely, and even began to consider the advisability of a penitent return in her tracks. But since she, with her mere animal eyes, could see no way of correcting the matter, she placed herself in the hands of Heaven and continued to plod ahead through the gloom, downcast in spirit and lopeared, plodding silently, as though her eyes were closed, across countless little piles of snow and brier-roots, plodding on and dragging the sleigh behind her together with all that was therein. Who knows where the mare might not have finally arrived had she not suddenly met with some obstacle? But the obstacle once met with, the sleigh overturned. Our two startled travelers woke up suddenly in a heap of snow, and found themselves surrounded by darkness and gloom.

"What's this?" gasped the rabbi in astonishment, struggling to get out of the snow. Suddenly he remembered all that had happened, and felt as though he had been struck over the head with a heavy hammer.

Was it possible? On the Sabbath?

The rabbi wished to cry a great and exceedingly bitter cry; he could not. The whole of his being cowered and stiffened in the dread thought of that single word, Sabbath! Yet, when at length the power of speech returned to him, a roar, like a lion's, burst from his throat:

"Ivan, Ai Vai!"

Within this roar, which burst from the depths of his heart and which comprised the only three words of the language of the Gentiles that were known to our rabbi, there could be found all this: a bitter outcry and a beseeching for mercy, the fear of God and an acceptance of the Evil Decree, remorse and complaint, and all sorts of other feelings that words are too poor to express . . .

Meanwhile Ivan stood cursing and attending to the overturned sleigh and tangled reins. From time to time, he kicked at the belly of his mare, reproaching her with the transgressions of her equine forefathers and foremothers for a thousand generations back. When his repairs were completed, he invited the "Rabbin" to seat himself again. Reb Lippe raised his eyes to the night. Whence was his aid to come? But aid there was none.

For a moment he thought that he would not budge. Here in the field let him stay, and here in the field let him celebrate the Sabbath. Let him be slain rather than transgress! Were there then so few tales of pious men and men of righteous deeds who had hallowed the seventh day in forests and deserts? Why, for example, there was the tale of Ariel! Hadn't the Holy and Blessed One sent that pious soul a lion in the desert to guard him until the *Havdalah* [3] ceremony, and for riding upon after the Havdalah? Yet when Reb

3. Ceremony marking the conclusion of the Sabbath.

Lippe looked round him at the darkness once again, his courage died. Toward the left his eyes could distinguish a real kind of forest, a forest dark and dire with dread, filled with noise and the howlings of the tempest; and we know by tradition that even an ordinary forest must be regarded as potentially perilous, containing robbers and wild beasts. And to the right—why, there was bare, desolate, open country, all shrouded in white. Out of the snow rose and thrust themselves all kinds of half-shapes and lumps in which black and white were mingled and which looked like tombstones in the graveyard. His Blessed Name alone knew what those queer things might be: devils, wild beasts, dead men—or just plain briers and brambles . . . from every side through the darkness there massed whole legions of panthers and basilisks to leap upon him.

"Nay indeed!" Reb Lippe changed his mind. "A matter of life sets the Sabbath aside! 'And live according to them,' it is written. We are not required to die for them, and miracles are not to be counted on. Anyway, who knows whether I am worthy of having a miracle done for my sake . . ."

And now Reb Lippe could clearly recognize a huge panther, huge and exceedingly dreadful, which stood facing him, sending sparks flying toward him out of its phosphorescent eyes, and gnashing cruel, crooked fangs at him. Reb Lippe's flesh began to creep, and his eyes all but bulged from their sockets.

"Nay indeed and nay again!" Reb Lippe decided the question once for all in very fear of death as he clambered back into the sleigh. "In all full truth, according to the deepest intention of the Law, I am in no way called upon to sacrifice my life for this thing. Rather the reverse! Travel on the Sabbath is not prohibited in the Five Books of the Torah; it is a later rabbinical addition. Refraining from labor—and, as to that . . ."

By this time Reb Lippe found himself sitting right within the sleigh. But still he tried, sighing and moaning and groaning, to seat himself there uncomfortably, in an unnatural sort of way, to prove the urgency of the case. The sleigh made its smooth way through the darkness, while Reb Lippe began whispering to himself the service for the Inauguration of the Sabbath, his heart broken and dejected.

May it never befall you, all you who use the roads! That

winter's night was as long and eventful for Reb Lippe as any
jubilee of years. The poor mare was already weary and walked on
without any more strength within her. The sleigh bumped on the
uneven surface of the ground and set the shaken body of Reb
Lippe quivering. His bones were all but shaken out of him along
the road. The trees of the forest, grave ancients, with broad snow-
burdened branches, passed before his eyes in silent reproach and
great wrath. Thickets of dwarf oaks, the little folk of the forest,
stared gaping with their pointed heads under their snow caps and
wondered in astonishment who and what this Reb Lippe might
be, this Rabbi of the Town and Master of the City, whose heart
had led him to travel on the Sabbath day. Thorns and briers
bowed their heads to the ground in shame, and the wind in the
weeping willows sorrowed and wailed and howled: oh and woe for
the profanation of the Name, and oh and woe for the shaming of
the Torah!

V

At about midnight the sleigh finally reached an inn standing
lonely by the wayside, sunk to its windows in the snow. The mare
was covered with lather and white frost, weary to death, while
the travelers were all but falling to pieces. The beard, earlocks,
moustache, and overcoat of the rabbi had become one solid piece
of glass. There could be no question of traveling beyond this point.
The hostler of the inn, an old Gentile, came out to them. The rabbi
entered the inn and the sleigh disappeared into the courtyard.

The room which the rabbi entered was dominated by a desolate chill and the mournful gleam of a sooty lantern. From the
neighboring room came the snoring of the family. On the table
stood two brass candlesticks in which the candles had burned out,
and on the thick homewoven linen tablecloth were scattered dishes,
crumbs, and bones, the relics of a Sabbath meal. Reb Lippe turned
his head away so as not to look at them. Frozen almost into one
lump and burdened with his heavy clothes, he flung himself down—
while yet there was life in him—on a hard bare bench next to the
wall, and buried his head in the bosom of his overcoat.

Yes, that's how it was. He, the rabbi, had profaned the Sabbath.
How great and mighty the profanation of the Holy Name! How

would he look people in the face on the morrow? And what would
he say on the Day of Judgment? Alas and alack for the shame and
reproach!

And he wept. His thawing beard and earlocks and moustache
wept with him. His head and limbs felt as heavy as lumps of lead.
He wanted to move but could not. Has the hour of death arrived?
he thought, and trembled with the fear of death. Yes indeed, this
must be the hour of death: it was time to confess.

The rabbi's lips, of themselves, began to repeat the formula
for confessing sin. "Oh, oh, merciful and gracious God, long suffering and mighty in lovingkindness and truth . . . . Prithee do it
not, have mercy! Lord of the Universe, forgive and have pity, we
being flesh and blood, and very worms . . . . How a man is led
off by his own legs! In sooth I have sinned, I have gone astray,
I have transgressed. Yet these sheep, my wife and my children,
wherein have they sinned?"

For a long, long time he suffered from sleeplessness. All his
body was washed in cold sweat, yet it seemed as though fire were
flaming in his bones. Through his fever he dimly whispered all
kinds of strange verses. He combined extracts from the Mishnah
with verses from the Five Books of Moses, sayings of our Sages of
blessed memory with prayers and entreaties. Heavenly thoughts
regarding such matters as reward and punishment, Hell and
Paradise, the beating in the grave and the Angel of Death whirled
in his disordered mind in confusion together with domestic affairs—
his wife a widow, his children orphans, a daughter ripe for wedding, the rabbinical dues, the communal impost on yeast.

The poor rabbi struggled with all these unhappy thoughts,
and moaned and groaned until dawn. Only then did he pass into
a hard uneasy sleep, a slumber born of and bearing with it suffering,
bringing with it short, uneven breathing. And so he slept.

VI

Reb Lippe lay in the inn on the bench, wrapped in his overcoat,
sweating and dripping from his thawing beard and earlocks, and
sleeping through unhappy dreams. Meanwhile the Holy and
Blessed One up in His Heaven was engaged in His work, setting
the cocks crowing at the dawn, and rolling the darkness away
before the light. And once the cock crew, and through the little

frost-covered windows there broke into the room the stern, pale, chill light of a winter's dawn, Feivka the Innkeeper sneezed, belched, said "Pah!" and woke up. At a single bound he was out of bed, put on his heavy kneeboots, set his short coat round his shoulders, and went out into the big room to see who had arrived at his inn during the night. He entered and looked, then stood gazing stupefied. In front of him on the bench, rolled up in his overcoat, lay the rabbi, Reb Lippe!

At first Feivka thought this must be illusion and some devil's hocus-pocus. He bent down and gazed again, staring long and thoroughly. He gazed—above, below, and from the side. "By my life, it's the Rabbi! Himself! Here's that trumpet of a nose and his wizened face."

It seemed to Feivka that he must be crazy. "What's this?" he said to himself. "Sabbath—and the Rabbi? Am I drunk or mad?" Suddenly he smote himself on the forehead with his fist. "O-ho, Feivka, ignoramus and son of an ignoramus that you are! There must be a mistake here, and a nasty mistake at that. Fancy getting the days of the week mixed up, Feivka! Yes, yes, Feivka, you've fallen in properly, and all the worse for you and your life. You've been living with Esau, and by reason of your many sins you've confused the proper order of the days. O-ho, a nice affair, a fine business, as I'm a Jew. Tomorrow the whole village will know about it. Pah!"

The moment Feivka realized what had happened, he dashed off to remove all the signs of Sabbath from the house before the rabbi woke up and caught him. To begin with, he put away the brass candlesticks, the remains of the Sabbath meal, and the white tablecloth. Then he rushed into the bedroom and brought his startled wife and daughter out of bed.

"Get to work quick, you lazy carcasses, you carrion! Come on, come on, may the plague take you!" he ordered.

"What's the matter, who's here?" his wife started, awake.

"To hell with you, may the earth swallow you up, you stupid cow; don't raise your voice! Get up at once and take the food out of the stove, quick . . ."

For a while she could not understand what her husband was talking about. But when a heavy blow of his fist had made the matter quite clear, she jumped up and dressed and hurried to the stove.

"Out with it, out with everything, may the plague take you," said her husband impatiently. "Porridge and pudding and all. Into the waste barrel with it, empty it all out. Don't keep as much as a sign of it!"

And straightway the whole appearance of the house was transformed. Sabbath departed and weekday arrived. Fire burned, crackling in the wide-mouthed stove. The potbellied samovar was stoked with fuel and began humming. Hammer and axe were heard. Yuchim the Hostler was chopping wood and fixing things and knocking in nails where they were needed, and also where they were not needed. Feivka himself had condescended to take up his stand at the trough, kneading dough for all he was worth. His daughter, a tall fat-cheeked girl with a dirty face, who stood confused in the middle of the house unable to understand what was going on, received a couple of boxes on the ear and one pinch from her father's dough-covered hands, and promptly began to peel potatoes into a big pot. "Peel, peel away, the plague take you both!" Feivka urged his womenfolk, while he himself kneaded the dough with all his might. He was expecting the rabbi to wake up any moment, was Feivka; but when he finished his kneading and the rabbi still slept, he hurriedly put on his old, crushed and shapeless round fur hat from the rents of which hung bits of thread, bared his arm, and began to wind his *tefillin* strap round his arm as befits a weekday, and to repeat the morning prayers to their ordinary weekday tune.

Meanwhile the door turned ceaselessly on its hinges and peasants in their overcoats, holding their whips, began tramping in and out. The room filled with steaming breath and chill of snow and *machorka* smoke, and the smell of the coats and stamping feet and tongues wagging.

While praying, Feivka took particular care to walk up and down in front of the spot where the honored rabbi slept, singing his hallelujahs in their weekday tune at the top of his voice. He kept an observant corner of his eye on the rabbi while doing so, as if to say, "Sleep, Rabbi, sleep, and may you enjoy it. Now I'm not afraid of you anymore. Now you even have the right to get up."

And sure enough, the rabbi chose just that moment to shift his weary body somewhat. "Good luck to you, Feivka," said the innkeeper to himself. "Just look, but don't spoil things."

And at once Feivka vanished amid the machorka smoke and

the multitudes of overcoats. And from his newfound spot he continued to keep a watchful eye on the rabbi and to sing at the top of his voice, in the weekday tune, "Hallelujah, hallelujah!"

VII

Now when our rabbi woke up, all his pains and aches awoke with him. "Oh, oh, oh! My whole head is sick and my bones feel as though they have been torn apart!" He raised half his body with great difficulty and opened his eyes. What was this? Where was he? At the bathhouse? No, in an inn. And where was the Sabbath? There was no sign or memory of the Sabbath! Peasants, a weekday crowd. And a samovar was boiling just over there.

"In that case," came a dreadful thought that set all the rabbi's bones trembling and made his purple face even more purple, "in that case I went on sleeping all through the Sabbath and the night of the departure of the Sabbath as well. Here on the bench, in the presence of Feivka and in sight of the Gentiles, I lay and slept through a full twenty-four hours. And without hallowing the Sabbath, and without Sabbath prayers, and without celebrating the end of the Sabbath and the beginning of the week. Lord of the Universe, what have you done to Lippe?"

Black dread fell on the rabbi and despair took his heart by storm. He all but fainted. God had made things exceedingly bitter for him, too bitter . . . "and why?" the heart within him cried out. "Lord of the Universe, tell me why?"

Through the cloud of machorka smoke came the Gentile Ivan, whip in hand:

"Time to start, Rabbi. The sleigh's ready."

The rabbi rose groaning and turned to the door. He reeled like a drunkard and forced his way between the peasants with difficulty. At the door the broad horny hand of Feivka gripped his own.

"Peace be with you, R-r-rabbi!"

"Peace, peace," the rabbi evaded him and hurried out. "I've no time."

"Peace, peace," responded Feivka after him. "Go in peace, R-r-rabbi, and the Lord prosper your way."

Both sides preferred things so at the moment and neither detained the other. Feivka hastened to slam the door shut after the fleeing rabbi, as much as to say, "Bless you!" while the rabbi set his heart upon climbing into the sleigh.

"Haya, Ivan, Ivan," he began to urge the driver.

But what was the hurry? To flee? Whither? The rabbi himself had no idea what to answer to these questions. But just at the moment Reb Lippe was not asking many questions or cogitating deeply. Whatever he was doing seemed to be done automatically, without his knowledge or attention. There was one sole and solitary thing for which his soul ceaselessly prayed: "Lord of the Universe, bring about a miracle and turn the road into a vast length and distance of thousands upon thousands of leagues. Let years and decades pass and jubilees be gone, and meanwhile let me journey and journey and journey. If I am not worthy of a miracle, then I pray Thee take my soul, Lord of the Universe, I am willing to forego everything—but take my soul . . ."

But the prayer of Reb Lippe went unanswered. The sleigh bore him as though with the wings of eagles, and the polished, smooth road seemed to bound below them. The cloudy night was followed by a wintry sun and the white countryside was bright and cheerful. The ravens picking along the road made way for the hasting sleigh, and welcomed it with their hoarse cries of "Kraa, kraa!"

Reb Lippe was ashamed in the presence of the ravens and in the presence of the shining sun and the white snow. He bowed his head and hid it within the collar of his coat, and once again reverted to his despairing thoughts. And from that point he neither saw nor heard nor felt anything more. He placed his spirit in the hands of the God of Spirits, and left his weary body in the speeding sleigh:

"Let be whatever must be . . ."

VIII

And at the noon hour, when the congregation left the synagogue and, in all the glory of the Sabbath, was returning home at the sides of the road and in the midst thereof, and when everybody was wishing everybody else a good Sabbath, in that selfsame moment there sped toward them from the outskirts a speedy sleigh. And in that selfsame sleigh—woe unto the eyes that did the like behold!— sat the rabbi, Reb Lippe!

Translated by I. M. Lask

REVEALMENT
AND CONCEALMENT
IN LANGUAGE

H. N. BIALIK

INTRODUCTION

THIS COMPACT PIECE *of speculation on the metaphysical matrix of language, dense with allusive imagery and rich in insight, is probably the most original of Bialik's essays. Written a year and a half before the influential "Halakhah and Aggadah," during the period when his own long silence as a poet was becoming final, it represents the opposite pole of his imagination. In "Halakhah and Aggadah," Bialik, very much the disciple of Ahad Ha-am, is the proponent of national continuity, of collective cultural coherence, of containment and definition as necessary categories for man's self-realization. In "Revealment and Concealment," on the other hand, there is no national perspective: instead, the poet, working only with his individual perceptions as poet, confronts the cosmos, and what he discovers it to be is a realm of inhuman chaos, in some ways exciting but also profoundly frightening, from which mankind has always shielded itself with the protective screen of language.*

For a writer immersed in the turbulence of twentieth-century experience, Bialik was in many ways remarkably a traditionalist, both in the formal aspects of his poetry and fiction and in the ideology of culture he articulated and tried to translate into action. "Revealment and Concealment," however, gives us Bialik the

*modernist. His central perception of reality here is of an abyss
(tehom) or void (belimah) over which all the solid-seeming structures
of civilization and all the pleasing designs of human meaning are
erected. The nothingness at the heart of existence that Bialik evokes
here has its counterpart in many of the modern masters of European
and American literature, beginning as far back as Melville, but
especially notable in modernist contemporaries of Bialik like Franz
Kafka, Hermann Broch, Andrey Biely, and, in the next generation,
William Faulkner, Jean-Paul Sartre and the Existentialist writers
who followed him. This essay also provides the best possible commentary on Bialik's own later poetry (from the early 1900s to about
1915), where a terrible abyss often gapes beneath the powerfully
realized images of the poems. Indeed, one suspects that an important
reason for Bialik's subsequent silence as a poet was that he found
himself too much in touch with the unbearable void through his use
of the poetic medium where, as he says here, "between concealments
the void looms." The world of halakhah, in the broad figurative
sense he gave the term, became the only viable one in which he
could work.*

*If the perception of ontological nothingness tends to be a com-
mon one in modern literature, what is noteworthy about its formulation by Bialik is that it is couched in the theological language of
Jewish tradition itself. In this regard, there is an instructive parallel
between Bialik and Kafka. Both finally see reality in radically post-
traditional terms, bereft of divine authentication and of the cer-
tainties of revelation. Yet both remain imaginatively attached to the
fundamental categories of Jewish tradition: exegesis as the means
for discovering the truth, law as the measure of human actions,
commandments as the form of human obligation, a metaphysics in
which man struggles to establish contact with an ultimate power that
offers the promise of revealing itself but remains in constant hiding.
One of Kafka's expositors, Erich Heller, has suggestively spoken of
a "negative transcendence" that is the ultimate, inverted theological
state in which Kafka's protagonists seem to find themselves. An
analogous concept is implicit in this essay of Bialik's. More specifically, what Bialik formulates here is a negative Kabbalah.*

*In the traditional Kabbalah, language is the embodiment of
inexhaustible meaning: it was through the letters and words of the
Hebrew language that God created the world and revealed Himself,
and each minute component of this language is thus a dynamic,*

potentially explosive reservoir of Divine Truths. In some Kabbalistic formulations, language is actually seen as the necessary mediator between man and God, a kind of radiation screen that protects man from the intolerable absoluteness of divinity itself. This, of course, is precisely the key concept of "Revealment and Concealment in Language," with one crucial difference: the devastating Absolute which is mediated by language here is not God; but nothingness. The Kabbalistic image of "husks" is invoked as a concealment not of Divine light but of the dark seed of an eternal enigma. "For man shall not look on me and live," God says to Moses in Exodus, but here, in one of Bialik's boldest transpositions of traditional language, it is the void that speaks these words. This is hardly a comforting essay, but it touches on something profound about the nature of language and culture as the poet, Bialik, possesses the courage of his own insights in using an inherited vocabulary to convey a metaphysically radical conception of being.

REVEALMENT AND CONCEALMENT IN LANGUAGE (1915)
H. N. BIALIK

EVERY DAY, consciously and unconsciously, human beings scatter heaps of words to the wind, with all their various associations; few men indeed know or reflect on what these words were like in the days when they were at the height of their power. Many of these words came into the world only after difficult and prolonged birth pangs endured by many generations. Others flashed like sudden lightning to illuminate, with one leap, a complete world. Many were paths through which living hosts passed, each leaving behind its shadow and aroma. These were words which served as receptacles for delicate and profound thoughts and exalted emotions. Some words were like the high mountains of the Lord, others were a great abyss. Sometimes all the vital essence of a profound philosophic system, its complete immortality, were hidden in one small word. There were words that laid low nations and lands in their time, deposed kings from their thrones, shook the foundations of heaven and earth. But there came a day when these same words, having fallen from their height, were thrown aside, and now people wallow in them as they chat, as casually as one wallows in grass.

Is this cause for wonder? The laws of nature are not to be questioned. That is the way of the world: words rise to greatness, and, falling, turn profane. What is essential is that language contains

no word so slight that the hour of its birth was not one of powerful
and awesome self-revealment, a lofty victory of the spirit. So, for
example, it was with the first man, when, taken aback by the sound
of thunder ("The voice [sound] of the Lord is in the power, the
voice of the Lord is in the glory"), overcome by amazement
and terror stricken, he fell on his face before the divinity. Then a
kind of savage sound burst spontaneously from his lips—let us assume, in imitation of nature—resembling a beast's roar, a sound
close to the r . . . r to be found in the words for thunder in many
languages. Did not this wild cry vastly free his confounded soul?
Was a smaller measure of the power, the fearfulness, and the exul-
tation of creative victory revealed in this echo of a spirit shaken
to its depths than are revealed in the happy phrases on exalted
subjects expressed by any of the great seers in their moments of
spiritual elevation? Did not this meager syllable, this seed of the
future word, embrace a complete volume of primordial emotions,
powerful in their novelty and vigorous in their savagery, resembling
terror, fear, amazement, submission, astonishment, preparedness for
self-defense? And if this was true, was not the first man himself at
that moment an artist and lofty seer, an intuitive creator of an
expression—and a very faithful expression, for himself, at any rate—
pointing to a deep and complicated inner disturbance? As one
thinker commented, how much of profound philosophy, of Divine
revealment was there in that small word *I* that the first man uttered!

Nevertheless, at this very moment these same words, and a great
many others like them, are being lost in language—and it does not
matter. We are inwardly almost untouched. Their core is consumed
and their spiritual strength fades or is hidden, and only their husks,
cast out from the private domain to the public, still persist in language, doing slack service within the limited boundaries of logic
and social intercourse, as external signs and abstractions for objects
and images. It has come to the point where the human language
has become two languages, built upon one another's destruction:
one, an internal language, that of solitude and the soul, in which
what is essential is "how?" as in music—the domain of poetry; the
other, the external language, that of abstraction and generalization,
in which the essential is "what?" as in mathematics—the domain
of logic.

Who knows whether it is not for the best that man should
inherit the husk of a word without its core—for thus he can fill

the husk, or supply it constantly from his own substance, and pour his own inner light into it. "Every man prefers his own measure." If the spoken word were to remain throughout history at the height of its glowing power, if the same complex of emotion and thought which became attached to it in its prime were to accompany it always, perhaps no speaking creature would ever attain to its self-revealment and particular illumination. In the final analysis, an empty vessel can hold matter, while a full vessel cannot; if the empty word enslaves, how much more is this true of the full word?

What is there to wonder at? This: the feeling of security and the satisfaction that accrue to human beings when they speak, as though they are really leading their thoughts or feelings beside the still waters and across the iron bridge of the Messiah, without their having any conception of how shaky is their bridge of mere words, how deep and dark the void is that opens at their feet, and how much every step taken safely partakes of the miraculous.

For it is clear that language with all its associations does not introduce us at all into the inner area, the essence of things, but that, on the contrary, language itself stands as a barrier before them. On the other side of the barrier of language, behind its curtain, stripped of its husk of speech, the spirit of man wanders ceaselessly. "There is no speech and there are no words," but only a perpetual search, an eternal "what?" frozen on man's lips. In truth, there is no place even for this "what?", implying as it does the hope of a reply. Rather there is—"nothingness"; man's lips are closed. If, nevertheless, man does achieve speech and with it contentment, it is only because of the extent of his fear at remaining alone for one moment with that dark void, face-to-face with the nothingness, with no barrier between them. "For man shall not look on me and live," says the void, and every speech, every pulsation of speech, partakes of the nature of a concealment of nothingness, a husk enclosing within itself a dark seed of the eternal enigma. *No word contains the complete dissolution of any question.* What does it contain? *The question's concealment.* It makes no difference *what* the particular word is—you can exchange it for another—just as long as it contains the power

momentarily to serve as concealment and barrier. Dumb music and
symbolic mathematics—two hostile kin at two parallel extremes—
attest unanimously that the word is not necessarily what it seems,
that it is nothing but a manifestation of the void. Or rather, just
as physical bodies become sensible to the eye and determinate because they serve as barriers before light in space, so the word's
existence takes place by virtue of the process by which it closes
up the small aperture of the void—constructing a barrier to prevent
the void's darkness from welling up and overflowing its bounds.

He who sits alone in the depths of darkness, trembling, speaks to
himself: he confesses his sins, or whispers a word. Why? *Because the
word is a talisman which serves to divert him and to dissipate his
fear.* It is the same with the spoken word—or with complete systems
of words. The word's power does not consist in its explicit content—
if, generally speaking, there is such a thing—but in the diversion
that is involved in it.

Averting one's eyes is, in the final resort, the easiest and most
pleasant means, although an illusory one, of escape from danger;
in situations where keeping one's eyes open constitutes the danger
there is really no securer refuge, and "Moses did well to conceal
his face."

Who knows? Perhaps the truth is that from the time of Creation, speech has not been cast as a social vessel to pass between two
men; it has not been speech for its own sake. It may have always
had its source in men sitting alone, speaking to themselves, as a
spiritual need, i.e., "speech for its own sake" falling in the class of
"When my spirit within me is dumb, I shall speak unto my heart.
. . ." The first man was not content until he had spoken *himself*
aloud for himself to hear. For the sound that at the time of creation drew man's self-recognition up from the depths of the void—
that very sound suddenly stood as a dividing wall between man and
that which is on the other side, as though to say: "Henceforth, O
man, thou shalt direct thy face toward that which is 'on this side.'
Thou shalt not look *behind* thee, and if thou shouldst—it shall
not avail thee, for man shall not see the 'void' face-to-face and live.

The dream that is forgotten shall not be recalled. Thy desire shall
be to the 'void' and speech shall rule over thee."

And, in truth, "knowledge and speech" rule only over that
which is on this side, within the four cubits of space and time.
"Man walketh in the shadow merely"; the nearer he approaches
the illusory light *that is before him,* the larger grows the shadow
behind him, and the surrounding darkness is never lessened. Perhaps, on this side, everything can be explained—strictly or liberally
—but explained. What is essential is that man's atmosphere of
knowledge must never for a single moment be rid of words, crowded
and consecutive like the links in a suit of armor, without so much
as a hair's breadth between them. The light of knowledge and
speech—the glowing coal and the flame—is an eternal light that
must not be extinguished. Indeed, the very area on this side that
lies within the bounds of the illusory light—in the final analysis,
of what importance is it compared with the endless sea of universal
darkness that still remains, and will always remain, *outside?*

And again, in the final analysis, it is that very eternal darkness
that is so fearsome—that darkness that from the time of Creation
has always secretly drawn man's heart to it, arousing his hidden
yearning to gaze on it for a brief moment. Every man is afraid of
it, and every man is drawn to it. With our very lips we construct
barriers, words upon words and systems upon systems, and place
them in front of the darkness to conceal it; but then our nails
immediately begin to dig at those barriers, in an attempt to open
the smallest of windows, the tiniest of cracks, through which we
may gaze for a single moment at that which is on the other side.
But alas, vain is the labor of man! At the very moment when the
crack is apparently opened—another barrier, in the shape of a new
word or system, suddenly stands in the place of the old, shutting
off the view again.

Thus, there is never an end. A word cometh and a word goeth, a
system riseth and a system falleth—and the old eternal enigma
remains as powerful as ever, unalterable and irreducible. Signing
a note, or listing a debt in a ledger, is far from being the debt's

liquidation; it merely momentarily removes the note's burden from one's memory—and no more. The same is the case with definitive speech: the assignment of names and the putting up of orderly fences around images and their associations. No reply to the question of essence is ever possible in the process of speech. Even the express reply to a question is really no more than another version of the question itself—"this is amazing" we understand as meaning "pause and think" (a form of concealment instead of revealment). If we were to strip all the words and systems completely bare to their innermost core, in the end, *after the last reduction,* we should be left with nothing in our hands but one all-inclusive word. Which? Again, the same terrible "what?" behind which stands the same X, even more terrible—the nothingness. Man chooses to tear the debt into small pieces under the false illusion that he is thus easing the final payment. When this illusion fails him, he exchanges the present word for another, the present system for another—he writes a new note to take the place of the old, and delays or gives himself more time for the final payment. In either event the debt is never paid in full.

So, a word or system declines and yields to another, not because it has lost the power to reveal, to enlighten, to invalidate the enigma either totally or in part, but for the very opposite reason—because the word or system has been worn out by being manipulated and used, is no longer able to conceal and hide adequately, and can, of course, no longer divert mankind momentarily. Man, gazing for a moment through the open crack, finding to his terror that awesome void before him again, hurries to close the crack for a time—with a new word. He seizes the new talisman, like its predecessor; a proven momentary diversion—and is saved from the terror.

Do not wonder at this! The talisman is effective for those who believe in it, for faith itself is no more than a diversion. Do not the speaking creatures themselves provide an analogy? So long as man moves and breathes—he occupies space and everything is apparently comprehensible; "everything is all right." All the flow of life, all its content, is nothing but a continuous effort, an unremitting toil to be diverted. Every moment spent in "pursuit of" is at the same time a "flight from," and flight, and flight alone, is its wages. The wages of pursuit is flight. At every moment the pursuer finds his momentary happiness not in that which he attains to, but in that which he escapes from, a fact which gives him a momentary shadow of security. "For to him that is joined to all the living there is security."

But man dies—and his space becomes unoccupied. There is nothing to serve as a diversion—and the barrier is down. Everything suddenly becomes incomprehensible. The hidden X descends upon us in all its fearful shape—and we sit mourning on the earth before it for a moment in darkness and dumb as a stone. But for a moment only. For the Master of all life anticipates the opening with a closing. He immediately furnishes us with a new talisman with which to divert ourselves and dissipate the fear. Before the covering stone is sealed over the dead, the space that was emptied is again occupied with a word, whether it be one of eulogy, or solace, or philosophy, or belief in the soul's immortality. The most dangerous moment— both in speech and in life—is that between concealments, when the void looms. But such moments are rare both in speech and in life, and for the most part men skip over them unaware. "The Lord preserveth the simple."

From all that has been said, it would appear that there is a vast difference between the language of the masters of prose and that of the masters of poetry. The former, the masters of exposition, find their sanction in the principle of analogy, and in the elements common to images and words, in that which is established and constant in language, in the accepted version of things—consequently, they walk confidently through language. To what may they be compared? To one who crosses a river walking on hard ice frozen into a solid block. Such a man may and can divert his attention completely from the covered depths flowing underneath his feet. But their opposites, the masters of allegory, of interpretation and mystery, spend all their days in pursuit of the unifying principle in things, of the solitary something, of the point that makes one body of all the images, of the fleeting moment that is never repeated. They pursue their solitary inwardness and the personal quality of things. Therefore, the latter, the masters of poetry, are forced to flee all that is fixed and inert in language, all that is opposed to their goal of the vital and mobile in language. On the contrary, using their unique keys, they are obliged themselves to introduce into language at every opportunity—never-ending motion, new combinations and associations. The words writhe in their hands; they are extinguished and lit again, flash on and off like the engravings of the signet in the stones of the High Priest's breastplate, grow empty and become full, put off a soul and put on a soul. By this process there takes place, in the material of language, exchanges of posts and locations: one mark, a change in the point of one iota, and the old word shines with a new light.

The profane turns sacred, and the sacred profane. Long established words are constantly being pulled out of their settings, as it were, and exchanging places with one another. Meanwhile, between concealments the void looms. And that is the secret of the great influence of the language of poetry. And to what may those writers be compared? To one who crosses a river when it is breaking up, by stepping across floating, moving blocks of ice. He dare not set his foot on any one block for longer than a moment, longer than it takes him to leap from one block to the next, and so on. Between the breaches the void looms, the foot slips, danger is close. . . .

Nevertheless, some of this group, too, "enter in peace and leave in peace," crossing in safety from one shore to the other, "for the Lord preserveth not merely the simple."

So much for the language of words. But, in addition, "there are yet to the Lord" languages without words: song, tears, and laughter. And the speaking creature has been found worthy of them all. These languages begin where words leave off, and their purpose is not to close but to open. They rise from the void. They *are* the rising up of the void. Therefore, at times they overflow and sweep us off in the irresistible multitude of their waves; therefore, at times they cost a man his wits, or even his life. Every creation of the spirit which lacks an echo of one of these three languages is not really alive, and it were best that it had never come into the world.

Translated by Jacob Sloan

THE WAY OUT

Y. H. BRENNER

INTRODUCTION

OF ALL MODERN *Hebrew writers, Yosef Haim Brenner (1881–1921) is the most ruthless critic of Jewish life, and one of the most tormented figures as well. His novels, short stories, and essays have something of the troubled intensity of Dostoevsky, whom he translated from the Russian, but without Dostoevsky's belief in a power of saving grace.*

His whole enterprise as a writer of fiction is in fact qualified by paradox, for in his peculiar moral asceticism he had little patience for the aesthetic dimension of imaginative fictions: "A single particle of truth," he once said, "is more valuable to me than all possible poetry." He seems to strive for a direct, often understated, "unliterary" prose that will serve as the stylistic equivalent of sincerity. The cultivated flatness of statement—the avoidance of editorial comment and dramatic effect—of "The Way Out," is typical of Brenner: here, as elsewhere, he pointedly wants the brutally depressing facts to speak for themselves, without any obvious authorial intervention or literary heightening.

Born in the Ukraine, Brenner left Russia as a young man, first for a brief period in London, then to settle in Palestine in 1909. He tried to work in the new Zionist community as a simple laborer, in keeping with his labor-socialist Zionist ideals, but he ended up as an editor, writer, lecturer, translator. He was murdered by Arabs during the general riots against the Jewish settlers in May 1921.

"The Way Out" is pointedly set in a time of public crisis and general disorder—a moment when the British and Turkish armies were struggling for the control of Palestine during World War I— that puts the greatest possible strain on moral values and ideals. As his protagonist, Brenner has deliberately chosen a relatively colorless and ineffectual figure. In his well-meaning weakness, the old teacher becomes a general image of the morally average man, of all of us. He is a teacher (of pioneer workers), that is, a man whose calling is to educate, to instill ideals. He is in a sense the conscience of the community, virtually the only one who has some conscience and is not selfishly callous to the suffering of the refugees. Yet he is a con- science powerless to translate its impulses into action, over against the hard-headed, tightfisted men of power who run the community. His being a teacher, then, may suggest something further about him—that he represents in some sense the intellectual, the man of books, who by the very nature of the grim world of action is unable to give his ideals substance in action.

The narrator at once attaches his point of view to the teacher's, who is seen standing on a balcony—an elevated and separated post of observation—looking down and out at the morass of wartime horror that has overtaken the public world. The refugees enter the story as an unspecified, dreaded "they" awaited by the "I" of the protagonist. The teacher immediately shows himself to be a man of realistic moral imagination, for it is his mind that projects the grim vision of "that nightmare-ridden waste, where the soil lay desolate," strewn with stinking, wretched, half-dead human beings. This night- marish vision, with which the first section of the story begins and ends, is the "window" through which we first look into the world of the story, is the ultimate reality of the story.

The teacher's stammering response to the arrival of the refugees is that "surely we have to do something," but the point is that he does not know exactly what he should do, or what in general can be done. His taking bread to the refugees is a reverent if futile symbolic gesture: bread is the staff of life, but this loaf-and-a-half will do little to alleviate the suffering of the refugees. The basketful of bread-scraps he gathers from the neighbors suggests a charitable gesture on the part of the whole community through the teacher's urging, but even that is no more than a momentary stopgap mea-

sure. At the end of the story the teacher will discover that the remaining half-loaf is now hard and inedible and will think what a waste it is that he did not take that, too, with him on his first trip to the refugees.

The beginning of Section IV in many ways epitomizes the general moral quandary of the protagonist. At the distance of a short walk, people are dying, "but all around, throughout the colony, life went on as usual." The man of conscience finds himself outside the locked door of the administrative powers of the community. At first, in his imagination, he can see himself pounding furiously on the council table and thundering prophetic castigation on the members of the council. But after half an hour of waiting, "he felt a kind of numbness creep over him." Pointedly, the head of the council has been sleeping all this time.

When the council doors open, the room fills with "grain merchants and brokers," and the chief consideration is material profit ("A wagon's worth its weight in gold at this time of the year"), not human lives. The coarse joke asserting that the refugees will eat what pigs would refuse obviously reflects how the villagers have ceased to think of the refugees as human beings. In this dismal situation, the teacher, assuming the role of prophetic rebuker, though ineffectually, quotes the Bible to his fellow townsmen. "Our hands have not shed this blood" (Deuteronomy 21:7) is a formula in a ritual of communal disavowal of guilt when the body of a murdered man is found near a town. The relevance of the verse to the present situation is clear. "You mustn't go against the rules of hygiene," the townsmen warn, but of course there is no concern for higher rules of moral responsibility.

The ultimate frustration of the teacher's efforts to help is the child's death at the end of the story. The only aid he can now offer is the "last kindness," the human act that expresses reverence for life in burying the dead. Even in this, the community is unwilling to help—no one calls the burial society, no one will so much as lend the teacher a hoe. Brenner strikes a bitterly ironic note when he likens the carrying of the tiny corpse to a godfather carrying a child at a circumcision—a communal rite of induction into life. As with the two Arab carters, earlier in the story, it is an outsider, the Turkish soldier, who steps forward to help. The soldier and the teacher join as an image of human solidarity—"they returned to the colony, now as comrades, united by the bond of their shared deed"—and also an image of suffering mankind's pathetic weakness in the face of bleak reality—a bedraggled, emaciated peasant soldier whose tarbush has lost its tassel and a limping, malaria-ridden old man carrying an infant's corpse. The enormous sense of relief that the teacher feels at the end of the story is itself ironic. His "way out" may well be his own imminent death; in any case, it is an escape through total impotence that is the moral equivalent of death.

THE WAY OUT (1919)
Y. H. BRENNER

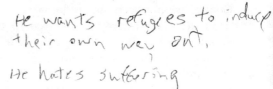

[handwritten annotations:] How is water & bread "way out"?

He wants refugees to induce their own way out. He hates suffering

He must then have Confruntations with: 1) Community 2) Refugees 3) Himself

I

EACH MORNING, day in, day out, when the tiny train was due to arrive from Tulkarm to fetch wood to stoke the engine, the old pioneer teacher would go out onto the balcony of his attic room on the farm. Shading his eyes, he would peer into the distance to see whether they were coming.

They were sure to come. They could be expected any day now.

They would be on that little train that came to fetch the wood. They would be arriving from back there, from that nightmare-ridden waste, where the soil lay desolate, the trees hewn down and the dwellings in ruins; from that dead region where the handful of farmers who were left paid the soldiers billeted in their houses to chop the remaining almond trees into firewood; from the place where the only food was unground millet, to fill the belly and still the pangs of hunger; from the place where damp huts, infested with mice and vermin, soggy with filth and permeated with the accumulated stench of months, gave sorry shelter to women and children who were chilled to the marrow and contorted with disease; from the place where out of the surviving hundreds, half a dozen dead were carted away daily for burial; from the place where there was no longer any room

145

to lay the scores of new victims that succumbed daily to the disease, nor a garment to cover them, nor even a sheet to spread under them; from the place whose denizens did nought to alleviate their plight— all they did was to listen to the guns firing, argue among themselves about military tactics, groan and grumble: "Oh, that Evacuation Committee has been our undoing! . . . it has been the end of us!"; from the place where those versed in the art of trickery and theft accumulated Napoleons [1] and made a fortune, and the privileged few healthy young men who had come down from the north ate eggs and jam, played cards round the clock and merely waited for the "liberation" that was so late in coming.

"Did you hear that? They're shooting again!"

"It's our side [2] shooting . . ."

"What are you talking about? Those aren't our guns . . ."

"Then where do you think our side is stationed, and where is that shooting coming from . . . ?"

"And even if it is ours, it means that they [3] are advancing . . ."

"The planes have been flying around here all day . . ."

"This morning there was one flying around for almost two solid hours . . ."

"And did you see the *golem*? . . . I saw it . . ."

(The golem, or dummy, was what they called the military observation balloon.)

"It's the weather that's holding them back . . ."

"No doubt about it. As soon as the rainy season's over, we'll be going back to Jaffa!"

But the rainy season went by, and Passover too, without unleavened or even leavened bread, and the wretched exiles, instead of returning to the south, to Jaffa, were again forced to pack their miserable rags and chattels and drag themselves wearily in the opposite direction, to the north.

What was going to happen to them? How would it all end? They were all broken in body and spirit, worn out, naked and starving, ravaged by contagious disease, and they would be coming here; they would be disgorged by the train to lie around out in the open, ex-

1. The French gold twenty-franc piece was used as legal tender in Turkish Palestine Y. S.
2. By "our side" the refugees refer to the Turkish Army. Y. S.
3. "They" were the British Forces under General Allenby. This was no indication of their sympathies, however, for they were eagerly awaiting the British victory that would deliver them from their desperate plight. Y. S.

posed to the scorching rays of the sun by day and to the chill and the dank dew by night, to be consumed by malaria, the dread swamp fever. Broken hollow shells of humans, hardly able to move, unable to do anything for themselves . . . who was going to feed them, give them drink, tend to them? What was going to happen to them?

II

As the days went by and they failed to arrive, the rumor went round that they had been sent straight to the Galilee and would not show up here. People began to breathe more freely and gradually went back to their everyday matters.

All of a sudden, one sweltering morning in June, the news struck like a thunderbolt:

"Forty-two of them!"

"Where?"

"Over there. Don't you see? In among the tree stumps, that's where they're lying around . . ."

"In that case," it was the old pioneer teacher. "In that case," he stammered, confused, "surely we have to do something . . . water . . ."

"They're filling a barrel with water already . . . take it out to them over there . . . they musn't come here to drink our water . . . we've got our children to think of . . . the doctor from the colony said we mustn't have anything to do with them before everything's been disinfected first. It's only that the horses haven't come back yet . . . there's nothing to carry the water in . . ."

But the old man in his excitement hardly heard what he was being told of this latest setback. "And what about bread?" he said. "We have to fetch them some bread, at least a few loaves for the meantime . . . something for breakfast . . ."

The farm was small and had only one oven, and there was very little bread to go round. The teacher himself had two loaves. He put one loaf into a basket, broke a chunk off the other one and put it into the basket too, then went round to each of the houses on the farm—there were five in all—to "borrow" some loaves or even a few slices for the newly arrived refugees; there were forty-two of them after all . . .

The housewives could not refuse, hard as it was to leave their families without any bread, for had not the exiles been breadless all through the long winter, and had just come in from their arduous trek, starving, thirsty and in a sorry state. The basket was soon filled with the loaves, half-loaves and crusts that the women scraped together, and the old man hurried to bring it to the newcomers. The drum of water had not yet been carted over; there were unaccountable delays.

III

Ghastly shadows. Old men and old women, sprawling inert near their meager bundles. Women in tattered blouses, their emaciated breasts exposed. Young girls, their shriveled faces long devoid of the bloom of youth. Seven or eight sickly orphans.

"Folks, don't snatch, don't crowd around him!" a short, yellow-bearded fellow rose to his feet and hurried over to the old man who had come up with his basket of bread. "It's got to be divided out properly, everyone gets an equal share, according to the list of names . . . sh . . . sh . . . here's the list . . . now let's share it out . . . not like that . . . you'll tear the old man to pieces . . ."

"Why, there's bread!" An old woman refugee was jubilant. "This must be England, they're giving us bread."

"What about the wagons?" demanded a red-headed man, his hair providing the only spot of color among the exiles. He was standing next to a pile of five stout crates reinforced with steel hoops. "Is that all the committee sent us, the rogues? They're all rogues in that Evacuation Committee, everyone of them, damn them! In Kfar Sava they made us a lot of fine promises, and here they let us lie out in the open. Aren't they ever going to transfer us to the colony?"

The old pioneer teacher patiently explained that he was not from the Evacuation Committee of the neighboring colony, but had brought the bread on his own initiative from a nearby farm. He would be going into the colony very soon to notify the local evacuation committee of the new arrivals.

"And what can we get in the colony to go with the bread?" a young woman asked. "I myself divided out the bread in Kfar Sava . . . but they say there's honey here, plenty of honey . . . and butter . . . and how much would a pound of meat cost?"

"Suppose I wanted to settle in this colony?" asked the red-haired man's wife after receiving her ration of bread. She volunteered the

information that she was the sister of the young woman who had
doled out the bread in Kfar Sava. "Would I be able to find a place
to live, nothing much, just a room with a ceiling over it? I don't
want it for nothing, God forbid . . . I'm quite ready to pay whatever they might ask for it. I'm just sick of having no place to live
. . ."

"Oh, dear," complained the woman distributing the bread,
"everybody knows I had such a fine flat in Kfar Sava."

Another woman fastened herself onto the old man. "A doctor,"
she said, "a doctor is what we need here. Please come and see for
yourself . . . a baby's dying . . . can't eat any bread . . . two
years old she is and looks like two months . . . her father stayed
behind in Petah Tikva . . . hasn't even had a spoonful of water
for two days . . . her mother hasn't eaten a thing, can't suckle the
baby, has nothing to nurse her with." She began tugging the old
man. "Please come and see for yourself."

A young woman of about twenty sat alone among the trees
apart from the others. She was barefoot and as thin as the dry twigs
that lay around her. In her arms she rocked a naked child whose
white body was covered with the bites of mosquitoes, lice, fleas, and
other vermin and with festering sores. Inert and silent, the child
stared out of wide-open glassy eyes.

"If only . . . a drop of milk . . ." the mother articulated the
barely heard syllables.

"What we need here is a doctor, a doctor," insisted the woman
who had called the old man over.

"D'you hear that!" A woman nearby flared up. "A doctor and
milk they need, if you please, and my child hasn't even got any
water . . ."

"There's no milk to be had on the farm," the old teacher
stammered in embarrassment. "But there's water there and they'll
be bringing some very soon." He turned to the harping woman,
"Have you got a pot, or some other container? Come along with
me and I'll let you have some water. It's only ten minutes' walk . . ."

"There's water to be had much nearer," spoke up the officious
little man with the list. "Over there near the bridge."

"Heaven forbid!" the old man exclaimed in alarm. "Don't you
drink that water, it's swamp. On the farm we have good water . . .
who's coming along with me to fetch some?"

Nobody offered to go with him. Who was going to walk all that distance? Furiously, the young woman thrust a kettle into the hands of an orphan who had volunteered for the task and sent him over to the bridge to fetch some water for her baby. The water there was nearer.

IV

The office of the village council, which also dealt with refugee relief, was closed, but all around, throughout the colony, life went on as usual. Sitting on the veranda outside the office, the old pioneer teacher sensed, to his alarm, that the enthusiasm which had prompted him to run from the "station" near the farm into the colony was now beginning to wane, sobered by the closed door of the office. Not so long ago he had seen himself pounding the council table with his puny fist, shouting at them, even plunging his nails into the council chairman's beard, fulminating: "Murderers! Why don't you do something!" But now that he had been waiting outside the closed door for half an hour, he felt a kind of numbness creep over him. The janitor, who had passed by a little while ago, had told him that the head of the council was asleep but would be along shortly. But even when the head of the council came, what would he, the teacher, tell him, and what could the council actually do?

The head of the council arrived an hour later.

"I've come to tell you," the old man began in a low voice, "that some refugees, forty-two of them, have arrived . . ."

"I know that," the head of the council replied curtly.

"Then what's going to happen?" the old teacher was embarrassed.

"Whatever's got to happen. I've given instructions that they aren't to be allowed into the colony before they've all undergone disinfection. Altogether, they'll be moving on from here . . . they've got nothing to do in the colony."

"Good, so they'll get the wagons today?" the teacher was pleased.

"I'm afraid it's a bad business about those wagons," said the deputy council head who had just come in. "It's the peak of the season right now, and who of the farmers will want to hire out his wagon? A wagon's worth its weight in gold at this time of the year."

"In any case, by tomorrow morning we'll have requisitioned two carts," said the head of the council importantly.

"Two carts for forty-two people?" protested the teacher.

"Well . . . to carry their belongings. The people will have to walk."

"But most of them are ill, diseased . . . there are children . . ."

"We know all about that," the deputy broke in. "A wagon if we can get it, means a hundred and twenty gold francs."

The council head kept silent.

"And they'll spend tonight out in the open?"

The deputy did not reply. After a few minutes' silence he began telling the council head about his phone call to the central office of the Evacuation Committee. As there were Turkish officers in the post office while he was making his call, he didn't want to say over the phone exactly how much money he wanted the committee to send to cover the cost of feeding the new arrivals, but he hinted at it by saying "twice as much as you sent the day before yesterday," which meant a hundred and fifty napoleons. The money had already arrived by special messenger.

"So we can buy the millet now?" asked the council head.

"They're asking thirty-nine medjidahs a bushel."

"Is that so?" exclaimed the head of the council. "Never mind, we've got to buy. We can't afford to be particular about the price right now."

"If I'm not mistaken," the deputy said to the council head, "you must also have a few bushels of millet for sale."

Very soon, the room was crowded with grain merchants and brokers. From time to time, the deputy would plunge his hands into his pockets and pour out streams of gold napoleons. One broker cracked a joke:

"Never mind. The refugees aren't pigs. They'll even eat this millet."

"But it's half sand!"

"*Malesh,* no matter!"

The old teacher tried to make himself heard above the din of the transactions. "So it's all decided then. They're to spend the night out in the open! And we'll be able to say" he quoted from the Bible, " 'Our hands have not shed this blood'."

Receiving no answer he flung another verse at them: " 'How have their hearts turned unto stone!' "

"But they're used to it by now," one of the farmers who had been called in to see about hiring the carts tried to set his mind at rest. "They have spent the whole winter at Kfar Sava."

The head of the village council was apologetic. "As long as they haven't been disinfected, we mustn't have anything to do with them . . . doctor's orders . . ."

"In that case you'd better be careful of me," shouted the old teacher. "I've been there, and I haven't been disinfected. I'm carrying all the germs!"

"That wasn't very clever of you," the deputy grew dead serious and stopped jingling the gold coins. "You shouldn't have come here, really."

"One doesn't play around with these things . . ."

"You mustn't go against the rules of hygiene . . ."

The negotiations were at an end.

V

The teacher stayed in the colony overnight, unwilling to go back to the farm. He was not at all sure that the carts would be sent in the morning, and if he was not there to push things, who else would?

At midnight the whole countryside was blanketed by a chill, dank mist. For a long time he stood outside watching the swirling vapors and shivering slightly, unable to go inside. No, he would stay out. All night long he roamed about the slumbering colony, and dawn found him standing outside the closed door of the village council office.

It was nine o'clock by the time the two carts set out for the timber-loading station. The mist had not yet lifted completely. Sitting on one of the lumbering carts, he reflected: if a new batch doesn't arrive today, those who came yesterday will manage somehow. The poorest ones will be packed off. Those who are better off— if they insist on staying and particularly if they indicate that they won't become a public burden—will probably be allowed to enter the colony after undergoing disinfection. But if a new batch should arrive today, what with the general mismanagement and indifference prevailing in the colony, all's lost!

As he drew near and peered through the mist at the shivering people, he saw to his relief that no new ones had arrived. His heart seemed to contract in a spasm and tears welled up in his eyes.

The red-haired man was ensconced in a makeshift hut he had thrown up with the help of two Yemenites; the hut was made of his crates, some canvas, and eucalyptus branches. All the others—men, women and children—lay huddled in the damp open field, panting with thirst and shivering.

"Sodom, that's what this colony is!" spat the little yellow-bearded fellow. He seemed to have shrunk even smaller during the night.

"And what are you going to feed us today?" the old teacher was accosted by the woman who had been so impressed by "England" the day before.

"They'll be bringing you some bread," the old man promised, feeling obliged to add "millet bread."

He looked about him for the sick child (he had brought her a can of milk, about half a pint, which he had finally managed to procure in the colony), but he did not see her anywhere. He was told her mother had taken her into the colony to the doctor, without being disinfected first, in defiance of the orders.

"What do you advise us to do?" the old man was bombarded with questions on all sides. "Should we stay here or go on?"

In the meantime, the red-haired man's crates had been loaded onto the carts with the help of the carters and the officious yellow-bearded little man. The crates, which contained bales of cloth, were extremely heavy and it was only by dint of a great deal of heaving and straining, grunting and puffing, that they were finally hoisted onto the carts. A new difficulty now arose. One of the carters, a Jew from the colony, stubbornly refused to accept any additional load, not even as much as a straw (there were only two crates on his cart). In the ensuing argument, the orphans were placed on the cart and removed a dozen times. The carter remained obdurate: he was not going to kill his pair of mules for the refugees, there were plenty of other carts in the colony, the Evacuation Committee could jolly well hire as many as were needed. The other carter, an Arab drayman, who did not understand all this talk about the all-powerful Evacuation Committee, was more amenable: he agreed to take, in addition to his three crates, a few bundles and an impatient old couple, who, in their eagerness to get away at all costs, boarded the cart like martyrs ascending the scaffold.

The carts lumbered off.

"Aren't they going to send us any more carts?" the refugees who had been left behind looked at one another in blank amazement.

"What about me and my children? Aren't we going to get a

cart?" The woman who had demanded water the day before did not
yet grasp what had happened.

Very soon there was a storm of protests, oaths, recriminations,
and gnashing teeth, with violent plans of action followed by witty
rejoinders, but all the refugees remained out in the field in the end.
A squabble broke out over possession of what was left of the
red-haired man's hut. "I had it first!" "No, I did!" and as the argument raged hotly, the few poles and branches were pulled down and
strewn about. The orphans sat playing with the branches and squirt-
ing water at one another—the good water that had at last been
brought over from the farm.

The old teacher returned to the colony to report on the situation. Some of the younger men of the colony had not gone to work
that day, having undertaken to see to the disinfection and to put
up tents for the refugees in the colony, so that they should not
have to spend another night out in the open. There was a serious
hitch, however. The village council claimed that the authorities
would not permit the refugees to be brought into the colony: this
was an army depot—the deputy head of the council explained—
and the authorities did not want the soldiers to catch the disease
carried by the refugees. The tents were therefore left unpitched.
The bathhouse-keeper firmly refused to allot his premises for the
disinfection and another large boiler was not to be had at any price.

The refugees remained where they were and the old teacher
stayed with them, tired, and helpless. Exposed to the night's dew,
he was seized by a violent fever. Next morning, the train from
Tulkarm brought a new batch of 174 refugees. There was no way
out.

VI

With the attack of fever still on him and overwhelmed by a sense
of great loss, the old man rushed away from the refugee encampment in the direction of the colony. The way out lay across his path.

On the rise overlooking the colony, in among the trees, stood a
knot of people—including some tattered, hungry scarecrows of Turkish soldiers—looking down at an emaciated woman who sat barefoot on the ground, with her dead child at her side.

The body of the child, stark naked the day before yesterday,
was now dressed in a little frock.

"The doctor tried to pour a spoonful of milk into her mouth, but she couldn't swallow it. It was plain there was nothing to be done," said one of the bystanders.

The mother sat silent for some time. She looked just the same as she had looked two days ago. When she finally spoke, she said she wanted them to bury her dead baby, and that they should not forget to bring her the day's millet-bread ration. She was hungry, she said, and wanted to eat.

The child, too, apart from the frock it was wearing, looked the same as it had looked when alive: the mouth was closed, the eyes wide open, the cheeks just as hollow, and the sores still festering.

"Why don't they bury the child?" one of the bystanders protested.

"They've been over to the village council three times already," answered another. "There's nobody to talk to . . . nobody wants to call the burial society . . . they keep putting it off. . . ."

"I'll bury her," the old pioneer teacher announced. "Who can give me a hoe?"

They waited while some of the people went into the colony to fetch a hoe, asked for one at every house, and came back empty-handed.

Someone noticed that one of the soldiers carried a trench tool. Wordlessly, the old man took a bishlik [4] out of his pocket and held it out to the soldier, as if to say: "Will you come along with me?" The soldier nodded. The old man picked up the little corpse, and carrying it in front of him laid across his outstretched arms—the way a godfather holds a child at circumcision rites—he began walking in the direction of the cemetery.

For half an hour they trudged through the deep sand, the soldier with his tassel-less tarbush in front, the malaria-racked old man dragging after him, his strength flagging. No longer able to bear the child's body in front of him, he placed it under his arm, where the tiny corpse sagged and dangled limply.

The cemetery fence had been pulled up, and where the railings had been, the earth was now pockmarked with deep, narrow potholes.

4. A small Turkish coin. Y. S.

The old corpsebearer was drenched with perspiration, as if he
had taken a large dose of quinine to force the fever down. He could
hardly carry his load any farther, though the tiny frail body weighed
far less than the basket of bread he had brought to the refugees two
days ago. He looked around him, eyes sightless with exhaustion.
Hugging the little body, he murmured: "My little girl, my child.
How beautiful you are. What a beautiful woman, a loving woman,
you could have grown up to be. Who knows whose happiness you
are taking with you to the grave today? My little girl!"

His foot caught in one of the potholes. He extricated it without
noticing that he had sprained the large toe of his left foot, and went
on. Suddenly he stopped. "Here!" he said to the soldier.

The soldier unshouldered his trench tool and set to work
simply, without asking any questions. He dug steadily for ten minutes, very much like an overgrown child playing in the sand, then
raised his childlike eyes questioningly to his new commander, the
old man who had given him the bishlik. The latter, who had meanwhile laid the body on the heap of sand, motioned him to dig
deeper. "We can't have the dogs getting at the body," he thought.

The soldier obeyed, and when the grave was ready, he straightened his back and stood, waiting. The old man did what was necessary. Removing the child's frock, for some reason, he placed the poor
little body, ravaged with starvation and mosquito bites, in the
ground and began shoveling the damp earth over it with both
hands. The soldier picked up the discarded frock and placed it under his tassel-less tarbush as an additional headgear, but immediately
removed it from his head to tuck it into a gaping rent in his tunic
where there had once been a pocket, and then helped the old man
shovel the earth into the grave. With a strange devotion, he joined
in the burial of this child of a faith alien to his.

They returned to the colony, now as comrades, united by the
bond of their shared deed.

The old man was limping badly, the excruciating pain in his toe
turning each hobbling step into torment. But he felt that his task
was still unfinished, that he could not simply say good-bye to his
dark-skinned friend, the Turkish soldier, without some further
token of friendship. He wanted to offer him a glass of wine, drink
with him, say to him: "Your health, fellow sufferer! Your good
health, Anatolian peasant, who has known so much hardship!" But
there was not a drop of wine to be had in the colony's only store:

the Mukhtar [5] had taken it all for the Mudir [6] who was billeted in his house.

"That's all to the good!" thought the old man, remembering that Moslems are forbidden to take wine and that the soldier might have felt embarrassed if offered some. Instead, he bought him a packet of cigarettes and a chunk of hard cheese, pressed another bishlik on him, and warmly shook him by the hand. Full of gratitude and high spirits, the Turkish soldier went his way, the child's frock peeping out from the erstwhile pocket of his tattered tunic. The old man, however, was now unable to walk a single step. The jagged stump of the rail which had been torn out of the cemetery fence—for military purposes, no doubt—had made a deep, serious wound in his toe. Night had fallen by the time one of his laborer-students came to take him back to the farm on a donkey. At his request, the laborer-student brought a bowl of cold water to his room and then left.

He lay alone in the dark room. He had tried bathing his toe in the cold water, but the throbbing pain had become unbearable and he was no longer able to move, not even to ease himself. Yet he felt strangely relieved, completely absolved of all his obligations toward others. Relief had come.

He dimly made out the half loaf of bread lying on the table amid his books and soiled underwear, reminding him that he had not eaten a thing for three days—but the agonizing pain in his toe drove out all thought of eating. Obeying some obscure impulse, he stretched out his hand to finger the bread, saw that it had gone stale and hard, and was swept by remorse at not having taken the two whole loaves along with him. "What a great pity," he thought, "to let even a crust of bread go to waste right now. . . ." His sorrow quickly passed, however, to make way for the sense of relief that flooded him. Ten minutes' walk away, the ruthless night spread over the third batch of refugees. They had arrived unexpectedly that afternoon, his pupil told him on their way to the farm, sixty-nine of them. But they were no longer his concern, he would not go to them, he was unable to go. He felt relieved.

Translated by Yosef Schacter

5. Village headman.
6. Turkish local military governor.

AT HEAVEN'S GATE

ASHER BARASH

INTRODUCTION

ASHER BARASH (*1889–1952*), *who was born in Galicia and settled in Palestine in 1914, wrote novels, short stories, and critical essays. In his fiction he first portrayed the rural life of Galician Jewry and later, Palestinian scenes and episodes from Jewish history. He is not a major creative figure, but his work as an editor and general literary entrepreneur contributed significantly to the development of the new Hebrew literary center in Palestine after World War I. From the 20s on, with the European landscape darkened by Russian pogroms and then Nazism, he dealt frequently in his fiction with questions of Jewish suffering and survival, and in two or three memorable instances—one of them is "At Heaven's Gate"—he managed to give this troubling historical theme a powerful fictional focus.*

The Ukraine region, which is the setting for the story, was historically an area where mutually alien national groups lived in a state of high tension that often broke into violence. At the time of the action, the region was under the rule of Poland. The Haidamaks—bands of Cossack brigands—rebelled against their Polish overlords in 1768, eventually besieging the key city of Uman where 20,000 Jews had taken refuge, along with many thousands of Poles. The fate of Uman is a good example of the whole ugly Ukrainian spectacle of national hatred and ruthlessness—at first the Jews and the Poles, fighting together, drove off the Cossacks; then the Haidamaks approached the Poles and promised to spare them if they would agree to hand over the Jews; after the agreement, the Haidamaks proceeded to massacre the Jews, then turned on the Poles and slaughtered all of them, too; subsequently, the king of Poland appealed for help to Catherine II of Russia, and her troops, marching into the Ukraine, savagely murdered thousands of Cossacks.

It should be noted that there is a religious as well as a political basis for the Cossack hatred of the Poles. The Poles were Roman Catholics, the Cossacks Greek Orthodox. This is why in the story both the Polish church and the synagogue are turned into stables by Gonta's men.

The first concrete object focused upon in the story, at the beginning of the second paragraph, is the large wooden crucifix with its frail Christ-figure exposing "the nakedness of its twisted body." The main action of the story, literally and figuratively, takes place in the shadow of this crucifix. There is more here than the simple irony of suffering inflicted in Christ's name by Christians, for the hero of the story is a kind of Christ—a Jew exposing the nakedness of a body twisted in hideous pain, a saintly sufferer bearing the sins of mankind, lovingly forgiving his torturer. The initial description of the scene, which sets the church against the synagogue as though the two were "locked in a mute trial of strength," is an obvious foreshadowing of the grim struggle between Christian persecutor and Jewish victim that is the heart of the story. Indeed, one might object that Barash's insistence on the opposed houses of worship here is heavy-handed, except that the story comes close to being an allegory of Gentile persecution and Jewish suffering through the ages, and in that quasi-allegorical context, such explicitly symbolic detail may be justified.

In keeping with this general symbolic conception of his subject, Barash makes no attempt at a truly psychological differentiation of character but conceives each of the personages as a representative type, excluding any characteristics that would mitigate the "pureness" of the type (the cunning, drunken Cossack leader; the saintly Jewish victim; the brawny, dim-witted, obedient executioner). Thus there are only four named characters in the story, each with a neatly assigned role. Section I pointedly concludes, "Only two Jews remained in the whole of Tetayev: the one that served liquor to *the drunken Gentiles, and the other, who crouched like a lion at the entrance to the Lord's House to preserve its sanctity." In this fashion, the actual, variegated historical response of Ukrainian Jewry to the threat of annihilation is polarized into a saintly defender of Jewish sanctity and a mercenary purveyor of liquor to the murderers, who announces, "Don't despair of doing a stroke of business, even at the gates of hell."*

The narrator's viewpoint through most of the story is sharply visual, taking in a great deal of the external appearance of things. Leisurely panoramas, like the description of Gonta and his parade of followers at the beginning of Section II, may remind us of the typical cinematic treatment of historical subjects in the delight in colorful pageantry; there also could well be a conscious effort to approximate the method of the epic, which so often gives a vivid physical solidity to its personages and actions. But the descriptive method here is finally ironic, because the climax of the story is a wholly inner event that occurs between Zorbilo and Israel Michal— the manifestation of a conquering strength that is beyond the realm of muscles and swords and which cannot be rendered visually.

The story is carefully divided in three: a relatively brief introductory section sets the scene for the action; a middle section, filled with action, which reports the weird "battle" between Israel Michal and the Cossacks; a final section, equal in length to the preceding one, which seems to move immeasurably more slowly as it focuses on two men, fatally fixed in one spot, following the stages of Israel Michal's last agony. Structurally, then, the slow execution of the beadle turns out to be the real climactic battle (or epic action), and the culminating revelation of meaning in the historical confrontation between Gentile and Jew that is the subject of the story. The combination, in the concluding section, of a kind of epic patience in the report of detail (with deliberate repetition) conveys a sense of being virtually suspended in—or out of—time, and this, of course, jibes with Israel Michal's inner experience.

From the nightmare of Cossack mayhem, Israel Michal's mind moves back in time to a sweet dream of happy earthly life in a community fulfilling the Divine commands; then still farther back to a sense of unity with the luminous eternal Source of being. As he is pinned down and beaten to death, he undergoes a progressive inner disengagement from his torturers, so that, from hour to hour, he becomes more and more a free man. Zorbilo, on the other hand, becomes more and more enslaved to the mechanical and exhausting movements of the grisly execution, to the psychological rhythm and "orderliness" of his executioner's role, until he falls vanquished, at the end, at the feet of the Jew he has physically destroyed.

One wonders whether the large contrast between the triumph of the victim's spirit and the impotence of the victimizer's violence is not too schematic, too easy; but there is powerful resonance in the whole hypnotic rendering of the torture, in the eerie aspects of love that reveal themselves through the hideous stages of the torture, in the terrible commitment of both Jew and Christian to their respective roles in this ritual of destruction.

AT HEAVEN'S GATE (1925)
ASHER BARASH

I

WHEN "PAPA" GONTA bore down on Tetayev at the head of his Cossack army in the summer of 1768, the little town had a strange look about it: the houses, large and small, stood desolate—their shutters drawn, no smoke wreathing up from their chimneys to the clear morning skies. Only from one low-roofed house that stood awry could voices—hoarse drunken voices—be heard. From the countryside that fringed the township a few stray farmers, wearing their Sunday best and their well-waxed top boots, lumbered at a leisurely pace in the direction of this house, the only one that was *alive*. They were drawn, slowly and irresistibly, to the flame of the tavern like heavy moths.

Nailed to the large wooden crucifix that drowsed in the heavy summer's heat, the frail figure of the Christ exposed the nakedness of its twisted body to the empty desolation of the central square. Facing one another above the rooftops of the Jewish houses and shops, the tall synagogue with the mildewed old walls of stone looked across at the timbered church, blackened with age, with its tiers of small toylike turrets and spires. The two seemed to be locked in a mute trial of strength.

It was now three days since the townspeople had got word that Papa Gonta was marching on Tetayev. The Polish army had entrenched itself at Uman, and Gonta, joining forces with Zheleznik, commander of the Haidamak revolt, directed his campaign against the Polish stronghold, leaving a wide swath of blood and fire in his wake. The news that came through told of the merciless butchery of masses of Jews and the firing of all their property. There was no hope of deliverance, all will or ability to resist crumbled. The strongest weakened at the approach of the ravaging beasts, whose destructive progress left open only one path—headlong flight. The entire Jewish community of Tetayev fled in good order, salvaging such chattels as they could carry with them (while the farmers, their wagons hitched, stood at the gates of their farmyards with their hands in their pockets, watching the flight of the refugees). They made for the provincial capital, a town with thousands of Jewish inhabitants, three days' journey away. The score of Poles who lived in the town joined them in their flight, blindly hoping that this road led to safety and little realizing that in a week's time they, too, would be slaughtered.

Even before the town had emptied of its Jewish inhabitants the Gentiles, who lived on the outskirts, were deliberating whether to set about plundering the Jewish property right away, or wait for Papa to arrive. Those in the know said that Papa did not like anything to be done without his being present, and at the local council meeting, therefore, it was decided to wait. The tavern presented a problem, however: how could they allow the tavern to remain closed with all those hogsheads of liquor full to the brim inside? A way out of this difficulty was suggested by one of the shrewder villagers: as soon as the Jewish exodus started, a score of fearless village lads, armed with axes, would lie in wait for "Chamka" (Nehemiah), the Jewish innkeeper, at the edge of the wood. They were to seize him and bring him back to the inn, where he would be forced to serve them drinks willy-nilly—and all this quite legal as far as Papa was concerned.

This plan was indeed carried out. Rudely hustled back to his deserted inn, Nehemiah was at first stunned at having been torn away from his family and people, crazed with terror at being surrounded by hostile, jeering Gentiles. His yellow beard and earlocks seemed to go ashen-grey and limp, and his frightened eyes stared with the uncomprehending sorrow of a chained beast. The next day, however, he was able to take stock of the situation; he served generous drinks to his tormentors—old friends of his—and acknowledged their coarse jests. He even jotted down the figures in his notebook out of some obscure hope: "Cast your bread upon the waters . . . you can never know," he thought. "Don't despair of doing a stroke of business, even at the gates of hell!"

There was a Jewish beadle living in Tetayev at the time, Israel Michal, a thick-bearded, taciturn man in his prime, who had officiated at the synagogue for more than twenty years—an office that had been in his family for generations. He had never been known to do or say anything unseemly for a man who held this post, having humbly served even the meanest of the congregants. When the community, at a meeting held in the synagogue, decided on flight, Israel Michal slipped away unobserved and hid in a large barrel that stood in the garret where dilapidated leaves from holy books were stored. Only when the community had departed, leaving behind an empty silence, did he come out of hiding and noiselessly descend to the courtyard, where there stood a heap of heavy, rough-hewn stones that were to have been used for renovating the old synagogue building. With strong, trembling hands he carried the stones singly into the vestibule and there arranged them in a pile. He knew only too well that before long the unclean Gentile hordes would storm in to defile the House of the Lord, bemire the large tomes of the Talmud and other sacred books (the refugees had taken the Scrolls of the Law with them, but had been unable to carry the other holy books in addition to their vital provisions), and scatter the torn leaves that were so zealously stored away. But he would not allow them to enter the House of Prayer! He would keep them at bay, hurl stones at the heads of any who dared approach!

He locked the heavy door on the inside. Then he placed a table against it, set a chair on the table and clambered up. He smashed the stained-glass fanlight—shaped like a Star of David in six colors—making an aperture large enough to fling the stones through when the moment arrived. This done, he again tried the door to make sure that it was locked, then lay down on the cold floor next to the table. He lay like that for two days, without food or drink, waiting for the destroyers to arrive. Unremembered were his wife and five children, who had fled with the others, forgotten was the whole community, dispersed and scattered. His mind was filled with but one thought: the inviolate sanctity of the House of Worship, and his visions of the broken heads of those that would defile it gave him strength and vitality.

It was thus that only two Jews remained in the whole of Tetayev: the one that served liquor to the drunken Gentiles, and the other, who crouched like a lion at the entrance to the Lord's House to preserve its sanctity.

II

Papa Gonta sat firmly astride his mount, a squat but fiery Cossack horse, thick of shank, small-headed, and somewhat shaggy. Gonta wore his large Cossack *kalpak* at a jaunty angle over one ear. His long sword almost trailed on the ground. His little, cunning eyes were deep-set in his fat, glistening face. His long brown moustache coiled down like snakes' tails on either side of his full, red lips. After him walked a motley crowd of minstrels playing a variety of instruments, followed by a large troop of horsemen, their drawn swords laid across the pommels of their saddles. Behind them came, on foot, a ragged mob of rebels, armed with picks, axes, scythes, and other farmyard implements. A train of carts, loaded with provisions and plunder, brought up the rear. The procession was marshaled by mounted officers, who rode up and down the line on either side.

All the villagers, men, women and children, had turned out in their holiday attire and lined the road on either side. They cheered boisterously, waved scarves and flags, and some even threw flowers at the marchers. The skies were distant, clear, and serene—as they were in the Sinai Desert before the Giving of the Law; the Feast of Pentecost was a week away.

The procession came to a halt in the center of the town, filling the circular marketplace around the large cross and the Christ in the last throes of agony. The jostling crowd poured into the square, were pressed back against the walls of the shuttered houses. Without dismounting from his horse, Papa Gonta made a short speech; the enthusiastic mob cheered wildly and flung caps into the air. Then his aides briskly set up his tent in the shadow of the cross, and laid out a carpet of coarse red wool at the entrance. The Cossack chief then sat down to conduct the business of the day.

To begin with, he ordered the leading members of the *Haromada,* the local council, to be brought before him. The next instant, a dozen village notables stood around him in a half-circle, fur caps in hand, bowing obsequiously.

"I want every zhid and liach [1] brought here at once," Gonta roared.

"They have run away, Papa, all of them," the farmers answered in abject apology.

"What, are none of them left?"

"Not a single one of the liachs."

"And the zhids?"

"All gone, Papa. There's only Chamka the Innkeeper, whom we kept behind to wet our thirsty souls. If Papa will give orders to let him live . . . for the good of the town . . ."

"Very well, we'll keep him alive for the time being. Now I want two of you to go and fetch me some of that liquor, the best there is. The rest of you go and see to it that your people are armed. At sunrise tomorrow we march on Uman."

After the farmers left, two Cossack officers wearing Polish kalpaks came over and stood respectfully before him.

"Well?"

"What shall we do about the horses, Excellency?"

"Put half of them in the Polish church and the other half in the zhid synagogue," their commander told them.

The officers having left to carry out his orders, Gonta settled down to the two large, potbellied bottles of vodka that had been brought from the inn. Ever since he had launched the insurrection against the Poles, allying himself with his fellow Haidamaks, he had progressively doubled, then trebled, his daily dose of liquor.

There were more than a hundred horses to be stabled in the synagogue. The Cossacks led them there by their bridles at a slow walk. The horses had beeen washed and were dripping wet, their shaggy coats had been combed down, their saddles and trappings hung from them loosely, and their long, swishing tails almost reached their small ears. The Cossacks carried pails of oats in their hands, and some bore sacks of fodder on their shoulders. They went about their business calmly, almost innocently, looking for all the world like the serfs that served the rich farmers or Polish noblemen. Little did they suspect what trouble lay ahead.

---

1. Derogatory names for Jew and Pole. Y. S.

From afar they saw that the doors of the synagogue were barred.

"The dogs shut the place up!" said one of them, shaking his head in annoyance.

"Pity they ran away," another joked. "We could have rammed the door open with their mangy heads."

"Let's get something to use as a battering ram."

"Nah! You can break that door down with an ordinary club!"

"Just let Tarras put his behind to it, and it'll fly open."

"Ho-ho, that's a good one! When Tarras farts, it can bring a fortress down!"

They continued exchanging their coarse jests till they came to the doors of the House of God.

Hearing the noise of the approaching crowd of men and horses, Israel Michal was buoyed by a wave of vigorous excitement, which turned his arms to tempered steel and set his heart afire. He leaped up from where he lay and crouched to peer through the keyhole. Then he raised his arms toward the Holy Ark and offered up a silent prayer to the Lord for having brought his enemies within his reach, that he might wreak havoc among them. Taking a stone from the pile, he sprang lightly onto the table, like a boy, mounted the chair, and then, without taking aim, hurled the stone through the broken fanlight onto the massed crowd below. The stone tore the ear off one of the Cossacks and dislocated his arm. At his agonized yell, his bewildered comrades pressed forward against the front of the building to see what had happened. Men and horses were bombarded by the heavy stones which came down in a steady stream, one by one. Before they had time to draw back to see what was happening, a number of dead and wounded lay on the ground. The frightened horses neighed wildly, rearing up on their legs.

"By god! Their God's fighting back at us!" cried one.

"Jesu and Maria! Did you see those stones! Straight down from the sky!"

"By the life of Papa! No man could lift such a stone!"

"They're magicians, they are! Damn their mothers!"

"We've got to bring up the battering rams!"

"Don't be a ninny! We've got to get Papa. He'll tell us what's to be done."

The stones kept falling, one by one, at regular intervals, but now they landed with dull thuds on the soft earth, or on the bodies of the slain.

Before long Papa Gonta arrived in person, his squat, blubbery body waddling in rhythm with the song of the liquor that swilled about inside him. After surveying the battlefield, he ordered his men to shoot at the door with their muskets. The door was soon riddled like a sieve, but still the stream of stones did not cease.

"The place must be full of devils!" the commander roared in fury. "Sons, lay logs all round this stable and set it on fire."

That same moment, a solitary shot having been fired at the door, the hail of stones let up.

After a few minutes of amazed silence, the Cossacks were ordered to break down the door with their hatchets. Great was their astonishment, however, when, bursting in, they found the vestibule deserted save for an elderly Jew who sat on the floor next to a pile of stones, nursing a wounded leg and biting his lips in agony; his hair was disheveled, blood and sweat streamed down his face, and his eyes gleamed with a mad light. They leaped over his crouching form and erupted into the synagogue with drawn swords to look for any others that might have barricaded themselves inside. They found not a soul; the whole synagogue—the dais, the curtainless Holy Ark that stood wide open, the lecterns, the candelabra—all was as silent as death. Rushing back to the vestibule, they dragged the wounded beadle outside and flung him at the feet of their commander.

"Here he is, Papa, the devil that's been killing our brothers. It's all we found."

Papa Gonta regarded him speculatively for a moment, kicked him, turned him over with his foot, spat on him, then ordered him to be dragged out of the way while the horses were taken into the "stable." With much heaving and tugging the frightened horses—strangely reluctant to enter—were finally stabled in the synagogue.

This done, the Cossack chief turned to the business of passing sentence on the beadle, who had caused the death of three soldiers and one horse and had injured four soldiers and five more horses. Flanked by his officers he faced the crowd, his head slightly canted under the weight of his Tartar fur cap. For a moment he toyed with the silver hilt of his long, curved saber, and then, clearing his throat loudly two or three times, he pronounced judgment slowly, deliberately, as though counting out money:

"Strip him naked and tie him down, with his head against that door," he waved his head in the direction of the synagogue. "Four guards will stand over him, two at his head and two at his feet, and

Ivan Zorbilo," a burly giant of a Cossack pushed his way through the crowd and stood before his chief, "will flog him with his knout. Flog him slowly. D'you hear, you whoreson? Give it to him slowly, easy, easy, like this, one after the other. Don't lay it on too hard, d'you hear? And take your time over it, easy, easy. But don't stop, d'you hear? Don't stop for a moment. Just keep at it till that black-bitched soul of his packs up and clears off. Easy now, carefully, lovingly, gently, with all your heart, till his devil's soul flies off, haw-haw-haw!" The Cossacks guffawed boisterously in wild appreciation of their chief's wit.

"Easy now, d'you hear?" Gonta sternly reminded Ivan, then a smile flitted under his moustache. "And now, my little ones, let's have some dancing at the tavern. My daughters back home in Rosschov are probably dancing too right now—on the red-hot stoves of the goddamn Polacks." Tears glistened in his eyes, and the admiring mob was moved to compassion. "Come children, let's go."

"The whoresons! No matter, Papa, we'll kill them off, cut their throats to the last mother's son!" Roaring these and other words of comfort at their chief, the crowd surged in a mighty wave toward the tavern.

III

The yard in front of the synagogue emptied, save for the four guards, the giant Ivan Zorbilo who was to administer the flogging (the dead and wounded had been evacuated to the main square), a few idle spectators who had been too lazy to go to the tavern, and the condemned man. Israel Michal lay spread-eagled on the ground, naked, genitals exposed, his head on the threshold of the Lord's House, his hands and feet bound, his wounded leg dripping blood.

The giant Cossack set about his task. To begin with, he unplaited the leather thongs of his knout, and they became four sharp, flickering tendrils. Then he stared appreciatively at the butt, patted it once or twice, and balanced it in his palm. Tears welled up in his eyes, but the strange light there quickly dissipated them. The guards smoothed their moustaches in anticipation, gazing down at the victim.

Zorbilo began to administer the flogging.

The fiery thongs enlaced the gaunt frame lovingly, endearingly, as though seized with a passionate desire to cling to the holy body.

Silently, with barely a swish, but with a violence as restrained as an ardent kiss, they came to rest on the chest, curled round and embraced the ribs, leaving four red weals when the knout was raised. At its first touch, the body quivered and writhed slightly, the face contorted and the beginnings of a moan escaped, but was immediately stilled. The tortured man shut his eyes, bit his lips, and was henceforth silent.

The giant performed his task dutifully, with painstaking deliberation. He was careful not to strike the same spot twice, enjoying the pattern of bloody weals he was raising on the naked body. He directed the lashing downward from the chest to the thighs, but carefully avoided striking the genitals. In his childhood—he remembered—his father had once hit him there with a whip, and he had never forgotten the gnawing agony of it. No, he wouldn't lay it on there! But there were still other places! The lashes curled round the thighs, the knees, the shinbones, adorning the legs with a series of crimson bangles and anklets. The rope that pinioned the legs snapped, but the legs remained together, motionless and taut. The lash flicked up again from the toes to the chest, and thence up to the head, but stopped at the neck. No, he wouldn't disfigure the face! He began all over again from the place where he had started.

The guards and onlookers, tired of standing, squatted down on the ground and watched tensely. The victim's face was contorted. The pain, lacerating at first, had made way for an agonizing dullness that crept through his whole body and which, reaching his heart, seemed to rend it with fiery pincers. His bound arms and legs felt numb, especially his wounded leg; the dripping blood had formed a little pool on the ground, which coagulated and glistened in the sun for a brief moment, with the further drops of fresh, warm blood floating on top.

From the tavern came the beating of drums and blowing of fifes and the sounds of drunken carousing. Seared with pain and hunger, Israel Michal's mind succumbed to strange visions. His eyes tightly closed, he saw in his tortured imagination how his brethren, the whole Jewish community of Tetayev, were being hounded and butchered in the streets of the town. He saw the Haidamaks riding them down with drawn swords and whistling knouts, trampling them under their horses' hooves, impaling babies on their lances. He saw his wife sprawled across the threshold of their house, her skull smashed in her attempt to bar the way to the ravaging

Cossacks. He saw his sons and daughters lying on the floor bathed in their own blood. But he was undisturbed by these visions. On the contrary, these bloody scenes filled him with a pleasurable sensation. The lashes that kept descending in a regular rhythm, too, had begun to mean for him an orderliness, an established scheme of things, quite understandable and justified. He was now possessed by a single fear—that the flogging would stop and upset this order.

The noonday sun beat down. From the tops of the tall trees that fringed the synagogue the birds twittered in reply to the sounds that came from the tavern. In some deserted farmyard, a lone cock crowed his protests with stubborn persistence. Zorbilo flogged on, his pillarlike legs planted firmly apart on the ground, his back slightly bent forward, his face reddening with the exertion. He whipped off his fur cap and flung it into the lap of one of the guards, baring a close-cropped fair head which gleamed in the sunlight. Rivulets of sweat streamed down his boorish face onto his corded neck. The guards sat cross-legged, waiting for the two boys they had sent to the tavern to fetch them something to drink. On the boys' return with a massive flagon of spirits, the guards took swigs at it in turn, their heads thrown well back. They offered the bottle to Zorbilo, but he refused it with a shake of his head. No, he mustn't stop. Papa had ordered him not to. He must keep at his flogging.

Israel Michal's mood underwent a change. A sweet sensation of utter weariness crept over his body and spirit. There was still that gnawing at his heart, his sinews seemed stretched to breaking point, his whole body was a swollen, bluish-red mass, but he felt no pain, and was at ease. Gone also were the nightmarish, bloody pictures of the Haidamaks' butchery, having made way for pleasant visions: festival services of the synagogue, wedding celebrations, circumcision rites. He heard the cantor and his choir chant the joyous, radiant melody of a New Year prayer; he saw himself spreading out the large prayershawl on the Feast of the Rejoicing of the Law; he was walking in the pleasant, dewy coolness of daybreak to wake up the worshipers for the early morning prayers. The scenes came through to him, through his closed eyelids, with such sharp clarity, with such radiance and glory. He had never felt a happiness such as this before.

His eyes remained closed, and Zorbilo flogged on.

A few reeling drunks came out of the tavern. They lurched

over to see what was going on, spat on the prostrate figure and went their way. Zorbilo did not stop.

Israel Michal had plunged into the dreamworld of childhood, into that Eden where the trees are ever in blossom and cherubs walk about in human form. His heart pounded in furious ecstasy, his soul smiled. Zorbilo swayed as if in prayer.

The sun had swung down from its zenith, plunging the synagogue in shadow—long shadows which swallowed in darkness the head of the tortured beadle, then slanted across to the church that looked on from afar. The sounds that came from the tavern rose to a menacing pitch, soon followed by the noises of windows being smashed and doors battered down. The Jewish houses were being ransacked and looted, now permitted by Papa Gonta in his expansive drunken benignity. Horses whinnied, wagons creaked under the loads of spoils that were being carted to the surrounding villages. Here and there flames leapt up among thick coils of smoke.

Doggedly, Zorbilo flogged on. His knees wavered from long standing, his heart was fit to burst with hunger and thirst and exertion. But he must not stop. So long as the chest of the prostrate figure heaved—though ever so faintly—there was no stopping. A few times already, the guards had run their hands over the lacerated body, but it was still warm, and Zorbilo went on flogging.

Suddenly Israel Michal opened his eyes, looked up with a clear, untroubled gaze that shone with the purity of the soul's light. He saw the gigantic Gentile looming over him, and the thongs that descended to cut into his flesh in ceaseless rhythm, yet he did not move an eyelid. He saw the two guards squatting at his feet, the cluster of idle onlookers, the synagogue yard, the wooden palings of the fence, the branches of the solitary tree that stood next to the church opposite—and all appeared so clear, so lucid and sharply defined. What might have been a smile hovered on the bloodless blue lips, but it was swallowed in the deep shadow that had now crept half down the neck, seemingly cutting it in two.

Zorbilo swayed wearily. His giant's strength was failing, becoming spent. Countlessly he had changed hands, but this no longer relieved the numbness in his arms, which moved mechanically as though of their own accord. He was *afraid* of stopping. He feared —not Papa Gonta, whom he had completely forgotten—that if he stopped now he would never again be able to move an arm. He had put his entire spirit, his very heart and soul, into the whipping. His whole attention was now focused on the face of the tortured man, riveted there ever since the eyes had opened. The calm gaze seemed to flow into his soul, merge with his inner being, thawing and softening the hardness there; the purity and holy innocence it gave out made him oblivious of all, of yesterday's butchery and tomorrow's battles, of his commanders, of the march on Uman and the fort that was to be stormed—all was forgotten. There was only himself communing with the soul of the tortured man. He lashed on, and his heart went out in prayer to the Jew who lay before him.

The guards untied his hands, but not a limb stirred. He lay inert on his back, his face waxen, only his eyes alive, gazing from the depths of his soul into the depths of Zorbilo's soul as the executioner stood over him, lashing him with deadened arms.

Israel Michal felt himself being taken up and borne aloft, higher and higher, to the Gate of Heaven, to the eternal serenity and the Hidden Light beyond. But before his eyes stood a tormented man, gasping painfully as he labored futilely in the last stages of exhaustion. He felt the need to speak to the sufferer, to comfort him.

The shadows had crept down to the lifeless waist, when Zorbilo suddenly noticed a faint movement of the blue lips and the saintly eyes beckoning to him to bend down. He answered this mute call, the whip in his deadened arm still flailing at the outstretched legs, the sweat streaming down his ashen face onto his sodden shirt. And as he stooped, his ears straining to hear, the lips parted slightly to whisper to him, distinctly, in his own language:

"You are tired, my son. Rest, rest a while, rest . . ."

A strangled cry, like the raucous rasp of a dying man, burst forth from the giant's heaving chest, the knout slipped from his hand, and he sank to his knees at the feet of the martyred man.

The guards and onlookers leaped up in alarm. On the tortured man's lips the last smile was already frozen, alight with the radiance of the Lord of mercy and forgiveness.

Translated by Yosef Schacter

AGUNOT

S. Y. AGNON

INTRODUCTION

SHMUEL YOSEF AGNON (*1888–1970*) *is the undisputed master of modern Hebrew fiction. Born in Galicia into a pious and learned family, he emigrated to Palestine at the age of nineteen, spent a ten-year period in Germany during and after World War I, then returned to Jerusalem where he lived and wrote for nearly half a century till his death. His novels and stories range from artistic reworkings of folktales and folklore to realistic psychological studies and social satires, to boldly experimental dream-fictions and intricate symbolic tales, sometimes puzzling, often haunting. His style is the crowning achievement of modern Hebrew prose, weaving together the Hebrew of centuries of sacred texts—predominantly rabbinic ones—into a beautifully lucid and flexible language that is often the instrument of subtle irony. His imagination is deeply rooted in the old world of pious tradition, yet he also responds profoundly to the terrible inner and outer shocks of twentieth-century history. Awarded the Nobel Prize for Literature for 1966, he is the one Hebrew novelist who clearly belongs among the major modern writers of the world.*

"Agunot" was Agnon's first story published in Palestine after his arrival there in 1907, and it announces some of the major themes and techniques of his later work. Asked by his editor to use a Hebrew name (his original name was Chachkes), the young writer

chose "Agnon," after the title of the story. An aguna *is the wife of a husband who has disappeared without conclusive evidence of his death. According to Jewish law, she may not remarry and so remains pathetically in a state of "living widowhood."* Agunot *in the title, then, suggests a world of mismatched souls sundered forever from their true mates, and Agnon's very choice of a name for himself expresses tragic, irreparable separation—one of his recurrent concerns as a writer. If the story seems to reflect astonishing artistic maturity for a nineteen-year-old, it should be observed that Agnon later subjected the story to two extensive revisions, mostly a matter of boiling down lyrical excesses, sometimes reducing a long effusive paragraph to a single compressed sentence. The translation is based on the last revised version.*

"Agunot" combines two familiar folkloristic themes—star-crossed lovers (as in Romeo and Juliet*) and the tragic, irreversible mistake. The "folk" narrator is an artful creation of the author's— a God-fearing soul who punctuates his narrative with pious ejaculations ("Mercy shield us!"), who believes in sin and retribution, wandering spirits, lurking evil presences, and so forth. This narrator is a figure firmly set within a tradition, addressing his audience almost as though he were telling the story orally, and pointedly calling attention to the narrative as a wondrous tale: "this is the theme of the tale recounted here, a great tale and terrible." Because the narrator himself is fully within the tradition, he can exploit its expressive resources naturally and uninhibitedly, as a conventional, modern writer could not. And because the narrator makes the assumptions of belief of the traditional world, he can infuse magical or supernatural events in the story with a genuine excitement and a kind of credibility. The archaic style of the story—and it is more obtrusively archaic than most of Agnon's prose elsewhere—fits such a narrator perfectly. Baruch Hochman's translation does a remarkable job of working out an English equivalent for Agnon's medieval Hebrew. The poetic inversions, the obsolete locutions, the wordplay ("their feasts are fasts, their lot is dust instead of luster") all resemble features of the original.*

The first introductory paragraph finely illustrates Agnon's virtuosity in the adaptation of traditional literary modes. The vehicle of the traditional Midrash is used to establish exactly the desired context of meaning for the story. The paragraph starts and ends on a note of Divine harmony, but the heart of the passage is devoted to a fatal error. The weaving of the prayershawl and the unraveling of its thread announce a formal motif of weaving and tearing that recurs in the story. The ark cast down into the garden will be covered with a "mantle of black silk" like a shroud over which the moon weaves "its silvery web," tracing a Star of David. At the wedding, "sadness attacks the bridal canopy, and rips it into shreds." At the end, the Divine Presence appears to the rabbi in the form of a woman "garbed in black" and when he awakes, he rends his own garments as a sign of mourning. After the unraveling of the prayershawl in the initial paragraph, all Israel "know they are naked"—a pointed echo of the phrase in Genesis describing Adam and Eve after the first sin.

The opening Midrash quotes the Song of Songs several times, which is, of course, the Bible's great poem of joyous young love, but here it is used to express the pain of loss and violence. The tale will continue to play artfully with echoes from the Song of Songs, eventually moving from that book to echoes from the gloomy Ecclesiastes. The story begins with the allegorical level of the Song of Songs (the lover is God, the beloved the Congregation of Israel) and then moves down to the literal level of human lovers. But by beginning in this way, Agnon establishes a cosmic perspective for the events to follow: we start with God and his Creation, then move on to Dinah and Ben Uri, so that it is not a matter of a single aguna but of a world of agunot, where tragic separation is an endemic condition.

The style in which the main action is conveyed might be characterized as a magic lyricism. Frequently we are introduced to a process in which metaphors imperceptibly turn into literal, and supernatural, fact. In the crucial first three paragraphs of Section II, Dinah does not just fall in love with the singer but it is "as though —God save us!—a spell had been cast." Or perhaps, we begin to wonder, a spell literally has been cast. Ben Uri, the artist, pours his soul into his work not only figuratively but, apparently, quite literally. (Note the arresting statement later on: "Among the trees in the garden he sleeps, like a lyre whose strings are rent [again the motif of tearing], whose melodies have forsaken it.") Or again, at the beginning of Section III, we are told of Dinah's mirror that "It had been her mother's glass, but held no trace of her mother's image"—as if it were quite natural to assume, in this spooky world of flitting spirits, that people left vestiges of their images in mirrors.

In the same passage the wind that puts out the candle "as in a sickroom" is a conscious, purposeful presence, not just a chance gust of air. The double image of Dinah with her candle and Dinah with her candle in the mirror is itself artfully doubled when the reflected moon in the water rises to meet the moon in the clouds and the two together are likened to Sabbath candles, thus reinforcing our sense of a world of uncanny correspondances.

These and related artistic means for translating popular belief into fictional vision give resonance to the fabulous ending of the story. The rabbi is converted into a legendary figure, a kind of Flying Dutchman, and as we imagine him floating across the world trying to reunite "the forsaken in love" (agunot), the sense of a cosmic dimension to the theme of sundered souls that was established in the opening Midrash is completed. It is no accident that the Shekhina appears as a lovely woman garbed in black—in this world of tragic separation, the Divine Presence itself is, as it were, an aguna. The effect of a tale of marvels told by an oral storyteller is again stressed at the end. The narrator has rumors to report ("They say he wanders still."), "innumerable tales" to allude to, a witness to cite ("Rabbi Nissim, of blessed memory") who is so factual about the miraculous—the strategem is typical of Agnon— that he apologizes for not knowing the name of the child carried off by a figure floating across the sea on a kerchief.

AGUNOT (1908)
S. Y. AGNON

I

IT IS SAID: A thread of grace is spun and drawn out of the deeds of Israel, and the Holy One, blessed be He, Himself, in His glory, sits and weaves—strand on strand—a prayershawl, all grace and all mercy, for the Congregation of Israel to deck herself in. Radiant in the light of her beauty she glows, even in these, the lands of her Exile, as she did in her youth in her Father's house, in the Temple of her Sovereign and the city of sovereignty, Jerusalem. And when He, of ineffable Name, sees her, that she has neither been sullied nor stained even here, in the realm of her oppressors, He—as it were —leans toward her and says, "Behold thou art fair, my beloved, behold thou art fair." And this is the secret of the power and the glory and the exaltation and the tenderness in love which fills the heart of every man in Israel. But there are times—alas!—when some hindrance creeps up, and snaps a thread in the loom. Then the prayershawl is damaged: evil spirits hover about it, enter into it, and tear it to shreds. At once a sense of shame assails all Israel, and they know they are naked. Their days of rest are wrested from them, their feasts are fasts, their lot is dust instead of luster. At that hour the Congregation of Israel strays abroad in her anguish, crying,

"They struck me, they wounded me, they took away my veils from me!" Her beloved has slipped away, and she, seeking him, cries, "If ye find my beloved, what shall ye tell him? That I am afflicted with love." And this affliction of love leads to darkest melancholy, which persists—Mercy shield us!—until, from the heavens above, He breathes down upon us strength of spirit, to repent, and to muster deeds that are pride to their doers and again draw forth that thread of grace and love before the Lord.

And this is the theme of the tale recounted here, a great tale and terrible, from the Holy Land, of one renowned for his riches— Sire Ahiezer by name—who set his heart on going up from the Diaspora to the holy city Jerusalem—may she be rebuilt and established—to work great wonders of restoration in the midst of her ruins, and in this way to restore at least a corner of the anteroom which will be transformed into our mansion of glory on the day when the Holy One, blessed be He, restores His presence to Zion— may it be soon, in our day!

And credit him kindly, Lord—credit him well for his wishes, and for his ministrations to his brethren, sons of his people, who dwell before Thee in the Land of the Living, and this though he ultimately failed.

Sire Ahiezer fathered no sons, but he praised the Ineffable sevenfold daily for the daughter who fell to his lot. He cherished her like the apple of his eye, and set maidservants and tirewomen to wait on her, that her very least wish might be honored. And, surely, she was worthy of all this respect, for she was the pattern of virtue, and all the graces were joined together in her person: royal the radiance of her countenance; like the matriarchs', her straitness of virtue; her voice pleasing as the harp of David; and all her ways modest and gentle. But all this pride was inward, and dwelt apart, in the innermost chambers, so that only the intimates of her father's house might behold her, at twilight, when—at times —she went down to walk in the garden, among the spice trees and the roses, where the doves fluttered about her in the twilight, murmuring their fondness in her ears and shielding her with their wings, like the golden cherubs on the Ark of the Sanctuary.

And when her season came, the season of love, her father sent couriers to all the dispersions of Israel, to spy out a youth that would be her match, such a paragon, a cluster of virtue, as had no peer in all the world. Here it was that the Evil One intervened, and not in vain were the words bruited about, by the men of Jerusalem, to the effect that Sire Ahiezer had slighted all the seminaries and academies, all the seats of learning in the Land of Israel when he sent to find a match for his daughter among the sons of the Exile abroad. But who might admonish so mighty a man—who might tender him counsel? They all began eagerly to await the match that the Holy One, blessed be He, would provide for this cloistered grace, glorious child, vaunted daughter of Jerusalem.

And then, months having passed, a scroll was received from the emissaries, declaring: "We hereby proclaim with joy: with the aid of the Lord we have found in Poland a boy, a wondrous lad, in virtue clad, with wisdom blest, head and shoulders above all the rest; pious, modest, pedigreed; model of virtue and good deed; paragon and worthy son, wreathed in blessings from the sages, who bless this match with all their hearts and wages." And so forth.

The grandee, Sire Ahiezer, seeing his designs were prospering, thought it only fitting that the above-mentioned bridegroom hold forth at a great academy in Jerusalem, that scholars might stream from the ends of the earth to hear the Law from his lips. What did he do? He convened all manner of craftsmen, built a great mansion, adorned it inside and out—painted it and gilded it, and furnished it with several cartloads of precious texts, no jot of godly wisdom lacking among them. And he designated a hall for prayer, adorned it with all manner of adornment, and called on the scribes to prepare the Scrolls of the Law, and on the gold- and silversmiths to design the ornaments of the Scrolls—and all of this in order that the prayers of the sage might be neighbor to his studies, so that he might truthfully say, "Here is my God, and I will praise Him." The grandee, wishing to consummate his work of glorifying the Sanctuary, set his heart on an Ark for the Scrolls—an Ark such as the eye of man had never seen.

He began to ask after a proper craftsman. Among the journeymen he came on one said to be versed in the subtlest of crafts, one Ben Uri by name—a man both modest and diffident, a mere craftsman as met the eye were it not for the spark that flashed from his glance, and was reflected in the work of his hand. Ahiezer took note, and placed the work of the Ark in his hand.

II

Sire Ahiezer took Ben Uri and lodged him by the garden, at the bottom of his house. Ben Uri brought his tools and readied himself for the task. Immediately, another spirit possessed him. His hands wrought the Ark; his lips uttered song all the day.

Dinah, lovely child of Ahiezer, stood by her window, gazing into the trees, and heard. Dreaming, she was drawn to the singer as though—God save us!—a spell had been cast. So she went down, she and her handmaidens with her went down, to examine the work of the man. She peered into the Ark, she stirred his paints, examined his carvings, and picked up his tools. All the time Ben Uri worked, singing as he worked, working even as he sang. Dinah heard his song and did not know her heart. And he, even as he wrought, all the time aimed his song at her heart, to wrap it in his rapture, so that she might stand there forever, never depart.

But as Ben Uri pursued his work, he cleaved more and more to it, until both eyes and heart passed into the Ark; no part of him was free of it. Memory of Dinah fled him; it was as though she did not exist. Not many days passed before he stopped singing altogether; his voice rang out no more. Ben Uri stood by the Ark all day, carving figures on the Ark and breathing the soul of life into them. Lions mounted upon it, a mane of gold on each of the pair, their mouths brimming with song, uttering the glories of the Lord. On the hangings that draped the doors of the Ark, eagles poised above, their wings spread, to leap toward the sacred beasts above. At the sound of the golden bells when the Ark was opened, they would soar in their places, flap their wings, and wrap the universe in song. Already the worthies of Jerusalem awaited the day the Ark would be borne up to the House of the Lord the hand of the grandee had builded, when the Scrolls of the Law, crowned with silver and lapped in gold and decked out in all the jewels of sanctity, would find their place within this Ark.

Rapt, Ben Uri wrought, possessed by a joy he had never known before. In no kingdom, in no province, in the course of no labor had he exulted as he exulted here, in the place where the Divine Presence was revealed and then reviled, in the multitude of our transgressions. Not many days passed before his labors were ended. Ben Uri looked at the work of his hands and was astonished how the Ark stood firm while he himself was like an empty vessel. His soul was sad and he broke out in tears.

Ben Uri went out to seek the air among the trees in the garden, to restore his spirits a little. The sun set in the west; the face of the heavens crimsoned. Ben Uri went down to the far corners of the garden, he laid himself down, and he slept. At just that moment Dinah left her chamber. Her robe clung to her flesh; fear was on her countenance. It was many days since she had heard Ben Uri's voice, since she had looked on the man. She went to his chamber to look at the Ark. She came, but did not find him there. Dinah stood in Ben Uri's chamber, and the Ark of God stood at the open window, where Ben Uri had worked. She stood near the Ark, and examined it. The Evil One came, and poured a potion of vengeance into her heart. He pointed at the Ark and said, "It is not for nought that Ben Uri takes no thought of you; it is the Ark that separates you twain." At that moment Dinah lifted her arms, and smote the Ark. The Ark teetered, and fell through the open window.

The Ark fell, but no part of it was broken, no corner of it was blemished. It lay there among the trees in the garden below. Roses and lilies nodded over it, like mourners at the ark of the dead. Night drew a mantle of black silk over the Ark. The moon came out of the clouds, and weaving its silvery web, traced a Star of David on the shroud.

III

On her couch in the night Dinah lies and her heart wakes. Her sin weighs heavily upon her: who could bear her burden of guilt? Dinah buries her head in her pallet, oppressed by sorrow, by shame. How can she look to Heaven, how call to it for grace? Dinah springs from her couch and lights the taper in her room. In the mirror opposite, light flares out in her eyes. It had been her mother's glass, but held no trace of her mother's image. Were Dinah to look into it now, it is only her own countenance she would see—the countenance of a sinner. "Mother, Mother!" her heart cries out. But there is no answer.

Dinah rose and crossed to the window, she rested her chin on her hands, and looked out. Jerusalem is cradled in mountains. The wind swept down and entered her chamber, extinguishing the light, as in a sickroom, where some invalid sleeps. It played around her hair and through her ears, whispering sweet melodies, like the songs Ben Uri had sung. Where, oh where, is he now?

Among the trees in the garden he sleeps, like a lyre whose strings are rent, whose melodies have forsaken it. And the Ark lies prone, in the garden. The Guardian of Night unfurls his pinions of darkness, and the lions and eagles in the Ark nestle under his wings. An unspotted moon slips out of the clouds; another moon rises to meet her in the waters of the pond. They stand, face-to-face, like a pair of Sabbath candles. To what might the Ark have been compared at that moment? To a woman who extends her palms in prayer, while her breasts—the Tables of the Covenant—are lifted with her heart, beseeching her Father in Heaven: "Master of the Universe, this soul which Thou hast breathed into him Thou hast taken from him, so that now he is cast before Thee, like a body without its soul, and Dinah, this unspotted soul, has gone forth naked into exile. God! Till when shall the souls that dwell in Thy kingdom suffer the death of this life, in bereavement, and the service of Thy habitation sound out in suffering and dread?"

All Israel which was in Jerusalem had foregathered to consecrate the Ark, to bear it up from Ben Uri's chamber to the synagogue. They thronged into Ben Uri's chamber, but the Ark was not there. Bewildered, they cried, "Where is the Ark?—the Ark of the Lord?" "Where is the Ark?" "The Ark, where is it?" They were still crying out when they spied it, under the window, prone in the yard. Directly they began to heap abuse on its creator, saying that the ne'er-do-well, the scoundrel was surely an infamous sinner, quite unqualified for the hallowed work of the Ark: having presumed to undertake it, he had surely called down the wrath of the Heavens, which had overturned it. And, having revered the Ark, they loathed it. The rabbi immediately condemned it to banishment. Two Ishmaelites came, and heaved it into the lumber room. The congregation dispersed in torment, their heads covered with shame.

The morning star glimmered and dawned, lighting the skies in the east. The folk of Jerusalem awoke as from an evil dream. The Ark had been banished, their joy had set, Ben Uri had vanished, none knew whither. Misery reigned in the house of the Sire.

Night and day Dinah keeps to her window. She raises her eyes

to the heavens, and casts them down again, like a sinner. Sire
Ahiezer is dogged by worries. The synagogue his hands had builded
stands desolate, without Ark, without prayer, without learning. Sire
Ahiezer bestirred himself and commissioned an Ark to replace Ben
Uri's. They installed it in the synagogue, but it stood there like an
emblem of loss. Whoever comes to pray in the synagogue is at once
struck by dire melancholy; he slips away from that place, and seeks
some place of worship, humble and poor, where he can pour out
his heart before God.

IV

The time of rejoicing is come; the wedding day is near, and in the
house of Sire Ahiezer they knead and they bake and they dress all
the viands, and prepare fine draperies to hang in the gateway, for
the day his daughter will enter under the bridal canopy with her
partner in joy, the esteemed and the learned Ezekiel, God preserve
him.

And—see!—upon the hillsides the feet of a courier—a special
emissary with scroll in hand: " 'Twill be the third day hence!" They
were preparing themselves to delight in the bride and the bridegroom on the day of their joy, saying, "A precious pearl it is the
couriers have drawn from the sea of learning which is Poland, and
the festivities will be such as Jerusalem shall not have seen the likes
of, since the day her sons were driven into Exile." All the men of
Jerusalem went forth to welcome the bridegroom, and they brought
him into the city in great honor, with tabor and cymbal and dancing. They escorted him to the house of Sire Ahiezer, and the great
ones of the city, assessing his virtues, were dazzled by a tongue
dropping pearls, and by his regal presence. Then the wedding day
arrived. They accompanied the bride to the house of the rabbi, to
receive her blessing from his lips. Suddenly, she raised her voice
in weeping, and cried, "Leave us alone!" They left her with the
rabbi. She told him all that had happened, how it was she who
had overturned the Ark. The rabbi stood mute with terror, his very
vision was confounded. But, deferring to the eminence of the bride
on this, her day of grace and atonement, he began to ply her with
comfort. "My child," he said, "our sages of blessed memory tell us
that when a person takes a wife to himself, all his sins fall away.
Notice that it was person they said, not man, and thence we gather

that it was not man, the male, that was meant, but mankind in general, so that man and wife are one in this, that on the day of their marriage the Holy One, blessed be He, pardons their sins. And should you ask, How is a woman to earn her absolution, on whom the yoke of works weighs so lightly?—know that the good Lord has called you to the greatest of all works. And should you ask, What could that be?, I will tell you: it is the rearing of children in the ways of the Lord." And he proceeded to speak the praises of her bridegroom, to endear him to her, and draw her heart to his virtues. And when the rabbi came to the matter of the Ark, he intimated that silence would be seemly, and held that the Ark would be restored to its rightful place, to the synagogue, and that merciful God would grant Dinah forgiveness. After the bride had left the house of the rabbi, the latter sent Sire Ahiezer word regarding the restoration of Ben Uri's Ark to the synagogue. They sought it, but did not find it. Stolen? Hidden? Ascended to Heaven?—who could presume to say?

Day ebbed and the sun set. All the great ones of Jerusalem foregathered with Sire Ahiezer, in his house, to celebrate his daughter's marriage. Jerusalem glowed in precious light, and the trees in the garden were fragrant as spices. The musicians plied their instruments, and the servants clapped for good cheer. Yet, nonetheless, a sort of sadness has found a place among them. This sadness attacks the bridal canopy, and rips it into shreds. They assemble at the grandee's table, to partake of the wedding feast. The throats of the scholars are filled with delicate viands and wines, with song and hymns of praise. The jester calls for a dance for the righteous, and they move out in a ritual ring to cheer the bride and the groom. But this dear pair are afflicted by some sadness; it drives a wedge between them, and forces their elbows apart. And neither drew near to the other all that night, even in the seclusion of their chamber. The groom broods in one corner, his thoughts straying elsewhere. He dwells on his father's house, on Freidele, whose mother had tended his father and him since his sainted mother had died. And Dinah broods in the other, her thoughts going back to the Ark and its builder who has vanished from the city, no one knowing where he has turned.

At morning prayers the young man stands wrapped in a prayer-shawl and crowned with phylacteries. He reigns as bridegroom all the seven days of the feast, and is not left alone, lest envious spirits assail him. But how to ward off the spirits that hold sway in his heart, and afflict him greatly? Just when he is preparing to give himself over, heart and soul, to the *Shema,* and shields his eyes with his palms in order to shut out anything that might intrude on his devotions—just then his Freidele slips into the palm of his hand, and stands there before his eyes. And once she has accommodated herself there, she stays there till the end of the service, when he unwinds his phylacteries and lays them in their reticule. This reticule —Freidele has made for him with characters embroidered upon it! He folds the reticule, and wraps it in his prayershawl, and furtively puts it away. His father, come from Poland for the nuptials, watches him, angry and troubled. What might he be wanting in the house of Sire Ahiezer? If wealth he craved, here was wealth, so prodigal; if love of woman, his wife was comely and gracious; if a home, this one was fit for a king. Why, then, was he restless? They went in to breakfast, and chanted the seven blessings of nuptial felicity, and seated the couple side-by-side. Their bodies are close, but their hearts have been given to others.

V

And they never drew near. Month comes and month goes. In numbers the scholars assembled, to attend the Law from Ezekiel's lips, and the academy was filled with holy lore. Gracious learning was on his tongue, and whatever his mode of expounding—simple or subtle or mystic—bright angels gathered around him, shedding the light of the Law on his brow. But even as he teaches, anguish gnaws at his heart, as though—God forbid!—he lacks gratitude for having been deemed worthy to go up to the Holy Land.

And Dinah—Dinah sits, despondent. At times she goes out for awhile, and stands by the spot where Ben Uri had wrought, and stares at his implements, which are gathering dust. She clasps her hands, and murmurs some few of the songs Ben Uri had sung, sings until her eyes are dimmed by tears. Her soul weeps in secret for her pride. Once, as Rabbi Ezekiel was passing by, he heard a pleasing melody rising within that chamber. When he paused to listen, they told him that it was no mortal voice he heard singing, but rather the evil spirits that had been created out of Ben Uri's breath as he sat and sang at his work. Rabbi Ezekiel hastened away. Thenceforth, when forced to walk in that part of the house, he averted his head, in order to avoid lending his ears to the chants of such as these.

Toward evening, Rabbi Ezekiel goes to walk in the hills. The mighty ones of Israel walk out at that hour, and their retainers go before them, striking the earth with their staffs, and all the people hasten to rise in awe and deference before them, and the sun casts purple canopies over each of the righteous as it goes down to greet its Creator. The elect, who are deemed worthy of this, are granted the privilege of finding their place in the Holy Land in their lifetime, and not only this, but those deemed worthy of dwelling there in their lifetime are privileged to enjoy the Holy Spirit for ever and ever. But Rabbi Ezekiel? His feet are planted in the gates of Jerusalem, and stand on her soil, but his eyes and his heart are pledged to houses of study and worship abroad, and even now, as he walks in the hills of Jerusalem, he fancies himself among the scholars of his own town, strolling in the fields to take the evening air.

It is told that once they found Freidele sitting there with her friends, singing:

They have borne him far away
To wed a dowered maiden.
His father did not care to know
Our hearts were heavy laden.

One day an emissary of the rabbis returned to Jerusalem from the Diaspora, and brought a letter for Rabbi Ezekiel. His father was pleased to inform him that he had negotiated the home journey in safety, and now, as ever before, was bearing up under the burdens of justice and learning in their town. In passing, he thought his son might care to know that Freidele had found her mate and had moved—together with her mother—to another city, so that the sexton's wife was therefore looking after his needs. Rabbi Ezekiel read the letter and began to weep. Here was Freidele, decently wedded, and here was he, fancying her still. And his own wife? When they pass each other she stares off in one direction, he in another.

Month comes, month goes, and the academy grows ever more desolate. The scholars, one by one, steal away. They cut a staff from some tree in the garden, take it in hand, and set off on their

separate ways. It is obvious for all to see—Heaven help us!—that
Rabbi Ezekiel's soul is tainted. Sire Ahiezer perceived that his works
had not prospered, that the couple was ill-matched, that the marriage, in fact, was no marriage at all.
The couple stand silent before the rabbi, their eyes downcast.
Rabbi Ezekiel is about to divorce his wife. And just as he did not
look at her at the hour of their marriage, so he does not look at her
in the hour of their parting. And just as Dinah did not hear his
voice as he said to her, "Lo, thou art sanctified unto me," so she
does not hear it as he says, "Lo, I cast thee forth." Our sages of
blessed memory said that when a man puts his first wife away from
him, the very altar weeps, but here the altar had dropped tears
even as he took her to wife. It was not long that Sire Ahiezer left
Jerusalem with his daughter. He had failed in his settlement there;
his wishes had not prospered. He went forth in shame, his spirit
heavy within him. His house was deserted, the House of Study stood
desolate. And the quorum that had gathered in the synagogue to
honor Sire Ahiezer so long as he was there, now did not assemble
there for even the first round of afternoon prayers on the day of
his departure.

VI

That very night, after the departure, the rabbi, seated at study,
nodded over his Talmud. In a dream he saw that he would suffer
exile. Next morning, following the counsel of our sages, he put the
best possible interpretation on his dream, and fasted all day. After
he had tasted a morsel and returned to his study, he heard a voice.
He raised his eyes and saw the Divine Presence in the guise of a
lovely woman garbed in black, and without adornment, nodding
mournfully at him. The rabbi started out of his sleep, rent his
garments, again made good his dream, and sat fasting for a day
and a night, and in the dark of the following evening inquired as
to the signification of his dream. Providence disclosed to him a
number of things concealed from mortal sight, and he beheld with
his eyes of spirit the souls of those bereaved of their beloved in
their lifetimes groping dismally in the world for their mates. He
peered hard and saw Ben Uri. Ben Uri said to him, "Wherefore
hast thou driven me out, that I should not cleave to my portion in
the Kingdom?" "Is it thy voice I hear, Ben Uri, my son?" the rabbi

cried, and he lifted his voice and he wept. Weeping, the rabbi woke
out of his sleep, and knew that his doom had been sealed. He washed
his hands, drew on his mantle, took up his staff and his wallet, and,
calling to his wife, said, "My daughter, seek not after me in my
going forth, for the doom of exile has been levied upon me, to redeem the forsaken in love." He kissed the *mezuzah,* and slipped
away. They sought him, and did not find him.

They say he wanders still. Once an aged emissary from the
Holy Land stopped at a House of Study in the Diaspora. One night
he nodded at his devotions, and in his sleep he heard a voice. He
awoke, and saw that selfsame rabbi, holding a youth by the hem of
his robe and trying to draw him away. Frightened, the emissary
cried out, "Rabbi, are you here?" The rabbi vanished. The youth
then confided to the emissary that when the House of Study was
emptied of its worshipers, he had begun to fashion an ornament
for the easterly wall of the synagogue, and the emissary had borne
witness to the loveliness of that ornament, and to the craft with
which it was fashioned. But as soon as he had begun, that old man
had stood at his side, drawn him by the hem of his robe, and
whispered, "Come, let us rise and go up to Jerusalem."

Since that time innumerable tales have been told of that rabbi,
and of his sojourning in the "world of confusion," Mercy shield us!
Rabbi Nissim, of blessed memory, who traveled about in the world
for many years, used to say, "May I forfeit my portion in the redemption of Israel, if I did not behold him once floating off into
the Great Sea on a red kerchief, with an infant child in his arms.
And even though the hour was twilight, and the sun was setting,
I swear by all that we yearn for in prayer that it was he, but as for
that child—I do not know who that was."

At the present time it is said that he has been seen wandering
about in the Holy Land. The worldly wise cavil and quibble, and
even—some of them—mock. But little children insist that at times,
in the twilight, an old man hails them, and peering into their eyes
drifts into the gathering dusk. And whoever has heard the tale here
recounted surely knows that the man is that rabbi, he, and no
other. But God alone knows for a fact.

Translated by Baruch Hochman

THE LADY
AND THE PEDDLER

S. Y. AGNON

INTRODUCTION

THIS IS, *on the most obvious level, a horror story, told in a grotesquely humorous vein, drawing on both popular folklore (the Jewish peddler invited to bed by the frustrated Gentile lady) and on Gothic literary motifs (the vampire luring victims into its luxurious den in the midst of the forest). It can certainly be enjoyed simply as an artfully told tale of horror, but a careful reading reveals that the tale of horror, as the Israeli critic Baruch Kurzweil has shown, is actually the vehicle for an allegory of assimilation and its deadly spiritual, or even physical, dangers. (The story, one should note, was written at the very moment when Hitler was murdering millions of Jews, by a writer who had grown up in the German-language cultural sphere where assimilation had been considered a beckoning adventure.)*

Briefly, the symbolic outline of the story is as follows: The Jew is a peddler, a characteristic trade for Jews in many stages of the Exile. An image of the wandering Jew of the Exile, he goes from place to place, with no home, no family, no sustaining community, at the mercy of the elements and of those from whom he seeks to make a paltry profit. The lady, then, is the eternally hostile Gentile host. Her name is Helen, which suggests the generic name for the Greeks (Japheth as opposed to Shem), Helen frequently

*appearing as the name of Gentile matrons in the Midrash. At first
she scorns the Jew, then takes him in grudgingly, finally woos him
to her way of life, but only with the aim of destroying and consuming him. His name, like that of the biblical sojourner in an
alien land, is Joseph, but he is a Joseph who quickly succumbs to
the blandishments of Potiphar's wife. At one point in the story,
there is an actual verbal echo of a verse from the story of Joseph
and Potiphar's wife (Genesis 39:6): "everything she had she put in
his hands, except for the bread which she did not eat at the same
table with him." The biblical Joseph, especially as he is represented
in rabbinic legend, is the exemplar of the Jew who zealously preserves his fitness for a Divine destiny in the most trying circumstances, while this Joseph does precisely the opposite. In rabbinic
law, a Jew is supposed to give up his life rather than commit the
three cardinal sins of murder, idolatry, and incest. As Kurzweil
observes, the lady is implicated in each of the three: murder, most
obviously; idolatry and incest not as they would be legally defined
but as they were understood popularly among East European Jews
(her praying as a Christian to the stone icon, her promiscuity). The
peddler, then, enters by stages into the realm of darkest sin, until
he is scarcely able to extricate himself, and is almost destroyed.*

*What in large part saves this whole scheme from the effect of
excessive symbolic insistence is the oddly wry humor with which
the narrative events are conveyed. Humor is often generated by
incongruity, and there is a studied incongruity throughout the story
between the placid, controlled, matter-of-fact style and the horror
of the subject. Note, for example, at the very end: "she had already
forgotten the science [in the Hebrew, Torah] of eating ordinary
human food, as it was her practice to eat the flesh of her husbands
whom she slaughtered and to drink their blood." Since this is a
monitory tale about the dangers of complacent naiveté in spiritual
matters, much of the humor is in a peculiar sense satirical, emerging
from the peddler's incredible obtuseness about seeing the lady's
transparent identity and intentions. Thus he insists on repeating
to her his most unwelcome wish that the police will catch the
murderers of the lady's husbands, and when she grimly tells him,
"They won't find them. Not every murderer is meant to be caught."
He innocently volunteers, "If I only knew how I could cheer you up,
I'd give half my life to do it." Later, when she embraces him, calling
him her "sweet corpse" and telling him that she eats human flesh*

and drinks human blood, he thinks "this is the kind of poetic language that noblewomen must use when they address their husbands with affection." As the story progresses, this grotesque humor becomes a grisly farce, most strikingly apparent in the scene where Helen counts her dead husbands on her fingers and Joseph's hair first stands up like pig bristles, then comically settles down with a part in the middle as cold as ice.

At the beginning, the peddler thinks, "Let me abandon myself . . . to the mercy of heaven, and I'll ask no favors of ungenerous people." But this is exactly what he ends up doing, substituting her mercies for heaven's: "the peddler thanked the mistress of the house for bestowing such bounties upon him, and he swore that he would never forget her kindness to him." At first, he hesitates to eat forbidden food, a chicken fried in butter, its neck cruelly wrung before his eyes, but he soon becomes accustomed to committing such transgressions with a hearty appetite. His problem is not lack of belief but a falling off from obedience to God's law and a dissociation from the community of Jews ("And is it possible not to believe in God?" he answers the lady's question). At the end, what saves him from destruction, as Kurzweil has noted, is a practice recalled from the pious training of his earliest years—the recitation of the bedtime Shema, which leads him to leave the house in order to be away from the presence of the crucifix. Joseph in the dark and snow, wandering wearily, lost, crying out, "Father in Heaven, how far away I have gone! If I don't return at once, I am lost," is the essential image of the self-estranged Jew's spiritual condition, desperately needing to return (the word for "return" in Hebrew, teshuvah, *also means "repentance") but having neither the strength nor the insight to do so.*

The unsettling progression of the couple's relationship suggests the role the peddler plays in his own fate. Here the allegorical scheme takes on an aspect of psychological truth on the level of individual characterization. At first Joseph is all obsequiousness. The lady buys a hunting knife from him, so the beginning of their relationship involves a mutual complicity in the means of destruction. "Don't you yourself sell knives with which it is possible to slaughter a man?" she later asks him. The knife expresses her own identity: "she looked at his throat and her blue eyes glittered like the blade of a new knife." The peddler persuades himself that he has succeeded in the adventure of assimilation: "He took off his peddler's clothes and put on the garments of aristocracy, and he fell in with the people of the place until he was like one of them" (emphasis added). *The lady is attracted to the peddler because she can use him sexually for the time being and gastronomically later on. He is attracted to her first because of the shelter she affords, then sexually, and finally because of the very enigma she represents for him. There is, clearly, no intimate mutuality here but an attraction-repulsion of opposites that know nothing about one another. The attraction, however, is so powerful for the peddler that he cannot bring himself to leave the lady, though he resolves to do so repeatedly in the latter part of the story. In the last episode, a moment after he has clenched his teeth in hatred of her, when he thinks she has come to his bed, he hastily undresses and crawls under the covers, again prepared to join sexually with her—which hardly suggests that he has "returned" to his Father in Heaven. At the end of the story he merely goes back to the precarious condition in which we found him at the beginning of the story—wandering in Exile from place to place, crying his wares.*

THE LADY AND THE PEDDLER (1943)
S. Y. AGNON

A CERTAIN JEWISH peddler was traveling with his stock from town to town and village to village. One day he found himself in a wooded region far from any settlement. He saw a lone house. He approached it and, standing before the door, he cried out his wares. A lady came outside and spoke to him. "What do you want here, Jew?" Bowing, he wished her well and said, "Perhaps you can use something of these lovely things I have?" He took his pack off his back and offered her all sorts of goods. "I have no use for you or your wares," she said to him.

"But look and see, perhaps even so? Here are ribbons and rings and kerchiefs and sheets and soap and fine perfumes that the noblewomen use." She looked at his pack for a few moments, then averted her eyes from him. "There's nothing here. Get out!" Again he bowed before her and took things out of the pack to offer to her. "Just look, my lady, and don't say there's nothing here. Perhaps you might want this, or perhaps this lovely piece of goods pleases you. Please, my lady, look and see." The lady saw a hunting knife. She paid him for it and went back into her house. He put his pack on his shoulders and went on his way.

By that time, the sun had already set and he could no longer make out the road. He walked on, and on again further, weaving his way in among trees and out and in among them once more. Darkness covered the earth and no moon shone in the sky. He looked all around and began to be afraid. Then he saw a light shining. He walked toward the light until he arrived at a house. He knocked on the door. The mistress of the house peered out at him and shouted, "Are you here again? What do you want, Jew?"

"Since I left you, I've been wandering in the darkness and I can't find any town."

"And so, what do you want from me?"

"Please, my lady, give me permission to sit here until the moon comes out. Then I'll be able to see where I'm going and I'll be off." She looked at him with an angry eye and granted him permission to spend the night in an old barn in her courtyard. He lay down on the straw and dozed off.

That night it rained heavily. When the peddler rose in the morning, he saw that the entire land was one great swamp. He realized that the lady was a hard person. Let me abandon myself, he thought, to the mercy of heaven, and I'll ask no favors from ungenerous people. He put his pack on his shoulders and prepared to leave. The lady looked out at him. "It seems to me that the roof needs mending. Can you do anything about it?" The peddler set down his pack. "I'll be glad to jump right up and take care of it." She gave him a ladder and he climbed up to the top of the roof, where he found shingles torn loose by the wind. At once, he set them back in place, paying no heed to himself while all his clothes gushed water and his shoes were like two buckets. What difference does it make to me, he thought, whether I'm on the top of a roof or walking through the forest? There's as much rain in the one place as in the other. And perhaps because I'm helping her out, she'll show some kindness to me and let me stay in her house till the rains stop.

The peddler fixed the shingles, sealed the leaks in the roof, and climbed down. "I'm sure that from now on the rain won't get into your house," he told the lady. "You are a real craftsman," she answered. "Tell me what your fee is and I'll pay you." He put his hand over his heart and said, "God forbid that I should take a single penny from my lady. It is not my practice to accept payment for anything which is not part of my trade, certainly not from my lady, who has shown me the kindness of allowing me to spend the night in her house." She looked at him with suspicion, for she thought that he spoke in this manner in order to ingratiate himself with her and get more money out of her. Finally she said, "Sit down and I'll bring you some breakfast." He stood up to wring out his clothes, then he emptied the water from his shoes, and looked all around. From the many antlers hanging on the walls, it was clear that this was a hunter's house. Or perhaps it wasn't a hunter's house at all, and those antlers were simply hung up for decoration, as is the custom of forest dwellers, who decorate their homes with the horns of wild animals.

While he was still standing and looking, the mistress of the house returned, bringing with her hot liquor and cakes. He drank and ate and drank. After he had eaten and drunk, he said to her, "Perhaps there is something else here that needs to be fixed? I'm ready to do whatever my lady wishes." She cast a glance around the house and told him, "Look and see." The peddler was happy that he had been granted permission to stay in the house until the rains passed. He began to busy himself, fixing one thing and then another, and he asked no payment. In the evening she prepared supper for him and made up a bed for him in a room where she kept old things no longer in use. The peddler thanked the mistress of the house for bestowing such bounties upon him, and he swore that never would he forget her kindness to him.

By the next morning, new rains were falling. The peddler looked first outside and then at the face of the lady: Who was prepared to have pity on him sooner? The mistress of the house sat huddled in silence and a great feeling of desolation arose from the furniture all around. The animals' horns on the walls were enveloped in mist and they gave off an odor like the odor of living flesh. Perhaps she wanted to relieve that feeling of desolation which gripped the heart, or perhaps she was moved to pity for this fellow who would have to walk through rains and swamps. Whatever the reason, the lady began to speak to him. About what did she speak and about what didn't she speak! About rains that did not stop and winds that blew without let up, about roads that were becoming impassable and grain that would rot, and much of the same sort. The peddler

thanked her in his heart for every word because every word extended
his time in the house so that he did not have to drag himself along
the ways in rain and cold and storm. And she also was pleased, that
she had a living creature there. She took up her knitting needles
and told him to sit down. He sat before her and began to tell of
noblemen and noblewomen, of lords and ladies, of all that he knew
and all that was pleasant for her to hear. In the meantime, they
had drawn closer together. He said to her, "My lady lives all alone.
Has she no husband or friend and companion? Surely there must
be here many distinguished gentlemen to seek the company of such
a fine lady."

"I had a husband," she said. The peddler sighed, "and he
died." "No," she corrected, "he was killed." The peddler sighed
over her husband who was killed and asked, "How was he killed?"
She answered, "The police don't know, and now you want to know!
What difference does it make to you how he was killed, whether an
evil beast ate him or whether he was slaughtered with a knife? Don't
you yourself sell knives with which it is possible to slaughter a man?"

The peddler saw that the lady was not inclined to discuss her
husband, so he kept silent. And she too was silent. After a little
while the peddler spoke again. "May the Lord grant that they find
the murderers of your husband to exact vengeance from them."

"They won't find them," she said, "they won't find them. Not
every murderer is meant to be caught." The peddler lowered his
eyes. "I am sorry, my lady, that I have reminded you of your sorrow.
If I only knew how I could cheer you up, I'd give half my life to
do it." The lady looked at him and smiled a queer smile, perhaps
in contempt or perhaps in gratification, or perhaps just an ordinary
smile that one person smiles to another and the other interprets
as he wishes: if he is naive, then he interprets it in his own favor.
The peddler, who was a naive man, interpreted the laughter of that
woman in his own favor and for his own benefit. And since he was
sorry for this woman who, to judge by her age and beauty, should
have had men courting her, he suddenly looked upon himself as
just such a man. He began to speak to her the sort of things that
the ear of a young woman loves to hear. God only knows where
this simple peddler learned such a style of talking. He soon found
courage and began to speak of love, and even though she was a lady
and he was a poor peddler, she welcomed his words and showed him

affection. And even when the rains had passed and the roads had dried, they did not part.

૪◊ઙ

The peddler stayed with the lady. Not in the old barn and not in the room for old things that were no longer used. No, he stayed in the lady's room and slept in her husband's bed, while she waited upon him as though he were her lord. Every day she prepared him a feast from all that she had, in house and field, every good fowl and every fat fowl. And if she broiled the meat in butter, he did not hold back from it. At first, when he would see her twisting the neck of a bird, he would be shocked. Afterward, he ate and even sucked the bones dry, as is the way of worthless folk: at first they are unwilling to commit a sin and afterward they commit all the sins in the world with a hearty appetite. He had neither wife nor children, he had no one to miss, and so he lived with the lady. He took off his peddler's clothes and put on the garments of aristocracy, and he fell in with the people of the place until he was like one of them. The lady did not allow him to labor, neither in the house nor in the field. On the contrary, she took all the work upon herself while she treated him royally with food and drink, and if she was short-tempered with him in the daytime she was loving to him at night, as it is a woman's nature to be sometimes one way and sometimes the other. And so passed one month and then two months, until he began to forget that he was a poor peddler and she a lady. She on her part forgot that he was a Jew or anything of the sort.

And so they lived together in one house under one roof, and he ate and drank and enjoyed himself and slept in a properly made bed—in short, it would seem that he wanted for nothing. But about one thing he was amazed: all that time he had never seen her eat or drink. At first he thought she might think it degrading to eat with him. After he became used to her and had forgotten that she was a lady and he a Jew, he wondered more and more.

Once he said to her, "How is it, Helen, that I've been living with you several months and I've never seen you eat or drink? You haven't put a feeding trough in your belly, have you?" She said to him, "What difference does it make to you whether I eat or drink? It's enough that you don't want for anything with me and you have plenty to eat always." "It's true," he answered, "that I eat and drink and I lead a more comfortable life now than ever before, but even so I would like to know how you sustain yourself and how you nourish yourself. You don't eat at the same table with me, and I've never seen you eat away from the table either. Is it possible to exist without eating and drinking?" Helen smiled and said, "You want to know what I eat and what I drink? I drink men's blood and I eat human flesh." As she spoke she embraced him with all her might and placed her lips against his and sucked. "I never imagined," she said to him, "that a Jew's flesh would be so sweet. Kiss me, my raven. Kiss me, my eagle. Your kisses are sweeter to me than all the kisses in the world." He kissed her, thinking, this is the kind of poetic language that noblewomen must use when they address their husbands with affection. And she on her part kissed him and said, "Joseph, in the beginning, when you showed yourself here I wanted to set the bitch on you, and now I myself am biting you like a mad bitch, so much that I'm afraid you won't get out of my hands alive. O, my own sweet corpse!" And so they would while away their days in love and affection, and there was nothing in the world to upset their affairs.

But that one thing kept gnawing away in the heart of the peddler. They lived together in one house in one room, and her bed was next to his, and everything she had she put in his hands, except for the bread which she did not eat at the same table with him. And she observed this to such a degree that she would not even taste from the dishes which she prepared for him. Since this thing was gnawing away in his heart, he would ask about it again. And she would tell him, "He who delves too deeply digs his own grave. Be happy, my sweet corpse, with everything that is given to you, and don't ask questions that have no answer." The Jew reflected on this. Perhaps she's really right. What difference does it make to me whether she eats and drinks with me or somewhere else? After all, she is healthy and her face looks fine and I want for nothing. He decided to keep quiet. He went on enjoying her board and all the rest of it. He neither pressed her with questions nor bothered her with excessive talk. Rather, he loved her even more than before, whether because he really loved her, or perhaps because of that enigma which had no solution.

Anyone who has to do with women knows that a love which depends upon the physical bond which alone will come to an end before long. And even if a man loves a woman as Samson loved Delilah, in the end she will mock him, in the end she will oppress him, until he wishes he were dead. That is the way it was with this peddler. After a while she began to mock him, after a while she began to oppress him, after a while he began to wish he were dead. Nevertheless, he did not leave her. And she on her part did not tell him to get out. He stayed with her month after month: they would quarrel and make up, quarrel and make up, and he not knowing why they were quarreling and why they were making up. But he would reason thus to himself: here the two of us are intimate with each other, living side-by-side, never apart from one another, and yet I know no more about her today than I knew yesterday, and yesterday I knew no more than I knew about her the day I came here for the first time when she bought the knife from me. As long as they continued to live together in peace, he didn't ask many questions, and if he asked, she would stop up his mouth with kisses. When the peace between them disappeared, he began to think more and more about it until he said to himself, I won't let her be until she tells me.

One night he said to her, "Many times now I've asked you about your husband and you've never said a thing to me."

"About which one did you ask?"

"You mean you had two husbands?"

"What difference does it make to you if there were two or three?"

"So then I'm your fourth husband?"

"My fourth husband?"

"Well, from what you say, that is what it comes to. Doesn't it, Helen?"

"Wait a minute and I'll count them all," she said to him. She held up her right hand and began counting on her fingers, one, two, three, four, five. When she had counted all the fingers on her right hand, she held up her left hand and went on counting. "And where are they?" he said to her.

"Now, didn't I tell you that he who delves too deeply digs his own grave?"

"Tell me anyway." She patted her belly and said, "Some of them perhaps are here."

"What do you mean, 'here'?" he asked. She narrowed her eyes and smiled. She looked at him for a few moments. "And if I told you," she said, "do you think you would understand? Mother of God! Look, see what a face this corpse has."

But from the moment she had begun to count on her fingers, he no longer had his wits about him. Now he lost the power of speech as well. He sat in silence. She said to him, "Darling, do you believe in God?" He sighed and answered, "And is it possible not to believe in God?"

"You're a Jew, aren't you?" He sighed. "Yes, I'm a Jew."

"Well, the Jews don't believe in God, for if they believed in Him they wouldn't have murdered Him. But if you do believe in God, pray to Him that you won't end up the way they did."

"The way who did?"

"The way those you asked about ended up."

"You mean your husbands?"

"Yes, my husbands."

"And how did they end up?"

"If you don't understand," Helen answered, "it doesn't pay to talk to you." As she said this she looked at his throat and her blue eyes glittered like the blade of a new knife. He took a look at her and shuddered. She also looked at him and said, "Why did you turn so pale?" He touched his face and asked, "Did I turn pale?"

"And the hair on your head," she continued, "is standing up like pig bristles." He felt his hair. "My hair is standing up?"

"And the strands of your beard," she said, "are clotted together in patches like goose feathers. Pfui, how ugly the face of a coward is!" She spat in his face and left him. As she was walking away, she turned her head back toward him and called out, "Take good care of your Adam's apple. Mother of God! it's trembling as though it saw the knife. Don't worry, my little sweetheart, I haven't bitten you yet."

The peddler was left sitting by himself. One moment he would feel his face with his hand and the next moment his beard. The hair on his head had already settled and was lying in place as before, half on one side and half on the other, with a part going down the middle that was as cold as though ice had been laid on it. From the next room he could hear Helen's footsteps. At that moment he neither loved her nor hated her. His limbs began to grow numb, as though he had lost control over them. His thoughts, on the other hand, became more and more active. I'll get up and take my pack and be on my way, he said to himself. But when he tried to leave, his limbs became even weaker. Again he heard Helen's footsteps. Then her feet were still and he heard the clattering of utensils and the smell of cooking. The peddler began to consider again. I have to get out of here. If not now, then tomorrow morning. How glad he was when he had been permitted to spend the night in the old barn. Now even the bed made up for him shrieked, "Pick up your feet and run!" By that time it had already grown dark. Despite himself, he decided to spend the night in that house. Not, however, in his wife's room, in the bed of her murdered husbands, but in the old barn or in some other room. When day broke, he would be on his way.

Helen came in and said, "You look as if I had already swallowed you." She took him by the arm and brought him into the dining room, sat him down at the table and told him, "Eat." He lifted up his eyes and looked at her. Again she said, "Eat." He broke off a piece of bread and swallowed it whole. "I see you need to have your bread chewed for you," Helen said. He wiped the remnants of bread from his hands and got up to leave. "Wait, and I'll go with you," Helen said. She put on a sheepskin coat and went outside with him.

Walking along, they spoke nothing either good or bad, but they just talked, like people who have quarreled and want to take their minds off themselves. As they were walking, they came upon a stone image. Helen stopped, crossed herself, stood and recited a brief prayer. Afterward she took Joseph by the arm and returned with him to their house.

During the night Joseph awoke from his sleep in terror and screamed with all his might. It seemed to him that a knife had been thrust into his heart, and not into his heart but into that stone image, and not into the stone image, but into another image made of ice, the kind the Christians make on the river during their holidays. And though the knife had not struck him, even so he felt pain in his heart. He turned over and sighed. Sleep fell upon him and he dozed off. He heard a clinking sound and saw that the bitch was pulling off the chain around her neck. He closed his eyes and did not look at her. She leaped up on him and sank her teeth into his throat. His throat began to spurt and she licked up his blood. He screamed with all his might and thrashed about in the bed. Helen awoke and shouted, "What are you doing, raising the house with your noise and not letting me sleep!" He shrank under his covers and pillows and lay motionless until daybreak.

In the morning Joseph said to Helen, "I disturbed your sleep."

"I don't know what you are talking about."

"Why, you shouted at me that I wasn't letting you sleep."

"I shouted?"

"Then you must have been talking in your sleep." Helen's face paled and she asked, "What are you saying?"

That night he moved his bedding to the room where old things were kept which were no longer in use. Helen saw and said nothing. When it was time to go to sleep, he said to her, "I haven't been sleeping well and I keep turning and tossing in bed, so I'm afraid that I'll disturb your sleep. That's why I've moved my bed into another room." Helen nodded in agreement. "Do whatever you think is best for you."

"That's what I've done."

"Then good."

From then on they spoke no more of the matter. Joseph forgot that he was only a guest and continued according to his practice. Everyday he thought of leaving her house, of abandoning all her favors. A day passed, a week passed, and he did not leave her house. And she on her part did not tell him to get out.

One night he was sitting at the dinner table and Helen brought in a dish. Her mouth gave off an odor like the smell of a hungry person. He grimaced. She noticed and said to him, "Why are you twisting your mouth?"

"I didn't twist my mouth." She smiled a queer smile. "Maybe you're bothered by the way my mouth smells?"

"Take a piece of bread and eat," he entreated her. "Don't worry about me, I won't go hungry," Helen answered. And again a queer smile played over her face, worse than the first one.

After eating and drinking, he went off to his room and made his bed ready. It occurred to him suddenly to recite the bedtime Shema. Since there was a crucifix hanging on the wall, he got up and went outside to recite the Shema.

That night was a winter night. The earth was covered with snow and the sky was congealed and turbid. He looked up to the sky and saw no spark of light, he looked to the ground and he could not make out his own feet. Suddenly he saw himself as though imprisoned in a forest in the midst of the snow around him that was being covered over by new snow. And he himself was also being covered over. He uprooted his feet and began to run. He bumped into a stone image that stood in the snow. "Father in Heaven," Joseph shouted, "how far away I have gone! If I don't return at once, I am lost," He looked one way and then another until he got his bearings. He directed himself toward the house and went back to it.

A tranquil stillness prevailed. No sound could be heard except for a muffled sound like snow falling on piles of snow. And from that arose another sound of his feet sinking in the snow and struggling to get out. His shoulders grew very heavy, as though he were carrying his heavy pack. After a while he reached the house.

The house was shrouded in darkness. There was no light in any of the rooms. "She's sleeping," Joseph whispered and stood still, his teeth clenched in hatred. He closed his eyes and entered his room.

When he came in he sensed that Helen was in the room. He put aside his hatred for her. Hurriedly, he took off his clothes and began to grope among the covers and pillows. He called out in a whisper, "Helen," but received no answer. Again he called and received no answer. He got up and lit a candle. He saw his bedding filled with holes. What's this? What's this? When he had left his room, his bedding had been undamaged, and now it was filled with holes. There could be no doubt that these holes were made by human hands, but for what reason were they made? He looked and saw a blood spot. He stared at the blood in wonder.

Meanwhile, he heard the sound of a sigh. He looked and saw Helen sprawled on the floor with a knife in her hand. It was the hunting knife that she had bought from him the day he came there. He took the knife out of her hand, lifted her from the floor, and stretched her out on his bed. Helen opened her eyes and looked at him. As she looked at him, she opened her mouth wide until her teeth glittered.

Joseph asked Helen, "Do you want to say something?" And she said not a word. He bent down toward her. She pulled herself up all at once, sank her teeth into his throat, and began to bite and suck. Then she pushed him away and shouted, "Pfui, how cold you are! Your blood isn't blood. It's ice water."

The peddler took care of the lady a day, and two days, and another day. He bound her wounds, for on the night that she came in to slaughter him, she wounded herself. He also prepared food for her. But whatever food she tried to eat she would throw up, for she had already forgotten the science of eating ordinary human food, as it was her practice to eat the flesh of her husbands whom she slaughtered and to drink their blood, just as she wanted to do with the peddler.

On the fifth day she gave up the ghost and died. Joseph went to look for a priest but found none. He made her a coffin and a shroud and dug in the snow to bury her. Since all the land was frozen over, he could not manage to dig her a grave. He took her carcass, placed it in the coffin and climbed up to the roof where he buried the coffin in the snow. The birds smelled her carcass. They came and pecked away at the coffin till they broke into it, and then they divided among them the carcass of the lady. And that peddler took up his pack and traveled on from place to place traveling and crying out his wares.

Translated by Robert Alter

AT THE OUTSET
OF THE DAY

S. Y. AGNON

INTRODUCTION

IN THE 1930s *Agnon had begun experimenting with an expressionist mode of dreamlike stories that offered obliquely confessional images of his own spiritual quandaries. "At the Outset of the Day," written during his greatest period of formal innovation, adopts this mode to reflect his relationship as an artist, after the Holocaust, to the historical legacy of European Jewry.*

Geography is telescoped here, historical chronology blurred, the whole external world converted into a series of images of the first-person narrator's inner state. An anonymous enemy has destroyed the narrator's home, after which he flees with his daughter to the city. Agnon's own home in Jerusalem was actually ruined by Arab marauders in the riots of 1929, but it is clear that "the city" here alludes most directly to his memories of his native Buczacz in Galicia. In a story written in 1951, the "enemy" suggests all the hostile forces that have made the Jew a displaced person in the modern world, threatened him with physical and spiritual destruction, with the perpetrators of genocide especially in mind.

The role of the daughter is a key to what happens in the story. From elsewhere in Agnon's writings, one can safely assume that he uses the little girl as a symbol of the soul, and within the story itself, he provides a clear enough clue of that symbolic meaning, written on the scrap of paper the narrator once found in the store-room: "At times she takes the form of an old woman and at times the form of a little girl." The little girl suggests the soul (always feminine in Hebrew) in its desire to return to childlike purity. "The fool substitutes the form for the need," imagining the purity has already been achieved, while "the wise man substitutes will for need," summoning, that is, the necessary inner resolution for repentance. The soul as old woman is the soul in its sickness, its deathliness, as we see in the story when the image of the narrator, "green as a wound," becomes confused in the mirror with the wrinkled face of the hideous old woman. It is thoroughly characteristic of Agnon that he should disguise his own key clue with an almost teasing comment: "I remember that I once found something . . . it is by no means allegorical but a simple and straightforward affair."

The story, then, is about a desperate last attempt to return—to God, to the spiritual sources of the past, to the houses of worship of the narrator's childhood (which, as a matter of historical fact, had themselves been ravaged by the Nazis). For this reason the action occurs on the evening of the Day of Atonement, the great day of returning (teshuvah) in the Jewish calendar, and the narrator finds himself in the fifty-ninth minute of the eleventh hour, racing against the clock to get back before it will be too late. The story is filled with pointed contrasts between then and now: men once knew how to pray, but now there are cantors who merely want to show off their voices. Men once knew how to choose their implements (like the grandfather's pipe), live in their houses, order their time, but now this basic capacity to be at home with life has been lost. The narrator returns with his daughter to his native city in hope of finding life and renewal, but everywhere he is confronted with images of inner disease, corruption, death. Sickly green and slimy, fishy textures abound; at the house of Reb Alter, representative of the traditional world, a ghoulish crowd of old people has gathered. Each of the individuals the narrator encounters is in some way repulsive, and coldly indifferent to his needs—like the two synagogue-goers who in turn look at the father and the naked girl obscenely and make a mockery of them.

The narrator wants something to give warmth and protection to his trembling, war-weary soul in a world full of physical and spiritual terrors. Paradoxically, when he seeks refuge in the old synagogue, he finds a reminder of death in the courtyard (the *memorial candle, lit for the dead), and it leaps out to burn the last garment off the little girl. (One might recall the theme of torn garments and exposure in "Agunot.") Before long, the daughter-soul is still closer to death in the synagogue courtyard, "pressed against the wall next to the purification board on which the dead are washed." In the sweet sleep the daughter enters into at the end of the story, the narrator seems to have found a garment for her: the clause, "My soul fainted within me," hinges on an untranslatable double meaning of the Hebrew verb hit'atef, which makes it equally possible to construe the statement as, "My soul wrapped itself up within me."*

The role of language and writing in this seemingly sudden resolution of the story's tensions should be carefully observed. The narrator's childhood friend Gad, mysteriously and ominously, disappeared the day after a dream in which a bizarre bird's plume shrieked the first letters of the Latin alphabet. The plume would appear to be a writer's quill—Gad has left the studyhouse to enter into the world of alien, Gentile learning that negates the spiritual values upon which he was raised. By contrast, the narrator's daughter is able to put together the first two letters of the Hebrew alphabet to form the Hebrew word for "father," and as her own father goes on to tell her, all the Hebrew letters "join together to make words and words make prayers and the prayers rise up before our Father in Heaven . . ." The Hebrew language, in other words, is the lifeline, the indispensable bridge between man and God, between the Jew and his spiritual past. The unexpected moment of deliverance at the end of the story must be understood in the light of this alphabet theme. The narrator's attempted return suddenly succeeds when he sees in the open Ark the resplendent Torah scroll that he himself "had written in memory of the souls of days departed." This scroll would seem to be Agnon's image for his own writings, through which—as the painstaking Hebrew artist often preoccupied with the vanished Jewish world of his childhood and his forebears—he has managed to remain in touch with the past imaginatively, to capture its living presence for himself and his readers, and thus to achieve a qualified kind of personal redemption. Agnon was not always so affirmative or so traditionalist in his conception of his role as artist, but here he gives highly condensed expression to one side of his vacillating self-image as a writer of fiction.

AT THE OUTSET OF THE DAY (1951)
S. Y. AGNON

AFTER THE ENEMY destroyed my home I took my little daughter in my arms and fled with her to the city. Gripped with terror, I fled in frenzied haste night and day until I arrived at the court-yard of the Great Synagogue one hour before nightfall on the eve of the Day of Atonement. The hills and mountains that had accompanied us departed, and the child and I entered into the courtyard. From out of the depths rose the Great Synagogue, on its left the old House of Study and directly opposite that, one doorway facing the other, the new House of Study.

This was the House of Prayer and these the Houses of Torah that I had kept in my mind's eye all my life. If I chanced to forget them during the day, they would stir themselves and come to me at night in my dreams, even as during my waking hours. Now that the enemy had destroyed my home my little daughter and I sought refuge in these places; it seemed that my child recognized them, so often had she heard about them.

An aura of peace and rest suffused the courtyard. The people had already finished the afternoon prayer and, having gone home, were sitting down to the last meal before the fast to prepare them-selves for the morrow, that they might have strength and health enough to return in repentance.

A cool breeze swept through the courtyard, caressing the last of the heat in the thick walls, and a whitish mist spiraled up the steps of the house—the kind children call angels' breath.

I rid my mind of all that the enemy had done to us and reflected upon the Day of Atonement drawing ever closer, that holy festival comprised of love and affection, mercy and prayer, a day whereon men's supplications are dearer, more desired, more acceptable than at all other times. Would that they might appoint a reader of prayers worthy to stand before the Ark, for recent generations have seen the decline of emissaries of the congregation who know how to pray; cantors who reverence their throats with their trilling, but stupefy the heart, have multiplied. And I, I needed strengthening—and my little daughter, too, a babe torn away from her home.

I glanced at her, at my little girl standing all atremble by the memorial candle in the courtyard, warming her little hands over the flame. Growing aware of my eyes, she looked at me—a frightened child, finding her father standing behind her, and sensing that his thoughts were muddled and his heart humbled.

Grasping her hand in mine, I said, "Good people will come soon and give me a prayershawl with an adornment of silver just like the one the enemy tore. You remember the lovely prayershawl that I used to spread over your head when the priestly *kohanim* would rise up to bless the people. They will give me a large festival prayerbook filled with prayers, too, and I will wrap myself in the prayershawl and take the book and pray to God, who saved us from the hand of the enemy that sought to destroy us.

"And what will they bring you, my dearest daughter? You, my darling, they will bring a little prayerbook full of letters, full of all of the letters of the alphabet and the vowel marks, too. And now, dearest daughter, tell me, an *alef* and a *bet* that come together with a *kametz* beneath the *alef*—how do you say them?"

"*Av*," my daughter answered.

"And what does it mean?" I asked.

"Father," my daughter answered, "the way you're my father."

"Very nice, that's right, an *alef* with a *kametz* beneath and a *bet* with no dot in it make *Av*.

"And now, my daughter," I continued, "what father is greater than all other fathers? Our Father in Heaven, who is my father and your father and the father of the whole world. You see, my daughter, two little letters stand there in the prayerbook as if they were all alone, then they come together and lo and behold they are *Av*. And not only these letters but all letters, all of them join together to make words and words make prayers and the prayers rise up before our Father in Heaven who listens very, very carefully, to all that we pray, if only our hearts cling to the upper light as a flame clings to a candle."

Even as I stood there speaking of the power of the letters, a breeze swept through the courtyard and pushed the memorial candle against my daughter. Fire seized hold of her dress. I ripped off the flaming garment, leaving the child naked, for what she was wearing was all that remained of her lovely clothes. We had fled in panic, destruction at our heels, and had taken nothing with us. Now that fire had consumed her dress I had nothing with which to cover my daughter.

I turned this way and that, seeking anything my daughter might clothe herself with. I sought, but found nothing. Wherever I directed my eyes, I met emptiness. I'll go to the corner of the storeroom, I said to myself, where torn sacred books are hidden away, perhaps there I will find something. Many a time when I was a lad I had rummaged about there and found all sorts of things, sometimes the conclusion of a matter and sometimes its beginning or its middle. But now I turned there and found nothing with which to cover my little girl. Do not be surprised that I found nothing. When books were read, they were rent; but now that books are not read, they are not rent.

I stood there worried and distraught. What could I do for my daughter, with what could I cover her nakedness? Night was drawing on and with it the chill of the night, and I had no garment, nothing to wrap my daughter in. I recalled the home of Reb Alter, who had gone up to the Land of Israel. I'll go to his sons and daughters, I decided, and ask clothing of them. I left my daughter as she was and headed for the household of Reb Alter.

How pleasant to walk without being pursued. The earth is light and comfortable and does not burn beneath one's feet, nor do the Heavens fling thorns into one's eyes. But I ran rather than walked, for even if no man was pursuing me, time was: the sun was about to set and the hour to gather for the evening

prayer was nigh. I hurried lest the members of Reb Alter's household might already be getting up to leave for the House of Prayer.
It is comforting to remember the home of a dear friend in
time of distress. Reb Alter, peace be with him, had circumcised me,
and a covenant of love bound us together. As long as Reb Alter
lived in his home I was a frequent visitor there, the more so in
the early days when I was a classmate of his grandson, Gad. Reb
Alter's house was small, so small that one wondered how such a
large man could live there. But Reb Alter was wise and made
himself so little that his house seemed large.

The house, built on one of the low hills surrounding the Great
Synagogue, had a stucco platform protruding from it. Reb Alter,
peace be with him, had been in the habit of sitting on that platform
with his long pipe in his mouth, sending wreaths of smoke gliding
into space. Many a time I stood waiting for the pipe to go out so
I could bring him a light. My grandfather, peace be with him,
had given Reb Alter that pipe at my circumcision feast. "Your
grandfather knows pipes very well," Reb Alter told me once, "and
knows how to pick just the right pipe for every mouth."
Reb Alter stroked his beard as he spoke, like one well aware
that he deserved such a pipe, even though he was a modest man.
His modesty showed itself one Friday afternoon before sunset.
As he put out the pipe, and the Sabbath was approaching, he said,
"Your grandfather never has to put out his pipe; he knows how
to smoke more or less as time necessitates."
Well, then, I entered the home of Reb Alter and found his
daughter, together with a small group of old men and old women,
sitting near a window while an old man with a face like a wrinkled
pear stood reading them a letter. All of them listened attentively,
wiping their eyes. Because so many years had passed I mistook
Reb Alter's daughter for her mother. What's going on? I asked
myself. On the eve of the Day of Atonement darkness is falling, and
these people have not lit their memorial candles. And what sort of
letter is this? If from Reb Alter, he is already dead. Perhaps it was
from his grandson, my friend Gad, perhaps news had come from
Reb Alter's grandson Gad, who had frequented the House of Study
early and late. One day he left early and did not return.
It is said that two nights prior to his disappearance, his wet

nurse had seen him in a dream sprouting the plume of a peculiar bird from his head, a plume that shrieked, "A, B, C, D!" Reb Alter's daughter folded the letter and put it between the mirror and the wall. Her face, peeking out of the mirror, was the face of an aged woman bearing the burden of her years. And alongside her face appeared my own, green as a wound that has not formed a scab.

I turned away from the mirror and looked at the rest of the old people in Reb Alter's home and tried to say something to them. My lips flipped against each other as when a man wishes to speak but, seeing something bizarre, is seized with fright.

One of the old men noticed the state of panic I was in. Tapping one finger against his spectacles, he said, "You are looking at our torn clothing. It is enough that creatures like us still have flesh on our bones." The rest of the old men and old women heard and nodded their heads in agreement. As they did so their skin quivered. I took hold of myself, walked backward, and left.

I left in despair and empty-handed—with no clothing, with nothing at all—returned to my daughter. I found her standing in a corner of the courtyard pressed against the wall next to the purification board on which the dead are washed. Her hair was loose and wrapped about her. How great is Thy goodness, O God, in putting wisdom into the heart of such a little girl to enable her to wrap herself in her hair after her dress has burned off, for as long as she had not been given a garment it was good that she covered herself with her hair. But how great was the sadness that enveloped me at that moment, the outset of this holy festival whose joy has no parallel all the year. But now there was no joy and no sign of joy, only pain and anguish.

The stone steps sounded beneath feet clad in felt slippers and long stockings, as Jews bearing prayershawls and ritual gowns streamed to the House of Prayer. With my body I covered my little girl, trembling from the cold, and I stroked her hair. Again I looked in the storeroom where the torn pages from sacred books were kept, the room where in my youth I would find, among the fragments, wondrous and amazing things. I remember one of the sayings, it went approximately like this: "At times she takes the form of an old woman and at times the form of a little girl. And when she takes the form of a little girl, don't imagine that your soul is as pure as a little girl; this is but an indication that she passionately yearns to recapture the purity of her infancy when she was free of sin. The fool substitutes the *form* for the *need*; the wise man substitutes *will* for *need*."

A tall man with a red beard came along, picking from his teeth the last remnants of the final meal, pushing his wide belly out to make room for himself. He stood about like a man who knew that God would not run away and there was no need to hurry. He regarded us for a moment, ran his eyes over us, then said something with a double meaning.

My anger flowed into my hand, and I caught him by the beard and began yanking at his hair. Utterly astonished, he did not move. He had good cause to be astonished too—a small fellow like me lifting my hand against a brawny fellow like him. Even I was astonished. He would not have let me go whole had he laid hold of me.

Another tall, husky fellow came along, one who boasted of being my dearest friend. I looked up at him, hoping that he would come between us. He took his spectacles, wiped them, and placed them on his nose. The whites of his eyes turned green and his spectacles shone like moist scales. He stood looking at us as though we were characters in an amusing play.

I raised my voice and shouted, "A fire has sprung up and has burned my daughter's dress, and here she stands shivering from the cold!" He nodded his head in my direction and once more wiped his spectacles. Again they shone like moist scales and flashed like green scum on water. Once more I shouted, "It's not enough that no one gives her any clothing, but they must abuse us, too!" The fellow nodded his head and repeated my words as though pleased by them. As he spoke, he turned his eyes away from me so that they might not see me, and that he might imagine he had made up the story on his own. I was no longer angry with my enemy, being so gripped with fury at this man; though he had prided himself on being my friend, he was repeating all that had befallen me as though it were a tale of his own invention.

My daughter began crying. "Let's run away from here." "What are you saying?" I asked. "Don't you see that night has fallen and that we have entered the holy day? And if we were to flee, where would we flee and where could we hide?"

Where could we hide?

Our home lay in ruins and the enemies covered all the roads. And if by some miracle we escaped, could we depend upon miracles? And here were the two Houses of Study and the Great Synagogue in which I studied Torah and in which I prayed and here was the corner where they had hidden away sacred books worn with age. As a little boy I rummaged about here frequently, finding all sorts of things. I do not know why, on this particular day, we found nothing, but I remember that I once found something important about *need* and *form* and *will*. Were it not for the urgency of the day I would explain this matter to you thoroughly, and you would see that it is by no means allegorical but a simple and straightforward affair.

I glanced at my little girl who trembled without a stitch of clothing. The night was chill and the song of winter birds resounded from the mountains. I glanced at my daughter, the darling of my heart, as a father will glance at his little daughter, and a loving smile formed on my lips. This was a very timely smile, for it rid her of her fear completely. I stood then with my daughter in the open courtyard of the Great Synagogue and the two Houses of Study which all my life stirred themselves and came to me in my dreams and now stood before me, fully real. The gates of the Houses of Prayer were open, and from all three issued the voices of the readers of prayer. Where should we look and whither should we bend our ears?

He who gives eyes to see with and ears to hear with directed my eyes and ears to the old House of Study. The House of Study was full of Jews, the doors of the Ark were open and the Ark was full of old Torah scrolls, and among them gleamed a new Scroll clothed in a red mantle with silver points. This was the Scroll that I had written in memory of the souls of days that had departed. A silver plate was hung over the Scroll, with letters engraved upon it, shining letters. And even though I stood far off I saw what they were. A thick rope was stretched in front of the Scroll that it might not slip and fall.

My soul fainted within me, and I stood and prayed as those wrapped in prayershawls and ritual gowns. And even my little girl, who had dozed off, repeated in her sleep each and every prayer in sweet melodies no ear has ever heard.

I do not enlarge. I do not exaggerate.

Translated by David S. Segal

FOREVERMORE

S. Y. AGNON

INTRODUCTION

THE PROBLEM *of the artist, which had concerned Agnon as early as "Agunot," particularly preoccupied him in his major period of experimental symbolism during the late 40s and 50s. This was the time when he was at work on* Shira, *his last, long novel (an incomplete version was published posthumously), which focuses on the relationship between art and sexuality, and on the claims of art as a unique source of truth. "Forevermore" shares these thematic concerns, approaching them through more obliquely symbolic distortion than does the novel; and like* Shira, *the story explores the connection between art and disease, or wisdom and disease (lepers figure centrally in both the novel and the story). "Forevermore" should also be read against the background of the novella,* Edo and Enam *(1952; English translation in Agnon's* Two Tales, *Schocken: 1966).* Edo and Enam *is still another story of a scholar delving into an archaic civilization, and it is the one other fiction of Agnon's that adopts the curious device of beginning virtually all proper names within the tale with the consonants* gimmel *or* ayin.

That device, it should be said, is much more prominent in the Hebrew than it can be in any translation. The ayin, *to begin with, is not visible as an initial consonant in transliteration. Then Agnon compounds the effect of the alliterative names—frequently in the* story, occasionally in the novella—with fantastic set pieces of inventive wordplay in which long strings of nouns and verbs are made to begin with the letters gimmel and ayin. In the version of the translation revised for this volume, some intimation of this bizarre technique is provided at several points. Now, the ayin and the gimmel are clearly some sort of signature, since they are the first two consonants of the author's own last name. Perhaps we are invited to infer that all the imagined acts and personages of the story are to be taken as the special private property of S. Y. Agnon, an intimate expression of his inner world as an artist and as a Jew that has to be conveyed in fantastic camouflage because of its very intimacy.

Other, more cryptographic implications of the two key letters may suggest themselves: gimmel ayin is a standard abbreviation for gan eden, Garden of Eden, and of course this is a paradoxical account of a paradise regained—in a leper hospital; in the opposite order, ayin gimmel constitute the Hebrew verb that means "to circle," and the story gives us a world of characters and seemingly opposed spheres that in fact are all held within the same magic circle, opposites linked in unsettling ways.

In any case, the most general effect of the repeated use of these two initial consonants is to endow everything in the story with a prominent quality of grotesqueness and through that to challenge our conventional vision of men, history, truth, fulfillment. "Forevermore" might be described as an anti-allegory. That is, it entices the reader into reading it allegorically, but then confronts him with such ambiguities, contradictions—and plain bizarreness—that the comfortable neatness of allegorical significance is denied him. Thus, the name Adiel Amzeh means "God's-Ornament This-People": the lepers recall a midrashic image of the degraded condition of the Jewish people in exile, and the tear-stained book that recounts the glory and destruction of an ancient people invites comparison with the Bible. Following this simple line, one would conclude that "Forevermore" is an allegory of the single-minded devotion to the Torah of the afflicted Jewish people, a people prepared to renounce worldly glory and wealth (Gebhard Goldenthal, whose very name is redolent of lucre) and to sequester itself in order to pursue the one dependable source of truth in this world. If such an allegory is intended, it is couched in such a way that it expresses the profoundest feelings of ambivalence toward the act of commitment described, for the treasured book is a hideous thing, covered with the suppura-

*tions of the running sores of untold leprous readers: Eden is a place
of disease, and the price Adiel Amzeh pays for his precious source
of wisdom is, after all, a terrible one.*

*What the enigmatic details of the book of the city of Gumlidata
do is to scramble such schemata of meaning and thus to suggest that
the reality conveyed in the work of the true writer—the Hebrew*
sofer *which is given considerable resonance in the story means both
"scribe" and "author"— defies our ordinary categories of explanation and moral classification. A clue to Agnon's procedure here is
provided by a biblical verse from which terms are borrowed, and
insisted upon, at several key junctures in the story. In Deuteronomy
23:18–19, the Israelites are enjoined as follows: "There shall be no
temple prostitute from the daughters of Israel, and no male temple
prostitute from the sons of Israel. You shall not bring a harlot's pay
nor a dog's price to the house of the Lord your God in payment of
any vow, for they are both an abomination to the Lord your God."
Temple prostitutes of both sexes, harlot's pay, dogs and their prices,
figure prominently in Adiel Amzeh's studies of Gumlidata at the
outset of the tale; he even sometimes has imaginary conversations
with the dogs of the city about their price; and at the end of the
story, he is telling his fellow inmates at the leper hospital about
the official and familiar names, all of course beginning with* gimmel, *
assigned to the temple prostitutes of both sexes and to the temple
dogs.*

*If we were inclined to see some symbolic correspondence be-
tween the Book of Gumlidata and the Torah, these details instead
indicate how Gumlidata is* par excellence *the sphere of paganism,
with the vividness of its exotic culture, the secret of its abiding appeal for the scholar-hero, consisting precisely in acts and institutions
defined by the Bible as abominations to the Lord. The intimations of ritualized and secular sexual promiscuity and of homosex-
uality, the bizarre commingling of the animal and human realms,
put Gumlidata (the name suggests "Retribution Cult," "Reward
Cult," or even "Weaning Cult") at the opposite pole from the world
of firm prohibitions and clearly demarcated spheres that the Bible
tried to legislate.*

*The story celebrates the power of the true writer, "who does
not abandon his work even when the sword of death hangs over
his neck, who writes with his very blood, in his soul's own script,
what his eyes have seen." What the writer's eyes have seen, however,*

is by no stretch of the imagination edifying, though it may be stirring, frightening, perplexing, arresting. What we can make out of it in the story is a panorama of sexual crisscrossings, weird animality, treachery, armed mayhem. Adiel Amzeh, at the end, has found the truth and renounced the world for it—but is it an aesthetic truth, or a purely antiquarian historical truth, with no reference to any set of values, and if so, where does that leave him?

There is surely nobility in Amzeh's final act of commitment, but what he is committed to remains ultimately ambiguous. The female figure of Wisdom, drawn from both Proverbs and Greek mythology, who whispers so sweetly to the scholar in the story's conclusion might even be whispering seductively, enslaving the discoverer of truth to his own ruin: that final turn of the screw would be entirely in keeping with the multiple ironic perspective Agnon has devised for this haunting fiction.

FOREVERMORE (1954)
S. Y. AGNON

I

For twenty years Adiel Amzeh worked on his history of the great city of Gumlidata, the pride of mighty nations until it was reduced to dust and ashes by the Gothic hordes, and its people enslaved.

After he had gathered all his researches together, examined and tested them, sorted, edited, and arranged them, he decided that his work was finally ready for publication and he sat down and wrote the book he had planned for so many years. He took the book and made the rounds of the publishers but without success. He looked about for patrons and benefactors but had no luck. During all the years he had been occupied with his research he had not taken the trouble to ingratiate himself with the learned men of the universities—nor with their wives and daughters—and now when he came to them seeking a favor, their eyes shone with such cold anger that their glasses seemed to warp. "Who are you, Sir?" they said to him. "We've never seen you before."

Amzeh shrugged his shoulders and went away, disappointed and dejected. He understood that in order to be recognized he would have to become friendly with them and he had no idea of how to go about it. Many years of painstaking research had made him a slave to his work from dawn till night, neglectful of all worldly cares. When he left his bed in the morning, his feet would carry him to the desk, his hands would pick up pen and paper, and his eyes, if not pursuing some obscure vision, would plunge into a book or into maps and sketches of the city and its great battles; sometimes he would add to what he had written, sometimes he would erase many days worth of writing. And when he lay down to sleep he would go over his notebooks again, sometimes in despair, sometimes with a sense of satisfaction. And sometimes laughing over his own mistakes that would make him ponder and rework things. Years passed and his book remained unpublished. You know, a scholar who is unable to publish his work often benefits from the delay, since he can reexamine his assumptions and correct his errors, testing those hypotheses whose ingenuity may take them far from historical reality and truth. So Adiel Amzeh revised and refined his work and brought it to the purest state, without, however, finding a publisher for it.

II

Finally, when he had despaired of ever seeing the results of his work in print, his luck took a turn for the better. Gebhard Goldenthal, the richest man in the city, informed him that he would publish the book. How did it happen that the name of a humble scholar had reached the ear of this famous man? And why would such an eminent personage want to publish a work which was sure to bring no profit? Some said he felt so uneasy about his great wealth that he had decided to become a patron of learning because his wealth gave him no inner satisfaction. He closely followed the world of scholarship and somehow had heard the story of Adiel Amzeh's book. According to another explanation, Gebhard Goldenthal secretly believed that his ancestors were among the unhappy people who were driven out of Gumlidata, that they had belonged to the city's aristocracy and that one of them had been an army general, the head of the palace guard, who fought valorously until the Goths destroyed the city. Of course, this was obviously untrue since Gumlidata was destroyed during the first wave of the Gothic invasions, and no person can say with any certainty that he is a descendant of the exiles of Gumlidata.

But whatever the reason, Gebhard Goldenthal was ready to

publish Adiel Amzeh's book, even though printing this kind of work would involve many extra expenses. Several colored maps were necessary, requiring many expensive inks: one for a general view of the city, another for its temples, a third for each of its gods —Gomesh, Gush, Gutz, Guach, and Guz; one for the founding mothers of the city, one for their offspring, another for Gomed the Great, one for Gichur and Amul—the twin pillars of prayer—and one each for all the remaining holy men, the priests and priestesses, not to mention the temple prostitutes of both sexes, the whores of noble lineage and those who were plebeian on their fathers' side, and the dogs—for each and every one a different color, to denote position and function, harlot's pay, or price. Add to all these the Goths and their allies, the Gazaens and their dwarfs, their carts and wagons, their weapons and battle defenses, and you can see how much money was needed to print such a work.

Nevertheless, Gebhard Goldenthal was ready to publish the book and make it a fine volume with beautiful printing and good paper, carefully detailed maps, expensive binding—perfect in every respect. His staff had already consulted with illustrators, engravers, and printers, and all that remained was for the author and publisher to meet, for in all his business affairs Gebhard Goldenthal would allow his staff to take care of the preliminaries—but the final arrangements had to be conducted between the client and the head of the business himself. If the client was unknown, he would be invited to Goldenthal's office; if the man was recognized in his field, he might be invited for a cup of tea to Goldenthal's home; and if he was important, he would be invited for dinner. Adiel Amzeh, who was more than a nobody but not well-known enough to be considered important, was invited by the rich man for a cup of tea.

So it was that one day Adiel Amzeh received an invitation for afternoon tea at the home of Gebhard Goldenthal. He was asked to be prompt and to come at the designated hour since Mr. Goldenthal was soon to leave for abroad and was pressed for time.

An author who for years has searched without avail for a publisher is not likely to be late for an appointment with the one he has finally found. Almost before he put down his publisher's invitation, he took out his best suit of clothes—untouched since the day he received his doctor's degree—shook it out and pressed it. He hurried to the barber, and from the barber to the bath; from there he ran to a shop where he bought a new tie, and from the shop back home to look over his book again. By morning of the day of his appointment, he had made all his preparations for his visit to the publisher. Never in his life had he experienced such a day as this. Adiel Amzeh, who for the sake of a city's destruction had put aside all personal affairs, who cared nothing for clothes or any human vanity, was utterly changed. He had become like most celebrated learned men who neglect their work for the sake of the honor they receive from others who know nothing of learning and scholarship. He sat and stared at his manuscript, rose and inspected himself in the mirror, glanced at his watch, examined his clothes, and rehearsed his gestures.

This is the regimen of all who wish to meet with a rich man. You must preen yourself and be careful of your demeanor and graces: the rich, even those who honor learning, prefer to honor it when it comes wrapped in a pleasing mantle. Yet that same love of learning which had used up so much of his energy and strength, furrowing his brow and bowing his shoulders, had touched his face with a special kind of radiance that one doesn't find except among those who are truly devoted to seeking wisdom. It's a pity Goldenthal did not see him then; had he done so he might have realized that a pleasant and happy face can be shaped from things other than money. But you see, my friend, for the sake of a little moralizing, I have gone and given away the ending at the very beginning of my story.

Well, Amzeh sat for a while, then got up, sat down again, rose again—all the time thinking of the future when the printer would take up his manuscript and transform it into attractive pages; he thought of how he would correct proofs, add and delete, omit and include certain passages; of how the printer does his work and how his book would finally be published and received. Sitting there dreaming he might have missed the appointed hour, except that all the years he had devoted to his work had sharpened him in his external affairs as well. When the moment came for him to leave for his appointment, he jumped up from his chair, picked up his house key, and made ready to leave and lock the door behind him. He stared at himself in the mirror once more and glanced about his home, astonished that his house had not changed as he had. There ought to have been some transformation, he thought, for this would have been only just for a man who was about to undergo a blessed metamorphosis.

III

At that moment, he heard the sound of footsteps and suddenly became alarmed. Perhaps Mr. Goldenthal had to leave before the appointed time and someone was coming to tell him the interview had been postponed. Amzeh stood transfixed and could hardly catch his breath; his reason was gone, only his senses functioned. His entire body seemed to become one big ear. As he listened intently to the footsteps, he realized that he was hearing the slow shuffling of an old woman. In a moment, his rationality returned and he understood that a gentleman like Goldenthal would not send an old woman to deliver a note canceling their appointment. When the sound of the old woman's footsteps came closer, he recognized them as those of a nurse who visited him once each year in order to collect journals and illustrated magazines to take to the inmates of the lepers' hospital where she worked. It was difficult for Amzeh to put the old woman off by telling her he was busy and asking that she come the following year; he had high regard for this nurse who devoted her entire life to those whose existence was a living death. But it was equally hard for him to tarry on her account, for if he was delayed, with Mr. Goldenthal about to go abroad and no one knowing when he would return, then the publication of his book would also be postponed. I should mention another factor as well, which might seem absurd but perhaps was decisive. To a man whose home is his whole universe, every unnecessary article in the house can cause annoyance. So it was with our scholar. When his mind was occupied with Gumlidata and he strolled through its ruins carrying on long conversations with the temple dogs about their price, he would occasionally raise his eyes and notice a pile of dusty old magazines. Now that the old woman had come, here was an opportunity to get rid of them; if he didn't act now, they would accumulate and gather dust for another year.

At the very moment when he was deciding what to do, whether to get rid of the superfluous volumes or to devote all his efforts to his own book, the old woman knocked on the door. He opened it and greeted her. The old woman understood immediately that he was worried and preoccupied, like a man uncertain whether to take an affirmative or negative course. "I see, Herr Doctor," she said, "that I have come at an inconvenient time. I'll leave and go about my business."

He was silent for a moment and didn't answer her. When she finally turned to go, he realized how tired the old woman must be from her long walk. After all, the lepers' home was far from the city, and she had to come on foot. She was unable to travel by bus for fear that if recognized she would be thrown off—most people are still terrified by the sight of someone who works with lepers.

"I'm sorry," Amzeh said to her as she was about to go, "but I can't take care of you the way I would like. I have been invited to afternoon tea by Gebhard Goldenthal, the famous industrialist whose name you have probably heard." (As a matter of fact, forty years previously Gebhard Goldenthal had courted the nurse and wanted to marry her, but she refused him because she had already given her heart to God's maimed, the poor prisoners of the lepers' home.) "I have a very important matter to discuss with Mr. Goldenthal," Adiel Amzeh went on. "I'll be back in an hour or so. Please sit down until I return, and later I'll fill your basket with books and journals and pamphlets and anything else I have about—they take up so much room here I can hardly breathe."

"I would like to sit here and wait for you, Herr Doctor," the old woman answered, "but I can't leave my good people for more than a short while. They are used to me and I am used to them, and when I'm away from them I miss them as much as they miss me. They are used to receiving all their needs from me. I'll go now, Herr Doctor, and if God grants me life and peace, I'll come back next year."

But Amzeh was unable to let her go away like that, without an explanation of why he was in such a hurry. Without thinking about how little time he had, he began to explain: "Perhaps you have noticed my appearance today. For many years you have been coming to visit me and you have always found me with slippers on my feet and a cap on my head, unshaven, my collar open, my hair disheveled. Today I'm dressed in a good suit and wearing shoes and a hat and a nice tie. The reason for the change is simple: for twenty years I have worked on a book and it is finally ready for publication. Mr. Gebhard Goldenthal has decided to publish it, and I'm now going to see him. He's waiting for me and for my book."

The old woman's face glowed. "You mustn't delay a moment, Herr Doctor. Hurry, hurry, don't wait, an hour like this doesn't come every day, don't put off even a minute what you have waited many years for. It is good that you found Mr. Goldenthal. He's an honest man. He keeps his promises. I, too, in my poor state owe him a debt of gratitude. I remember when I began to serve in the lepers' hospital, the rooms were full of dust and broken beds and chairs, the roof was caved in, the walls tottering and moldy. If he hadn't given us money to put the place together again, to buy new beds and equipment and make all the necessary repairs, it would have been impossible to get along there."

After the old woman had recounted all of Gebhard Goldenthal's good deeds, she let out a deep sigh. "Are you unhappy?" Adiel Amzeh asked her. "Unhappy?" she replied with a shy smile. "I've never been unhappy." He was quiet for a moment. "You are unique, Nurse Eden, you are the only one in the world who can make such a declaration," he said.

The old woman blushed with confusion. "I really should correct what I just said, Herr Doctor. I have had great unhappiness, but not on my own account." Her face turned scarlet and she lapsed into silence.

"You stopped right in the middle of what you were saying, Nurse Adah," Amzeh said, "and perhaps at the crucial point. I'm certain it would be worthwhile to hear."

"Worthwhile?" the old woman cried, stammering in her confusion. "How do we know what is worthwhile and what isn't? I'm an old woman whose grave is waiting for her—let me boast once that I told the whole truth. I flattered myself falsely when I said that I've never been unhappy. On the contrary, I haven't known a day without sorrow, a sorrow greater than that of my good people who suffer more than any other creatures in the world. For the merciful God who inflicts suffering on man provides him with the strength to withstand his woes; but if one is healthy and without physical disability, then he has no special allotment of strength, and when he looks on those who suffer and on their pain he is tormented and has nothing with which to withstand his sorrow. And especially someone like myself, who has to look after the suffering ones. I'm always afraid that I won't fulfill my obligations, that I don't do the right thing for the good people. A healthy person cannot know the inner needs of the sick. Since I don't leave them for a moment, my suffering does not leave me. . . . But I'm talking too much. I've forgotten that you are in a hurry. Now I'll be going. I hope, Herr Doctor, that your business will bring you a full life and peace. Only it's too bad about the poor people who must see me return empty-handed, without any books."

"Why is it too bad?" he asked, facing her. "Have they finished all the books? They've read them all?"

"They've read them dozens of times," answered the old woman.

"What kind of books do they have?"

"Oh, I can give you the names of all of them."

"All of them? Surely you're exaggerating."

"No, there aren't very many. I've been there so many years, every article and every book is familiar to me."

The old woman then recited the name of each book in the hospital library. "Not many, not very many at all," Amzeh said after she had finished. "I can imagine how happy they must be to receive a new book. But," he went on, jokingly, "I'm sure you have forgotten one or two, and perhaps they were the best books of the lot. For that's the way we are—we always forget the most important thing. Isn't that so, Nurse Adah?"

The old woman smiled. "I have no love of dialectics. But I must say for truth's sake that there isn't a book in our library that I haven't mentioned—except for one, which is hardly worth discussing, since it isn't read anymore."

"Why isn't it read anymore?"

"Why? Because it has decayed with age, and on account of the tears."

"On account of the tears?"

"Because of the tears, yes, because of the tears that every reader of the book sheds on its pages after reading the awful tales it contains."

"What are these terrible stories?"

"I don't know what they are," the old woman answered. "Whatever I know I've told you already. It's an old, worn-out book, written on parchment. They say it was written more than a thousand years ago. Had I known you would ask, I would have made inquiries. There are still old men in the hospital who can tell the story, which I remember many years ago the old men before them used to tell with tears—the same story that is in the book. But they say that even then, years ago, the old men already had difficulty in reading the book because its pages were torn and the words blurred. The manuscript is a heap of moldy, decayed matter. They even tried to burn it. In my time one of the caretakers was all set to destroy it, but I asked him to return it. I told him that a book which had found shelter with us mustn't be treated like a rag. I believe, Herr Doctor, that a piece of work done by an artist gives joy to the creator as long as it endures."

"Tell me, Nurse Adah," Amzeh said, mulling over the old woman's words, "perhaps you have heard something about the contents of the book. What do your old men say about it? I'm sure if they say anything at all, they must know more."

"I've heard that all its pages are of parchment," the old woman answered. "As far as what is written in it, I've heard that it contains the history of a city which was destroyed and disappeared from the face of the earth."

"A city which was destroyed and disappeared from the world!" Amzeh repeated excitedly. "Please tell me, Nurse Eden, perhaps you have heard the name of the city?"

"Yes, I have heard the name. The name of the city is Gumlidata. Yes, Gumlidata is the name."

"What? What? What?" Amzeh stammered, his tongue caught in his mouth. "Have . . . have . . . you heard the name correctly . . . ? Gum . . . Gum . . . Gumli . . . lidata . . . you said. Please, my good nurse, tell me again, what is the name of the city you mentioned? Guml. . . ."

She repeated what she had said. "Gumlidata is the name of the city, and the book is an account of its history."

Adiel Amzeh grasped a table in front of him, leaning forward so that he would not collapse and fall. The old woman noticed his sudden paling and moved to help him. "What is the trouble, Herr Doctor," she said staring at him, "are you ill? Is it your heart?"

He straightened up and pulled himself together. "It's nothing, my good nurse," he began with a smile, "there's nothing wrong with me. On the contrary, you have given me new life. Let me tell you about it. For twenty years I have devoted myself to the history of this same city. There isn't a piece of paper which mentions the city's name that I haven't read. If I were king, I could build the city anew, just as it was before its destruction. If you want, I'll tell you about the historical trips I have taken. I have walked in the city's markets, strolled in its streets and alleys, seen its palaces and temples. Oh, my good nurse, what headaches I've suffered from the walks I've taken there. And I know how it was destroyed, who took part in the destruction, the name of each and every tribe that helped reduce it to ruins, how many were killed by the sword, how many died of starvation and thirst, and how many perished from the plague that followed the war.

"I know everything except one detail—from which side Gediton's brigades entered the city, whether from the side of the great bridge which was called the Bridge of Valor, or whether they entered secretly by way of the Valley of Aphardat, that is, the Valley of the Cranes . . . the plural of crane in the language of Gumlidata is *aphardat;* the word does not mean ravens or chestnut trees or overshoes as is claimed by Professor Alpha, Professor Beta, or the true private advisor to the court, Professor Gamma, whose pictures you may have seen in the magazines when they were given honorary titles and medals by the empire. In point of fact, 'raven' in the language of Gumlidata is *eldag* and in the plural *elgadata,* since when the letters 'd' and 'g' come together in the plural they reverse their order. I don't know the words for chestnut trees or overshoes in the language of Gumlidata. I really don't know what they are."

Suddenly his expression changed, his voice dropped, his lips twisted, and he let out a hoarse, stuttering laugh. His knees began to shake and he pinched his mouth. "I'm surprised at you, Nurse Adeh," he said, "after all, you are an intelligent woman. You should be more careful about what you say. How can you believe something which doesn't make any sense. How can you say that your hospital possesses a book containing the history of Gumlidata. Gumlidata was destroyed in the days of the first Gothic invasions. And you say that a book from these ancient times has come down to our day, and the old people in the hospital have read it. Now really, my dear nurse, how can you reconcile this kind of nonsense with simple reality? How could a book like this ever get to the hospital . . . to the hospital which you, my dear nurse, serve so well. . . . How? How?

"Pardon me, my dear Adinah, if I tell you that this is a very doubtful story. A gelded goat has got in your grange: you have heard a silly old folk tale and it has enchanted you with its romance. Or perhaps you have confused Gumlidata with . . . with . . . I don't know with what city you might have confused Gumlidata. What did you hear about this manuscript? How did it get to the hospital? You have made me curious, my dear lady, very curious for more information. I feel just like a psychoanalyst. Aren't you surprised at me, the author of a book myself, being so curious about someone else's book? It's not enough that my house is filled with books, I must go looking for others. Let me tell you, just between us, all these books in my cabinet are not there for reading, they're there for effect. And if you want, I'll tell you the real reason: self-preservation. People see the books and start talking about them, and I don't have to discuss my own work with them. Please tell me, though, how did this history of Gumlidata ever get to your hospital?"

"I haven't read the book," answered the nurse Adah Eden, "and when it was taken out of the reading room some time ago I forgot it. I don't devote much time to books generally. When I come to your house for books, it's not for myself, of course, but for the sake of my good people, in order to ease their suffering. Sometimes books can do that. As for the parchment pages, I remember how surprised I was when I first saw them about forty years ago—like most nurses, I had to know everything about every article I saw where I worked. An old man noticed that the volume of parchment interested me and he told me what he had heard about the book. I still remember a little of what he said. If old age hasn't confused my memory, I'll try to pass on his story. May I sit down and tell you what I heard?"

Amzeh was suddenly embarrassed. "My God!" he cried out in confusion. "How could I let you stand all this time! Sit down, do sit down . . . here, on this chair. Not that one, this chair over here . . . it is the most comfortable one in my miserable house. Please sit down and tell me your story."

The old woman sat down in the chair that he brought her, gathered up the folds of her dress, clasped her hands together, and, taking a deep breath, began. "As far as I can remember, this is the story. After the Gothic hordes had conquered the great city of Gumlidata and reduced its strength to dust, they found the tyrant ruler of the city, Count Gifayon Glaskinon Gitra'al, of the house of Giara'al, just as he was scheming to flee. He moaned and wept and pleaded for his life, asking that he be made a slave to their nation and their king, Alaric. The Goths allowed him to live, and carried him off with them as a slave. He had with him a chronicle which contained stories of the city's might and valor, stories that might be read to Alaric the King, so he should hear of the glory and greatness of Gumlidata's grandees. On the way he was struck with cholera, and the Goths left him for dead and went on.

"He wandered about in the fields until some lepers, who were following the soldiers for scraps of food and clothing, came upon him. They took pity on him, released him from his chains, and nursed him until he revived. He soon realized who his saviors were and began to groan and curse, declaring that death was better than life with the lepers. For in those days a leper was looked upon as a dead man and anyone who came in contact with an untouchable was himself considered to be infected. They tried to comfort him by saying that if he went away he might fall into the hands of the Goths and their allies who would surely kill him, or else he might be waylaid by roving packs of wild beasts who would surely eat him alive; but if he stayed with them he would be saved from the punishments of both men and beasts and have food to sustain him. They took him to their camp and gave him a noisemaker to carry, so that if he were approached by a healthy man he might warn him away by shaking the noisemaker, and they hung a small cup about his neck, for merciful people would sometimes throw scraps of food to the lepers.

"He lived with them for some time, eating what they ate and drinking what they drank. He saw how well they treated him and began to repay them in kind. On long winter nights he would read to them from his book, entertaining them with stories of the great city of Gumlidata and tales of his ancestors, the tyrant counts who governed over Gumlidata and its dependencies. In time, both the Count and his benefactors died. No trace remained of them except the book. Men live and die, but their instruments remain and live on.

"The Count's friends died, but their place was taken by a new generation, whose lot was no better than that of their forebears. They discovered the book and read it from cover-to-cover, joining their tears to those of the first generation. After many generations the world began to change and people began to realize how great was the suffering of the lepers, how difficult and terrible their ordeal. Not only was their sickness a great tribulation, but they were forced to live in forests and deserts and wander about in search of food. And there were times during the hard winter days when they had no sustenance and were unable to beg for food and they simply died of starvation. Eventually, benevolent groups were formed and a shelter established for the lepers, where they were brought together and their needs taken care of. That is the story of the place where I serve as a nurse, and that is the story of the book the lepers brought with them. Herr Doctor, I doubt whether there is anyone else in the world who knows more than I have told you about these sheets of parchment. But you want to leave. I hope you aren't late for your appointment."

"No, I'm not late for my appointment," answered Adiel Amzeh. "In fact, this is only the beginning of my appointment. Take a little more time, sit a little while longer, and we'll fill our hands with books and take them to the good people. Sit where you are, Nurse, sit a while and forget about my book. My book is used to waiting." Amzeh went over to the cabinets lining his walls and began to take books down. When he had accumulated a large pile, he tied them into packages. He took down more books, muttering: "They'll enjoy them, they'll enjoy these books." Several times he repeated the process, searching and ransacking his shelves, whispering and muttering all the time, "What more can I give?" If the old woman had not stayed his hand, he would have taken all his books from their shelves, with all his possessions, and given them to her.

"You take a bundle and I'll take a bundle," he said when he finished, "and we'll deliver them to your patients. As for Mr. . . . as for Mr. what's-his-name . . . Mr. Goldenthaler, Gebhard Goldenthal, who is waiting for me to come, well, I'm sure he will find something else to occupy himself with. And now, my dear Adah Eden, let's hurry so that we arrive before the sun sets, and you will open the gate for me and take me to see the book—the book of which you have spoken. What's the matter, Nurse? Why do you make such a face? Don't you think they'll allow me to enter? I swear on my mother's grave that if they don't let me in, I'll lie down on the steps of the hospital and won't move an inch until they say I can enter.

"Are you unhappy? Are you sorry about something? If it's because of me, don't be sorry. This is the most glorious day of my life, sweeter than any day I have ever lived, and what you have told me is sweeter than anything I have ever heard since . . . since . . . I'm really confused now, I don't know since when. Look, look, it's already going down. I mean the sun, the sun. The sun is more beautiful when it sets than when it rises. For twenty years a man must be hidden in wisdom's shadow in order to be able to utter such a simple piece of wisdom."

IV

They went out of the city, the two of them walking together, Amzeh in long strides, the old woman with short steps. He chattered as he walked; she managed every so often to bring forth a word which sounded more like a sigh. Everyone who passed by and recognized her stepped aside, and she avoided them as well. She knew these people were afraid of her and was careful not to arouse any unnecessary terror, for something is more frightful when one runs away from it. But Adiel Amzeh was not conscious of the passers-by avoiding them as they went along. He turned to his companion suddenly. "Do you remember whether I locked the door?" he asked. He put down his package and saw that the key was still in his hand. "I'm carrying the key with the package and am not conscious of what I'm doing," he said with a laugh. "It's because of the heaviness of the burden I have to bear." For a minute he was silent. Then he cried out, "My God!" with a mixture of impatience and reproach, for at the edge of his consciousness he saw himself reading the book of Gumlidata in the hospital and a mumbled jumble of words confused his reading. Because of this book, too, he had forgotten his own book which he had worked on for twenty years, and he had forgotten Mr. Goldenthal who had agreed to publish it. After a while, they arrived at the lepers' hospital.

I don't know through which gate they entered or how much time it took before he was granted admittance. And I can't describe the condition of the book itself, which was so covered with pus that even the lepers felt a loathing for it. I don't know all the details and have no love for suppositions. Let me put aside the doubtful and come back to what is certain.

Amzeh, then, came to the house of the untouchables and after much argument he finally was allowed to enter. He went in and they tied him in an antiseptic apron which reached from his neck to his feet. They took the book out of the chest it was stored in, and gave it to him with a warning not to touch it. Amzeh stared at it until his eyes seemed to occupy half his face. He looked at it for a long time, then jumped up quickly to open it. They took hold of him and told him to wait. He was fitted with a pair of white gloves, carefully tied, so they would not slip. Then they warned him again not to touch the book unless his hands were protected with gloves. They described to him the dire fate of the foolhardy ones who had taken the warnings lightly, telling him both fact and fabrication to scare him, so that he should not fail to take the disease seriously. I don't know whether he heard them or not. This I do know: his eyes grew so large they seemed to cover his entire face—and half his neck as well. When they saw that they would not get rid of him very quickly, they left, providing him with a table and chair in the hospital garden among the trees which are known as the "Trees of Eden," after Nurse Eden, with one of the hospital functionaries to stand by him. Adiel Amzeh sat there and painstakingly read every letter, every word, column, and page which the book contained, the assistant standing by his side and turning the pages as he progressed. They were still afraid he might be so excited that he would not exercise the necessary restraint. The book had been infected by the hands of many untouchables, and it seemed almost as if it were not written on parchment, but on the skin of a leper, and not ink but pus had been used to inscribe the words.

What more can I say? After he had carefully gone over every sentence in the book, he found the answer to the riddle that had troubled him for many years: how Gumlidata had been conquered, from which side of the city the first bands of the Goths had entered. For Gumlidata had been surrounded by a solid wall of stone and protected on all sides by bristling natural fortifications. And so, within a few short hours, Amzeh solved the problem that had caused him so much trouble during his years of exhaustive research. For your sake, my friends, and for the sake of the whole House of Israel, let me tell you the story the dead words told our scholar. I'll try to summarize what was written there at great length.

The book of parchment told the story of one of the Hun women, a young girl named Geldag or Eldag, who one day left the camp of the Huns, the allies of the Goths, and rode about on a wild ass. She reached the cisterns behind the city of Gumlidata where she was caught and brought to the city. The servants of the tyrant, the old Count Gifayon Glaskinon Gitra'al of the house of Giara'al, grandfather of the young Count Gifayon Glaskinon Gitra'al Giara'al, noticed her and brought her for a gift to their master. She was horrified by the old man and his city, disgusted by his groaning and drooling, his soft bed and his strange manners, and nauseated by the smell of the city and its sacrificial altars. She tried to flee at once, but was caught and returned to the Count. The same thing happened three or four times; each time she was caught.

Finally, she saw that escape was impossible and she sat brooding how to gain revenge on her captors.

At about the same time the girl was held captive, the Goths, with Gaditon the Brave at their head, rose up and waged war with Gumlidata. The city's inhabitants held the Goths in great terror, for they knew that every place the barbarians conquered they slaughtered and burned, and if Gumlidata was vanquished, their future was annihilation. The tyrant Count saw that his city was doomed, and he fell into a deep melancholy. Had it not been for Eldag, the Hun girl, who had changed her manner and begun to show him hidden and daring ways of love he had known with no other woman or lad, he probably would have died of sorrow before the Goths had a chance to behead him.

When the court guards saw that Eldag had changed her attitude toward the Count, they ceased watching her as carefully as before. Eldag took advantage of the guards' carelessness and began to take long walks through the city, wandering everywhere. She even visited the city wall near the Valley of the Cranes, which most people avoided for fear that it might collapse. Years before, an earthquake had struck the city and shaken the wall in several places. The citizens of Gumlidata were careful not to bother Eldag, for they knew that only the power of her charms had saved their king from melancholy. So enamored of the girl was their king that he had his tailors make her a mantle as a gift, a kind of priestly garment called *izla* normally worn by a queen, woven with bands of calves' eyes arranged in the shape of the Valley of the Cranes.

One day Eldag remained in the king's garden, playing with her wild ass among the tall trees. This ass was one of many animals in the garden, each of which had suckled at a woman's breast, for there was a strange custom in Gumlidata. If a woman conceived and it was not known who the father was, her relatives waited until she gave birth and then took the infant and brought it to these animals to be suckled. They looked for an animal that had recently given birth, and left the infant to be suckled, taking the animal's young to the human mother for suckling. If they could not find the young of a wild animal, they brought her the young of a tame one. They were most careful about the children of the noblewomen, *Givyatan* in their language, for if a noblewoman had given birth and the father was unknown, the infant was killed and the young of an animal was brought to the mother, so that her noble

blood would not be mixed with the blood of the common people.
So Eldag played with her pet in the garden among the tall trees.
She was quite unafraid of animals, having spent most of her life
with them: her father, Gichul the Clown, was the owner of a dancing
bear. A young ass saw them and, growing jealous, began snorting
and hee-hawing, as though he were being slaughtered. Eldag heard
the young animal's cries. "An ass always sounds like an ass," she said
with a laugh, "even if it has been suckled by a duchess. What is it
you want? Do you want this mantle which covers my heart? Come
and I will wrap round your neck an ornament more beautiful than
any that has been worn by your noble wet nurse." The young ass
heard her and came close. She took the izla from her bosom and
tied it about the animal's neck, and made him bow his head as if
in thanks, as she had seen Gothic noblemen do when they received
gifts from their ladies.

Suddenly the girl was overwhelmed with a deep longing for
her home, her family, and her people, whose camp was far away,
who were all free, with no walls or locks and bolts to restrain them.
She was filled with rage and her anger turned against the ass who
reminded her of her former happiness. She was angry at the ass
because he was more faithful than she was: even after she had
placed the izla around his neck, the ass continued to protest. She
grabbed him by the ears in order to strike him. The calves' eyes,
woven into the mantle, shone before her. Her heart began to beat
wildly. She tried to gain control of herself so that she would not
cry out and give away her plan. She forced herself to smile and
dragged the ass to the city wall near the Valley of Cranes; there,
she found the place which had collapsed during the earthquake
and had not been completely repaired. She broke through the opening and pushed the ass with the mantle around his neck outside.
And Eldag was happy, for she knew that if the Goths saw the ass,
they would understand he had been sent as a sign that they should
enter the city through the Valley of Cranes. She controlled her joy
and returned to the old Count, assuming a happy countenance for
him, his court, and his city. So charmed was the population by
Eldag's grace and beauty that they forgot about the fierce Gothic
soldiers who were besieging their city.

The ass went out of the city and reached a nearby forest. His
nose sniffed the odors of trees and flowers and he began to snort
loudly like a wild ass who has returned to his home. The noise was

heard by some Gothic soldiers. They were surprised to see the ass with the mantle around his neck, for they had never seen an animal adorned like this. They brought the animal to Gaditon, their general. Gaditon the Brave saw the mantle. "Is there a place known as the Valley of the Cranes?" he asked his soldiers. "Is there one of our people in Gumlidata?" Gichul the Clown heard of the matter: He groaned and he grunted and he groveled on his gut in the grass for Eldag who was gone. "If this is not my daughter's work," he said, "I am not her father. The glorious girl was gone from me, but now I know she's in Gumlidata." The Goths sent soldiers to inspect the wall near the Valley of Cranes, and when they saw the place through which Eldag had sent the ass, the Goths entered the city. They set the city on fire, killing everyone in their path: old and young, infant and aged, male and female. Not a man or woman was left alive except little Eldag, the Hun girl, who was released from her bondage, and the grandson of the old Count who was made a slave. . . .

All this was written on the last page of the book as a kind of epilogue by the city's scribe. And when Adiel Amzeh read the story, he shed many tears. How great is the true writer, he thought, who does not abandon his work even when the sword of death hangs over his neck, who writes with his very blood, in his soul's own script, what his eyes have seen!

Adiel Amzeh read many other things in the book. There were pages which supported some of his theories, and there were other pages which completely contradicted what he previously thought. It seems he had relied too much on earlier scholars, even though he realized that much of what they wrote was confused. Adiel Amzeh remained at the hospital throughout the summer, reading the book.

When the days grew colder and the land was covered with frost, he had to stop working outside. He took a room at the hospital and had a heater brought in. He sat there studying the text, joining letter to letter and word to word until he could read whole passages without trouble. And if he discovered something unusual he would read the passage aloud to the patients in the great hall. "My friends and brothers," he would say, "listen while I read to you." And he would read to them about the people of the great city of Gumlidata, who had been a mighty nation, full of greatness and grandeur, proud-eyed and joyous, until the Gothic hordes conquered them and reduced the city to dust and ashes. He would tell them about Gomesh and Gush and Gutz and Guach and Guz, the gods of Gumlidata; and about its infants, offspring of their loins, about its great temples, its priests and priestesses, the *Gorgani,* the *Gnogani,* and the *Gechoni*—each one named according to its function. He would also tell them about the *Galmudi* and the *Golanae,* which were the dogs and the temple prostitutes, affectionately called *Golshani* and *Golshanae.* And sometimes Adiel Amzeh would tell them about his new theories.

He had thought out many new hypotheses and some of them he had written down. But his book never reached the hands of the living, for it was forbidden to remove any article or letter or book from the lepers' house. Nevertheless, in some way or other, some of his new ideas became known to his colleagues. When a true scholar discovers a thing that is right, even if he himself is isolated and hidden away in the innermost chambers of his house, something of what he has found reaches the world. Many times, when Adah Eden had brought from his house the scientific journals which he received regularly, he would read his ideas in articles signed by others. He was shocked that something which he had worked on so long and hard was now published under another scholar's signature. "If this kind of thing can happen," he would ask himself, "then why do I work? I ought to be satisfied with what the others say."

Yet learning bestows a special blessing on those who are not put off easily. Yes, Adiel Amzeh would ask himself for what and for whom he was working. But Wisdom herself would take hold of him and whisper: "Sit, my love, sit and do not leave me." So he would sit and discover new things which had been unknown to all the learned men of the ages until he came and revealed them. And since there were many things and learning is endless and there is much to discover and investigate and understand, he did not put his work aside and did not leave his place and he remained there forevermore.

Translated by Joel Blocker
Revised for this volume by Robert Alter

RAHAMIM

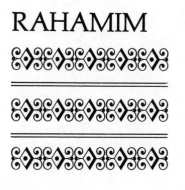

HAIM HAZAZ

INTRODUCTION

AFTER LIVING THROUGH *the turmoil and hardships of the Russian Revolution, to which he would later recur in his stories and novels, Haim Hazaz (1898–1972) left Russia in 1921, spent the next ten years in Paris, with occasional stays in Berlin, and then settled in Palestine. His work is, in some respects a continuation of the tradition of Mendele, and his bustling, energetic prose—sometimes humorous, sometimes lyrical—carries to an ultimate Mendele's stylistic fusion of traditional Hebrew sources, with the possibilities of lexically rich synonymity in style pushed as far as imaginable. In the 40s and 50s, Hazaz turned from Russian to Yemenite Jews, and astonished many Hebrew readers with his convincing reconstruction of Yemenite life in all its varied customs. A dedicated secular Zionist, Hazaz repeatedly used his fiction to express his opposition to Exile, to the mentality of Exile, and to the religious world view which he conceived to underlie life in Exile. He has, frequently been accused of tendentiousness because of his ideologically polemic impulse. Older critics used to see him as a complementary opposite and competitor to Agnon. Most younger critics now would rank him lower than that. His long novels often seem to lack selectivity and subtle development of character, but some of his short fiction*

253

*gives striking expression to certain underlying concerns of the
Zionist enterprise.*

*"Rahamim" takes place in the Jerusalem of the Mandate period,
probably in the early 1930s. (Rahamim first set out for Palestine
from Iraq during the "war with the Turk," that is, World War I.)
Menashke Bezprozvani presumably has come to Palestine from
Russia in the Third Aliyah, the wave of immigration that followed
World War I. Zionists like him, who came as settlers out of
ideological conviction, and whose whole vision of Jewish character
and life was based on the East European Jewish experience, were
sometimes startled by the unguessed possibilities of Jewishness—or
of simple human identity—revealed by the Jews from the Arab
world whom they now encountered for the first time in Palestine.
This story, of course, is built on such an encounter. The two
protagonists, therefore, are deliberately conceived as opposite polari-
ties, both as human types and as examples of different cultures—the
introspective, restless, uprooted, Russian Jewish intellectual, and
the simple, earthy, Kurdish Jew. "Rahamim" in Hebrew means
mercy. Rabbinic thought sets up two opposing categories on which
the world is supposed to be founded,* midat ha-rahamim, *the quality
of mercy, and* midat ha-din, *the quality of justice, law, severity. If
the Rahamim of the story is associated with midat ha-rahamim,
then clearly Menashke is to be associated with midat ha-din. The
porter's name, Rahamim, is a Hebrew name used almost exclusively
by Sephardic Jews, while Menashke Bezprozvani, with all its Slavic
syllables, is meant to sound Russian.*

*The contrast between these two characters is drawn through a
deployment of Hazaz's characteristic stylistic resources, here artfully
adapted to the subject. Hazaz's style is highly emphatic, full of
verbal energy, swirling around and around the objects of its description to make them more vivid and concrete and particular through
an accumulation of descriptive phrases and comparisons. Hazaz
shows a caricaturist's love for the grotesque, frequently describing
human beings in terms of inanimate objects: Menashke is "lean as
a pole," Rahamim's face is "bright as a copper pot."*

*The initial description of Menashke is almost entirely in terms
of negatives—a catalogue of discomforts and vexations and frustrations. The description is not very visual, as though the man himself
were made up of mere abstractions and internal divisions. By contrast, Rahamim will be described in terms that emphasize the*

solidity *of his physical presence (his face like a copper pot, "doubled-over" girth, and so forth). The transition from Menashke to Rahamim is then effected through a descriptive paragraph that introduces nature for the first time in the story, a kind of nature that is fiercely inhospitable and hostile to Menashke who, as a man, is not at home in the world. Rahamim, on the other hand, is part of that burning-hot Middle Eastern landscape; in fact, with his coppery glint, he is a little sunlike himself. The transition from Menashke concludes, aptly, with an explosion, after which Rahamim, on his donkey, suddenly appears—almost like a miraculous apparition after the detonation.*

Rahamim is clearly meant to be Menashke's antithesis in every possible respect: if Menashke is a Quixotic ghost of a man, Rahamim is a Sanchesque solid "double man"; where Menashke is intellectual, malcontent, sterile, Rahamim has the proverbial wisdom of a peasant ("no belly without belly button, no man without a missus"), is happy in his world, a virile husband and the father of a swarming brood. Since Menashke is above all isolated from his fellowmen, we are keenly aware of Rahamim as a family man, and his first, unintroduced question cuts directly to the heart of Menashke's predicament —"Got a missus?"

Menashke, walking alongside Rahamim, imagines him at home with his two wives (before the founding of the State of Israel, polygamy was still legal for Sephardic Jews). The thematic point in assigning two wives to Rahamim is to extend the image of him as a superabundant double man. Emphasizing physical solidity and fertility, Menashke thinks of the two wives "heavy and solid as two blossoming garden plots." The apparent incongruity of the old dying father, "a heap of rags in the corner," in this happy scene by the merry crackling of the hearth fire suggests that the chain of generations—the cycle of life and death—is naturally bound together, naturally accepted, in Rahamim's world as it is not in Menashke's; so we have wives, children, elders, the dying and the newly born, together in one great bundle.

There is a kind of recapitulation of the past of each of the two protagonists before the end of the story. Rahamim's, appropriately, is external and involves sweeping geographical movements—his account of his travels until he came to Jerusalem. This, in turn, triggers a chain of inner recollections in Menashke ("the days at Migdal, the baths at Tiberias . . ."), with the saddening memory of a lost love. Rahamim's repeated concern for Menashke's sadness, his last turning back to cheer up the Russian Jew, suggest that a real moment of human communication has taken place between these two opposites. At the end, Menashke is more tranquil than he was before because of his meeting with the Kurdish porter. He begins to sing, but it is a song remembered from a past that is at best bittersweet. The words of the song, moreover, indicate emptiness, drought and, perhaps by implication, sterility—which is just where the story began.

RAHAMIM (1933)
HAIM HAZAZ

ONE SUNNY DAY Menashke Bezprozvani, lean as a pole, wandered through the streets of Jerusalem, his face seamed and sickly looking, his mouth unusually fleshy and red, his eyes discontented and disparaging.

Bitterness gnawed at his heart, piercing through him like some venom—a bitterness of heart which was unconscious rather than clearly expressed, resulting from the years he had spent without achieving anything, neither contentment for himself, nor property nor a family; the bitter, gloomy quintessence of fever and hunger, of unsettled wandering from one agricultural commune to another, of vexations and suffering and troubles enough to drive a man out of his mind and make him lose his strength, and all the other effects of his past experiences, his lack of employment, and his present sickness.

His despair set him in a fury. All sorts of evil thoughts possessed him, recriminations and accusations directed against the Labor Federation and Zionism, against, "the domination of the Zionist Imperialism"; against everything in the world, it seemed. As though one might claim that everything was fine and bright, he would have had a job, his spirit would be refreshed, he might have everything he desired and the whole of life could be brilliant, were it not for the worthless leaders and the Zionist Imperialism that hindered things.

All these were the complaints of a dejected, despairing person who, more than he wanted comfort, wished to torture himself, to cry out aloud and rebel and remonstrate against the whole state of affairs. But his complaining was only halfhearted. Like it or not, he possessed a great love for the Land and a great love of the Hebrew language; a strong, deep, irrational, obstinate love that went past all theories and views, and led beyond all personal advantage. And since his complaints were no more than halfhearted, he complained all the more, denying everything and destroying everything in thought without getting anywhere, and just making himself uncomfortable.

Apart from all his bitterness, the excessive heat was tiring him. It was the middle of July. The heat was like that of an oven stoked with glowing coals, and the white light dazzled to blindness and distraction. The roadway quivered uncertainly in the light as though in a dream; it might have been so much barren soil or else a field left fallow because of drought; or it might have been anything you like in the world. The sun quarreled with the stones and the windows. The slopes of the mountains on the horizon shone yellow-brown through the dryness, while the skies in their purity of blue called eternity and worlds-without-end to mind.

A yell stopped him as he walked. A dozen or so Arabs dashed excitedly among the crowd in the street, yelling at the top of their voices as though attacked by robbers:

"*Barud! Barud!*" (Blasting going on!)

Menashke Bezprozvani stood among the group of stationary folk pressed together, until the road echoed to a loud explosion and stones flung aloft scattered around and fell here and there in confusion. When he began to resume his walk he found himself accompanied by a man riding a donkey.

"Noise, eh!" said this stranger, turning his face to him with a smile of satisfaction and wonder.

He was a short fellow with thick black eyebrows, a beard like a thicket, his face bright as a copper pot and his chest uncommonly virile and broad. He was dressed in rags and tatters, rent upon rent and patch upon patch, a rope girded round his loins, and a basket of reeds in front of him on the donkey's back.

Menashke Bezprozvani glanced at him and made no answer, but the stranger entered into conversation and drew him to reply.

"Got a missus?" he turned on the donkey's back to ask.

"What do you want to know for?"

"Ain't got one, a missus?" wondered the man on the donkey.

"No, I haven't, I haven't!"

"Not good," the owner of the donkey commiserated with him, as though he saw something strange and impossible before his eyes. "Take you a missus!"

"I'm poor and I have nothing. How shall I keep a wife?" Menashke Bezprozvani answered, half-mocking, half-protesting.

"His Name is merciful!"

"How's His Name merciful? I'm an old bachelor already and so far He hasn't shown me any mercy!"

"His Name is merciful!" maintained the owner of the donkey. "Him, everything He knows. Me, got nothing, and His Name never forsook me."

"That's you and this is me."

"What's a matter, huh? Must be everything all right. I had sense and got missus! Plenty all right."

He lowered his head between his two shoulders and closed his eyes tight with satisfaction and contentment.

"Plenty all right, His Name be blessed!" He opened his eyes and went on speaking. "Plenty all right . . . one day was in shop, I brought boxes. I saw there's one missus there . . . first, long, long before men gave me a missus and wasn't luck. His Name never give . . . I heard they told me, it is a missus come from Babylon wants to marry. Goes to Kiryat Shaul—and that's the missus from the shop. . . . From heaven, eh! No money I had—not got money what'll you do! Look, look, took six pound in Bank and did business. At Muharram I made five pound also—and married! His Name be blessed, plenty all right . . . take you a missus, a worker, a fat one, be all right. His Name is merciful . . ."

He rapped his two soft sandals on the belly of the donkey which was plodding slowly under him, while his face expanded and broadened till it beamed like two copper pans.

"Never get on, no man, without a missus!" He moved from where he was sitting toward the donkey's crupper, speaking in a tone of absolute and assured finality. "No mountain without top, no belly without belly button, no man get on without a missus!"

"And how many wives have you?" asked Menashke Bezprozvani, looking at him from the corner of his eye. "Two? Three?"

"Two is two." He raised his outstretched palms aloft as though saying, Come and see, I have no more than two . . .

"Do they live at peace?"

"Eh! Mountain looks at mountain and valley between them." He turned a mouthful of strong white teeth toward him. "If a young one in house, old one always brrr, brrr. . . ."

"And how much do you earn? Are you a porter or what?"

"Yes, mister."

And having found himself a comfortable part of the donkey's back to sit on and having settled himself firmly there, he began telling him all his affairs. To begin with, he said, he had been a plain porter, and now he was porter with a donkey! This donkey under him was already his eighth, and from now on, nobody swindles him anymore. He was already a big expert on donkeys, an experienced and well-versed donkey-doctor! Through a bad donkey and a bad wife, said he, old age comes leaping on a man, but a good donkey and a good wife, nothing better than they in the world. Like a fat pilaf to eat, or the hot pot on the Sabbath! And His Name be blessed, he earned his daily bread. His Name is merciful! Sometimes one shilling a day, sometimes two shilling a day, and sometimes one mil. . . . There were these and those, all sorts of days!

"Then was all right, long before," he passed his hand over the back of his neck as he spoke, "earned four shilling a day also! Then was all right."

He put his hand into the reed basket before him and took out a few dirty eggs.

"Take the ecks." He held them out to his companion. "Take, mister. Fresh as the Cooperative!"

Menashke Bezprozvani did not wish to take them.

"Have you a chicken run?" he asked, in a better humor.

"His Name be blessed! Got seven hens!" replied the other contentedly and with pride. "All make ecks, eck a day, eck a day . . . take, mister! Please, like the Cooperative . . . chickens all right, His Name be blessed!"

Were it not, said he, for the money he needed, he himself would eat the eggs his hens laid, so all right were those eggs! But his little daughter lay sick in the Hadassah and not a farthing did he have. Yesterday he had bought her bananas for half a piaster and she ate . . . .

"Eating already!" he said as one who announces great tidings, while his face lit up in a smile of good nature and happiness. "Eating already, blessed be His Name!"

While he put the eggs back in the basket, Menashke Bezprozvani noticed that he wore two rings on his fingers, two copper rings set with thick projecting colored stones. He asked:

"What are these?"

"This? Rings. And you haven't got?"

"Haven't got."

"That's it," he smiled into his beard. "I'll tell you saying they tell by us in Babylon . . ."

And he began telling him the story of a certain man who loved a beautiful woman. "Once it happened he had to go a long journey. He said to her, to that beauty: Lady! because that I love you much, you give me your ring, and as long as I see it on my finger I remember you and long for you. And that beauty who was sharp, never wish to give him her ring but said to him: Not so, only every time you look at your finger and see my ring not there, you remember me because I never give you ring, and you long for me . . ."

Ending his tale, he burst into a peal of laughter.

"Ha-ha-ha!" He threw his head back and filled the whole road with his powerful, noisy laughter. "And so you also, ha-ha-ha!"

His laughter and the yarn he had spun turned Menashke Bezprozvani's mind in a different direction. Despite himself, he began to think of his own girl—her merits, her queernesses, and the whole of that chapter.

The donkey, left to its own devices, was proceeding lazily and heavily while the porter sat shaking on its back, his face ruddy as copper and glinting, his beard spread in his satisfied smile, and his mood good as though he found everything in the whole world satisfactory. Menashke Bezprozvani turned his eyes to him and observed the way in which he sat on the donkey's back among his wooden vessels and ropes and pieces of metal; short and broad, a sort of doubled-over and redoubled-over man. It looked almost as though his height had been doubled over into breadth, his backbone was double, and the teeth in his mouth were double;

echoing from one end of the road to the other, his laugh with childhood in it scattered itself throughout the universe; and the Holy and Blessed One was with him, near to him, at home with him among his children and his wives, his chickens and his donkey. . . .

Menashke walked slowly beside him and pictured the other at home. Here, his thoughts gradually emerged in clear pictures: the porter sits at the entrance to his home of an evening in the closed courtyard beside the cistern built over with stones. The children— a mixed heap of children—hang round him and tumble over him from every side, squalling and yelling. The womenfolk are busy at the fire. They cook the evening meal and quarrel between themselves on his account with vituperations and curses. Both are heavy and solid as two blossoming garden plots, and he makes peace between them looking at one with affection and at the other with even more; every glance of his falls like rain upon thirsty soil. At the side lies his sick father, a heap of rags in a corner—an old man, his days drawn near to die. The fire crackles cheerfully and brightly, the pot boils, and one of the wives begins singing, rolling her voice toward the stars and drawing out her song. . . .

"How did you come to the land of Israel?" he interrupted his reverie to ask.

"With the help of His Name!"

And ere a moment had elapsed he was telling him all his wanderings. Thus and thus, he was a Kurd from Zacho. Did he know Zacho? . . . One day he heard there's a legion in the land of Israel, warriors of the Children of Israel. He said: wish to be a Jewish warrior—what is! He rose and went from Zacho to Mosul and from Mosul to Baghdad and from Baghdad to Basra. And already in Basra he is a servant to a Jew who has a shop to wear clothes, a rich man, plenty blessing he has, His Name be blessed. He made bread, he made food, everything, everything . . . because a man is better fit for work than a missus, fit much more . . . and then from Basra he went to Bombay, as the way to Damascus was then—long, long before—closed because of the war with the Turk. He stayed in Bombay two months, and every day, every day walked in the garden of Señor Sassoon, eating and drinking and walking . . . until at last he went to the land of Israel. Did he know Haifa? . . . As yet then in Haifa the Commercial Center wasn't, eh! The lads told him there in Haifa: stay with us, Rahamim! But he didn't want—to Jerusalem, to the Jewish Legion! So he came to Jerusalem and the Legion wasn't. . . .

"None there!" He clapped his hands together, speaking in a downcast, long drawn-out voice.

For a while he was silent, shifting on his saddle. He turned his eyes and casually glanced at Menashke Bezprozvani, and his face changed. It was as though something astonishing had occurred to him just then.

"What for you're so sad?" he asked in a slow, soft voice.

Since Menashke Bezprozvani did not answer, he scratched the back of his neck two or three times and stirred himself.

"Late already," he said, raising his head aloft.

He kicked his heels into the donkey's belly and tugged at the reins in his hand. The donkey tossed its head, put its feet one here and one there, and began kicking up its heels and galloping.

"Take a missus! His Name is merciful!" he turned his head and shouted back to Menashke. "Peace! Peace to Israel!"

The donkey changed its gait, began to move precisely, and its tiny hoofs tapped in the roadway like castanets.

Menashke Bezprozvani remained alone and walked on, his body heavy and his spirit worn-down and weary. Strange feelings were pricking at his heart, chop and change, piecemeal, in turn, then all tossing within him in confusion; half-recollections of his childhood, the affairs and misadventures of his girl, and all his suffering and distractions. For some reason he remembered the days at Migdal, the baths at Tiberias, Ras al Ain and Kfar Gileadi; and the rhythm of a tune which was still indistinct to himself began to trouble him, half-remembered, half-forgotten—half-forgotten, half-remembered; he could not bring it fully to mind. . . .

Until he heard the sound of a donkey's hoofs clacking on the roadway like castanets. He raised his eyes and saw that the porter had turned back toward him. He stood in surprise, blinking his eyes in the sun, and stared.

When the porter reached him, he pulled up his donkey, and stopped.

"Mister! Mister! . . . Listen!" He lowered his head to him with a wayward smile, his face strangely affectionate and humble. "Mister! . . . Don't be sad! By my life! . . . Be all right! By my life! His Name is merciful!

"His Name's merciful . . ." he explained again, with a modest, almost maternal, smile. "Don't be sad! My life! On my head and eyes! Be all right!"

Menashke Brezprozvani stood astonished with nothing to say. His heart leaped within him, and the beginnings of a confused smile were caught frozen at the corners of his mouth. The other had already left him and vanished along the road, but he still stood where he was as though fixed in the ground, his heart leaping and his spirit in a protracted, dark turmoil, like a distant echo caught and hanging all but still of an evening. And he could not understand it. It was as though something had happened within him, something big, but he did not know what. As though—as though—the guilty and soothing smile of that porter and his face which had been bright with love and humility did not disappear from his thoughts, but soothed him, comforting him and raising his spirits above all the errors and mistakes and recriminations and bitterness.

After a while he moved and turned and stirred to go. He descended into an open space covered with dry thorns, with many sunken stones in it, and a few twisted old olive trees. Under one of the trees stood five or six sheep pushing their heads one under the other and standing as though bewitched.

Menashke Bezprozvani sat himself down on a stone. He looked up at the Mountains of Moab—desolate in their blue, indistinct in outline—as though they had been swallowed by the sky or, perhaps, as though the sky had been swallowed by them. Before his eyes stood the likeness of the porter with his smile; his spirits rising within him, his thoughts divided, he sighed, almost tearful, then began to hum to himself the words of the song which the children had been accustomed to sing at Kfar Gileadi in those days of hardship and hunger:

In Kfar Gileadi, in the upper court,
Next to the runnel, within the big butt
There's never a drop of water . . . .

Translated by I. M. Lask

THE SERMON

HAIM HAZAZ

INTRODUCTION

"THE SERMON," *which was written in the later years of the Mandate period, when the prospect of Jewish statehood seemed likely, stirred considerable debate after its initial publication, and has remained a recurrent text for discussion on the question of Zionism and Jewish continuity. For the issues raised by Yudka are still ones that trouble Israel, the ideologically anti-Jewish position he articulates being more or less the position taken by the so-called Canaanite intellectuals and their successors.*

Since the story is, from one point of view, a kind of rambling, polemical essay on the nature of Jewish history, with nothing like a plot, it is worth considering the utility of the fictional form for Hazaz. On a rather simplistic level, one might say that the argument reads better in fictional form, is more lively and colorful, and relieved by interruptions from Yudka's impatient listeners. More important, the story form gives Hazaz the opportunity to try out extreme or heretical ideas without having to take full responsibility for them himself, since they are spoken in passion by a fictional character. Still more important, perhaps, is the fact that Hazaz is not interested in ideas in the abstract, but in ideas as the average Jew has to live with them, wrestle with them, doubt them, turn them inside out. For this reason, not only the character of Yudka is im-

portant but the interplay between him and his audience, who constitute a kind of small-scale model of the community as a whole. While the troubled individual is wracked with doubts, the representatives of the community sit "all clean-cut and positive, like captains and heroes in council," paring their nails, growing impatient, making a joke of the whole affair.

Yudka means little Jew, *and he is pointedly represented as a member of* amkha, *the ordinary people—not an intellectual, not a man of words, but a simple laborer who has come to Palestine because he was fed up with life in Exile, and who has been rebuilding the Land with his own two hands. Yudka's simplicity cuts two ways: on the one hand, much of his argument shows the impressive soundness of instinct about national feelings of a man who has lived close to the people; on the other, his knowledge is limited, his points are made in a passionate outburst, not from a careful examination of the assumptions behind them.*

When Yudka announces that the Jews have no history, to take his most central assumption, he presupposes that to have a history one must make it—that is, a people must be a physically powerful, politically autonomous entity initiating action and determining its own destiny. But of course no people is ever really in that position. Autonomy is a relative thing, and the destinies of even the most powerful nations are determined in part by other nations, sometimes actually by much smaller and weaker nations, as recent history has so abundantly illustrated. One might also wonder whether Yudka, in using the example of schoolchildren bored with Jewish history, is not adopting childish criteria for deciding what authentic history is: he wants a "world full of heroism," complains that Jewish history has "no glory or action, no heroes and conquerors, no rulers and masters of their fate."

Yudka tends to see all of Jewish history in terms of the poverty-stricken, pogrom-ridden existence of Jews in the Russian Pale of Settlement—which was as grim as Jewish life has been anywhere in the Diaspora. To be sure, Jews elsewhere and earlier were often in highly vulnerable positions or actually subjected to ghastly persecutions, but it is a sweeping over-simplification to say, as Yudka does, that there is nothing but "oppression, defamation, persecution, and martyrdom" in the last 2,000 years of Jewish history. The distinguished Jewish historian, Salo Baron, who has demonstrated that Jews were often very comfortable and legally advantaged before the

Emancipation, has stigmatized this common view as "the lachrymose version" of Jewish history.

"The Exile," says Yudka, "that is our pyramid, and it has martyrdom for a base and Messiah for its peak. And . . . and . . . the Talmud, that is our Book of the Dead." Yudka is in essence going back here to a common outcry among the nineteenth-century proponents of Hebrew Enlightenment and among the Hebrew Nietzscheans of a later generation: that traditional Jewish life in the Diaspora, under the yoke of rabbinic law, was a kind of living death. As in his acceptance of external power as the measure of autonomous history, the criteria for life that he assumes might be challenged, but his whole argument seems most probing in its general critique of Diaspora psychology. That "moonlight psychology" (the Hebrew literally means nocturnal psychology), with its capacity to believe and yet not quite believe in redemption, with its underside of masochistic complicity in the victimhood of the Exile, is finely perceived by Yudka, and may be the most convincing point of his attack.

The advantage of using a fictional character to grapple with ideas about history is vividly illustrated about three-quarters of the way through the story when Yudka, who is clearly expressing in his whole tirade one powerful side of a basic ambivalence, suddenly turns around and wonders whether all his assumptions about Jewish history might be completely wrong ("What if it's true that Judaism can manage to survive somehow in Exile, but here, in the Land of Israel, it's doubtful?"). Here, Yudka tries on for size the values and outlook of the very Diaspora Judaism he has been attacking so fiercely, and by so doing he gives recognition to their possible cogency. In a related manner, the manifestly inconclusive ending of the story is a particularly appropriate one. Yudka has been facing (for us, as well as for himself) questions that have no answers, and therefore it seems right that at the end he claims he is just getting started, that he hasn't yet begun to say what he really meant to say. The fictional form, as we noted, has given Hazaz a vehicle for the exploration of the possibilities of ideas—including dangerous possibilities—rather than a medium for the fixed, final expression of ideas, and that is why the ending intimates another beginning.

There is a finely directed irony in the concluding statement of the story—the chairman's urging Yudka to go on, but without "philosophy" (roughly: intellectualizing and theorizing). The chairman is a hardheaded, practical kibbutznik, and "philosophy" is foolish *nonsense for him. The burden, however, of Yudka's speech is only "philosophy," can only be "philosophy," because it is an inquiry into first principles of historical experience and national identity and purpose. Yudka's sermon is an assault against the idea that Zionists can continue to be Jews, yet he himself remains deeply Jewish in his troubled introspection about his identity, his uneasy grappling with a problematic past, his hopeless involvement, against his own will and inclination, in all that goes under the name of* philosophy.

THE SERMON (1942)
HAIM HAZAZ

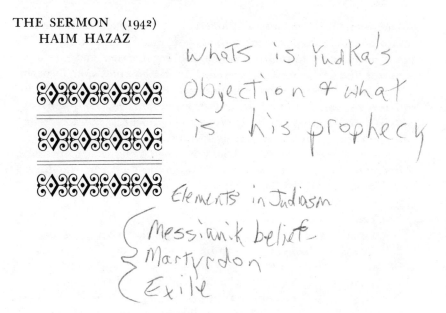

[handwritten annotation: What's is Yudka's objection & what is his prophecy]

[handwritten annotation: Elements in Judiasm — Messianik belief, Martyrdom, Exile]

YUDKA WAS NO SPEAKER. He didn't make public addresses, never took part in the debate at general meetings or at conventions—not even to make a point of order. So he was considered a man whose strength was not in self-expression. And, even though he was not just as he was considered to be, his reputation had its effect. It became second nature to him, so that he quite forgot how to open his mouth in public and say something in proper form, whether it was important or no more than a jest. That was why the boys were astounded when they heard he proposed to deliver a formal statement before the committee—and the committee, whose proceedings were open only to its members and to individuals called in before it, was convened at that time for no other reason than to hear him speak.

The committee members sat in a single row at the green table, right and left of their chairman, all clean-cut and positive, like captains and heroes in council. They eyed Yudka curiously, waiting to hear him say something not yet heard or known (except the chairman, who gazed straight at the table, apparently dreaming or drowsing, with cool eyes).

The chairman dutifully spoke a few words of introduction, fell silent, and sat down, just as though he hadn't opened his mouth, and there were no one else in the room.

Yudka drew himself up stiffly, looking harried and confused, so much did he have to say and so little did he know how to begin.

It was shocking, how confused and how harried he was! This quarryman, who split rocks and rent mountains, and went out fearlessly on night patrols, no sooner had to speak publicly before his comrades, than he completely lost himself from fright.

They waited, and he said nothing. Again the chairman spoke, directly to the green-covered table: "Comrade Yudka has the floor."

Yudka stood there crumbling inwardly, drops of sweat glistening on his brow.

"You wanted to make a statement," the chairman prompted, glancing slantwise at him, "Well then, speak. We're listening."

Some of the committee members looked aside, some stared off into space. All were silent.

At last Yudka passed his hand over his forehead, and said in the soft, slurred accent of the south of Russia: "I didn't come here to make a speech, only to say something important. . . . Really, I shouldn't say anything at all. . . . Do you know what it is to speak when it's best for you to keep still?"

He looked down the line of seats, parting his lips in an injured smile, faint and sickly.

"But I must speak!" He fixed his eyes in a blank stare, his face clouding. "I don't understand anything at all . . . I no longer understand. It's been years since I've understood. . . ."

"What don't you understand?" the chairman asked him calmly, like a judge trained to be patient with the public.

"Everything!" Yudka called out with passion. "Everything! But that's nonsense. Let's leave that for now. All I want to know is: What are we doing here?"

"Doing where?" The chairman did not follow him.

"Here! In this place, or in Palestine. In general. . . ."

"*I* don't understand!" The chairman spread his hands wonderingly, and his lips twisted in a mocking smile. "Now *I* don't understand either. . . ."

"That's a different way of not understanding," Yudka rejoined. "That's probably your way of mocking me."

One of the committee members broke into a broad grin and

tapped his fingers on the tabletop. Yudka felt his smile, but lowered his eyes, pretending not to see.

"Get back to the subject!" the chairman demanded. "Make the statement you want to make, without argument."

"I want to state," Yudka spoke with an effort, in low, tense tones, "that I am opposed to Jewish history. . . ."

"What?" The chairman looked about him to either side.

The committee members exchanged glances in astonishment. The one who had smiled at first could no longer control himself, and a short explosive laugh escaped him.

"I have no respect for Jewish history!" Yudka repeated the refrain. " 'Respect' is really not the word, but what I said before: I'm opposed to it. . . ."

Once again the same comrade—a lively fellow by nature—burst into laughter and all the others joined in.

Yudka turned and looked at him.

"You're laughing," he said in a voice dulled and measured and serious beyond words, "because you took my wife from me. . . ."

At once they all fell silent and shrank back, as if from some imminent danger, and the comrade who had laughed was thrown into confusion. Shifting and slouching, he sat with bowed back and restless eyes.

The chairman struck four or five strokes with all his might on the bell, and then again three more from sheer shock and helplessness, with no idea of what to say.

"I think that's how it is," Yudka went on, after the ringing had ceased. "If I were in his place, I would laugh too every time I saw him . . . not straight in his face, but like that . . . it's a different kind of laugh! I couldn't help laughing, I wouldn't dare . . . I couldn't manage to do anything else or say anything . . . for I would feel terribly ashamed then . . . terribly ashamed! I couldn't talk to him freely, for example, let's say about literature. Or perhaps make my confession and weep . . . I can't explain it very well, but it's clear! I've thought it all out and made sure that that's how it is. But it's not important. . . ."

For a while there was quiet—a total, final quiet in the room.

Then the chairman stirred, beetling his heavy eyebrows, and spoke with gruff, ironical severity: "Comrade Yudka, I call you to order! If you have something to say, please, say it briefly, no wandering off the subject. And if it's history you want to talk about, then the university is the place for you!"

"It's on the subject, it's on the subject!" Yudka hastened to reply with a propitiating smile. "I can't proceed now without history. I've thought a great deal about it, many nights, every night when I'm on guard. . . ."

The chairman shrugged and spread his hands skeptically. "Speak!" he ordered, to cut it short.

Yudka became as before: confused and harried, as though at that very moment some ill fortune had befallen him and he had come to pain and torment.

"You've already heard that I'm opposed to Jewish history." He coughed in shame and unease, as he began the sermon. "I want to explain why. Just be patient a little while. . . . First, I will begin with the fact that we have no history at all. That's a fact. And that's the *zagvozdka*. I don't know how to say it in Hebrew. . . . In other words, that's where the shoe pinches. Because we didn't make our own history, the goyim made it for us. Just as they used to put out our candles on Sabbath, milk our cows and light our ovens on Sabbath, so they made our history for us to suit themselves, and we took it from them as it came. But it's not ours, it's not ours at all! Because we didn't make it, we would have made it differently, we didn't want it to be like that, it was only others who wanted it that way and they forced it on us, whether we liked it or not, which is a different thing altogether. . . . In that sense, and in every other sense, I tell you, in every other sense, we have no history of our own. Have we? It's clear as can be! And that's why I'm opposed to it, I don't recognize it, it doesn't exist for me! What's more, I don't respect it, although 'respect' is not the word, still I don't respect it . . . I don't respect it at all! But the main thing is, I'm opposed to it. What I mean is, I don't accept it. . . ."

The storm within him made him shake from side-to-side like an ox refusing the yoke. He swung his hands about as if he were moving stone or sorting lumber, and he was so swept along in his speech that he could no longer halt.

"I don't accept it!" he repeated, with the stubborn insistence of one who has come to a final, fixed opinion. "Not a single point, not a line, not a dot. Nothing, nothing . . . nothing at all! Will you believe me? Will you believe me? You can't even imagine how I'm opposed to it, how I reject it, and how . . . how . . . I don't respect it! Now, look! Just think . . . what is there in it? Just give me an answer: What is there in it? Oppression, defamation, persecution, martyrdom. And again oppression, defamation, persecution, and martyrdom. And again and again and again, without end. . . . That's what's in it, and nothing more! After all, it's . . . it's . . . it bores you to death, it's just plain dull!

"Just let me mention one fact, just one little fact. It's well known that children everywhere love to read historical fiction. That's where you get action, see, bold deeds, heroes, great fighters, and fearless conquerors. In a word, a world full of heroism. Now, here now, in Palestine, our children love to read, unless they're stupid. I know this for a fact. I've looked into it. Yes, they read, but historical novels about goyim, not about Jews. Why is that so? It's no accident. It's simply because Jewish history is dull, uninteresting. It has no glory or action, no heroes and conquerors, no rulers and masters of their fate, just a collection of wounded, hunted, groaning, and wailing wretches, always begging for mercy. You can see for yourselves that it can't be interesting. The least you can say is it's uninteresting. I would simply forbid teaching our children Jewish history. Why the devil teach them about their ancestors' shame? I would just say to them: 'Boys, from the day we were driven out from our land we've been a people without a history. Class dismissed. Go out and play football. . . .' But that's all in passing.

"So, let me proceed. I'm sure you won't take me wrong. I know that there is heroism in the way we stood up to all that oppression and suffering. I take it into account. . . . But . . . I don't care for that kind of heroism. Don't laugh . . . I don't care for it! I prefer an entirely different kind of heroism. First of all, please understand me, it's nothing but the heroism of despair. With no way out, anyone can be a hero. Whether he wants to or not, he must be, and there is no credit or honor in that. In the second place, this heroism after all amounts to great weakness, worse than weakness, a kind of special talent for corruption and decay. That's how it is! This type of hero sooner or later begins to pride himself on his 'heroism' and brags about it: 'See what great torments I withstand! See what untold shame and humiliation I suffer! Who can compare with me?' See, we don't merely suffer torments. It's more than that, we love these torments too, we love torment for its own sake. . . . We want to be tortured, we are eager, we yearn for it. . . . Persecution preserves us, keeps us alive. Without it, we couldn't exist. . . . Did you ever see a community of Jews that was not suffering? I've never seen one. A Jew without suffering is an abnormal creature, hardly a Jew at all, half a goy. . . . That's what I mean; it's just such 'heroism' that shows our weakness . . . suffering, suffering, suffering! Everything is rotten around suffering. . . . Please notice, I said *around,* not *in* suffering. There's a tremendous difference. . . . Everything, everything around it rots: history, life itself, all actions, customs, the group, the individual, literature, culture, folk songs . . . everything! The world grows narrow, cramped, upside-down. A world of darkness, perversion and contradiction. Sorrow is priced higher than joy, pain easier to understand than happiness, wrecking better than building, slavery preferred to redemption, dream before reality, hope more than the future, faith before common sense, and so on for all the other perversions . . . It's horrible!

"A new psychology is created, a kind of *moonlight* psychology. . . . The night has its own special psychology, quite different from the day's. I don't mean the psychology of a man at night, that's something separate, but the psychology of night itself. You may not have noticed it, perhaps, but it's there, it's there. I know it. I feel it every time I stand guard. The whole world behaves quite differently too in the day, nature moves in a different way, every blade of grass, every stone, every smell, all different, different. . . ."

"Yudka," the chairman cut in, half-jesting, half-beseeching, "your thoughts are very fine, but have pity on us. Why did you have the committee convened?"

"Wait, wait," said Yudka hastily, "I haven't come to the main thing. You don't know yet . . . I have something in mind, I have something in mind. . . . You'll soon see. Just be patient a little . . ."

"Let him talk," one of the committee spoke up, "let him talk."

"But . . ." the chairman began dubiously.

At that moment Yudka unintentionally shouted at him: "Quiet!" The chairman was cowed and submitted in silence.

"I'm not wandering from the subject. I'm speaking about principles, about basic things. . . ." Yudka fumbled wide-eyed, his earnestness written on his face, his mind obviously entangled and exalted, laboring and driving toward something.

In a short while, he began again:

"I've already told you, and I beg you to remember that a

special, perverted, fantastic psychology has grown up among us, if I may say so, a *moonlight* psychology, altogether different in every way from other people's. . . . We love suffering, for through suffering we are able to be Jews; it preserves us and maintains us, it proves we are bold and heroic, braver than any people in the whole world. I admit, I am forced to admit that this is heroic indeed, in a way.

"People, you know, abuse many fine and noble words . . . in a certain sense suffering is heroic. And in a sense even decay is heroic and degradation is heroic . . . that is exactly the kind of people we are. We don't fight, or conquer, or rule. We have no desire, no will for it. Rather, we submit, we suffer without limit, willingly, lovingly. We actually say: You shall not conquer us, nor break us, nor destroy us! There is no power on earth strong enough for that . . . because power has its limits, but there is no limit, no end to our suffering. . . . In fact, the more we are oppressed, the greater we grow; the more we are degraded, the greater we think is our honor—the more we are made to suffer—the stronger we become. For this is our staple food, it is our elixir of life. . . . It's all so beautifully arranged! A character like that, imagine it, a nature so perfected . . . and that explains everything: Exile, martyrdom, Messiah . . . these are three which are one, all to the same purpose, the same intention. . . . Doesn't it say somewhere: 'The threefold cord'? . . ."

" 'And the threefold cord is not quickly broken,' " contributed one of the committee.

"That's it!" Yudka seized upon the verse excitedly. "Not quickly broken! Not quickly! Never, never. . . . These three support each other, aid and abet each other, so that never will the Jews be redeemed in all the world . . . so that they wander from nation to nation and country to country, age upon age to the end of all ages, the weight of the laws falling upon them, the fury of the lawless rising against them, everywhere trials and tribulations and foes and hatred on every hand. . . . Exile, Exile . . . Oh-oh, how they love it, how they hold it fast! This is the most sacred thing, the most beloved, intimate, closest to their hearts, nearer and dearer than Jerusalem, more *Jewish* than Jerusalem, deeper and purer. Far more, there's simply no comparison! Is this a paradox? But that's how it is. . . . Wait now, don't talk!" He hurriedly gestured to each side, though nobody made any attempt to interrupt. "Let me tell you how I look at it. . . ."

He rubbed his hand over his face and lips, as though coming out of a tub; he muted his voice and whispered, as though it were a deep secret.

"The Exile, that is our pyramid, and it has martyrdom for a base and Messiah for its peak. And . . . and . . . the Talmud, that is our Book of the Dead. . . . In the very beginning, as far back as the Second Temple, we began to build it. Even that far back we planned it, we laid the foundations. . . . Exile, martyrdom, Messiah. . . . Do you grasp the deep cunning hidden in this wild fantasy, the cold *moonlight* with which it flames . . . ? Do you grasp it? Just think, just think! Millions of men, a whole people plunging itself into this madness and sunk in it for two thousand years! Giving up to it its life, its very existence, its character, submitting to affliction, suffering, tortures. Agreed that it is foolish, a lunatic dream. But a dream, that is, a vision, an ideal. . . . What an uncanny folk! What a wonderful, awful people! Awful, awful to the point of madness! For look, it scorns the whole world, the whole world and all its fighters and heroes and wise men and poets all together! Fearsome and blind! A bottomless abyss. . . . No, one could go mad!"

He formed the last words soundlessly on his lips and stood as though in trance—pale—with his mouth open and a fixed stare.

The chairman invited him to be seated. "Sit down," he said, pointing to an empty chair.

"What?" He came to himself, speaking as out of a daze. "But it's not just a fantasy, it's more than fantasy . . . fantastic, to be sure. But a necessary fantasy. . . . Why necessary? What is its purpose? A very necessary purpose, let me tell you, a vitally necessary purpose! This madness is practical, it is very deliberate, it has a clearly understood aim, and it is thought out to the finest detail. . . . Look here, here we have a single element, as slight as can be, a trifling anecdote, with consequences as grave, as far-reaching as can be . . . I'm speaking of the belief in the Messiah. That's a typical Jewish fantasy, the most typical of all! Isn't it? . . . A single myth, all that is left of the whole past, the closing speech of all that great drama, after the Judges, the Prophets, and the Kings, after the First Temple and the Second, after the wars and wonders—well, and all the rest of it. . . . And that's what we are left with—a single, simple legend, and no more. Not much, you say? You are mistaken.

"On the contrary, it is a great deal. It is far too much. You might think, it's no more than a trifle, a kindergarten legend. But it's not so. It's by no means so innocent. It has such a cunning, do you know, like that of well-tried, ancient men, cunning of the greatest subtlety, so fated, so *podlaya*—that is, so corrupt a cunning. . . . Let me add, by the way, it's a wonderful legend, a tale of genius, although—apart from the philosophy and symbolism in it—not free of caricature, you know, not without a biting Jewish wit and humor; he comes on an ass! A great, a colossal, a cosmic image—not on a snorting steed, but precisely on a donkey, on the most miserable and insignificant of animals. . . . And this was enough to determine a people's fate and chart its course in the world for endless ages, for all eternity, this, and not the disputes of the schools of Shammai and Hillel. I'm not familiar with these things, I never learned Talmud, but it's quite clear. . . . It's an obvious thing, a certainty that if not for this myth, it would all have been different. For then, they would finally have had to go right back to Palestine or somehow or other pass on out of the world. At any rate, they would have had to think of something or do something, somehow or other, to bring it all to an end. . . ."

Once more the chairman thought of making him bring his speech to an end, for it seemed to him that the whole discussion was out of place in the committee. He turned to both sides, consulting the commitee members with a glance: "What do you think?" They signed to him to let him go on. He acquiesced and settled back.

Yudka did not notice the exchange of signals at all, but went on: "Now there is no need. Now they needn't think about anything or do anything, not a single thought or the slightest action. King Messiah will do it all for them, and they have nothing to do but sit and wait for his coming. In fact, it's forbidden to get involved in the whole matter, to force the end. Forbidden! What can this thing mean?" His voice shook. "What can it mean? . . . Under orders, under orders to stay in Exile until in *Heaven* they decide to redeem them. Not by their own will or their own acts, but from Heaven—not in the way of nature, but by wonders and miracles . . . you understand?"

His eyes passed down the seated line, and he stood there marveling, momentarily struck dumb.

"Do you understand?" he repeated, out of wonder and oppression of mind. "They do nothing, not an effort, nothing at all, just sit and wait. . . . They invented a Messiah in Heaven, but not as a legend out of the past, as a promise for their future. That's very important, terribly important—and they trust in him to come and bring their redemption, while they themselves are obliged to do nothing at all and there you have it. . . . How can they believe in such a thing! And so to believe! To believe for two thousand years! Two thousand years! . . . How, how can men who are by no means simple, who are no fools at all, on the contrary, very shrewd men, men with more than a touch of skepticism, men who are practical, and maybe even a bit too practical, how can they believe something like that, *a thing like that*—and not just believe, but trust in it, pin their whole life upon it, the whole substance of their life and survival, their national, historic fate? . . . And quite seriously, in full earnest! For truly they believe with perfect faith . . . the whole thing is that they really believe! And yet, and yet, in the secrecy of their hearts, you know, deep down, in some hidden fold, some geometric point down there in their hearts—*somewhat* they don't believe—just the faintest hint, at any rate—that he will come now, at this very moment, that he will come during their own lives, in their day, and this, of course, is the core of the matter. . . . It would not be possible for them not to *not* believe, even though, generally speaking, they believe with perfect faith! See? . . . This is a Jewish trait too, a very Jewish trait: to believe with perfect faith, with the mad and burning faith of all the heart and all the soul, and yet *somewhat* not to believe, the least little bit, and to let this tiny bit be decisive . . . I can't explain it well. But that's how it is. I am not mistaken! How complicated it all is! . . . Redemption is the chief of all their desires, the whole substance of their hopes, and yet they have bound themselves, locked their hands and feet in chains, and sealed their own doom, guarding and observing their own sentence with unimaginable pedantic strictness, not to be redeemed for ever and ever!

"Well, now then . . . now then . . . the birth pangs of Messiah. . . . That's an entire, separate chapter, a very interesting chapter. . . . Why must there be, according to the folk belief, why must a time of great troubles come before the end of days? What for? . . . Why couldn't they do without the troubles? After all, he is Messiah and he has unlimited power. . . . Why couldn't he come amid joy, with goodness and blessings, in the midst of peace? . . . And look: it's not troubles for Israel's enemies particularly, for the Gentiles, but especially for Israel! Nor are these troubles such, let's say, that would make them repent and so on, but just troubles for the sake of trouble, with no rhyme or reason, a whole flood of troubles, plagues, and oppressions and every kind of torment, until the eyes of Israel grow weary with beholding the grief and agony, till they can no longer bear it, and they despair of redemption. . . . What is this? A *Weltanschauung?* Historic wisdom? Or is it perhaps what one dare not hint: simply their own fear of redemption? . . . I am just lost!"

He really looked lost, standing there. He seemed for a moment to have forgotten himself completely, and not to know where he was.

"It seems to me," he said, with a vague, sickly smile, "I once heard there was a sage or a pious man, I forget which, who said it already: 'Let him come, and may I not see it,' or something like that. . . . Maybe it was a joke, a cynical remark, or just chatter. Or maybe it was a great truth, revealing a secret deep, deep buried. . . . How was this myth ever invented at all? Not invented, no. . . . I don't mean to say that . . . because in the beginning surely there was nothing but hope and longing for the kingdom of the House of David. . . . But how did it become what it turned into afterward, the classic creation of the people, one might say the creation of its highest genius, the eternal creation of the people of Israel? What made it, more than any other myth, sink so deep and spread so wide in the folk-mind that it became common to everyone, rabbis and thinkers and the mass of people, scholars and illiterates, man, woman, and child? What was there in it to let it dye our very heart's blood, and rise to a kind of dogma of faith and religion, the foundation of the whole people's life for all ages, our national idea, our vision in history, our political program, and so on? Whatever the answer—it did! That's the fact. It means there must be a profound kinship, a fundamental bond between this myth and the spirit of our people, if it thrust so deep! It means there is a basic harmony, a full and perfect unity between it and our people's ideal, between it and the people's will, and the direction it desires to go! . . . There's not the least doubt: it's quite clear!"

He stopped for a moment, and his face turned dull and pale. It was quiet in the room, as quiet as in the season just before the rains come—a waiting, oppressive, gloomy quiet.

"Ye-es . . ." he said with a long, groaning breath, as if speaking from his very heart, "such is that wild, enthusiastic, *moonlit* fantasy of theirs . . . the fantasy they need for such practical purposes, for their well-understood ends. Just as I've already told you . . . because . . . because. . . ."

He halted and could not speak on. But even half-paralyzed, he looked from one to another in a sort of driven frenzy.

"Because they don't want to be saved!" he blurted out all in one breath.

Again he was still, looking from side-to-side like one who fears he has been trapped by his own foolishness.

"Because they don't want to be saved!" he repeated, seeking assurance in speech. "That is the deliberate intent of this myth, that is its practical effect, not to be saved, not ever to go back to the land of their fathers. . . . I don't say that it is conscious, necessarily. But if it's unconscious, it's even worse. . . . They *really* believe redemption will come, I repeat it, again, they believe in all truth and sincerity, they hope for it, aspire to it, and yet they *intend* that it should not come. This is not deceit, it's not duplicity at all. I'm sure of it, I'm sure of it. . . . Here something is at work beneath the surface, something rooted in the depths of their heart, something unconscious. . . . It's not for nothing that that myth became so beloved among the people, and holds such sway that they became like some kind of poets, not concerned at all with the world as it is, but altogether given up to dream and legend. Two thousand years it has consoled them, and for two thousand more they will live by its warmth, in dream, in mourning, in expectation, and in secret fear of it, and never will they tire. And that's the whole essence of Judaism, the whole character of Israel, and of its love of Zion, and the holiness of the land, and the holy tongue, and the end of days, and everything altogether. . . . But let's leave this now.

"For what if they really have something to fear? What if it's true that Judaism can manage to survive somehow in Exile, but here, in the Land of Israel, it's doubtful? . . . What if this country is fated to take the place of religion, if it's a grave danger to the survival of the people, if it replaces an enduring center with a transient center, a solid foundation with a vain and empty foundation? And what if this Land of Israel is a stumbling block and a catastrophe, if it's the end and finish of everything? . . ."

A queer, weary, and ill-defined smile flickered on his lips.

"Well? . . ." He turned his eyes on them as though waiting

for an answer. "What if they're right? What if their instinct doesn't deceive them? . . . Just see how here, here, in Israel, they are against us, all the old settlers, all those pious old Jews, simple Jews like all those that ever lived in any other place or time. Don't their very faces tell us plainly: 'We are no Zionists, we are God-fearing Jews! We don't want a Hebrew state or a national home. What we want is to go up peacefully to be buried on the Mount of Olives, or down to pray at the Wailing Wall undisturbed. . . .' Now, that means something! I won't talk about our Mizrahi [1] people, those little naive semi-sophisticates of our Zionist movement. I'm speaking about the people, the people of the root and foundation. Well, then? . . . I'll tell you!

"To my mind, if I am right, Zionism and Judaism are not at all the same, but two things quite different from each other, and maybe even two things directly opposite to each other! At any rate, far from the same. When a man can no longer be a Jew, he becomes a Zionist. I am not exaggerating. The *Biluim* [2] were primarily very imperfect Jews. It wasn't the pogroms that moved them —that's all nonsense, the pogroms—they were falling apart inside, they were rootless and crumbling within. Zionism begins with the wreckage of Judaism, from the point where the strength of the people fails. That's a fact! Nobody has yet begun to understand Zionism. It is far deeper, far more pregnant with vast and fateful consequences than appears on the surface, or than people say. Herzl expressed no more than the rudiments of it. Ahad Ha-am said nothing at all, just another idea that came into the head of an inquiring Jew. At most, he went around advising Jews who had somehow determined to establish a new community that they'd do better to set up a Jewish study circle or build a school or cemetery first. . . . What?" He turned to one of the committee who had opened his mouth to speak.

"Oh, nothing," the interrupter chuckled, "I just remembered something. I had an uncle, he was a clever fellow. The Bolsheviks killed him. For nothing, just killed him. He used to say: 'Ahad Ha-am is the Habad [3] school of Zionism.'"

---

1. The modern Orthodox Zionist movement.
2. The first, small group of modern Zionist immigrants, who came from Russia to Palestine in 1882 out of ideological conviction.
3. A Hebrew acronym for Hokhma, Bina, De'a (wisdom, understanding, knowledge); *Habad* was a relatively intellectual and learned stream within the larger movement of Hasidism.

The committee enjoyed the remark, but the chairman felt it his duty to reprove him. "Don't interrupt!" he said.

Yudka may not have heard, or may not have understood. He stood bemused and smiling.

"I'll finish soon," he said with a deprecating smile. For a while he waited, collected his thoughts, and sought a new beginning. "Yes. . . ." He coughed two or three times. "Right away. . . . What was it I wanted to say? That is . . . about Zionism. Yes! In a word, no one has yet said the right . . . the . . . the hidden, the deepest . . . no one has revealed, or explained, fully . . . just talk, elementary things, banalities, you know, empty, meaningless phrases. . . ."

"Oh, they've explained," one of the committee broke in, jesting. "The Brit Shalom, the wise men of the University and all the other little professors. . . ."

"You can't prove anything by idiots," another spoke up in an offhand manner.

"Ernst Fäig . . ." went on the first, referring to a public figure who was regarded as something of a fool and an exhibitionist.

"*Ernst is' nicht fähig, und Fäig is' nicht ernst . . .*" rejoined the first with a witticism.[4]

"I ask you not to interrupt and not to talk across the table!" The chairman straightened up and took over control. "Please continue."

"All right." Yudka began again, struggling with the words. "Of course I'm not the one to say what Zionism is. I'm not the man for it. Even though I've wracked my brain and thought about it for a long time. But that's not important. . . . One thing is clear. Zionism is not a continuation, it is no medicine for an ailment. That's nonsense! It is uprooting and destruction, it's the opposite of what has been, it's the end. . . . It has almost nothing to do with the people, a thoroughly non-popular movement, much more apart from the people than the Bund,[5] more than assimilationism, more even

---

4. The Brit Shalom was a pacifistically inclined group of Jerusalem university intellectuals especially active in the 1930s in the cause of Arab-Jewish reconciliation and the fostering of bi-nationalism as a solution to the Palestinian conflict. Martin Buber was a leading figure in this group, and the *Ernst* of the punning German may refer to Buber's friend, Professor Ernst Simon. The meaning of the German is, "Ernst is not able, and Fäig is not earnest."

5. Yiddish labor movement in Eastern Europe, socialist in ideology, opposed to Zionism.

than communism. The fact is, it turns away from the people, is opposed to it, goes against its will and spirit, undermines it, subverts it and turns off in a different direction, to a certain distant goal. Zionism, with a small group at its head, is the nucleus of a different people. . . . Please note that: not new or restored, but *different*. And if anyone doesn't agree, well, I'm very sorry, but either he's mistaken or he's deluding himself. What? Perhaps it isn't so? I believe that this land of Israel already is no longer Jewish. Even now, let alone in the future. Time will tell, as they say. That's its hidden core, that's the power it will yet unfold. Yes! At any rate, it's a different Judaism, if you choose to fool yourselves and keep that name, but certainly not the same as survived for two thousand years, not at all the same.

"That is . . . well, nothing. You understand? And nothing will help, neither grandfathers and grandmothers nor antiquities, nor even Hebrew literature which has grown like a crust on the past, and clings to the old small towns of our Exile. All wasted! *Kaput!* I'll take the liberty of mentioning one detail, not directly related, but it has some bearing, a tangential bearing . . . a fine expression, you know," his lips twisted in a smiling grimace. "So round and smooth—tangential. . . . Well, then, it's well known that we're all ashamed to speak Yiddish, as though it were some sort of disgrace. I intentionally said 'ashamed.' Not that we dislike, or fear, or refuse, but we're ashamed. But Hebrew, and none other than Sephardic Hebrew, strange and foreign as it is, we speak boldly, with a kind of pride or vanity, even though it isn't as easy and natural as Yiddish, and even though it hasn't the vitality, the sharp edge and healthy vigor of our folk language. What's the meaning of this? What's the reason for it? For no reason at all, just to take on such an immense burden? But it's quite simple: This community is not continuing anything, it is different, something entirely specific, almost not Jewish, practically not Jewish at all. . . . In the same way, we are ashamed to be called by the ordinary, customary Jewish names, but we are proud to name ourselves, say, Artzieli or Avnieli. Haimovitch, you will agree, that's a Jewish name, entirely too Jewish, but Avnieli—that's something else again, the devil knows what, but it has a strange sound, not Jewish at all, and so proud! That's why we have so many Gideons, Ehuds, Yigals, Tirzahs . . . what? . . . And it doesn't matter that we had the same kind of thing before, that was with the assimilationists, that's easy to understand. There we were living among strangers, people who were different and hostile, and we had to hide, to dissimulate, to be lost to sight, to appear different from what we really were. But here? Aren't we among our own, all to ourselves, with no need for shame, or for hiding, or anyone to hide from? Well then, how do you expect to understand this? . . . That's it! That's the whole thing, point by point. It's obvious, no continuity but a break, the opposite of what was before, a new beginning. . . . A little detail, quite unimportant, it didn't deserve going into so much, but it is a symptom of far more . . .

"I've gone into side issues. I won't keep you much longer. I'm finishing. In a word, this is the aim—one people, and above all, a people creating its history for itself, with its own strength and by its own will, not others making it for it, and history, not the chronicles of a congregation, anything but *chronicles,* that's how it stands. For a people that doesn't live in its own land and doesn't rule itself has no history. That's my whole idea. I've already told you and I repeat again, and I'll say it again and again, day and night . . . is it clear? Is it clear?"

And all at once his words ran together and his voice broke and sputtered with feeling, his eyes flickered to and fro like one who doesn't know which way to go. "With this I've said a great deal, the whole thing . . . everything I had on my mind . . . and now I don't want to say anything more. I have nothing more to add. . . . Enough!"

He noisily pulled back a chair and cast himself heavily into it, wiping the sweat off his face with his palm, and sat there all in a turmoil, with his face flaming, his heart pounding, and his temples throbbing.

It grew quiet, like the stillness after a quarrel. The men were silent and sat uncertainly with changed faces, not sure in their hearts nor easy in their minds, as though in doubt whether something might not be lost or lacking, or as if they were in mid-passage between where they had been and where they were going.

Then the chairman lifted his eyes and spoke with a certain strain: "Have you finished?"

At that, Yudka sprang to his feet with a jerk.

"Right away, right away . . ." He spoke hastily and with some panic. "I said much too much. . . . That's not how I meant it, not the way I thought. It came out by itself. The devil knows how . . . such nonsense! Trifles, side issues like that, about Yiddish there, and the names. . . . It was ridiculous, quite unnecessary. I see it myself. . . . But just those side issues, those unimportant details, you know, they come to mind immediately. . . . Well, it's all the same. What I mean, I really just wanted to explain . . . I no longer know how to tell you . . . the main thing, what I'm after. It's not just . . . yes! Well, now. Now to the main thing. I beg just a few more minutes of patience. . . ."

The boys all straightened up in their chairs and felt more at ease, as though he had saved them from a great worry—especially the chairman, who bowed his head and sat staring at his fingernails.

"Say what you want," he said, "and let's see if we can't do without the philosophy. . . ."

Translated by Ben Halpern

THE PRISONER

S. YIZHAR

INTRODUCTION

S. YIZHAR *(pen name for Yizhar Smilansky, born 1916) is usually considered to be the major novelist of the war generation of 1948, the first generation of native Israeli writers. He began writing in the politically troubled period at the end of the 30s, and his novels and stories register the shock of coming of age in a time of brutal warfare. His immense stream-of-consciousness novel,* The Days of Ziklag *(1958), a subject of furious debate after its publication, was acclaimed by many younger Israelis as the definitive stocktaking of their generation's relationship to the War of Independence. Yizhar's continually inventive style, utilizing elements of the older literary Hebrew as well as the new colloquial language, together with a good deal of his own neologisms, decisively extended the range of descriptive prose in Hebrew. Yizhar was for many years a member of Knesset, the Israeli parliament, and, a high-school teacher by profession, he has repeatedly addressed himself to questions of education, national values, and the condition of Israeli society.*

"The Prisoner" was written in November 1948 during the first Israeli-Arab war. It was published in Molad, *a monthly then sponsored by Mapai, the ruling party, and so it appeared in wartime in what was indirectly a government-supported magazine. That fact is worth noting as an index of the openness of political discussion in*

Israel, even under conditions of grave crisis. For the radical critique here is conducted by a writer who is, after all, an establishment figure, using a literary organ of the Israeli establishment.

The familiar process by which power dehumanizes those who exercise it, set at the center of the story, had a special disturbing vividness for Yizhar's generation. Raised on the idealistic vocabulary of classical Zionism, these young Israelis, as a first act of manhood, suddenly found themselves thrust into the heart of violence, called on to kill or to be killed for the sake of the new State. In the result-ing psychological shock, many of the values they had been taught to cherish were severely tested, or exposed as mere slogans. From one viewpoint, this story is about such a test—and how easy it is to fail it.

Some attention to how Yizhar maneuvers his narrator may yield a more precise understanding of how he handles his moral theme. In the first part of the story, the narrator uses "we" repeatedly in describing the movements of the patrol, so he is obviously one of the soldiers. But, never identified, he remains an anonymous observer— which is of course appropriate, since he expresses in part the collec-tive awareness of the soldiers, and as a not-entirely-innocent by-stander, he speaks for the confused, wavering conscience of any average citizen in time of war. (Note that none of the soldiers is assigned a name: they are all gray citizens doing their ugly duty. Only the Arab has a name!) In the last third of the story, however, the "we" is dropped and the narrator now addresses the soldier in the back of the jeep as "you," who then appears to answer in paren-thetical paragraphs using "I." The most plausible explanation for this shift is that the anonymous soldier-narrator of the beginning of the story is the soldier in the back of the jeep at the end. As the action moves inside him, focusing on his inner struggle, he is no longer the passive observer, and in order to articulate his own con-flict, he splits himself into two voices: one a voice of conscience in which he buttonholes himself in the second person, the other a voice of his own weakness attempting to answer, in the first person, the accusations of conscience with conventional excuses.

In the body of the story, the kind of prose that predominates is made of a staccato series of brief sensory impressions, feelings, truncated thoughts, that constitute a kind of continuous summary of the way the soldiers feel as filtered through the awareness of the unnamed narrator. The narration of the story, then, might be de-scribed as a loose "stream-of-collective-consciousness." The very be-

ginning of the story, however, is written in a more elaborately literary style, striving for poetic effects through a highly wrought imagery, in the rendering of the natural scene. Instructively, the lyric attention given to nature here drops out of sight almost entirely until the last paragraph of the story. The narrator obviously can relate to nature joyously and deeply while relating to men and their ambiguous actions is more problematic for him, and this contrast shows in the prose. Still more important, the central action of the soldiers is framed by nature, and they appear in it at the outset as interlopers. The hills with their flocks and crops curve peacefully as in the days of Abraham, but the armed men in pursuit of an enemy are "designs of a different sort cast[ing] their diagonal shadows across the pastoral scene!" When the narrator's vision turns back to nature at the very end of the story—as he looks out on the endless shimmering expanse of the plain—it is to stress his essential aloneness with the burden of choosing to become a man, after all the ugliness and the moral untidiness of the power-wielding group.

The guiding moral idea of the story, that every man must assume the full weight of responsibility for his choices, as though he were alone in the world, would seem to derive from Sartre's Existentialist views, but it has special resonance in the Israeli situation. One need not assume that the beating of the Arab prisoner is in any way typical Israeli behavior (as, predictably, Arab propagandists, capitalizing on the story, have done), but it is clear that Yizhar has provided a sharp fictional focus for the inevitable moral quandary involved in a reversal of roles between the powerless and the powerful. One of the climactic moral shocks of the story occurs in the midst of the beating: "Have no mercy. Beat him! They have no mercy on you. Besides, a goy is used to blows." It takes only a little historical imagination to see what in the experience of young Jews growing up in Palestine of the 30s and 40s, repeatedly subject to murderous Arab incursions, would prompt this sort of feeling. The crucial point is that the plea in behalf of conscience is made here on the strength of values embedded in the historical memory of the Jewish people: a Jew knows from bitter experience what it means in concrete human terms to be the helpless target of ruthless fists; and Yizhar, as a writer many of his generation saw as their moral spokesman, argues that Israelis simply cannot afford to forget the hard lessons of their own antecedent history.

THE PRISONER (1948)
S. YIZHAR

SHEPHERDS AND THEIR FLOCKS were scattered on the rocky hillsides, among the woods of low terebinth and the stretches of wild rose, and even along the swirling contours of valleys foaming with light, with those golden-green sparks of rustling summer grain under which the clodded earth, smelling of ancient soil, ripe and good, crumples to gray flour at a foot's touch; on the plains and in the valleys flocks of sheep were wandering; on the hilltops, dim, human forms, one here and one there, sheltered in the shade of olive trees: it was clear that we could not advance without arousing excitement and destroying the purpose of our patrol.

We sat down on the rocks to rest a bit and to cool our dripping sweat in the sunlight. Everything hummed of summer, like a golden beehive. A whirlpool of gleaming mountain fields, olive hills, and a sky ablaze with an intense silence blinded us for moments and so beguiled our hearts that one longed for a word of redeeming joy. And yet in the midst of the distant fields shepherds were calmly leading their flocks with the tranquil grace of fields and mountains and a kind of easy unconcern—the unconcern of good days when there was yet no evil in the world to forewarn of other evil things to come. In the distance quiet flocks were grazing, flocks from the days of Abraham, Isaac, and Jacob. A far-off village, wreathed with olive trees of dull copper, was slumbering in the curves of hills gathered like sheep against the mountains. But designs of a different sort cast their diagonal shadows across the pastoral scene.

For a long time our sergeant had been carefully peering through his fieldglasses, sucking his cigarette, and weaving plans. There was no point in going further, but to return empty-handed was out of the question. One of the shepherds, or at least one of their boys, or maybe several of them, had to be caught. Some action had to be taken, or something be burned. Then we could return with something concrete to point to, something accomplished.

The sergeant, of medium height, had thick brows which met over his deep-sunken eyes; his cap, pushed back on his balding head, exposed a receding forehead and damp, limp wisps of hair to the wind. We followed his gaze. Whatever it was that he saw, we saw a world of green-wool hills, a wasteland of boulders, and far-off olive trees, a world crisscrossed with golden valleys of grain—the kind of world that fills you with peace, while a lust for good, fertile earth urged one to return to back-bending work, to gray dust, to the toil of the burning summer: not to be one of the squad which the sergeant was planning to thrust bravely into the calm of the afternoon.

And, in fact, he was about ready to take action because just then we noticed a shepherd and his flock resting in the leveled grain in the shadow of a young, green oak. Instantly a circle was described in the world: outside the circle, everything else; inside, one man, isolated, to be caught alive. And the hunters were already off. Most of the platoon took cover in the thickets and rocks to the right, while the sergeant and two or three others made an encircling movement down to the left in order to surprise their prey and drive him into the arms of the ambush above. Amid the tender, golden grain we stole like thieves, trampling the bushes which the sheep had cropped so closely, our hobnails harshly kissing the warm, gray, sandy soil. We "took advantage" of the "terrain," of the "vegetation," of the protection offered by "natural cover," and we burst into a gallop toward the man seated on a rock in the shadow of the oak. Panic-stricken, he jumped to his feet, threw down his staff, lurched forward senselessly like a trapped gazelle, and disappeared over the top of the ridge right into the arms of his hunters.

What a laugh! What fun! Our sergeant hadn't recovered before another bright idea struck him, astonishingly bold and shrewd: take the sheep too! A complete operation! Drunk with satisfaction, he slapped one palm against the other and then rubbed them together as if to say, "This will be the real thing!" Someone else, smacking his lips, said: "Boy, what a stew that will be, I'm telling you . . ." And we willingly turned to the task, roused to a genuine enthusiasm by the flush of victory and the prospect of reward. "Come on! Let's get going!"

But the noise frightened the sheep. Some tossed their heads, some tried to flee, others waited to see what the rest would do. But who knew anything about handling sheep? We were ridiculous and that's just what our sergeant said, and he claimed that *shlemiels* and idiots like us could only mess up a good thing. Raising his voice, he began calling the sheep with a br-r-r and gr-r-r and a ta-ah-ta-ah and all the other noises and signs used by shepherds and their flocks from the beginning of time. He told one of the men to get in front of the sheep and to bleat, while some of us paired off on either side, brandishing our rifles like staffs and striking up a shepherd's tune, and three or more brought up the rear the same way. Thus, with a show of energy and wild laughter, we might overcome our hesitation, and be, in fact, soldiers.

In the confusion we had forgotten that behind a rock on the slope, huddled between two rifle butts and two pairs of spiked boots, sat our prisoner shivering like a rabbit—a man of about forty, with a moustache drooping at the corners of his mouth, a silly nose, slightly gaping lips, and eyes . . . but these were bound with his kaffiyeh so that he couldn't see, although what he might have seen I don't know.

"Stand up," he was told as our sergeant came over to take a good look at his prisoner. "So you thought we wouldn't get a thing?" crowed the men. "We did, and how! With us there's no fooling around! Didn't have to waste a bullet: 'Hands up' . . . he got the idea right away."

"You're terrific," agreed the sergeant. "Just imagine—the shepherd *and* his flock! What won't they say when we get back! It's really great!" Only then did he look at the prisoner: a little man in a faded, yellow robe, breathing heavily behind the cloth over his eyes, his battered sandals like the flesh of his hooflike feet. On his hunched shoulders sat doom.

"Lift the blindfold, but tie his hands behind him. He'll lead the sheep for us." It was one of those crack commands which the intoxication of battle always inspired in our sergeant, and a spark of joy passed among us. Good. The men unwound the black cord of the shepherd's kaffiyeh, took his hands and bound them with it good and tight, and then good and tight again for safety's sake, and still again for the third time. Then the blindfold was pushed above the nose of the frightened man: "*Nabi el'anam kudmana!*" he was ordered. "Lead the sheep ahead of us!"

I don't know what our prisoner thought upon seeing daylight again, what he felt in his heart, whether his blood whispered or roared, or what stirred helplessly in him. I don't know—but he immediately began clucking and grunting to his sheep as if nothing at all had happened, dropping from rock to rock through the brush with accustomed ease, the bewildered animals behind him. We followed after with hoarse yells, our rifles slapping our backs as we stampeded along and descended with wanton abandon to the valley.

We were so absorbed that we did not notice the silhouettes of other shepherds on the ridges of the hills, now gathering silently to peer at us from the distance as they rounded up their flocks; nor had we looked at the sun which all this busy hour had slipped lower and lower, getting more golden, until, turning the corner of a steep slope, we were struck by an intense blinding light: the smoky, enflamed disc seemed a mute admonition from space! But, of course, we had no time for all that: the flock! the prisoner! The sheep were bleating and scattering in all directions, while he seemed to shrink within himself, dazed and stupefied, his mind a ruin in which everything behind him was loss and all before him, despair. And as he walked he grew quieter, sadder, and more confused and bewildered.

It's too long to tell in detail how we made our way through valleys and past hills in the peaceful ripeness of summer; how the frightened sheep kept tripping over their own feet; how our prisoner was enveloped by dumbness, the silence of an uprooted plant—his misery so palpable that it flapped about his head in a rhythm of terror, rising and falling with the blindfold (tied to his brow with a brute twist of disdain) so that he was pathetic but also ludicrous and repulsive; how the grain turned more golden in the splendor of the sun; how the sandy paths followed their course between hills and fields with the faithful resignation of beasts of burden.

We were nearing our base of operations.

Signs of the base, an empty Arab village, became more frequent. Interrupted echoes. An abandoned anthill. The stench of desertion, the rot of humanity, infested, louse-ridden. The poverty and stupe-faction of wretched villagers. The tatters of human existence. A sudden exposure of the limits of their homes, their yards, and of all within. They were revealed in their nakedness, impoverished, shriveled, and stinking. Sudden emptiness. Death by apoplexy. Strangeness, hostility, bereavement. An air of mourning—or was it boredom?—hovered there in the heat of the day. Whichever, it doesn't matter.

On the rim of the village, in those gray, greasy trenches, the other citizen-soldiers of our Home Guard company wandered aim-lessly—their food no food, their water no water, their day no day, and their night no night, saying to hell with what we'll do and to hell with what will be, to hell with everything that was once nice and comfortable, to hell with it all! We'll be dirty, we'll grow beards, we'll brag, and our clothes, wet with sweat, will stick to our unwashed bodies, infested with ulcers. We'll shoot stray dogs and let their carcasses stink, we'll sit in the clinging dust, we'll sleep in the filth, and we won't give a damn. It doesn't matter!

Nearing the trenches, we walked with heads high, proud of our loot! We fell smartly into step, almost dancing along. The bleating sheep were milling about in confusion. The prisoner, whose eyes had been covered again, dragged his sandles with clumsy uncertainty as we good-naturedly railed at him. We were happy and satisfied. What an adventure! What a job! Sweaty we were, caked with dust, but soldiers, real men! As for our sergeant, he was beside himself. Imagine our reception, the uproar and berserk laughter that broke loose like a barrel bursting its hoops!

Someone, laughing and sweating profusely, pointing at the un-seeing prisoner, approached our sergeant. "Is that the prisoner? Want to finish him off? Let me!"

Our sergeant gulped some water, wiped his sweat and, still grinning, said, "Sit down over there. It's none of your business." The circle which had formed around howled with laughter. The trenches, the troubles, the disorder, no leave, and all that—what were they compared to all this?

One man was taking pictures of the whole scene, and on his next leave he would develop them. And there was one who sneaked up behind the prisoner, waved his fist passionately in the air and then, shaking with laughter, reeled back into the crowd. And there was one who didn't know if this was proper or not, if it was the decent thing to do, and his eyes darted about seeking the support of an answer, whatever it might be. And there was one who, while talking, grabbed the water jug, raised it high over his head, and swilled the liquid with bared teeth, signaling to his audience with the forefinger of his left hand to wait until the last drop had been drained for the end of his slick story. And there was one wearing an undershirt who, astonished and curious, exposed his rotten teeth: many dentists, a skinny shrew of a wife, sleepless nights, narrow, stuffy room, unemployment, and working for "the party" had aggravated his eternal query of "Nu, what will be?"

And there were some who had steady jobs, some who were on their way up in the world, some who were hopeless cases to begin with, and some who rushed to the movies and all the theaters and read the weekend supplements of two newspapers. And there were some who knew long passages by heart from Horace and the Prophet Isaiah and from Haim Nahman Bialik and even from Shakespeare; some who loved their children and their wives and their slippers and the little gardens at the sides of their houses; some who hated all forms of favoritism, insisted that each man keep his proper place in line, and raised a hue and cry at the slightest suspicion of discrimination; some whose inherent good-nature had been permanently soured by the thought of paying rent and taxes; some who were not at all what they seemed and some who were exactly what they seemed. There they all stood, in a happy circle around the blindfolded prisoner, who at that very moment extended a calloused hand (one never knows if it's dirty, only that it's the hand of a peasant) and said to them: "*Fi, cigara?*" A cigarette?

His rasping voice (as if a wall had begun to speak) at once aroused applause from those with a sense of the ridiculous. Others, outraged by such impudence, raised their fingers admonishingly.

Even if someone were moved to think about a cigarette, it all ended in a different way—in military style. Two corporals and a sergeant came over from headquarters, took the prisoner, and led him away. Unable to see, he innocently leaned on the arm which the corporal had just as innocently extended in support. He even spoke a few words to guide the prisoner's groping steps. And there was a moment when it seemed as if both of them were laboring together peacefully to overcome the things that hindered their way and helped each other as if they went together, a man and another man, close together—until they had almost reached the house, when the prisoner repeated: "Fi, cigara?" These few syllables immediately spoiled the whole thing. The corporal withdrew his arm that had been interlocked with the prisoner's, raised his eyebrows angrily and, almost offended, shook himself free. "Did you ever see such a thing?"

It happened so suddenly that the sightless man stumbled and tripped on the front step of the house, lost his balance and, almost falling, plunged headlong into the room. In a desperate effort to right himself, he sent a chair flying and collided with the table. There he stood, helpless, clumsy, overwhelmed by the force of his own violence and the fear of what was to come. His arms dropped to his sides and he stood stupefied, resigned to his fate.

A group of officers, their faces frozen in severe formality, had been ceremoniously seated at the table. But the prisoner's sudden entrance completely upset their quiet preparations, disturbed the atmosphere, confused the sentry at the door, confused the corporals and the sergeant; in short, everything had to be put back together again and grudgingly reorganized from the very beginning.

The officer sitting in the middle was tall and muscular, with stubby hair and a fierce face. On his left sat none other than our sergeant. One could see now that he was quite bald; the hair above his forehead was still dark but what little hair he had at the temples was turning gray. Perspiring freely, a crumpled cigarette in his mouth, he was the hero of the day and only at the beginning of his glorious adventures. Near the wall, conspicuously removed from the others, stood a pale young fellow glancing about through half-lowered lashes like someone quite convinced of a particular truth but curious to see by precisely what means it stands to be revealed.

"What is your name?" The tall officer began his interrogation abruptly but the prisoner, still stunned, paid no attention. The lips of the young fellow leaning against the wall puckered with assurance: this was just what he had expected.

"What is your name?" repeated the tall officer, drawing out the syllables.

"Who? Me?" The prisoner trembled and reached for his blindfold with a faltering hand. Halfway there, he dropped it, as if it had been singed by flame.

"Your name?" the officer asked a third time in a tone that emphasized his patience.

"Hasan," he rasped, bowing his head, frustrated by his blindness.

"Hasan what?"

"Hasan Ahmed," he answered, now on the right course, and his head nodded affirmatively.

"How old?"

"Oh, so-so. Don't know exactly." He twitched his shoulders and slid his palms together uncertainly, wanting to be of help.

"How old?"

"Don't know, sir," he said, moving his thick lips. For some reason he chuckled and his drooping moustache performed a little caper. "Twenty, maybe thirty," he said, eager to cooperate.

"Well, what's going on in your village?" The tall officer spoke with a restraint which, more than it emphasized his calm, betrayed the coming storm—the restraint of an original, cunning deceit, a kind of slow circular descent that is followed by a sudden strike at the jugular, a swoop to the heart.

"In the village they are working, sir." The prisoner sketched a picture of country life, sniffing the trouble that was to come.

"Working, you say? As usual?" The interrogator was moving in like a spider when a trembling thread of the web announces the prey.

"Yes, sir." The fly had edged away from the intricate web.

It was clear he would lie at this point. He had to lie. It was his duty to lie, and we would catch him by his tongue, the dirty dog, and we would show him. And just as we understood that with these tactics he would reveal nothing, so we knew that this time he wouldn't fool us. Not us. It's his turn to talk!

"Who is in your village?" The hawk hovered over its prey.

"Eh?" The prisoner did not follow the question and licked his lips innocently, like an animal.

"Jews? English? French?" The interrogator continued his questions like a teacher setting out to trap a slow pupil.

"No, sir, no Jews, only Arabs," he answered earnestly, with no hint of evasion. Once again, as if the danger were over, he tugged absentmindedly at his blindfold. The interrogator was glancing about the room: take a good look! It's beginning. Just see how an expert does it!

"Are you married?" He was started on a new, oblique attack. "Any children? Where is your father? How many brothers? Where does your village get its drinking water?" He wove his delicate web painstakingly, and the prisoner struggled to satisfy him; he fumbled uselessly with his hands and made superfluous, meaningless gestures, bobbing his head and rolling his tongue, getting involved in petty details which threw him into confusion and annoyed his interrogators: some story about two daughters and a son, and how the son, neglected by his sisters, went out of the house and, as a result, fell sick and passed from the world. As he mumbled along, the prisoner innocently scratched his back ribs up and down, first with his thumb and then with a knot of four fingers, stammering as he tried to find the right words—he was unbearable.

There was a pause. The sentry shifted his weight from one foot to the other. From the expression on the face of the young fellow leaning against the wall and from the way our balding sergeant got up from the table, it was suddenly clear—not that the prisoner had nothing more to say, but that nothing would help but a beating.

"Listen here, Hasan," said the interrogator, "are there any Egyptians in your village?" (Now he'll talk! Now it's going to begin. Now he's sure to lie.)

"There are," answered the prisoner, so simply it was disappointing.

"There are," echoed the interrogator resentfully, like a man who has been paid in advance by his debtor. He lit a cigarette, deep in thought, contemplating his next move.

Our sergeant paced back and forth across the room, rearranged his chair, tucked in his shirttails, and with evident dissatisfaction turned his back to us and stared out the window. The young fellow by the wall, looking very wise, was passing his hand downward over his face, pinching his nose at the end of each stroke. You have to know how to handle these situations!

"How many are there?"

"Oh, so-so. Not many." (Now he'll start lying. This is it. Time for a beating.)

"How many?"

"Ten, maybe fifteen, about that."

"Listen, you Hasan, you'd better tell the truth."

"It's the truth, sir, all the truth."

"And don't lie."

"Yes, yes, sir." His hands, outstretched in surprise, dropped to his sides.

"Don't think you can fool around with us," the tall interrogator burst out. He felt it was the right moment to say this. "How many soldiers are there?"

"Fifteen."

"That's a lie."

The bald sergeant turned to us from the window. His eyes were smiling. He was enjoying that last sweet moment of anticipating all the joy still to come. To prolong it, he lit the cigarette held in the corner of his tightly pressed lips. The other five men in the room regarded one another with the same wide-eyed pleasure. The sentry at the door shifted his weight again.

"I swear, sir, fifteen."

"No more?"

"The truth, no more."

"How do you know there are no more?" The interrogator intended to make clear that he was nobody's fool.

"No more."

"And if there are more?" (How can one answer such a question?)

"No more!"

Suddenly a clumsy kick from too short a distance landed on the man at an awkward angle. The unsuspecting prisoner staggered and collapsed upon the table with a loud exclamation—more of surprise than of pain. The whole scene suggested some kind of unfairly matched game rather than a cross-examination, something unexpected, unnatural.

"Now talk and see that you tell the truth!"

"Sir, I swear by my own eyes, I swear by Allah, fifteen."

The young man by the wall was afraid that so gross a lie might be believed. He held a long stick which he drew through his fingers with the grace of a knight drawing his sword. Then silently, significantly, he placed it on the table.

The barrage of questions continued without a break. The kicks landed like lightning, more naturally and freely, cool, deliberate, increasingly skillful. If at times they seemed unavailing, they nonetheless continued.

Because if you want the truth, beat him! If he lies, beat him! If he tells the truth (don't you believe it!) beat him so he won't lie later on! Beat him in case there is more to come. Beat him because you've got him at your feet! Just as a tree when shaken lets fall its ripest fruit, so a prisoner if you strike him yields his choicest truths.

That's clear. And if someone doesn't agree, let him not argue. He's a defeatist, and you can't make wars with that kind. Have no mercy. Beat him! They have no mercy on you. Besides, a goy is used to blows.

Now they came to the question of machine guns in the village. A crucial point, this. Here you have to lay it on or you won't get anywhere. And if you don't, Jewish blood will be spilled, our own boys' blood, so this point must be completely clear. They questioned him again and again until it became nauseating, and they gained nothing but the certainty that he was lying. Then he was ordered to describe the village's fortifications. And there he got completely confused. He had difficulty with the description, the abstraction, the geometry, the mathematics. He tried to convince his questioners with gestures, freeing his arms from his sleeves and waving them about while he shuffled back and forth. But the cloth over his eyes reduced everything to a blur of confusion. It was clear to everyone in the room that all his talk was nothing but a tissue of lies.

"You're a liar," exclaimed the discouraged interrogator. "I can see in your eyes that you're lying," and he raised a menacing fist in front of the prisoner's blindfold.

This got nowhere. It had become boring. Everyone was fed up. The cross-examination blundered along, without enthusiasm, and the kicks fell listlessly. There was sudden surprise when the stick came whistling down on the prisoner's back, a disinterested, routine blow from an obedient hand.

O.K. And now about the guns. The prisoner kept insisting that their barrels were no longer than the distance from his shoulder to his palm. He struck his left palm like a hatchet against his right shoulder and then against his wrist: from here to there. He beat himself incessantly, unstintingly, to remove any trace of doubt. Even then he was uncertain whether he had done enough or must continue, and around his mouth was the expression of a blind man who has lost his way.

The questions petered out. At the door the sentry, shifting his weight from one foot to the other, was looking up at the sky, possibly searching in the glimmering light for something that was not in the dirty, gloomy room. He feared that something terrible was about to take place. It was inevitable! Take the stinking beggar, they would tell him, and get rid of him!

"Well, that's that," said the interrogator, slumping back in his chair, eager to relax now that it was over. He stubbed his cigarette impatiently on the floor.

"I'd better finish him off," volunteered the sergeant, flicking his cigarette through the doorway with a quick snap of his forefinger.

"He's a complete moron," concluded one of the corporals.

"He's only pretending to be," said the other.

"He needs someone who can handle him," said the young man by the wall, curling his lips in a sneer at this offense to truth.

The prisoner, sensing a respite, licked his thick lips, stuck out a thick hand, and said: "Fi, cigara?" Of course nobody paid attention to the fool. After waiting some time, the idiot dropped his hand and remained rooted to the spot, sighing softly to himself: Oh, Lord God.

Well, what now: to the village quarry or perhaps a little more torture to open his mouth? Was there any other way to get rid of him? Or . . . perhaps one could give him a cigarette and send him home. Get out and let's not see you again!

In the end someone telephoned somewhere and spoke to the captain himself, and it was decided to move the prisoner to another camp (at least three of the men in the room wrinkled their noses in disgust at this unfit procedure, so civilian, so equivocal), a place which specialized in interrogating prisoners and meted out to each just what he deserved. The sentry—who had been uneasy throughout the cross-examination without knowing what to do—went to get the dusty jeep and the driver on duty. The young man who came was griping, angry that he had been called out of turn. Not that he objected to leaving: it would be nice to get back to civilization for a while and to see some human faces, but it was the principle, the principle of the thing! Another soldier, charged with an order whose execution had been delayed for lack of transport, took his place alongside the driver. Now he was assigned another duty: accompany the prisoner! (Thus shall they go through the streets of the town: the machine gun in front and the prisoner behind!) He sat and loaded his machine gun. With two jobs, the trip—God forbid!—couldn't be counted as leave!

The prisoner was pushed and shoved like a bundle into the jeep where the only place left for him was the floor. There he was dropped, kneeling like an animal. In front of him were the two soldiers and behind, the sentry whose pocket held the official order, travel authorization, and other essential papers. The afternoon, begun long ago among mountains, oaks, and sheep, was now drawing to a close. Who could foresee how it would end?

The jeep left the moldering village behind, passed the dry river-beds, and spurted ahead at great speed through the fields, bouncing on all fours. Distant details of the landscape kept shifting to close view. It was good to sit and watch the fields now bathed in a rosy light trailing small, golden clouds, a light that seemed to envelop everything—all those things which are so important to you and me but mattered not at all to the driver and his comrade in the front seat. They smoked and whistled and sang "On Desert Sands a Brave Man Fell" and "Beautiful Green Eyes" in turn. It was difficult to know what the man who lay on the floor of the jeep was feeling because he was blind, stunned, and silent.

A cloud of dust, billowing up behind the jeep like a train of smoke, caught the rosy light in its outlines. The uneven gullies and shallow furrows of the fields made the racing jeep dance. The fields stretched to infinity, abandoned to the twilight, to something distant and dreamlike.

Suddenly, a strange thought pierces one's mind: *The woman is lost beyond a doubt.* And before there's time to wonder where the thought came from, one understands, with the shock of lightning, that here, right here, a verdict is being sealed which is called by so many different names, among them: fate.

Quick, escape this rotten mess! Join the harmonizing of the other two up front or journey toward a far distance with the deepening twilight. But the circle of that unexpected thought grows larger and larger. This man here at your feet, his life, his well-being, his home, three souls, the whole fabric of life, have somehow found their way into the hollow of your hand, as though you were a little god sitting in the jeep. The abducted man, the stolen sheep, those souls in the mountain village—single, living strands that can be joined or separated or tangled together inextricably—suddenly, you are the master of their fate. You have only to will it, to stop the jeep and let him go, and the verdict will be changed. But wait . . . wait . . .

An inner force stirs in the young man on the back seat of the jeep and cries out: Wait! Free the prisoner!

We'll stop the jeep right here in the gully. We'll let him out, unbind his eyes, face him toward the hills, point straight ahead, and we'll say: Go home, man, it's straight that way. Watch out for that ridge! There are Jews there. See that they don't get you again. Now he takes to his heels and runs home. He returns home. It's that easy. Just think—the dreadful, oppressive waiting: the fate of a woman (an Arab woman!) and her children; the will-he-or-won't-he-come-back; the what-will-become-of-me-now—all would end well, one could breathe freely again, and the verdict would be a return to life. Come, young man, let's free him.

Why not? Who's preventing you? It's simple, decent, human. Stop the driver. This time no more lofty phrases about humanity, this time it's in your hands. This time it's not someone else's wickedness. This time it's an affair between you and your conscience. Let him go and you'll save him. This time the choice (that terrible and important choice of which we always spoke with awe) is in your two hands. This time you can't escape behind "I'm a soldier" or "It's an order" or "If they catch me, what will they do?" or even behind "What will my comrades say?" You are naked now, facing your duty, and it is only yours.

So stop, driver! Send the man away! No need for reasons. It is his right and your duty. If there is a reason for this war, it must show itself now. Man, man, be a man and send him home. Spit on all this conventional cruelty. Send him away! Turn your back on those screaming slogans that paved the way for such an outrage as this! Free him! Hallelujah! Let the shepherd return to his wife and his home!

There is no other way. Years might pass before he is set free, by some magic, to return to the hills to look for his wife and family; meanwhile, they have become fugitives fleeing misery and disease— mere human dust. Who knows what can happen in this meanwhile, and where? Perhaps, in this meanwhile, someone will decide to get rid of him, to finish him off for some reason—or even for no reason at all.

Why don't you make the driver stop? It's your duty, a duty from which there is no escape. It's so clear that it's hard to wait for you to act. Here you must rise and act. Say a word to the driver. Tell him and his companion that this was the order. Tell them a story, tell them something—or don't even bother. Just let it happen. You are going to face the sentence, that's sure. Let him go!

(How can I? He's not mine. He's not in my hands. It's not true that I'm his master. I'm only a messenger and nothing more. Is it my fault? Am I responsible for the hard hearts of others?)

That's enough. That's a shameful evasion. That's the way every son-of-a-bitch escapes from a fateful decision and hides himself behind "I have no choice," those filthy and shopworn words. Where is your honor? Where is this independence of thought you boast about? Where is freedom, hurrah for freedom, the love of freedom! Free him! And what's more, prepare to be sentenced for this "crime." It's an honor. Where are they now, all your words, your protests, your rebellions about pettiness, about oppression, about the ways to truth and freedom? Today is your day of payment. And you shall pay, my son. It's in your hands.

(I can't. I'm nothing but a messenger. What's more, there's a war, and this man is from the other side. Perhaps he is a victim of the intrigues of his people but, after all, I am forbidden and have not the power to free him. What would happen if we all started to set prisoners free? Who knows, maybe he really knows something important and only puts on that silly face.)

Is that what you really think? Is he a soldier? Did you catch him with a weapon in his hands? Where did you find him? He's not a fighter; he's a miserable, stinking civilian. This capture is a lie— don't blind yourself to that. It's a crime. You've questioned him, haven't you? Now set him free. Nobody can get anything more out of him. And are you willing to suppress the truth for one more detail? The truth is to free him—now!

(It's so difficult to decide. I don't dare. It's involved with so much that's unpleasant: talk to the driver, persuade his companion, face all the questions, get into a rotten mess, and all because of a good-for-nothing wretch named Hasan, and what's more, I'm not sure it's good to free him before he's been thoroughly questioned.)

Nonsense! Someone with only a fraction of your feelings about truth and freedom would stop right here and send the man home and continue on his way, quickly forgetting the whole thing: short and simple, a man of action. And he wouldn't thank himself for being good! But you, with all your knowledge, arguments, proofs, and dreams, it's clear that you won't do it. You're a noble fellow. You'll meditate, enthuse, regret, reconsider, you'll be submerged in a sea of thoughts: Oh, why didn't I do it? And you'll cast the bitterness of your unfulfilled existence over the whole world: the world is ugly, the world is brutal. So make up your mind, and do it this time. Stand up to the test. Do it!

(I feel sorry for him. It's a shame they picked me for the job. I would do it if I weren't afraid . . . I don't know of what. If only I were alone with him here. It's bothering me like a desire almost within reach, and I can't begin. When I think that I'll have to explain, get all involved, go to people and argue and prove and start justifying myself, I simply can't. What can I do?)

Listen, man! Can you actually think of weighing these pitiful trifles against another's life? How would you look at this thing if you were the one crouched on the floor of the jeep, if it were your wife waiting at home, and all was destroyed, scattered to the winds like chaff?

The prisoner has already said all he can say, told all he can tell. What more do you want? And even if he has lied a hundred times, who is he and what is he? He is only a miserable nothing, a subdued, shriveled creature, a mask wrapped in a cloth, someone shrunken and stooped like a worthless sack, frightened, dissolving into nothingness, for whom being kicked is second nature (kick him—he's an Arab; it means nothing to him). As for you, his little god, it's your duty to free him, even if he himself laughs at you, even if he (or someone else) sees it as a sign of weakness on your part, even if your friends make fun of you, if they try to restrain you, even if they bring you up for court-martial, for twenty court-martials! It's your duty to break free of this habitual swinishness. Let there be one person who is ready—even at the price of suffering—to get out of this heap of filth which was piling up in the days when we were good citizens and which is now the celebrated, the accepted, the official way of the world, embraced by those bearing the proud title "soldier." And all that was frowned upon is now freely allowed!

Oh, Hasan Ahmed, you with a wife named Halima or Fatima, you with two daughters, you whose sheep have been stolen and who has been brought God-knows-where one clear afternoon, who are you and what is your life, you who can cleanse from our hearts all this filth—may it rot forever in darkness!

Of course you won't free him. That's clear. Beautiful words! It's not even cowardliness—it's worse than that: you are an accomplice to the crime. You. Hiding behind a stinking what-can-I-do-it's-an-order. This time you have the choice, and it's at your disposal. It's a big day. It's a day of rebellion. It's the day when, at last, you have the choice in your hands. And you hold the power to decide. And you can restore life to a man from whom it has been taken. Think it over. You can behave according to the dictates of your heart, of your love, of your own standard of truth, and—most important of all—of the freedom of man.

Free him! Be a man! Free him!

It's clear that nothing will happen. It was certain that you would evade it, that you would turn away your eyes. It's clear that all is lost. Too bad for you, prisoner, he does not have the strength to act.

And maybe, even yet. You, you right here, it will only take a minute: Driver, stop! Hey, Hasan, get out and go home! Do it! Speak! Stop them! Talk! Right now! This is the moment! You can become at last, you sufferer of many, long, empty days, you can become a man, the kind of man you've always wanted to be.

The glimmering plain was a thin, bright foil. Thousands of acres shone—a magical expanse without riverbeds or hills, ascents or descents, trees or villages. Everything was spread out to form a single, golden matrix, flat and gleaming, strewn with moving pinpoints of light, a single vast field stretching to infinity. And yet behind us (but no one is gazing there) in the misty evening coming over the mountains, there, maybe, there is a different feeling, a gnawing sadness, the sadness of "who-knows?," of shameful impotence, the "who-knows?" that is in the heart of a waiting woman, the "who-knows?" of fate, a single, very personal "who-knows?," and still another "who-knows?" belonging to us all, which will remain here among us, unanswered, long after the sun has set.

Translated by V. C. Rycus

THE TIMES
MY FATHER DIED

YEHUDA AMICHAI

INTRODUCTION

BORN IN GERMANY *in 1924, Yehuda Amichai came to Palestine at the age of twelve; he quickly took root in the new Hebrew environment, though modern German, then English, writers would be important influences in his work. The poems he began to publish after the War of Independence established a very new, colloquial and ironic tone for Hebrew poetry, and thrust him to prominence. Having served in the British army during World War II and then, repeatedly, in the Israeli army, he returns again and again in his work to the tensions between the demands of a warring public world and the need to live a private life. He is now widely regarded as the major Hebrew poet of his generation, and he has been accorded considerable international recognition. Amichai began experimenting with short stories in the 1950s, breaking sharply with the conventions of traditional realistic fiction in a way that Hebrew writers before him, with the one notable exception of Agnon, had not dared to do. His big book,* Not of This Time, Not of This Place *(1963), is one of the important achievements of the experimental novel in Hebrew, and a probing expression of an Israeli's sense of inner division in his life in a new world after the European Holocaust. Amichai continues today to write fiction as well as poetry.*

The operation of figurative language in "The Times My Father

Died" provides the key to its innovative narrative form, and that is true for all the stories in the collection where it first appeared, In This Terrible Wind (1961). Each simile or metaphor here begins to assume a life of its own, so that the imaginative action of the story is less the external events than the rapid movement from metaphor to metaphor, every figure of speech constituting a little explosion of revealed possibilities of meaning. At the very beginning, for example, the narrator, describing the father's features, moves from gaping door to fluttering flag to postage stamps to sails and "a little private beach at the edge of the world's sea," and so through an associative chain of metaphors an entire voyage is effected.

Metaphor-making, which involves the perception of generally unnoticed similarities or connections, is of course the basic activity of the poet, but in this story the metaphoric vision seems peculiarly appropriate to the child whose experience is retrospectively reconstructed. Many of the striking effects of the story come through Amichai's reproduction of the naive literalism of a small child. Thus the narrator recalls his father prostrating himself in prayer: "I thought he was drinking with his forehead. I thought that God must be flowing down there in among the legs of the tables." This naive literalism becomes a means of arresting conventional phrases and symbols, unmasking them, discovering unexpected implications in them. Thus, the narrator takes the idiom "flesh and blood" and, by thinking of it literally, sees through it the terrifying fragility of human life, the ghastly gap between the beauty of the living creature and the meaty horror of the dead thing: "He was flesh and blood that had come to life . . . You see, not flesh and blood, but skin and eyes, you see a smile and dark hair, hands and a mouth." This notion, once picked up, becomes a formal motif, recurring in a later reflection on war and killing: ". . . all one could see was flesh and blood, but no more smiles and hair and caressing arms and other fine arrangements of things."

As a rule, in this story where so much of the action is in the metaphors, when metaphoric activity becomes more intense, we are at a crucial juncture. Just after the typographical break in the middle of the story, figures of speech proliferate as the physically dying father is described. The father's eyes are "smashed like the glass tumblers they crush underfoot at a . . . Jewish wedding," the associations of the traditional wedding practice being pointedly incongruous for a deathbed scene, ironic, and finally quite poignant.

The bizarre shift from this tradition-linked, yet violent, simile to the image of the "oxygen bomb" (brilliantly, "bomb" and not "tank") and the sea divers and pilots is thoroughly characteristic of Amichai's poetry as well as his prose. The sudden movement from traditional ritual to modern technology mimics the larger pattern of remembrance in the story, in which the narrator feels himself cut off from that irrevocably ravaged world of piety to which his father belonged.

The concluding paragraph of the story beautifully illustrates the suggestive art of Amichai's imaginative prose. The dream or hallucination of a final encounter with the father is pointedly not differentiated from waking reality, for the effect of the whole story has been to break down the divisions between vision and factual experience. The father, who first died in Germany and last died in Jerusalem, is here seen in an ambiguous state between life and death in Rome, a location that may intimate the alienation of the son from his origins (Rome being traditionally a symbolic antithesis to Jerusalem). The son's love for his father, his desire to wish away his father's death, his guilty feeling that he ought to have been able somehow to sustain his father, and his assumption of his father's role after the parent's death, are all expressed through the huddled action in which the son carries his father on his shoulders, lays him by the roadside, futilely seeks a taxi for him, leaves him behind at the end, a distant object seen through the arches of San Sebastian's Gate.

This combination of melancholy tenderness and innovative technique is typical of Amichai. Through the inventive elaboration of imagery, the writer offers a subtle rendering of a father's distinctive presence and of a son's anxious love over the years. The story also develops a larger sense of what a human life is, in the son's remembrance of the father: what makes an individual life moving and precious is the fact that it must be cut off; that life, as the title suggests, is a series of little deaths, or a continuous dying. At a number of points, therefore, Amichai can shift from comment on the father to a resonant general aphorism on the human condition. "In a man's lifetime he gives off a large quantity of sweat, blood, body waste, poetry, and letters." This is the substance of a man's life, touching and sad, and the writer makes this sense of existence emerge from a steady metaphoric contemplation of his father.

THE TIMES MY FATHER DIED (1959)
YEHUDA AMICHAI

ONE YOM KIPPUR, my father stood in front of me in synagogue. I climbed up onto the seat to get a better view of him from behind. His neck is much easier to remember than his face. His neck is always at rest and unchanging; but his face is perpetually in motion —as when he speaks, his mouth gaping like the doorway of a dark house or fluttering like a flag. His eyelids and his eyes are postage stamps affixed to the letter of his face, which is always mailed to far-away places. Or his ears are sails on the sea of his God. And his face is either all red, or white like his hair. And his rippled forehead is a little private beach at the edge of the world's sea.

It was then that I saw his neck. A deep furrow, practically a groove, ran right across it. It was the first time I had seen this deep, sun-scorched creek, though I was still far away from that country. Perhaps my father had also started out from just such a creek. The rains hadn't come yet, and on that Yom Kippur the summer heat lay sweltering on the land where I was still to arrive.

I now see his face on the picture of him that I keep in my closet. It is the face of a man who has started eating his favorite food and is disappointed to find the taste not to his liking—as shown in the mouth drooping at the corners, as shown in the wrinkled nose, as shown in the mute sad birds lurking in the corners of the eyes.

I can garner a great deal of evidence from the face—not to use in passing judgment on him, but in judging myself.

That Yom Kippur he stood in front of me, completely absorbed in his grown-up God. He was all white in his Day of Atonement winding-sheet. All around him the world was black, like the charred stones left behind after a bonfire. The dancers were gone and the singers were gone, and only the blackened stones remained. That's how my father seemed to have been left behind, dressed in his white winding-sheet. It was the first time I remember my father dying.

When they got to the Alenu prayer, my father went down on his knees like all the other people and touched the floor with his forehead. I thought he was drinking with his forehead. I thought that God must be flowing down there in among the legs of the tables. Before he went down on his knees he laid out his velvet prayershawl bag on the floor so as not to get his knees dirty, but he didn't bother about dirtying his forehead. Then he came back to life again. He got up without moving his feet, which he kept close together. And after he got up, his face changed color a number of times and he was alive and my father again, and I climbed onto the seat to have a look at the groove in his neck. He was flesh and blood that had come to life. Why are living people called flesh and blood? You only see flesh and blood when somebody has been crushed and mangled, when his body is injured or when he's dead. When people are alive you see other things in them. You see, not flesh and blood, but skin and eyes, you see a smile and dark hair, hands and a mouth.

I went up to the women's gallery to tell my mother about how the dead came back to life. Up there, they had apples filled with spices to keep the women from fainting. I have always wanted to faint—to be wiped off the slate, to withdraw from everything aimlessly and unresisting—but I have never been able to. The women were holding the spiced apples in their hands; I was also in their hands, and so was the whole sphere of the world. They held me up to the large clock to check the time with me. They looked at me in the light of the fires that were going to burn down the synagogue. From up there in the gallery I saw them stripping the white mantles off the Scrolls of the Law. They took hold of a shoulder strap and pulled the mantle off, leaving the Scroll of the Law naked and cold. Then my father came back to life, and in the evening he broke his fast after the Ne'ilah service. The year was a huge hoop, a wall fencing in the days and seasons. An odd game! My sins and my atonements were still folded up, and both of them looked the same. That evening, the moon fluttered round the city like a gleaming white chicken, the one they used in the atonement ritual.

My father died many times more, and kept on dying from time-to-time. Sometimes I was there, and sometimes he died alone. Sometimes he died quite near my table, or when I was busy writing pretty words on the blackboard or looking at the colored-in countries in my atlas. But there were times when I was very far away when he died, like the way it happened in World War One. It's a good thing sons don't see their fathers at war. And it's also a good thing I wasn't in that war, otherwise we might have been killing one another; because he wore the uniform of Kaiser Wilhelm, while I wore the uniform of King George the Fifth, with a gap of twenty-five years in-between. I put his medals in the same box where I kept my own World War Two decorations, since I had nowhere else to keep them. One of his medals had a lion on it and two crossed swords, which looked like a duel being fought between two invisible swordsmen. Beasts of prey are prominent on most emblems: there are lions and eagles and bulls and hawks and all sorts of other ravening creatures. In the synagogue they have a pair of lions holding up the Tablets over the Holy Ark. Even our own laws, too, can only be protected and safeguarded by wild animals.

In Germany once, some time after the war, my father put on a black frock coat and shiny top hat, pinned on his decorations, and went to the dedication of a war monument. The names of all the dead were engraved on it in alphabetical order. They erected the monument in a public park near the playground, right next to the swings and sandboxes. I don't remember what the memorial looked like, but it must have had stone soldiers pointing stone rifles under stone flags, and stone mothers weeping stonily. There must also have been all sorts of wild beasts to immortalize the invincibility of man and the greatness of generals and emperors.

For four whole years my father died in the war. He dug a lot of trenches. They told him that sweat saves blood, and that the soldiers' blood saves the generals', and that the generals' sweat, in turn, saves the manufacturers and kaisers a lot of sweat and blood, and so on all down the line, a regular savings scheme. My father dug a lot of trenches and dug himself a whole lot of graves. He was wounded only once. All the other bullets and shrapnel missed. When he really died, much later, all the bullets and shrapnel that had missed him got together and smashed his heart all at once; and that's how he never got out of the last trench, which others had dug for him. He went through a great many battles and was very often among those statistically reported killed in action, or on the statistical roll of those killed while capturing enemy positions. His blood glowed like those luminous buttons you press to put the electric light on in hallways, so that if death should want to see him properly, all it had to do was to light up his body with his blood. But death never pressed the luminous-blood button and my father didn't really die. God, in whom he believed, hovered over him like a white protective umbrella, up above the path of the shells. He never involved his God in the war. He left God out of it, among the laws of nature and the stars, above it all, like a light foam that topped the dark, heavy beverage of his life.

Sometimes, when the war went hard, his body became like a tree that had shed its leaves. His nerves were then the branches from which all his life was shed. He sent back a great many letters from out there. At first the letters were few and far-spaced, but during the four years of the war the letters accumulated into packs and bundles, and the packs hardened like stone. This is what happenes to letters. At first they flutter in, white and soft like a dove's wings; later they get hard like stone. The hard bundles of letters were shifted about from place-to-place, from one chest of drawers to the other, into the closet and on top of the closet, up to the attic and later right under the roof tiles. When my father really died, a lot of what was in his letters went straight up from under the roof. When there is the true resurrection of the dead, he will have to undo all those bundles and read out his letters. In a man's lifetime he gives off a large quantity of sweat, blood, body waste, poetry, and letters.

Once he told us about some French prisoners at Verdun who asked him for water in their language, de l'eau, de l'eau, and he gave them all that was left in his canteen. Since then I have never forgotten those prisoners calling for water. Sometimes they come to me asking for some water. Perhaps my father told them about me, but I hardly think so since I wasn't born yet. But in war—which jumbles people and earth together and throws everything into confusion, making standing people sit down, and seated ones lie down, and turning recumbent ones into pictures on the wall—in war everything is possible.

Once, just before Hitler came along, my father's former brothers-in-arms invited him to a regimental reunion. They sent him a nice letter headed by the regimental emblem: a hunter's cap, antlers, and a pair of crossed rifles. It had this emblem because it was a hunting regiment with a glorious tradition behind it, a *corps d'élite*. Originally they used to hunt stag and hares, but later they went hunting human beings in the war. And they didn't only hunt them, they actually killed them. Nor was it in order to eat them, as they ate the hares, but simply to kill them and mangle their bodies. And then, all one could see was flesh and blood, but no more smiles and hair and caressing arms and other fine arrangements of things.

My father didn't accept the invitation and this, too, meant death for him, because his comrades liked him very much and used to call him David. During the war, they used to give him some of their rations before the Day of Atonement so that he would have strength for his fast. They would gather stars for his prayers and moments of silence for his quiet devotions. In return, he would keep their spirits up with the confidence he imparted and with the funny stories he told.

After that he died a great many times.

He died when they came to arrest him for throwing the Nazi pin I found into the garbage. The black uniforms came to our door and broke it down. And the top boots tramped in. It was terrible for me to see my father no longer able to defend our house against the enemy's onslaught. That was childhood's end. How could they just burst into our house like that against father's wishes!

If I had been bigger then, I would have covered up my father as he walked away, despondent.

He died when they stationed pickets outside his shop to keep people from buying there because it was a Jewish shop.

He died when we left Germany to emigrate to Palestine, and all the years that had passed died with him. When the train went past the Jewish Old-Age Home, which my father had supported, all the old people stood waving their bed sheets from windows and balconies. They were not waving them in surrender and farewell, for in either case, you wave white flags or handkerchiefs or even bed sheets.

He died a great many times, for he was made of stuff that kept changing all the time. Sometimes he was like iron, sometimes like white bread, sometimes like seasoned old wood, and all these had to die. There were times when I saw him covering his face with his hands so as not to let me see it stripped and bare. There were times when his thoughts overburdened his small body, which sagged and bowed under their load. But there were also times when he stood firm and strong like a chain of telephone poles, effortlessly sending out his marvelously brilliant thoughts like the wires stretched between them, and then even the songbirds would alight and perch on them.

When he really died, God didn't know whether he was actually dead or not. Till then, he always used to come back to life, but this time he didn't. A few weeks before he had had a heart attack. They call it a heart attack, but it's not at all clear what attacks what: does the heart attack the body, or the body the heart? Or does the world attack both?

When I came to see him one day, he was lying next to an iron oxygen tank, his eyes smashed like the glass tumblers they crush underfoot at a traditional Jewish wedding. When I went over to him, I heard the oxygen hissing out of the bomb-shaped tank. There was a time when the Angel of Death used to stand next to the sickbed, but now they have the hissing oxygen bomb. Sea divers and airplane pilots are also given oxygen tanks. Where was my father going? Was he going to dive, or maybe soar aloft? In any case, he was leaving us. He beckoned me to him. I said, "Don't talk and tire yourself out," and he said, "There's the cat mewing on the neighbors' roof. Maybe it's shut in and wants to get out." I went over to the neighbor's to release the cat. When I got back all we heard was the hiss of the oxygen. There was a pressure gauge fitted into the oxygen tank. My father had as much time left as there was oxygen in the tank. My mother stood at the door. If only she had been able to, she would have stood at his bedside like the oxygen tank giving him of her life force.

After that, my father slowly began to recover. Every day he regained a little of his color, as if all his colors had run away and dispersed when his heart had been attacked and were now creeping back, like refugees after an air raid. The oxygen tank was put outside on the balcony.

The day he died they gave him a cardiograph test. The doctor came and opened up a radiolike box and hooked it up to my father with all kinds of electric wires. When you love a person you don't need such a complicated contrivance in order to examine his heart, but you do when somebody's ill. The needle traced a lot of zigzags on a roll of paper, like a seismograph in an earthquake. My father was looking like a broadcasting station, what with the jumble of wires and antennae. That day he transmitted his last broadcast. I heard it.

The doctor said, "We're all right" using the plural, as if anybody had doubted that he himself was all right, too. He then dismantled the apparatus and showed us the zigzags, which he thought were all right.

In the evening, I took my wife to see a movie. When the close-up faces on the screen had stopped laughing or crying, we went out to the street, where my wife bought some flowers from a man who kept them in a bucket, just outside an arty cafe. This place was frequented by a motley crowd: young poets of sad mien, ever gazing into the distance; men who sported a variety of battle pins; men who limped because of war injuries, and those who limped because it looked aristocratic; men who brandished moustaches; war-lovers in civilian clothes and peace-lovers in uniform; and girls who liked keeping company with all of them. We bought red roses, possibly because we wanted to hasten the color back to my father's cheeks.

We went back to my father's side. My wife put the flowers in a vase, where they breathed more freely. We drew up chairs round the bed and my father started telling us about a man who had arrived in the country after he had jumped off a train and had been hidden by good Gentiles. Tears welled up in my father's eyes as he spoke of the good people who had given shelter to a refugee. His eyes filled with tears and an odd gurgling sound came out of his mouth. He stopped speaking all at once, like a film that has snapped in the cinema, or like a radio program when another station suddenly cuts in. What other station could be cutting in on my father's broadcast? I was asking myself, when suddenly both stations went dead, both his and the one that was making all the interference. His mouth opened wide, as if he still had a host of stories to tell about a lot of good people and all the stories were trying to crowd out and couldn't. I rushed over to him, clasped him to me and kissed his cold forehead. Perhaps I had just remembered how he had once touched the ground with his forehead on Yom Kippur, or did I wish to bring him back to life as Elisha had done? My mother came running in from the bathroom. My wife called the doctor, who confirmed what was already a confirmed fact. A good neighbor came in and saw to the arrangements. A rabbi, an acquaintance of my father's, came in and supervised the rites; he had the furniture shifted around and windows opened and shut—he was used to people dying. The rabbi placed a lighted candle on the floor, like a lantern near a building that is going up or a road under repair, then he opened a book and began whispering. The hissing of the oxygen tank was no longer necessary.

The next day they washed my father at home. They moved the furniture out of the room, poured out streams of water and wrapped him in rolls of cloth. After he was buried, a whole lot of relatives and acquaintances came visiting. Aunt Shoshana, who lives in the country, came too, glad to get away from her hundreds of chickens and to meet friends whom she hadn't seen for a long time.

There were many occasions for mourning. We let pass the occasion for the loud, bitter wail of grief. Perhaps it was because he died in the middle of telling a story, or because all the radio stations had suddenly closed down, or perhaps it was because the heart would have had to open up as wide as a trumpet mouth and it wasn't large enough for that. One could shriek like the train that went up to Jerusalem through the lowering, haunting mountains, or sigh in silent torment, like a window that has been left open.

We can express only a few emotions: sorrow, fear, a smile, and a few others, like the mannikins in shopwindows. Fate manipulates us, like a window dresser fixing his dummies into position, lifting an arm here and turning a head there, and that's the way they remain all through the season. It's the same with us.

I let my beard grow in mourning. At first it was bristly and stiff, but later it grew soft. Sometimes, when I lay down, I would hear shots or the rumble of tractors down in one of the valleys, or dynamiting from the stone quarries. My father was like those quarries; he gave me all his stone and depleted himself. Now that he was dead and I was built up, he remained gaping-void and deserted, with the forest closing in around him. When I go down to the coastal plain sometimes, I see the stone quarries at the roadside, and they are deserted.

I ordered a tombstone. The evening I went to order it I saw a girl standing near one of the tombstones, fixing the strap of her sandal. When she saw me coming she ran away in-between two tall buildings. I ordered a horizontal tombstone, with a stone pillow as a headpiece. The stonemason asked me about measurements and angles and materials, like a tailor taking measurements for a suit.

The cemetery lies near the border. When things get rough there, the dead are left to themselves, with only a few soldiers turning up from time-to-time. Next to my father lies a German doctor, who doesn't have a tombstone but only a little tin marker. As you look toward the city you can see the Tnuva Dairy tower. Towers don't help us very much anymore, but the Tnuva tower is actually a cooling system. There are also water towers, and they have to be high enough to fill the cisterns on top of all the houses. God, who is very high up, filled my father up to the brim. I was filled up with other things, and not always from high towers. Sometimes the pressure wasn't strong enough and I was only half-filled with dreams and ideas.

I was in the cemetery a few days ago. Every grave bears a name and an inscription. No one knows where Moses was buried, but we know where he lived and we still know all about his life. Nowadays everything is the other way round. We know only where the burial places are. Where we live is unfixed and unknown. We roam about, we change, we shift, and the only thing we know for certain is where the graves are located.

I, for my part, go my way, developing some of my father's qualities and some of his facial features and traits. I develop some, and discard others.

But, as I said at the beginning, my father still keeps dying. He comes to me in my dreams and I am afraid for him and say: take your coat, walk more slowly, don't talk, you mustn't get excited, take a rest from this awful war. I, myself, can't rest. I must keep going, but not to pray. I lay my phylacteries, not on my arm and forehead, but in the drawer which I never open anymore.

Once I was walking along the Appian Way in Rome. I was carrying my father on my shoulders. Suddenly his head sagged down and I was afraid he was going to die. I laid him down at the side of the road, with a stone under his head, and went to call a taxi. Once they used to call on God to help; now you call a taxi. I couldn't find one, and as I went searching I got further away from my father. Every few steps I would turn round to see if he was still there, and plunge on toward the stream of traffic. I saw him lying at the roadside, his head turned in my direction, watching me. I saw him through the ancient Arch of San Sebastian. Passersby stopped for a moment to bend over him and then went on. I finally got a taxi, but it was too narrow and looked like a snake. I got another one, and the driver said: We know him by now; he's only pretending to be dead. I turned round and saw my father still lying at the side of the road, his white face turned to me. But I didn't know if he was still alive. I turned round again and saw him, a very distant object, through the ancient arches of San Sebastian's Gate.

Translated by Yosef Schacter

BEFORE HIS TIME

AMOS OZ

INTRODUCTION

A prolific and precocious writer, Amos Oz (born 1939) had estab-
lished himself as an important figure in Israeli fiction before he was
thirty. He and A. B. Yehoshua are the two leading writers in what
the critic Gershon Shaked has called the New Wave in Israeli fiction.
Having grown up in the Jewish state, Oz, like Yehoshua, tends to
see statehood amid armed conflict not as an unexpected moral
trauma, in the fashion of S. Yizhar and the generation of 1948, but
as a troubling existential fact. Though his novels and stories typi-
cally use explicit and sometimes explosive political material, he
seems less interested in politics as such than in how politics can
provide a mirror for the subterranean life of the psyche. As an
Israeli citizen, he has participated in various efforts toward recon-
ciliation with the Arabs; as a writer, he has probed the hidden—or
suppressed—emotional netherworld of Israeli national existence. His
first novel, Elsewhere, Perhaps *(1966, English translation, 1973),*
explores the Israeli kibbutz—Oz has been a member of Kibbutz
Huldah since 1957—as a writhing tangle of thwarted egotism and
sexual desires. With greater artistic sureness, his next novel, My
Michael *(1968, English translation, 1972), evokes the disturbed*
emotional life of a young Jerusalem housewife, frightened yet power-
fully lured by fantasy-images of Arab terrorists which are fraught

with erotic attraction and the promise of release through destruction. After My Michael, Oz wrote two novellas, put together in a volume called Unto Death (1971), which was followed by a third novel, Touch the Water, Touch the Wind (1973, English translation, 1974).

"Before His Time" exhibits many of the characteristic themes and motifs of Jackal Country (1965), the early volume of stories in which it appears; but it is also remarkable in the way its sure artistic control and the innovative boldness of its narrative technique—in a writer twenty-two years old—adumbrate Oz's finest later work. More particularly, "Before His Time" anticipates his extraordinary novella, Crusade, in substituting for conventional narration a prose-poem method of exposition through imagistic motifs, and reiterated verbal formulas, an incantatory language used to evoke a mood, to intimate a subject beyond the grasp of words.

The narrative data of the story are minimal and, in the end, of secondary interest: a father has left his wife and two children on the kibbutz, eventually to become a geography teacher in Jerusalem; the son is killed during a reprisal raid; the father recalls a chance encounter in the Negev with his son two months before the young officer's death. The temporal sequence of these events is fractured and reconstituted, and the events are not so much laid out in a plot as circled around by the narrator's imagination which, as it works over them, elicits from them portentous images, eerie tonalities of implication.

A prominent instance of this whole technique is the use of the slaughtered bull as a ring-structure device to begin and end the story. At first, the bull would seem to be a symbolic analogue for Ehud, the slaughtered son (a connection reinforced by the fact that tableaux of the life of Jesus, the archetypal crucified son, are to be made from the bull's skin). As we read on, though, we come more and more to see that the deeper analogy is between the bull and Dov, the father, who, like the barnyard creature, has lost his virility —twice stricken by almost fatal heart attacks—and who proves vulnerable, at least symbolically, to the savagery of the jackal world by which Samson the bull is literally bitten and brought low. Our initial inclination to link the bull with Ehud, now corrected in the direction of Dov, leads us to a sense of overlap between the destinies of the father and the son. One is even tempted to speculate whether the nameless nocturnal visitor poised on Dov's steps might not be

Ehud, finally coming, from the kingdom of the dead, to fulfill his promise of a sudden nighttime visit to his father—perhaps as a grisly emissary of the third and lethal heart attack.

It is a measure of the story's richness that it swarms with such suggestions which are intimated in complex and oblique ways that never allow us to draw comfortably resolved conclusions about them. Images and motifs beget other images and motifs. They interlace, exfoliate, turn back on themselves with expanded meanings. At the outset, the slaughtered bull is immediately associated with alien Arab and alien Christian, with the coded enemy language of the church bells that will ring out again at the end of the story, with the color imagery that will play so central a role in the gray Dov Sirkin's geographical fantasies drawn in crayons on sheet after sheet of graph paper.

Perhaps the most crucial motif in the story, and in all Oz's fiction of kibbutz life, is that of enclosure. The kibbutz enterprise is seen as a dream of overweening rationality, an attempt to impose a neat geometic order on the seething chaos of the natural world. The kibbutz needs to fence out the natural world, and so, near the beginning of the exposition, the breaking in of a jackal from the realm without sets up disturbing resonances. Dov Sirkin in his earlier years had been the man of the kibbutz par excellence, "His walls solid, his kibbutz fenced." We come to realize, however, that his repeated activity of bolting doors, closing shutters, barring eyes (that same verb is used for the eyes of Samson the bull) is a reflex of turning away from the unsettling darkness of reality to an illusory light. In his ultimate withdrawal to the locked and shuttered Jerusalem apartment—into which fingers of darkness will nevertheless "insinuate" themselves—Dov undertakes a compulsive parody of the kibbutz rationalist enterprise by laying out on paper that pedantically geometric world of vast proportions and mad orderliness. Even in this fantasy world, moreover, unconscious forces erupt in the mountainous landscape with "wrathful labyrinths and bursting caves" that threaten to tear apart the delicate texture of willed order.

In a kind of fiction that moves through poetic language from the surface details of kibbutz life to a haunting meditation on how civilized man tries to contain uncontainable, inimical existence, much that is significant takes place in the operation of metaphor on what it purports to describe. Over against Dov's world, whose *emblems are the ruler and the compass, implements to trace artificial constructs of the human mind, the untamed realm of darkness and jackals roils with violent activity: whipping, biting, cutting, tearing, screaming. Oz's vision of hostile nature is, of course, extravagantly anthropomorphic, but that rhetorical choice seems right and convincing, perhaps because nature is envisaged so sharply as a projection of all that is suppressed within man.*

The synesthetic linking of color and sound here subtly reinforces this argument from man to the jackals and back to man again. A bull's flesh shrieks red, a bay drawn by Dov screams blue, kiosk counters scream yellow smells, dogs emit a greenish laughter akin to that of their wild cousins—but the jackal's howl itself has no color, coming from a place in existence where the bright demarcations of Dov's crayon box are useless. Precisely because what the image of the jackals nihilistically denies is so basic to humanity, these wild creatures must be described anthropomorphically as base, obscene, malevolent; and at the very end it is they who have the last word, or laugh, answering the annunciation of the church bells with peals of blasphemy.

BEFORE HIS TIME (1962)
AMOS OZ

I

HOT AND POWERFUL and hulking was the bull on the night of slaughter.

During the night Samson was butchered. Early in the morning, before five o'clock milking, a meat dealer came from Nazareth and took his carcass away in a gray truck. The joints hung on rusty hooks in the butchershops of Nazareth. In regimented phalanxes, roused by pealing church bells, big dung flies stormed the bull's flesh, to wreak a green vengeance upon him.

At eight in the morning an old effendi came, a transistor radio in his hand. He wanted to buy Samson's hide. Radio Ramalla threaded American tunes into the palm of the effendi's hand. Last bead threaded, top of the pops, the station transmitted the latest hit. Wild and unruly, the tune was cast abroad with the cymbal-like backing of church bells. The tune over, the bargaining stopped. The bull's hide has been sold. What will you do, ya Rashid Effendi, with this pelt of Samson, a lordly bull? Ornaments I will make of it, work of the cunning workman, souvenirs for wealthy lady tourists, parchment of variegated pictures: here is the alley of Jesus' dwelling; here a carpenter's workshop, Joseph in the middle; here angels beat clapper and bell and herald the birth of the Savior; and here the Babe himself, his forehead shining light. All work of the parchment workman—glorious creation.

And Rashid Effendi went to Café Za'im, to lay out his morning on a board of *Shesh-Besh.* In his right hand an instrument of joy, and wrapped in his sack a bundle of steaming hide.

A Nazarene wind, heavy-scented, plucks at bell-clappers and tops of cypress trees; its breath swings the butchers' hooks; the bull's flesh shrieks red.

II

At the height of his vigor was Samson the bull, pride of the kibbutz herdsmen, most glorious of the valley's bulls. Had not Samson's virility failed, Yosh would not have come upon him in the night, to tear his throat open with a knife.

Samson slept on his feet, his eyes barred, head bent, his exhalations hot and damp, the vapor of his breath mingling with the scent of sticky bull's sweat. The beam of a flashlight stroked the bull's body and lingered on his neck.

Poisoned baits, mused Yosh. The scream of the jackals came to his ear. A rabid jackal had broken into the shed at the end of November and bitten Samson in a leg. Samson had kicked the mad creature and had killed him. But that same bite destroyed Samson's virility. Then did he freeze and wilt, the most fiery of all bulls in the Valley of Jezreel.

With soft and quiet hand Yosh took hold of the bull's jaw and raised his darkling head. The bull exhaled deeply, and his dimmed eyes shuddered—a vibration very near blinking. Yosh drew the knife up to Samson's Adam's apple. The bull's nostrils suddenly widened, and his front leg stamped in the dung at his feet. Still his eyes did not open. They were barred for a long time after the blade had torn his skin and his flesh and the artery that goes from the bull's heart to his head.

Fine, inquisitive droplets sprouted. The bull grunted an uneasy sigh. He moved his head from right to left as if driving away an obstinate fly or as if refusing to accept the last statement of his interlocutor. A thin and hesitating trickle followed, as though spurting from a cut during a hasty shave. "Nu," said Yosh.

Samson lashed his muddy hind quarters with his tail and let out a nervous, warm sigh. "Nu," repeated Yosh, and delved into his pocket. The cigarette came to his mouth, damp and filthy. What made Yosh toss the lighted match straight at the bull's brow?

Samson lowed in faint pain, retreated with a clumsy step, and raised a splendid head to consider the man.

Now his blood burst forth in a rush and flooded in black cataracts, bubbling in the dim glow of the flashlight. Yosh was filled with nausea and impatience. "Nu," he said again. The view of the showering blood worked upon his full bladder. What stopped him from pissing in the presence of the expiring bull? Slowly, slowly, Samson expired. Hot and dense his blood. Upon his knees the bull knelt. Upon his front ones first. His softening horns tried to butt, and there was nothing to catch their thrust.

At first, the bull's eyes dimmed while his skin continued to twitch. Then the moving skin stilled, and alone, a front leg stamped in the mud, like a blind man's stick. Tranquillity came at the death of that leg. The bull's tail—lax—beat once, and again, like the wave of a parting hand. Last came a convulsion which rolled up the bull's body as if Samson were fitting himself to the mold of the vehicle brought by the dealer from Nazareth; or as if he were trying to die a fetus.

"Nu, nu," said Yosh.

Afterward, the kibbutz herdsman finished his cigarette and voided his bladder and directed his steps to the small kitchen of the night watchwoman.

Zashka, the divorced wife of Dov Sirkin, gave Yosh milk, hot and sweet, to drink from a porcelain cup.

Zashka is a wrinkled woman, and her eyes are deeply inlaid, like those of an owl. The porcelain cup is thick and clumsy. Zashka's small and shriveled body emits a sharp coldness. Hot, fragrant steam rises from the cup; a skin of fat floats upon the surface of the milk.

III

Until the gleam of dawn Zashka crouches in the small kitchen— the kitchen set aside for the cooking of the babies' food, as distinct from the common kitchen which stands near the dining hall—her sharp face resting upon her knees, her knees braced by her arms, all of her like a penknife with the blade drawn in and around back. At hourly intervals Zashka, muffled in a man's coat, goes to the children's quarters—straightens out a cover that has slipped, fastens a window to keep out the cold. Between the hours, she perches upon her stool: deedless and dreamless; a muted lingering in that no-man's land that is between the realm of waking and the kingdom of sleep.

Ever since the day Dov Sirkin abandoned kibbutz and family, something had sharpened in Zashka's face. Ever since the day that Ehud, her firstborn, was killed in a hard-hitting retaliation raid, something went limp in Zashka. More frequent were the long journeys to that no-man's land which is between the kingdoms. Had it not been for the frantic concern of the kibbutz women at their councils, something in her might very well have snapped. Zashka, however, did not lose her bearings; nothing snapped. Just another instance corroborating the tangible efficacy of the organizational patterns and institutions of the kibbutz.

Had the bull bellowed as it was slain, Zashka might have moved her head, and maybe whispered. But Samson chose to die with a groan, not with a cry; and Yosh, too, sipped his milk in silence. He did not linger in order to shorten the night with one of those soldiers' tales habitually on his lips. A young man comes from the dark: drinks, grumbles, takes leave, and back he goes into the dark. Until the morning light, far-away jackals fill the air of the valley with mangled cries. Salvos of weeping, salvos of laughing, whirlpooling hybrids, babies wailing and the jubilation of fools.

At five Zashka goes to her bed. On her way she stops at Geula's, knocks forcefully on her door, and issues a morning greeting. The tone is abrupt, not at all like one of greeting.

Geula Sirkin, the remaining daughter of Zashka and Dov, hurries to the dining room. Her gaze wanders and her hands busy themselves with the large vats. Her nails are chipped and the skin of her palms split; two bitter ravines dig into the ashen slope that is between the end of her nose and the corners of her mouth. It is coffee she's brewing for the early risers.

Geula is not like the rest of her companions—daughters of the kibbutz. They have tanned, well-rounded legs. She has thin, pale legs, covered with a mat of black hair. They have round faces, dark and alert eyes. Geula's features are thin and drawn, her eyes a clouded blue. Although Geula Sirkin is already twenty-six, her cheeks are pockmarked with acne, scratched and reddening. Coffee made in the large vats, muses Geula, will always taste flat. Coffee —the real stuff—has passed from the face of the earth. Ehud would brew coffee with reverence and great ceremony. His visits to the kibbutz were not many, but they were stirring. Ehud would minister over the coffee, like a magician, with spells and incantations. And how enchanted were the kibbutz girls during his visits. All of them. Since the day Ehud was cut down, the secret of the coffee ceremony had been forgotten—the order of precepts pertaining to the small cauldron—all the stages of the precise ceremony. Ehud did not leave the kibbutz; neither did he settle in it. From year to year his service in the army lengthened, he became famous and his return was delayed. He took part in all the reprisal raids; not one did he miss.

As Geula Sirkin's vats raise steam, the valley jackals withdraw, bound for their lairs. The smell of the blood of Samson the bull has troubled their night. Lean, very lean are the valley jackals, drooling and bleary eyed. The jackals' paws are soft, their tails threadbare. At times a jackal will go mad from hunger, and break in. Their night begins with wailing, ends in weird laughter.

In days gone by Dov Sirkin would plant poisoned baits for the jackals and small spring-loaded traps—his own invention. He who laughs last laughs best, Dov used to say long ago—before a future in which he would abandon his family and his kibbutz and go roaming over the land, leaving his fingerprints upon all.

Army regulations don't allow our soldiers to retreat from enemy territory until the wounded and the dead have been evacuated. Why Ehud's corpse was left in no-man's land is a matter better left to an investigating committee. Three nights Ehud remained in no-man's land. The enemy soldiers tried to get the body in order to display it and thus to cover up their defeat. Ehud's comrades foiled this plan by keeping up a steady fire from our territory. At night they would crawl up to him in order to get him out of there. The enemy mounted huge floodlights and banished the darkness. On the fourth night our men dragged him back under great risk. Jackals' teeth had torn the flesh of his cheeks and had demolished his square jaw. Dov came to his son's funeral and forced himself to a clumsy show of affection for his daughter.

Black. Black and bubbling the coffee revels in the wide vats. Seven times it will boil, decrees Geula. Seven times: none failing. Her lips held tight, sucked in. Her teeth are clenched, and her mouth arches like the bent blade of a saber.

IV

At six A.M., the noise of tractors being started reverberates from the shed, and the kibbutz members go out to damp fields. At eight the sun has reached its vexing strength. Human sweat flows in the orchards and rusty pipes gurgle.

In days gone by Dov Sirkin would rule over the orchards. His songs would bubble riotously and his voice would hold the orchards captive in a spirit of broad revelry.

He would glide lightly between ranks of saplings, naked to the waist. How wide and hairy were his shoulders, his chest, his back, his arms. His hips alone were bare of that thick fur.

During summer days there would be a child, with straight nose and square-set jaw, riding on Dov's shoulders. With small and sharp fists Ehud would drum upon his father's head, and Dov would avenge himself upon his son with a mighty swoop; would hurl the boy skyward and catch him again in his arms, this child who never cried for help.

Blocks upon blocks form the orchard. Furrows, ruler-straight and formal, mark one species from the next. The coarse apples known as Alexander the Great, trees of Galia, and trees of juicy Delicious, rows of peach trees with fruit rough and sharp as whisky, plums dark as wine, delicate guavas, and again a block of apples of the kind known as Nonpareil.

In days gone by Dov was master of the orchard. Twenty years have passed since the day he abandoned wife and children, without giving the kibbutz leaders one of those explanations which nourish ideologists whenever they undertake a deep examination of the problems of the kibbutz. The grandfather of Samson the bull reigned over the cattle sheds in those days. Generations of jackals have vanished, but their young ones preserve their heritage and do not incline to innovation. Generation upon generation fills the

reaches of the night with dirges and obscene jubilations—a ca-
cophony of vile hatred and abject flattery.

Dov's departure stirred an outcry of wonder and recrimination.
The deed was not performed in the manner of those days. In
those days, if members left the kibbutz, they were peripheral
figures in the group. And if it was one of the mainstays who left,
he would not do so without delivering an outspoken condemnation,
making a speech: exposing, stigmatizing, rocking foundations.

Dov, as was said, slipped away with no clamor and no con-
troversy, giving no account. He disappeared one morning and did
not return that evening—and not the next day, nor after days
and weeks.

As days went by the anger of the kibbutz faded, and was
replaced by shrugs and incomprehension. After a while, as is usual
in such cases, someone, whoever it was, fabricated a tale of a tourist
—a woman painter from Mexico—the kibbutz nodded knowingly
and doubled its sticky sympathy for Zashka and the children.

In the end the kibbutz settled back into its preoccupations and
its difficulties. As an encampment of world reformers, our activists
tell us, it is in its nature to leave behind weaklings and stragglers.
It is in the nature of things.

Dov went first to Haifa; thence to the desert project, and
thence his ways branched out and his activities varied. Finally he
settled in Jerusalem and became a geography teacher. A heart
attack turned his face gray. A second heart attack forced him to
retire from his post and to sit at home.

V

Dov Sirkin did not stretch, nor yawn, nor move in his chair, nor
blink with his cold steely eyes; and yet he was tired.

He sat at his bulky desk and drew with self-assured strokes.

Two A.M. The yellowish electric bulb is overheated, naked
without a lampshade. A tiny grain of plaster comes off the ceiling
and flutters down upon a very old, green, wooden chair. Dov's
room is orderly with the pedantry of early old age. Every object
rests in its accustomed way, in the same spot where it was laid
before the State's declaration of independence. And yet whoever
enters the room falls upon a loud whirlpooling herd of furniture

bellowing with thick voices. All this due to the odd and wild mixture of colors: a riot of diaphanous pinkish curtains, an antique chest, a round table leaning on mastodon legs, and a shabby black cupboard. Like a spurt of loud revels in the midst of all this, a flowery bedspread, in red and azure. And a black chandelier floats above the chaos: the type of chandelier our great-grandfathers used. In a corner of the room a large flowerpot twists about with its tangled serpents of African cactus. And in the middle—near a bureau decorated with brass embossings glittering in gold and silver shades—the man himself.

Dov lay down the compass and lifted the ruler. He lay down the ruler and sharpened his pencil to a fine point. He sharpened his pencil and picked red and black from a heap of crayons.

In days gone by Dov was a foreman in the Port of Haifa; a soldier in the Bedouin Raiding Unit of His Majesty; gunrunner in South America on behalf of the underground; general staff officer in the battles for independence; development adviser to one of the community leaders in the Negev; and in the end—a teacher of geography.

Dov's head is bent and his neck stretched. His face is cold and lean, each feature functional. An expression of absorbed miserliness spreads over it; a miserliness with no shadow of covetousness or avidity; a miserliness strong and self-assured. Only Dov Sirkin's eyebrows, only those are lavish, as if mocking the square brow above them. His pencil raps rhythmically upon the surface of a page torn from an arithmetic notebook.

Silence. The silence of a deserted Jerusalem suburb, at a deserted hour of night, was adrift in the road tearing off needles and more needles from the tops of pine trees standing in backyards. The torn needles emitted a fine, light rustle which penetrated barred shutters and bristled the hair of black cats upon rusty terrace railings. Dov turned toward the front door. It was barred as it should be. Doubt lingered.

A distant jackal screamed a squeaky fragment, like a first violin too hasty in tuning and giving the lead. Many years had passed since the day Ehud appeared at his father's home. He came once for a youth congress held in Jerusalem and stopped at his father's house. Six years later they chanced upon each other in

Beersheba, and Ehud promised half-heartedly to drop in. Some night or other, he said. In the summer we will hold maneuvers in the mountains of Adulam. Don't be startled if I come at night. Did he really intend to come or was it an empty promise? Shortly after that promise, he was killed. Dov barred his eyes and opened them wide, rocked his head, and crossed his legs to shake off drowsiness. Church bells from within the city walls sent out signals to the bells of Bethlehem, and both exchanged confidences with the church bells in Jerusalem outside the wall.

VI

Dov lay down the black and the red and marked a tiny arc with the compass. Concentrating then on the blue, he belabored the crayon for a long while.

A giant harbor stretched out upon the sheet of paper. Depths of azure waters floated up and cascaded in successive floods from gray eyes to long fingers and from fingers to bounding lead ranging over the graph-paper. Azure streamed from the crayon, spread, and came to rest upon the surface of the sheet.

The quays of Dov's harbor are wider than the widest quays. Its piers are longer than any ever built by human hand. Its cranes are more gigantic than the biggest that creak in any harbor of any land. Its warehouses are tall as the silence insinuating dark fingers through the cracks of Dov Sirkin's shutters. A tangle of ways, tracks, bridges, roads, twists about like a streaming coil of reptiles. Yellow machines shower sparks: hard-edged power. Steel and rubber ribbons are arrayed in festive frozen splendor, capable of unloading mountains of merchandise from the entrails of gigantic vessels. Gaping pumps overhang the water, poised to swallow mighty morsels with a metallic roar: snatched, unmasticated gulps. Had the biggest ocean liner been lured to drop its anchor by Dov's piers, it would have carried no more weight than a laughable, dwarfish object among the wharfs created by Dov.

The blue crayon filled the bay to the brim with mighty waters; it circled and capered with delicate strokes, shooting water with twitching spouts into the maze of crisscrossing canals.

A stranger's footsteps echoed and mounted from the stair-well. The stranger leaned heavily upon the railing, and the railing responded with a cracked and senile wail, a blunt ache.

Dov stirred from his seat and with a slam of his fist pulled down the shutter on a window—whose paint was peeling, its hinges unstuck. Spiderwebs of starlight stretch across the road, from balcony to balcony, from cypress tops to garbage cans, from stone wall-crests to cracks among the paving stones—a silent film upon the face of the earth. A bluish mist floats up to meet it from the sewers.

A piece of plaster fell from the ceiling, bigger than the previous one. Tiny crumbs of whitewash soiled the red and azure bedspread —that spread to which the room is hostile.

The footsteps on the stairs broke off. The stranger stood on the first landing. The steps stopped echoing, but no key was inserted in its keyhole, no door was opened, no doorbell clamored. Perhaps the stranger lingered as he fixed his piercing eyes upon the gray, peeling paint, on the doors of slumbering flats. Perhaps he was committing to memory the names of the tenants on the letterboxes. Dov clenched his teeth. His jaw tightened like a fist. He rose, concealed the sheet in one of the drawers of the brown chest, with a sudden swoop tore a sheet of graph paper from a thinned notebook, and drew the map of a mountainous country with a firm hand and cold eye. His chin jutted like the sword of a duelist.

VII

Dov Sirkin has gray eyes, a gray face and gray hair. On his body a light, boyish, bright blue shirt, hides a hairy body covered by a network of strong gray sinews. This body is built to stay at the height of its vigor for many long years. Its flaw is not apparent. The exterior is hairy and powerful. Thick hands, shoulders set at a fair angle, and the back of a stevedore. It is hard to believe from his appearance that he is hollow, corroded within. A weak heart sits inside him, the left auricle enlarged beyond its proper measure, its walls deformed and, after two warnings, about to give out.

Dov Sirkin is around sixty. Many years ago drops of lead were blended with his blood, and made him peerless among men. With the dead years the lead that was in his blood melted, until it was forced into the tips of his fingers, into the slopes of his jaw, and no more.

Dov drew a country of mountains. A green patrol car races

down the road, ripping the silence; and the silence sews up its tatters again with a great hand—soft, dreamy, cool. The car has slipped away, down the gradient, and penetrated the southern alleys, down toward the railway station.

A land of basalt mountains. Black, they stab the moon-and-star-embroidered silken sail with their snow-covered points and tear wide rents in it. Stone monuments, daggers of rock, summits drawn like bared knives in drunken alleys. Crazed ravines score the sides of boulders. Frightful mounds scheme to plunge into the abyss in primordial cascades of crushed cliff. Contorted fingers of stone point at herds of chaotic crevices indented with barriers, ten times deeper than the deepest crevices in creation. Crevice after crevice gapes in wrathful labyrinths and bursting caves; and then the roar, the horror, and all congeals.

In the end Dov came to a stop and considered the sheet. Hard, blue, and cool, the lead lay heavy on the lower part of his face. His pencil set down the altitudes of the summits. The slopes of the Sirkin Mountains could proudly defy the snow-covered peaks of the Alps.

VIII

Out of grief, or out of hunger and cold, a jackal of the Bethlehem jackals wailed. Instantly jackals, five in number, answered back in a frenzy of corrupt laughter; merry malice. The wind stopped blowing and listened intently.

The stairs began creaking again. A shudder ranged over a back, tickled a neck, entrenched itself in the soles of two feet. Fingers trembled, turned pale. The stranger trod heavily upon three steps, burst into a wet cough, cleared phlegm from his throat, then was silent. The creaking of the steps floated away like vapor. Dov rushes to his kitchen, bars a shutter, locks a door, seals a lattice.

In days gone by Dov was a teacher of geography. Hundreds of pupils passed through his hands, paying honor to his grayness, obeying his fluent voice, confabulating during breaks, exchanging whispers about the events of the history of the mysterious Mister X. His fingers were long and so thick as to cause wonder; always white with chalk, wielding a long ruler and wandering with self-assurance among mountains and borders and cities and the complexities of variegated maps.

At times he would joke in class. Threadbare, gray jokes. He was spare of enthusiasm. If he ever caught fire, he never kindled his students.

Twice or three times a year he would don khaki, pick up a bagful of maps and a small satchel—always small, enviable for its spare weight—and lead a school outing. The sight of him in hiking gear, gun in hand, was odd and startling. His pupils would talk of his heroic deeds during the years of Arab riots and of underground activities. Tales of wonder, partly schoolboy hyperboles, partly deeds performed by others, and the rest feats that Dov really accomplished in days gone by, in the days when he was a commander in the underground with cold voice and countenance.

He would climb the mountains of Galilee with several groups, or drag a column of sweltering, grumbling teenagers over the steep slopes leading to the gulleys of the Negev.

During one of those Negev excursions Dov and his pupils were stopped in Beersheba. The army representative instructed them to change their itinerary and to avoid wandering about in the desert of Par'an, because of the worsening of the security situation. He was a thin and tall army officer, his head curly, his eyes elongated and blinking, his jaw square, his uniform self-consciously slipshod, his name Ehud Sirkin. It was six years since Dov had seen his son's face. He once came to Jerusalem to a youth congress and spent the night at his father's house. The next day Dov had accompanied him to the vehicle returning to the kibbutz and tried to buy his sympathy with nervous backslapping and roughhewn phrases, seeking to imitate the clumsy diction of the kibbutzniks.

"If you head in that direction," said Ehud, "you will walk into an ambush. No kidding. Go past the gulleys and straight to Eilat. And that, too, you could do without."

The teacher pulled down his shoulders, embarrassed that suddenly all his greatness was dwarfed in the eyes of his pupils. In days gone by he had served as commander in the underground; and his rank was much higher than Ehud's today. "I know, I know," he stammered. The Negev sun pumped sticky sweat from all his pores. "I was in the Negev when you were a toddler."

"Fine," said Ehud. "If you know the area you won't get lost. That, too, happens around here. Tourists trip up the army all over the place. Absolute anarchy." Ehud pushed his hand to his head and dug into his abundant curls. After a couple of minutes he said good-bye and turned to go.

"Listen," Dov called after him with a hesitant, nervous voice. "Listen! In my time we would have chased that gang away within twenty-four hours. We wouldn't let it roam all over the place." Ehud stopped in his tracks and turned about, startled. "Listen," Dov added, "Geula stops by sometimes, why don't you?"

"Sure," answered Ehud with a careless, tired voice. "In the summer we'll come up for maneuvers in Adulam. Don't be startled if I come by at night. I'll see. I'll find an occasion."

Two months later, Dov had occasion to meet that same officer again. His jaw had changed: small nocturnal predators had demolished it.

During each outing Dov would raise his voice a little—only a little—and lecture, fluent and familiar with the subject: about terraced cultivation in the Galilee or about commercial routes to distant continents, via the approach to the Red Sea.

His eyes were wide open, fixing glances sharp as a compass point at the map. Of a sudden he would stop the column, trudging with indifferent weariness, and hurriedly point out a silent ruin, a secretive mound; the skeleton of a camel, a hyena or jackal; a spring hidden to the eyes of the inexperienced hiker.

During the days following the outing he would leaf through the composition books of his pupils which described in detail the outing, with all its trivial events. He would borrow the notebooks from the literature teacher. He would not tire of reading even a hundred or more compositions that recounted the wonders of that same outing. Never was this habit made known to his pupils. At times he would copy a short description from one of the books and hide it in a drawer, one of the drawers in the brown chest, so comically Berlin-style. Yet as a teacher he was strict. His teaching overflowed with names, numbers, tables, laborious home assignments, troublesome tests and merciless final marks, complaints and counter-complaints.

Each year Geula would come to her father's house. She would come on the eve of Independence Day. The day after she would go back to her kibbutz. All through the night and half the day she would sit on Dov's tiny terrace and look at people dancing and the wonderful entertainers; and she would become feverishly excited at the view of the military parade. How handsome Ehud looked, graceful and tall at the head of his soldiers. From the day Ehud was cut down Geula discontinued her visits.

At first, Dov was happy she had stopped coming. After a while he regretted his happiness. Perhaps her sharp features blurred in his memory, the bent saber of her lips softened, her pockmarks faded and the chill she emanated lost its sharp edge.

IX

Dov lay down the map of the land of mountains and drew a foaming river, not the kind of river flowing anywhere upon the face of man's earth. He slit a long canal, straight as a ruler, put up a system of rigorous secondary canals, cast out a complex network of slopes, inclines, dams, and reservoirs; all this with the exact calculations involved. He drew, and hastened to set figures for gradient degrees, cement strength, steel resistance, stone stubbornness, earth endurance, and the pressure of a great quantity of many waters.

An hour had passed since the sound of footsteps in the stairwell stopped. Now the stairs were trod heavily again with a rough and deliberate trampling. The heart attack had come near the end of the school year. Frequent nausea marked the days between the first and second attack. In the end Dov surrendered, abandoned his occupation, and withdrew into his room to attend to whatever it was he did. He decreed for himself rules of moderation and kept watch that he might not drive his heart to a new excess. A housebound old man, his face gray, congealed lead in his fingertips and in the underside of his jaw.

He would obtain his livelihood from writing hefty articles, brimming with complex tables, for geographic monthlies, development reviews, industrial yearbooks. For additional income he would photograph luminous, delicate landscapes, but the weekly would print them at the bottom of page sixteen, squeezed between a quiz and a recipe, leaving none of their beauty; nothing but a smear of print, gray and blurred.

Dov Sirkin's photographs end up in Zashka's heavy album. Week by week, one by one, the divorcée cuts out the smear of print that clouds the soft landscapes. With thick glue Zashka pastes Dov's photographs to her black pages. Her teeth are clenched during the

procedure, and her eyes shine. Cold, cunning wrinkles wind from
the corners of her mouth and twist her chin.

In the morning hours Dov habitually looks out through the window
facing east, exchanging scorching glances with the rising sun as it
gains height over the mountains of Moab, fixing its rays on the
boulders of the mountains of Jerusalem. Bare mountains, shadow-
etched mountains, mountains hiding shadowy monasteries with
weighty walls, gravid groves, and booming bells. At noon he would
sit in the easy chair on his tiny balcony, among cactus tins and
fern pots, looking at the street. A crooked Jerusalem street, stone
hedges and big barred windows. A caravan of garbage cans along
cracked tarmac sidewalks. Kingdom of cheating, evasive cats. His
eyes would take in the ringing steps of passersby and pull up from
the street endless strings of quiet brown yearning.

At dusk he would share the evening headlines with the
benches of the nearby avenue. As darkness closed in he would sip
orangeade at the kiosk, and his leaden fingers would tighten and
close around the glass tumbler. He enjoyed observing the man at
the counter wiping with a worn blue rag the cracked marble slab
that held soda faucets and brightly colored candy boxes.

At night he drew.

His cupboards overflowed with sketches, landscape photographs, and plaster molds; exact calculations of raw materials;
expenses for building, paving, and transportation; timetables of
trains, fastest in the world; winding rails flowing into long tunnels,
carved into the entrails of rocks, rocks of the lands of fancy.
Avenues carrying a thousand water fountains, bathed in streaming
light, crossing the centers of dream towns. High towns lifting
vaulted towers high above the peaks, looking down upon cleaved
sea bays screaming blue.

X

A wind wandered in the streets. It took into its arms the cover
of a rusted garbage can and hurled it against the pavement of the
road and the stone fences. The wind played cruel pranks with its
victim.

Light and quick elastic steps came up to the apartment threshhold. One wonders how many hours the stranger needed to come from the street to Dov's door. Why did he linger so long on the ground floor, not entering any of the apartments? Why did he advance barely three steps an hour ago, then stop? And what made him hurry now? It seems he's bounding up the stairs, swallowing steps two by two. Dov dragged his chair noisily and moved, shoulders drooping, to the door.

He who laughs last laughs best.

In days gone by Dov would bar his shutters and put on the light in his room at the kibbutz. His walls solid, his kibbutz fenced. The settlement guards, armed and awake, stand between him and the darkened fields. Lanterns on the fence posts warn off the jackals and whip the fields' flesh with blows of light. Dov in his clothes stretches upon his bed, enjoying a quick nap, his face covered with the morning paper. His small children roll on the straw mat, and Zashka's knitting needles click in soft rhythm. A choir of jackals howls. Ehud and Geula answer back with innocent, pampered laughter.

Lean, very lean are the jackals, bleary eyed and drooling. Soft are the jackals' paws, their tails threadbare. Their eyes glint with sparks of cunning, their ears perk in expectation, their mouths always open, their teeth shining hate.

The jackals circle round on tiptoe; their noses are damp and sniffly, and they do not dare approach the fence. Round about they creep; they gather in bands as for a celebration, a ring of tremulous jackals circling at the edges of the shadow, closing in on the island of light. Until morning they fill the air with wailing, and their hunger shatters in successive waves upon the shores of the fenced lighted island. At times one will be fired with madness, will burst with mouth dribbling saliva into the enemy fort, will spring to the sheds in muddled distraction, and will bite a horse or a bull until the enemy kills him.

The jackal's comrades take up a dirge, wailing of fear, impotence, abasement, anger, and expectation of a day to come.

A day will come. Slowly, like festive priests at a ceremony of mourning, they will approach the boy's body. With supple, caressing steps—with soft, damp nose. To begin with they will stop nearby and take up a stand in a circle, sniffing quietly. Then one will approach the victim and will bend till he touches with the tip of

the tongue the dead man's body. The next one will approach and
rip away the soldier's garments with sharpened fangs. A third and
a fourth and a fifth will come to lick his solid flesh. The first will
break forth with a low salvo of restrained laughter; and the whole
congregation will stiffen at the signal. Composed and festive, the
first one will approach, and with clear-cut movement lop off a
joint. The assembly will then roar in relieved laughter.

An eternal curse stands between the housedwellers and the
inhabitants of mountain and ravine. At times, deep in the night,
the pampered house dog makes out the voice of his accursed
brother. Not over the fields does the voice come. Deep inside the
dog his foe dwells. From the depths he sends forth salvos of
greenish laughter.

"My son," said Dov and his hand closed in fear around the
brass doorknob.

To begin with came a light cough.

After that followed a wild trembling; it hit, faded, fled. Weariness came in its place, heavy and bristling. Dressed in mauve, a
shudder hastened by, in coarse successive waves. Dim, dull, and
distant, the pain crouched. The pain is sly and stubborn; its face
that of a muffled monk repeating twisted verses by rote. A worn
bluntness had its say, and retreated in the face of clenching teeth.
With the gnashing came the sound of laughter from the choir of
jackals in the mountains of Bethlehem. The evil laughter runs, runs
along the length of empty night streets; climbs, as a loathsome ape,
along the drainpipes of the house; penetrates and shatters into
myriad jagged splinters.

At last came the convulsion, soft and lenient. True, when the
kibbutz was founded, Ehud, we attempted to introduce new ways;
until matters cried to high heaven that no remedy was possible.
I said to myself, it will be enough to perform worthy, handsome
deeds; and I did not know, Ehud, that our fingerprints do not
remain imprinted on the face of the waters. How loathsome is an
old age stained with masturbation, Zashka: I am last, and I do
not laugh.

XI

Some first cracks broke into the walls of night, and a light-hating
bird gave out a cry of hatred. As though stealing in, a pale red
something arrived and filtered fingers of light through the fissures

of the shutters facing east. A choir of sparrows whipped through the silence, with resonant hymns.

At last day came. Kerosene wagons sang out; children hastened to their studies; counters screamed yellow smells; newspaper vendors announced the revelation of secrets; shops opened, rolling up their shutters like eyes waking and blinking and opening slowly.

The car of a cabinet minister slipped by on whispering tires, escort motorcycles screaming before it.

A wrinkled old woman crossed the road with liquid legs and trembling hand. Children pointed derisively in her direction and plotted a prank. An onrushing car gave warning to the children with a wailing of brakes, and raced down other roads.

A coil of lady tourists, yellow hair and smeared cheeks, crowded enthusiastically around a tray of antiques: ornaments and holy pictures, all glory of art, work of the parchment workman, true bull's hide, strong and ancient—proclaims Rashid Effendi.

So festive are the bells of the monasteries. So base and obscenely riotous the jackals, answering the annunciation of the clappers with twisted laughter, derision of imbeciles. Evil instigations are secreted in their heart. Evil and blasphemy.

Translation by Gavriel Moses

FACING THE FORESTS

A. B. YEHOSHUA

INTRODUCTION

AVRAHAM B. YEHOSHUA *(born 1936) is generally regarded as one of the two most important figures of the generation of prose-writers that came to prominence in the 1960s (the other is Amos Oz). Except for some writing for the stage, he has limited his work to short fiction, and his production has been relatively small, but his symbolic stories established a new voice, a new narrative mode, for Hebrew fiction, and have won considerable critical esteem. Yehoshua's first volume of stories,* The Death of the Old Man *(1962), consists of short pieces, often parable-like, marked by vivid elements of fantasy, with signs of influence from both Kafka and Agnon.* Facing the Forests *(1968), a group of four longer stories, is more original in conception: the symbolic patterns here emerge more naturally from a faithful representation of indigenous Israeli characters, manners, social settings.*

Like Amos Oz, Yehoshua has repeatedly used his fictions to explore the shadowy underside of ambivalence in an Israeli consciousness beleaguered by unrelenting conflict with the Arabs. In political life, he has argued passionately for the need to continue an unremitting search for alternatives to armed confrontation; professionally, he is enough involved in the Establishment to have served

353

as Dean of Students at Haifa University. In his fiction, he has sought to face unflinchingly the fears and covert desires that may seem subversive both in the private life of the individual and in the individual's connection with his society.

The political symbolism of "Facing the Forests" is transparent, but one would unfairly reduce the story to read it merely as a political allegory. The national forest that has been planted over the site of a destroyed Arab village suggests, with the symbolic aptness of a guilt-ridden psychology though not necessarily with historical accuracy, the State of Israel itself. The fact that the graduate student is trying to do research on the Crusades provides a further clue to the political symbolism because Arab propaganda has frequently attempted to draw a historical analogy between Israel and the Crusader-state as a European intrusion eventually to be swept away. Gradually, the isolated student, staring day and night out into the manmade forest, develops a fascination with the idea of the village that once stood there, enters into a complicity with the mute Arab who is plotting the destruction of the forest, and finally experiences a sense of exhilaration when the awaited flames burst out and he can imagine the long-vanished village rising in the spirals of smoke.

Despite these obvious allusions to Israel's historical predicament, a more general human ambivalence is also implied in the story's use of the local situation. As we move in a typical Yehoshua pattern from the frustrations of impotence—here, the unwritten research paper—to the thirst for destruction, we get a sense of the balked consciousness of civilized man secretly longing for the cataclysm that will raze all the artificial hedging structures of human culture. The steadily generalizing perspective that characterizes virtually all Yehoshua's stories is clear from the opening sentences of "Facing the Forests." The unnamed graduate student, with his postponed exams, his unwritten papers, his bureaucratically approved documents, at once becomes an exemplar of contemporary futility. The first sentences of the story introduce us immediately to the characteristic Yehoshua world, which is a world of incompletions. These incompletions manifest themselves both in projects undertaken and in acts of communication attempted: frustration in both directions is what finally leads the graduate student to his eagerness for the consuming flame.

"Words weary him," we are told of the protagonist at the very outset, "his own, let alone the words of others." Language, having

proved a pathetically inadequate instrument of communication and of knowledge, only confirms the individual in his loneliness; and so the plot of the story is really a progressive disengagement from words. The student takes with him to his lonely post in the forest suitcases stuffed with words—the books he is to read for his research paper—but he soon neglects these entirely. His only human companions at the forest station are an Arab who cannot speak at all, and an Arab girl, whose language is unintelligible to him. As he contemplates the forest, "words . . . dropped away from him like husks," and, at a late point in the story, he concludes that "Trees have taken the place of words for me, forests the place of books." The contradictory nature of the forest itself, a vast growing thing planned and planted by man, is reflected in the plaques with words, the names of donors, bizarrely affixed to the wordless trees. In the protagonist's frustration with words—then his abandonment of them—fire becomes his language, the only common language between him and the mute Arab, and thus the whole process of disengagement from words, ending in smoldering destruction, has a certain grimly monitory aspect.

Yehoshua's view of the possibilities of human nature is bleak enough; what makes it distinctive is the quality of imaginative wit through which it is conveyed. Yehoshua's prose is colloquially terse, understated, quick-paced, avoiding all the obstrusively literary effects that marked the writing of Yizhar's generation and that, in another way, frequently characterize the work of Amos Oz. The general consequence is an astringent, ironic, shrewdly incisive presentation of character and situation. If the failure of human relation is a common theme of modern literature, Yehoshua's handling of it is noteworthy for the wryly comic effect of poignant farce, delineated in an efficient, unemphatic prose, through which this experience is represented.

Perhaps the ultimate act of derisively inadequate communication conveyed in this fashion in "Facing the Forests" is the visit paid to the fire-watcher in his lonely station by his former mistress: "Only toward sunset does he finally manage to undress her. The binoculars are still on his chest, pressed between their bodies. From time to time he coolly interrupts his kisses and caresses, raises the binoculars to his eyes and inspects the forest." The obsession of the fire-watcher, redoubling that condition of isolation in which we found him at the beginning of the story, has grown so imperceptibly that until this juncture we scarcely realized it had reached the point of mania. Now that realization suddenly explodes in a finely comic revelation through the single word of dialogue by which the student explains his bizarre interruption to his sexual partner as she lies beneath him: " 'Duty,' he whispers apologetically, smiling oddly to the naked, embarrassed woman." The moment illustrates Yehoshua's characteristic technique at its best: the situation has a psychological plausibility, even in its strange incongruity; it is sharply realized with a great economy of means; the sad comedy generated exposes that perverse capacity of humanity to act at cross-purposes with itself which is Yehoshua's recurrent subject.

FACING THE FORESTS (1963)
A. B. YEHOSHUA

I

ANOTHER WINTER lost in fog. As usual he did nothing; postponed examinations, left papers unwritten. He had completed all his courses long ago, attended all the lectures, and the string of signatures on his tattered student card testified that all had performed their duty toward him, silently disappeared, and left the rest of the task in his own limp hands. But words weary him; his own, let alone the words of others. He drifts from one rented room to another, rootless, jobless. But for an occasional job tutoring backward children he would starve to death. Here he is approaching thirty and a bald spot crowns his wilting head. His defective eyesight blurs many things. His dreams at night are dull. They are uneventful; a yellow waste, where a few stunted trees may spring up in a moment of grace, and a naked woman. At student revels he is already looked at with faint ridicule. The speed with which he gets drunk is a regular part of the program. He never misses a party. They need him still. His limp figure is extremely popular and there is no one like him for bridging gaps between people. His erstwhile fellow students have graduated since and may be seen carrying bulging briefcases, on their way to work every morning of the week. Sometimes, at noon, re-

turning from their offices, they may encounter him in the street with
his just-awake eyes: a gray moth in search of its first meal. They,
having heard of his dissipations, promptly pronounce the
unanimous, half-pitying, half-exasperated decree: "Solitude!"

Solitude is what he needs. For he is not without talent nor does
he lack brains. He needs to strengthen his willpower.

He, as a rule, will drop his arms by his sides in a gesture of pious
despair, back up against the nearest available wall, languidly cross
his legs and plead in a whisper:

"But where? Go on, tell me, where?"

For look, he himself craves solitude. He plainly needs to
renew his acquaintance with words, to try and concentrate on the
material that threatens ever to wear him down. But then he would
have to enter prison. He knows himself (a sickly smile): if there
should be the tiniest crack of escape through, he would make it a
tunnel at once. No, please, no favors. Either—or.

Some content themselves with this feeble excuse, shrug their
shoulders wryly, and go their way. But his real friends, those whose
wives he loves as well, two budding lecturers who remember him
from days gone by, remember him favorably for the two or three
amazingly original ideas that he had dropped at random during his
student days—friends who are concerned for his future—these two
are well aware that the coming spring is that much more dangerous
to him, that his desultory affairs with women will but draw zeal
from the blue skies. Is it any wonder, then, if one fine day they will
catch hold of him in the street, their eyes sparkling. "Well, your
lordship, we've found the solution to your lordship's problem at
last." And he will be quick to show an expectant eagerness, though
cunning enough to leave himself ample means of retreat.

"What?"

The function of forest scout. A fire-watcher. Yes, it's something
new. A dream of a job, a plum. Utter, profound solitude. There he
will be able to scrape together his crumbled existence.

Where did they get the idea?

From the papers, yes, from a casual skimming of the daily
papers.

He is astonished, laughs inordinately, hysterically almost. What
now? What's the idea? Forests . . . What forests? Since when do we
have forests in this country? What do they mean?

But they refuse to smile. For once they are determined. Before
he has time to digest their words they have burned the bridges over
which he had meant to escape, as usual. "You said, either—or. Here
is your solution."

He glances at his watch, pretending haste. Will not a single
spark light up in him then? For he, too, loathes himself, doesn't he?

II

And so, when spring has set the windows ajar, he arrives early
one morning at the Afforestation Department. A sunny office, a
clerk, a typist, several typists. He enters quickly, armed with impressive recommendations, heralded by telephone calls. The man in
charge of the forests, a worthy character edging his way to old age,
is faintly amused (his position permits him as much), grins to himself. Much ado about nothing, about such a marginal job. Hence he
is curious about the caller, even considers rising to receive him.
The plain patch of barrenness atop the head of the candidate adds
to his stature. The fellow inspires surely trust, is surely meant for
better things.

"Are you certain that this is what you want? The observation
post is a grim place. Only really primitive people can bear such
solitude. What is it you wish to write? Your doctorate?"

No, sad to say, he is still at the elementary stages of his study.

Yes, he has wasted much time.

No, he has no family.

Yes, with glasses, his vision is sound.

Gently the old manager explains, that in accordance with a certain semiofficial agreement, this work is reserved for social cases only
and not for how-shall-I-put-it, romantics, ha-ha, intellectuals in
search of solitude . . . However, he is prepared, just this once, to
make an exception and include an intellectual among the wretched
assortment of his workers. Yes, he is himself getting sick of the
diverse social cases, the invalids, the cripples, the cranks. A fire breaks
out, and these fellows will do nothing but stand and stare panic-
stricken at the flames till the fire brigade arrives. Whenever he is
forced to send out one such unstable character he stays awake nights
thinking what if in an obscure rage, against society or whatever, the
fire-watcher should himself set the forest on fire. He feels certain

that he, the man in front of him here, though occupied with affairs
of the mind, will be sufficiently alert to his duty to abandon his
books and fight the fire. Yes, it is a question of moral values.

Sorry, the old man has forgotten what it is his candidate wishes
to write? A doctorate?

Once more he apologizes. He is still, sad to say, at the elementary stages of his study. Yes, he has wasted much time. Indeed, he has
no family.

A young secretary is called in.

Then he is invited to sign an inoffensive little contract for six
months: spring, summer (ah, summer is dangerous!), and half the
autumn. Discipline, responsibility, vigilance, conditions of dismissal.
A hush descends while he runs his eyes cursorily over the document.
Manager and secretary are ready with a pen, but he prefers to sign
with his own. He signs several copies. First salary due on April the
fifth. Now he eases himself into his chair, unable to rise, tired still.
He is not used to waking so early. Meanwhile he tries to establish
some sort of contact, display an interest. He inquires about the size
of the forests, the height of the trees. To tell the truth—he runs on
expansively, in a sort of dangerous drowsiness—the fact is that he
has never yet seen a real forest in this country. An occasional ancient
grove, yes, but he hardly believes (ha-ha-ha) that the Authorities in
charge of Afforestation have anything to do with that. Yes, he keeps
hearing over the radio about forests being planted to honor this,
that, and the other personage. Though apparently one cannot
actually see them yet . . . The trees grow slowly . . . don't gain
height . . . Actually he understands . . . this arid soil . . . In
other countries, now . . .

At last he falters. Naturally he realizes, has realized from the
start, that he has made a bad blunder, has sensed it from the laughter
trembling in the girl's eyes, from the shocked fury coloring the face
of the manager who is edging his way to old age. The candidate has,
to use a tangible image, taken a careless step and trampled a tender
spot in the heart of the man in charge of forests, who is fixing him
now in a harsh stare and delivering a monologue for his benefit.

What does he mean by small trees? He has obviously failed to
use his eyes. Of course there are forests. Real forests. Jungles, no;
but forests, yes, indeed. If he will pardon the question: What does
he know about what happens in this country anyway? For even when
he travels through it on a bus he won't bother to take his head out of

his book. It's laughable, really, these flat allegations. He, the old man, has come across this kind of talk from young people, but the candidate is rather past that age. If he, the manager, had the time to spare, he could show him maps. But soon he will see for himself. There are forests in the Hills of Judea, in Galilee, Samaria, and elsewhere. Perhaps the candidate's eyesight is weak, after all. Perhaps he needs a stronger pair of spectacles. The manager would like to ask the candidate to take spare spectacles with him. He would rather not have any more trouble. Good-bye.

Where are they sending him?

A few days later he is back. This time he is received not by the manager, but by an underling. He is being sent to one of the larger forests. He won't be alone there but with a laborer, an Arab. They feel certain he has no prejudices. Good-bye. Ah yes, departure is on Sunday.

III

Things happen fast. He severs connections and they appear to come loose with surprising ease. He vacates his room and his landlady is glad of it, for some reason. He spends the last nights with one of his learned friends, who sets to work at once to prepare a study schedule for him. While his zealous friend is busy in one room cramming books into a suitcase, the prospective fire-watcher fondles the beloved wife in another. He is pensive, his hands gentle, there is something of joy in his expectations of the morrow. What shall he study? His friends suggest the Crusades. Yes, that would be just right for him. Everyone specializes in a certain subject. He may yet prove to be a little researcher all in his own right, just so long as he won't fritter his time away. He ought to bring some startling scientific theory back from the forests. His friends will take care of the facts later.

But in the morning, when the lorry of the Afforestation Department comes to fetch him out of his shattered sleep, he suddenly imagines that all this has been set in motion just to get rid of him; and, shivering in the cold morning air, he can but console himself with the thought that this adventure will go the way of all others and be drowned in somnolence. Is it any wonder that Jerusalem, high on its hills, Jerusalem, which is left behind now, is fading like a dream? He abandons himself to the jolts and pitches of the lorry.

The laborers with their hoes and baskets sit huddled away from him in the back of the car. They sense that he belongs to another world. The bald patch and the glasses are an indication, one of many.

Traveling half a day.

The lorry leaves the highway and travels over long, alien dirt roads, among nameless immigrant settlements. Laborers alight, others take their place. Everyone receives instructions from the driver, who is the one in command around here. We are going south, are we? Wide country meeting a spring-blue sky. The ground is damp still and clods of earth drop off the lorry's tires. It is late in the morning when he discovers the first trees scattered among rocks. Young slender pines, tiny, light green. "Then I was right," he tells himself with a smile. But farther on the trees grow taller. Now the light bursts and splinters. Long shadows steal aboard the lorry like stowaways. People keep changing and only the driver, the passenger and his suitcases stay put. The forests grow denser, no more bare patches now. Pines, always, and only the one species, obstinately, unvaryingly. He is tired, dusty, hungry, has long ago lost all sense of direction. The sun is playing tricks, twisting around him. He does not see where he is going, only what he is leaving behind. At three o'clock the lorry is emptied of laborers and only he is left. For a long time the lorry climbs over a rugged track. He is cross, his mouth feels dry. In despair he tries to pull a book out of one suitcase, but then the lorry stops. The driver gets off, bangs the door, comes around to him and says:

"This is it. Your predecessor's already made off—yesterday. Your instructions are all up there. You at least can read, for a change."

Laboriously he hauls himself and his two suitcases down. An odd, charming, stone house stands on a hill. Pines of all sizes surround it. He is at a high altitude here, though he cannot yet see everything from where he is. Silence, a silence of trees. The driver stretches his legs, looks around, breathes the air, then suddenly he nods good-bye and climbs back into his cab and switches the engine on.

He who must stay behind is seized with regret. Despair. What now? Just a minute! He doesn't understand. He rushes at the car, beats his fists against the door, whispers furiously at the surprised driver.

"But food . . . what about food?"

It appears that the Arab takes care of everything.

IV

Alone he trudges uphill, a suitcase in each hand. Gradually the world comes into view. The front door stands open and he enters a large room, the ground floor. Semidarkness, dilapidated objects on the floor, food remnants, traces of a child. The despair mounts in him. He lets go of the suitcases and climbs absently to the second floor. The view strikes him with awe. Five hills covered with a dense green growth—pines. A silvery blue horizon with a distant sea. He is instantly excited, on fire, forgetting everything. He is even prepared to change his opinion of the Afforestation Department.

A telephone, binoculars, a sheet covered with instructions. A large desk and an armchair beside it. He settles himself into the chair and reads the instructions five times over, from beginning to end. Then he pulls out his pen and makes a few stylistic corrections. He glances fondly at the black instrument. He is in high spirits. He considers calling up one of his friends in town, to say something tender to one of his aging ladyloves. He might announce his safe arrival, describe the view perhaps. Never has he had a public telephone at his disposal yet. He lifts the receiver to his ear. An endless purring. He is not familiar with the proceedings. He tries dialing. In vain. The purr remains steady. At last he dials zero, like a sober citizen expecting a sober reply.

The telephone breaks its silence.

The Fire Brigade comes on with a startled "What's happened?" Real alarm at the other side. (Where, where, confound it!) Before he has said a word, questions rain down on him. How large is the fire? What direction the wind? They are coming at once. He tries to put in a word, stutters, and already they are starting a car over there. Panic grips him. He jumps up, the receiver tight in his hand. He breaks out in a cold sweat. With the last remnant of words in his power he explains everything. No. There is no fire. There is nothing. Only getting acquainted. He has just arrived. Wanted to get through to town. His name is so-and-so. That is all.

A hush at the other side. The voice changes. This must be

their chief now. Pleased to meet you, Sir, we've taken down your name. Have you read all the instructions? Personal calls are quite out of the question. Anyway, you've only just arrived, haven't you? Or is there some urgent need? Your wife? Your children?

No, he has no family.

Well, then, why the panic? Lonely? He'll get used to it. Please don't disturb again in the future. Good-bye.

The ring closes in on him a little. Pink streaks on the horizon. He is tired, hungry. He has risen early, and he is utterly unused to that. This high, commanding view makes him dizzy. The silence. He picks up the binoculars with a limp hand and raises them to his eyes. The world leaps close, blurred. Pines lunge at him upright. He adjusts the forest, the hills, the sea horizon to the quality of his eyes. He amuses himself a bit, then lets go of the binoculars and eases himself into the chair. He has a clear conception of his new job now. Just watching. His eyes grow heavy. He dozes, sleeps perhaps.

Suddenly he wakes—a red light is burning on his glasses. He is bewildered, scared, his senses heavy. The forest has caught fire, apparently, and he has missed it. He jumps up, his heart wildly beating, grabs the telephone, the binoculars, and then it occurs to him that it is the sun, only the sun setting beyond the trees. He is facing west. Now he knows. Slowly he drops back into the chair. His heart contracts with something like terror, like emptiness. He imagines himself deserted in this place, forgotten. His glasses mist over and he takes them off and wipes them.

When dusk falls, he hears steps.

V

An Arab and a little girl are approaching the house. Swiftly he rises to his feet. They notice him, look up and stop in their tracks—startled by the soft, scholarly figure. He bows his head. They walk on but their steps are hesitant now. He goes down to them.

The Arab turns out to be old and mute. His tongue was cut out during the war. By one of them or one of us? Does it matter? Who knows what the last words were that stuck in his throat? In the dark room, its windows ablaze with the last light, the fire-watcher shakes a heavy hand, bends to pat the child, who flinches, terrified.

The ring of loneliness closes in on him. The Arab puts on lights. The fire-watcher will sleep upstairs.

The first evening, and a gnawing sadness. The weak yellow light of the bulbs is depressing. For the time being, he draws comfort only from the wide view, from the soft blue of the sea in the distance and the sun writhing in it. He sits cramped on his chair and watches the big forests entrusted to his eyes. He imagines that the fire may break out at any moment. After a long delay, the Arab brings up his supper. An odd taste, a mixture of tastes. But he devours everything, leaves not a morsel. His eyes rove hungrily between the plate and the thick woods. Suddenly, while chewing, he discovers a few faraway lights—villages. He broods a while about women, then takes off his clothes, opens the suitcase that does not hold books, and takes out his things. It seems a long time since he left town. He wraps himself in blankets, lies facing the forests. A cool breeze caresses him. What sort of sleep will come to one here? The Arab brings him a cup of coffee to help him stay awake. The fire-watcher would like to talk to him about something; perhaps about the view, or about the poor lighting perhaps. He has words left in him still from the city. But the Arab does not understand Hebrew. The fire-watcher smiles wearily in thanks. Something about his bald crown, the glint of his glasses, seems to daunt the Arab.

It is half-past nine—the beginning of night. Cicadas strike up. He struggles against sleep engulfing him. His eyes close and his conscience tortures him. The binoculars dangle from their strap around his neck, and from time to time he picks them up, lifts them to his eyes blinded with sleep, glasses clicking against glass. He opens his eyes in a stare and finds himself in the forest, among pines, hunting for flames. Darkness.

How long does it take for a forest to burn down? Perhaps he will only look every hour, every two hours. Even if the forest should start to burn, he would still manage to raise the alarm in time to save the rest. The murmur downstairs has died down. The Arab and his child are asleep. And he is up here, light-headed, tired after his journey, between three walls and a void gaping to the sea. He must not roll over onto his other side. He nods, and his sleep is pervaded by the fear of fire, fire stealing upon him unaware. At midnight he transfers himself from bed to chair; it is safer that way. His head droops heavily onto the desk, his spine aches, he is crying out for sleep, full of regret, alone against the dark empire swaying before him. Till at last the black hours of the first night pass; till out of the corner of his eye he sees the morning grow among the hills.

Only fatigue makes him stay on after the first night. The days and nights following after revolve as on a screen, a misty, dream-like screen lit up once every twenty-four hours by the radiant glow of the setting sun. It is not himself but a stranger who wanders those first days between the two stories of the house, the binoculars slung across his chest, absently chewing on the food left him by the un-seen Arab. The heavy responsibility that has suddenly fallen upon his shoulders bewilders him. Hardest of all is the silence. Even with himself he hardly manages to exchange a word. Will he be able to open a book here? The view amazes and enchants him still and he cannot have enough of it. After ten days of anguish he is himself again. In one brief glance he can embrace all the five hills now. He has learned to sleep with his eyes open. A new accom-plishment; rather interesting, one must admit.

VI

At last the other suitcase, the one with the books, gets opened, with a slight delay of but a fortnight or so. The delay does not worry him in the least, for aren't the spring, the summer, and half the autumn still before him? The first day is devoted to sorting the books, spelling out titles, thumbing the pages. One can't deny that there is some pleasure in handling the fat, fragrant, annotated volumes. The texts are in English, the quotations all in Latin. Strange phrases from alien worlds. He worries a little. His subject—"The Crusades." From the human, that is to say, the ecclesiastical aspect. He has not gone into particulars yet. "Crusades," he whispers softly to himself and feels joy rising in him at the word, the sound. He feels certain that there is some dark issue buried within the subject and that it will startle him, startle other issues in him. And it will be just out of this drowsiness that envelops his mind like a permanent cloud that the matter will be revealed to him.

The following day is spent on pictures. The books are rich in illustrations. Odd, funny ones. Monks, cardinals; a few blurred kings, thin knights, tiny, villainous Jews. Curious landscapes, maps.

He studies them, compares, dozes. On the hard road to the abstract he wishes to linger a while with the concrete. That night he is kept from his studies by a gnat. Next morning he tells himself: Oh, wondrous time, how fast it flies upon these lonely summits. He opens the first book on the first page, reads the author's preface, his grateful acknowledgment. He reads other prefaces, various acknowledgments, publication data. He checks a few dates. At noon his mind is distracted from the books by an imaginary flame flashing among the trees. He remains tense for hours, excited, searching with the binoculars, his hand on the telephone. At last, toward evening, he discovers that it is only the red dress of the Arab's little daughter who is skipping among the trees. The following day, when he is all set to decipher the first page, his father turns up suddenly with a suitcase in his hand.

"What's happened?" the father asks anxiously.

"Nothing . . . Nothing's happened . . ."

"But what made you become a forester then?"

"A bit of solitude . . ."

"Solitude . . ." he marvels. "You want solitude?"

The father bends over the open book, removes his heavy glasses and peers closely at the text. "The Crusades," he murmurs. "Is that what you're engaged in?"

"Yes."

"Aren't I disturbing you in your work? I haven't come to disturb you . . . I have a few days' leave."

"No, you're not disturbing me."

"Magnificent view."

"Yes, magnificent."

"You're thinner."

"Could be."

"Couldn't you study in the libraries?"

Apparently not. Silence. The father sniffs around the room like a little hedgehog. At noon he asks his son:

"Do you think it is lonely here? That you'll find solitude?"

"Yes, what's to disturb me?"

"I'm not going to disturb you."

"Of course not. What makes you think that?"

"I'll go away soon."

"No, don't go. Please stay."

The father stays a week.

In the evening the father tries to become friendly with the Arab and his child. A few words of Arabic have stuck in his memory from the days of his youth, and he will seize any occasion to fill them with meaning. But his pronunciation is unintelligible to the Arab, who only nods his head dully.

They sit together, not speaking. The son cannot read a single line with the father there, even though the father keeps muttering: "Don't bother about me. I'll keep myself in the background." At night the father sleeps on the bed and the fire-watcher stretches himself out on the floor. Sometimes the father wakes in the night to find his son awake. "Perhaps we could take turns," he says. "You go to sleep on the bed and I'll watch the forest." But the son knows that his father will see not a forest but a blurred stain. He won't notice the fire till it singes his clothes. In the daytime they change places—the son lies on the bed and the father sits by the desk and tries to read the book, which lies open still. How he would like to strike up a conversation with his son, stir up some discussion. For example, he fails to understand why his son won't deal with the Jews, the Jewish aspect of the Crusades. For isn't mass suicide a wonderful and terrible thing? The son gives him a kindly grin, a noncommittal reply, and silence. During the last days of his visit the father occupies himself with the dumb Arab. A host of questions bubbles up in him. Who is the man? Where is he from? Who cut his tongue out? Why? Look, he has seen hatred in the man's eyes. A creature like that may yet set the forest on fire some day. Why not?

On his last day the father is given the binoculars to play with.

Suitcase in hand, back bent, he shakes his son's hand. Then— tears in the eyes of the little father.

"I've been disturbing you, I know I have . . ."

In vain does the son protest, in vain mumble about the oceans of time still before him—about half the spring, the whole long summer, half the distant autumn.

From his elevated seat he watches his lost, blind father fumbling for the back of the lorry. The driver is rude and impatient with him. When the lorry moves off, the father waves good-bye to the forest by mistake. He has lost his bearings.

VII

For a week he crawls from line to line over the difficult text. After every sentence he raises his head to look at the forest. He is still awaiting a fire. The air grows hot. A haze shimmers above the sea horizon. When the Arab returns at dusk his garments are damp with sweat, the child's gestures are tired. Anyway you look at it, he himself is lucky. At such a time to be here, high above any town. Ostensibly, he is working all the time, but observing could hardly be called work, could it? The temperature rises day by day. He wonders whether it is still spring, or whether perhaps the summer has crept upon the world already. One can gather nothing from the forest, which shows no change, except thorns fading to yellow among the trees perhaps. His hearing has grown acute. The sound of trees whispers incessantly in his ears. His eyes shine with the sun's gaining strength, his senses grown keen. In a way he is becoming attached to the forest. Even his dreams are growing richer in trees. The women sprout leaves.

His text is difficult, the words distant. It has turned out to be only the preface to a preface. Yet, thorough that he is, he does not skip a single passage. He translates every word, then rewrites the translation in rhyme. Simple, easy rhymes, in order that the words should merge in his mind, should not escape into the silence.

No wonder that by Friday he can count but three pages read, out of the thousands. "Played out," he whispers to himself and trails his fingertips over the desk. Perhaps he'll take a rest? A pensive air comes over the green empire before him each Sabbath eve and makes his heart contract. Though he believes neither in God nor in all his angels, there is a sacredness that brings a lump to his throat.

He combs his beard in honor of the holy day. Yes, there is a new beard growing here along with the pines. He brings some order into the chaos of his room, picks a page off the floor. What is this? The instruction sheet. Full of interest, he reads it once more and discovers a forgotten instruction, or one added by his own hand, perhaps.

"Let the forest scout go out from time to time for a short walk among the trees, in order to sharpen his senses."

His first steps in the forest are like a baby's. He circles the observation post, hugging its walls as though afraid to leave them. Yet the trees attract him like magic. Little by little he ventures among the hills, deeper and deeper. If he should smell burning, he will run back.

But this isn't a forest yet, only the hope and promise of one. Here and there the sun appears through the foliage and a traveler among the trees is dappled with flickers of light. This isn't a rustling forest but a very small one, like a graveyard. A forest of solitudes. The pines stand erect, slim, serious; like a company of new recruits awaiting their commander. The ranging fire-watcher is pleased by the play of light and shadow. With every step he crushes dry pine needles underfoot. Softly, endlessly, the pines shed their needles; pines arrayed in a garment of mingling life and death.

The rounded human moving among trees whose yearning is so straight, so fierce. His body aches a bit, the ache of cramped limbs stretching; his legs are heavy. Suddenly he catches sight of the telephone line. A yellowish wire smelling of mold. Well, so this is his contact with the world. He starts tracing the yellow wire, searching for its origin, is charmed by its pointless twists and loops between the trees. They must have let some joker unwind the drum over the hills.

Suddenly he hears voices. He wavers, stops, then sees the little clearing in the woods. The Arab is seated on a pile of rocks, his hoe by his side. The child is talking to him excitedly, describing something with animated gestures. The scout tiptoes nearer, as lightly as his bulk will permit. They are instantly aware of him, sniff his alien being, and fall silent. The Arab jumps up, stands by his hoe as though hiding something. He faces them, wordless. It is the Sabbath eve today, isn't it, and there is a yearning in his heart. He stands and stares, for all the world like a supervisor bothered by some obscure triviality. The soft breeze caresses his eyes. If he did not fear for his status, he would hum them a little tune, perhaps. He smiles absently, his eyes stray and slowly he withdraws, with as much dignity as he can muster.

The two remain behind, petrified. The child's joy has shriveled halfway through her interrupted story, the Arab starts weeding the thorns at his feet. But the scout has retreated already, gone forth into the empire. He has been wandering in the woods for all of an hour now and is still making new discoveries. The names of donors, for example. It had never occurred to him that this wouldn't be just some anonymous forest but one with a name, and not just one name either. Many rocks bear copper plates, brilliantly burnished. He stoops, takes off his glasses, reads: Louis Schwartz of Chicago; the King of Burundi and his People. Flickers of light play over the letters. The names cling to him, like the falling pine needles that slip into his pocket. How odd! The tired memory tries to refresh

itself with these faceless names. Name after name is absorbed by
him as he walks, and by the time he reaches the observation post
he can already hold a little rehearsal. He recites the sorted names, a
vacuous smile on his face.

Friday night.

A wave of sadness wells within him. His mind happens to be
perfectly lucid at the moment. We'll clear out on Sunday he whispers
suddenly, and starts humming a snatch of song; inaudibly at first,
the sound humming inside him, but soon trilling and rising high to
the darkening sky. A hidden abyss behind him echoes in reply. The
light drips, drips. Strings of light tear the sunset across and he shouts
song at it, shrills recklessly, wanton with solitude. He starts one
song, stops, plunges into another without change of key. His eyes
fill with tears. The dark stifles his throat at last, suddenly he hears
himself and falls silent.

Peace returns to the forest. Remnants of light linger. Five
minutes pass and then the Arab and the girl emerge from the cover
of the underbrush and hurry to the house with bent heads.

The Sabbath passes in a wonderful tranquillity. He is utterly
calm. He has begun counting the trees for a change. Sunday he is
on the verge of escaping but then the lorry brings him his salary, a
part of the job he had forgotten. He is amazed, gushes his thanks to
the mocking driver. So there's a prize in the whispering world, is
there?

He returns to the books.

VIII

Hot summer. Yes, but we have forgotten the birds. Presumably the
observation post stands on an ancient crossroads of bird trajectories.
How else to explain the mad flocks swooping in from the forest to
beat their wings against the walls, drop on the bed, dive at the books,
shed gray feathers and green dung, shatter the dull air with their
restlessness—and vanish on their circuitous flight to the sea. A
change has come over him. Sunburned, yes, but there is more to it
than that. The heat wells up in him, frightens him. A dry flow of
desert wind may rouse the forest to suicide; hence he redoubles his
vigilance, presses the binoculars hard against his eyes and subjects
the forest in his care to a strict survey. How far has he come? Some
slight twenty pages are behind him, thousands still before. What

does he remember? A few words, the tail end of a theory, the atmosphere on the eve of the Crusades. The nights are peaceful. He could have studied, could have concentrated, were it not for the gnats. Night after night he extinguishes the lights and sits in darkness. The words have dropped away from him like husks. Cicadas. Choruses of jackals. A bat wings heavily across the gloom. Rustlings.

Hikers start arriving in the forest. Lone hikers some of them, but mostly they come in groups. He follows them through the binoculars. Various interesting ages. Like ants they swarm over the forest, pour in among the trees, calling out to each other, laughing; then they cast off their rucksacks all at once, unburden themselves of as many clothes as possible and hang them up on branches, and promptly come over to the house.

Water is what they want. Water!

He comes down to them, striking them with wonder. The bald head among the green pines, the heavy glasses. Indeed, everything indicates an original character.

He stands by the water tap, firm and upright, and slakes their thirst. Everyone begs permission to go upstairs for a look at the view. He consents, joyfully. They crowd into his little room and utter the stock formula of admiring exclamations. He smiles as though he had created it all. Above everything, they are surprised by the sea. They had never imagined one could see the sea from here. Yet how soon they grow bored! One glance, a cry of admiration, and they grow restless already and eager to be away. They peep at his notes, at the heavy books, and descend the staircase brimming with veneration for him and his view. The group leaders ask him to give some account of the place, but there is no account to give. Everything is still artificial here. There is nothing here, not even some archaeology for amateurs, nothing but a few donors inscribed on rocks. Would they be interested in the names? Well, for instance . . .

They laugh.

The girls look at him kindly. No, he isn't handsome. But might he not become engraved on one of their hearts?

They light campfires.

They wish to cook their food, or to warm themselves. A virtuous alarm strikes him. Tiny flames leap up in the forest, a bluish smoke starts blowing gaily about the treetops. A fire? Yes and no. He stays glued, through his binoculars, to the lively figures.

Toward evening he goes to explore his flickering, merrymaking empire. He wishes to sound a warning. Softly, soundlessly he draws near the campfires, the figures wreathed in flames. He approaches them unnoticed, and they are startled when they discover him beside them. Dozens of young eyes look up at him together. The leaders rise at once.

"Yes? What do you want?"

"The fire. Be careful! One spark, and the forest may burn down."

They are quick to assure him. Laying their hands on their young hearts they give him their solemn promise to watch with all the eyes shining in a row before him. They will keep within bounds, of course they will, what does he think?

He draws aside. Appeased? Yes and no. There, among the shadows, in the twilight of the fire, he lingers and lets his eyes rove. The girls and their bare, creamy legs, slender does. The flames crackle and sing, softly, gently. He clenches his fists in pain. If only he could warm his hands a little.

"Like to join us?" they ask politely. His vertical presence is faintly embarrassing.

No, thanks. He can't. He is busy. His studies. They have seen the books, haven't they? Now there is nothing for it but to withdraw with measured tread. But as soon as he has vanished from their view he flings himself behind the trees, hides among the needle branches. He looks at the fire from afar, at the girls, till everything fades, and blankets are spread for sleep. Giggles, girls' affected shrieks, leaders' rebukes. Before he can begin to think, select one out of the many figures, it will be dawn. Silence is still best. At midnight he feels his way through the trees, back to the observation post. He sits in his place, waiting. One of the figures may be working its way in the darkness toward him. But no, nothing. They are tired, sleeping already.

And the same next day, and all the days following.

Early in the morning he will open his book and hear wild song in the distance. He does not raise his eyes from the page but his hand strays to the binoculars. A dappled silence. Flashes of light through branches. His eyes are faithful to the written page, but his thoughts have gone whoring already. From the corner of his eye he follows the procession threading through the forest—sorting, checking ages, colors, joys of youth. There is something of abandon about them from afar, like a procession of Crusaders; except that these women are bare. He trembles, choking suddenly. He removes his glasses and beats his head against the books. Half an hour later they arrive. Asking for water to drink and the view to look at, as usual. They have heard about the wonderful view to be seen from up here. Perhaps they have heard about the scholar as well, but they say nothing. The group leaders take them, a batch at a time, into his room turned public property. No sooner have they scattered about the forest than the campfires leap up, as though that were their prime necessity. In the evening he rushes over the five hills, from fire to fire, impelled by his duty to warn them or by an obscure desire to reveal himself. He never joins any of the circles though. He prefers to hide in the thicket. Their singing throbs in his heart, and even more than that—the whisperings. Warm summer nights—something constantly seeping through the leaves.

Gradually the groups of hikers blend. One excursion leaves, another arrives. By the time he has managed to learn a few outstanding names, their owners are gone and the sounds alone survive among the branches. Languor comes over him. No longer does he trouble to caution against fire. On the contrary. He would welcome a little conflagration, a little local tumult. The hikers, however, are extremely responsible. They, themselves, take care to stamp out every dying ember. Their leaders come in advance to set his mind at rest.

The birds know how much he has neglected his studies; the birds whom he watches constantly lest they approach his desk. A month has passed since last he turned a page and he is stuck squirming between two words. He says: let the heat abate, the hikers be gone—then I shall race over the lines. If only he could skip the words and get to the essence. From time to time he scribbles in his notebook. Stray thoughts, speculations, musings, outlines of assumptions. Not much. A sentence a day. He would like to gain a hold upon it all indirectly. Yet he is doubtful whether he has gained a hold even upon the forest in front of his eyes. Look, here the Arab and the girl are disappearing among the trees and he cannot find them. Toward evening they emerge from an unforeseen direction as though the forest had conceived them even now. They tread the soil softly. They avoid people, choose roundabout ways. He smiles at them both but they recoil.

Friday. The forest is overrun, choking with people. They come on foot and by car, crowds disgorged by the faraway cities. Where is his solitude now? He sprawls on his chair like a dethroned king whose empire has slipped from his hands. Twilight lingers on the treetops. Sabbath eve. His ears alone can catch, beyond the uproar of voices, beyond the rustling, the thin cry of the weary soil cease-lessly crushed by the teeth of young roots. A hikers' delegation comes to see him. They just want to ask him a question. They have argued, laid wagers, and he shall be their arbiter. Where exactly is this Arab village that is marked on the map? It ought to be some-where around here, an abandoned Arab village. Here, they even know its name, something like . . . actually, it must be right here, right in the forest. . . . Does he know anything about it perhaps? They're simply curious.

The fire-watcher gives them a tired look. "A village?" he repeats with a polite, indulgent smile at their folly. No, there is no village here. The map must be wrong, the surveyor's hand must have shaken.

But in the small hours of the night, somewhere between a doze and a slumber, in the face of the whispering, burgeoning forest, the name floats back into his mind of a sudden and he is seized with restlessness. He descends to the ground floor, feels his way in the dark to the bed of the Arab, who lies asleep covered with rags. Roughly he wakes him and whispers the name of the village. The Arab does not understand. His eyes are consumed with weariness. The fire-watcher's accent must be at fault. He tries again, therefore, repeats the name over and over and the Arab listens and suddenly he understands. An expression of surprise, of wonder and eagerness, suffuses all his wrinkles. He jumps up, stands there in his hairy nakedness and flings up a heavy arm in the direction of the window, pointing fervently, hopelessly, at the forest.

The fire-watcher thanks him and departs, leaving the big naked figure in the middle of the room. When he wakes tomorrow, the Arab will think he has dreamed it.

IX

Ceremonies. A season of ceremonies. The forest turns all ceremonial. The trees stand bowed, heavy with honor, they take on meaning, they belong. White ribbons are strung to delimit new domains. Luxurious buses struggle over the rocky roads, a procession of shining automobiles before and behind. Sometimes they are preceded by a motorcycle mounted by an excited policeman. Unwieldy personages alight, shambling like black bears. The women flutter around them. Little by little they assemble, crush out cigarettes with their black shoes and fall silent—paying homage to the memory of themselves. The fire-watcher, too, participates in the ceremony, from afar, he and his binoculars. A storm of obedient applause breaks out, a gleam of scissors, a flash of photographers, ribbons sag. A plaque is unveiled, a new little truth is revealed to the world. A brief tour of the conquered wood, and then the distinguished gathering dissolves into its various vehicles and sallies forth.

Where is the light gone?

In the evening, when the fire-watcher comes down to the drooping ribbons, to the grateful trees, he will find nothing but a pale inscription saying, for example: "Donated by the Sackson children in honor of Daddy Sackson of Baltimore, a fond tribute to his paternity. End of Summer Nineteen Hundred and . . ."

Sometimes the fire-watcher, observing from his heights, will notice one of the party who is darting troubled looks about him, raising his eyes at the trees as though searching for something. It takes many ceremonies before the fire-watcher's wandering mind will grasp that this is none other than the old man in charge of Afforestation, who comes and repeats himself, dressed always in the same clothes, at every ceremony.

Once he goes down to him.

The old man is walking among his distinguished foreign party, is jesting with them haltingly in their language. The fire-watcher comes out of the trees and plants himself in front of him for the inevitable encounter. The distinguished party stops, startled. An uneasy silence falls over them. The ladies shrink back.

"What do you want?" demands the old man masterfully.

The fire-watcher gives a weak smile.

"Don't you know me? I'm the watchman. That is to say, the fire-watcher . . . employee of yours . . ."

"Ah!" fist beating against aged forehead, "I didn't recognize you, was alarmed, these tatters have changed your appearance so, this heavy beard. Well, young man, and how's the solitude?"

"Solitude?" he wonders.

The old man presents him to the party.

"A scholar . . ."

They smile, troubled, meet his hand with their fingertips, move on. They do not have complete faith in his cleanliness. The old man, on the other hand, looks at him affectionately. A thought crosses his mind and he stays behind a moment.

"Well, so there *are* forests," he grins with good-natured irony.

"Yes," admits the scout honestly. "Forests, yes . . . but . . ."

"But what?"

"But fires, no."

"Fires?" the old man wonders, bending toward him.

"Yes, fires. I spend whole days here sitting and wondering. Such a quiet summer."

"Well, why not? Actually, there hasn't been a fire here for several years now. To tell you the truth, I don't think there has ever been a fire at all in this forest. Nature itself is harnessed to our great enterprise here, ha-ha."

"And I was under the impression . . ."

"That what?"

"That fires broke out here every other day. By way of illustration, at least. This whole machinery waiting on the alert, is it all for nothing? The fire engines . . . telephone lines . . . the manpower . . . for months my eyes have been strained with waiting."

"Waiting? Ha-ha, what a joke!"

The old one hurries along. The drivers are switching on their engines. That is all he needs, to be left overnight in this arboreal silence. Before he goes he would just like to know the watchman's opinion of the dumb Arab. The lorry driver has got the idea into his head that the fellow is laying in a stock of kerosene. . . .

The watchman is stirred. "Kerosene?"

"Daresay it's some fancy of that malicious driver. This Arab is a placid kind of fellow, isn't he?"

"Wonderfully placid," agrees the fire-watcher eagerly. Then he walks a few steps around the old man and whispers confidentially: "Isn't he a local?"

"A local?"

"Because our forest is growing over, well, over a ruined village. . . ."

"A village?"

"A small village."

"A small village? Ah—" (Something is coming back to him anyway.) "Yes, there used to be some sort of a farmstead here. But that is a thing of the past."

Of the past, yes, certainly. What else . . . ?

X

One day's program as an example.

Not having slept at night, he does not wake up in the morning. Light springs up between his fingers. What date is today? There is no telling. Prisoners score lines on the walls of their cell, but he is not in prison. He has come of his own free will, and so he will go. He could lift the receiver and find out the date from the firemen bent over their fire engines, waiting in some unknown beyond, but he does not want to scare them yet.

He goes down to the tap and sprinkles a few drops of water over his beard to freshen it up. Then he climbs back to his room, snatches up the binoculars and holds a pre-breakfast inspection. Excitement grips him. The forest filled with smoke? No, the binoculars are to blame. He wipes the lenses with a corner of his grimy shirt. The forest clears up at once, disappointingly. None of the trees has done any real growing overnight.

He goes down again. He picks up the dry loaf of bread and cuts himself a rough slice. He chews rapidly, his eyes roving over a torn strip of newspaper in which tomatoes are wrapped. It is not, God forbid, out of a hunger for news, but to keep his eyes in training lest they forget the shape of the printed letter. He returns to his observation post, his mouth struggling with an enormous half-rotten tomato. He sucks, swallows, gets smeared with the red, trickling sap. At last he throws a sizable remnant away. Silence. He dozes a bit, wakes, looks for a long time at the treetops. The day stretches out ahead of him. Softly he draws near the books.

Where are we? How many pages read? Better not count them or he will fall prey to despair; for the time being he is serene, and why spoil it. It isn't a question of quantity, is it? And he remembers what he has read up to now perfectly well, forward and backward. The words wave and whirl within him. For the time being, therefore, for the past few weeks, that is, he has been devoting his zeal to one single sheet of paper. A picture? Rather, a map. A map of the area. He will display it on this wall here for the benefit of his successors, that they may remember him. Look, he has signed his name already, signed it to begin with, lest he forget.

What is he drawing? Trees. But not only trees. Hills too, a blue horizon too. He is improving day by day. If he had colored crayons he could have added some birds as well; at least, say, those native to the area. What interests him in particular is the village buried beneath the trees. That is to say, it hasn't always been as silent here. His curiosity is of a strictly scientific nature. What was it the old man had said? "A scholar." He strokes the beard and his hand lingers, disentangles a few hairs matted with filth. What time is it? Early still. He reads a line about the attitude of the Pope to the German emperor and falls asleep. He wakes with a start. He lights a cigarette, tosses the burning match out into the forest, but the match goes out in mid-air. He flings the cigarette butt among the trees and it drops on a stone and burns itself out in solitude.

He gets up, paces about restlessly. What time is it? Early still.

He goes in search of the Arab, to say good morning. He must impress his own vigilant existence upon the man, lest he be murdered some morning between one nap and another. Ever since the fire-watcher has spoken the name of the vanished village in his ears, the Arab has become suspicious, as though he were being watched all the time. The fire-watcher strides rapidly between the pines. How light his footstep has grown during the long summer months. His soundless appearance startles the two.

"Shalom," he says.

They reply in two voices. The child—a voice that has sweetness in it, the Arab—a harsh grunt. The fire-watcher smiles to himself and hurries on as though he were extremely busy. Chiseled stones lie scattered among the trees, outlines of buildings, ruins and relics. He searches for marks left by humans. Every day he comes and disturbs a few stones, looking for traces.

A man and a woman are lying here entwined, like statues toppled from their base. Their terror when the bearded head bends silently over them! Smile at them and run, you! A couple slipped away from a group-hike, no doubt.

What is he looking for? Relics of thoughts that have flitted here, words that have completed their mission. But what will he find one fine day, say even the day that we have taken for a sample? Small tins filled with kerosene. How wonderful! The zeal with which someone has filled tin after tin here and covered them up with the girl's old dress. He stoops over the treasure, the still liquid on whose surface dead pine needles drift. His reflection floats back at him together with the faint smell.

Blissfully he returns to the house, opens a tin of meat and bolts its contents to the last sliver. He wipes his mouth and spits far out among the branch-filled air. He turns two pages of a book and reads the Cardinal's reply to a Jew's epistle. Funny, these twists and turns of the Latin, but what a threat is conveyed by them. He falls asleep, wakes, realizes he has nearly missed an important ceremony on the easternmost hill. From now on the binoculars stay glued to his eyes and he mingles with the distinguished crowd from afar. He can even make out the movements of the speakers' lips; he will fill in the missing sound himself. But then the flames of the sunset catch his eye and divert his attention, and with a daily returning excitement he becomes absorbed in the splendor, the terrible splendor.

Afterward he wipes the dust off the silent telephone. To give him his due—he bestows meticulous care on the equipment that belongs to the Afforestation Department, whereas his own equipment is already falling apart. The loose buttons shed among the trees, the frayed shirt, the ragged trousers.

A private outing of joyriders arrives with loud fanfare to spend the night in the forest. Wearily he chews his supper. Nightfall brings the old familiar sadness.

The Arab and his daughter go to bed. Darkness. The first giggle that emerges from the trees is a slap in his listening face. He turns over a few dark pages, swats a gnat, whistles.

Night. He does not fall asleep.

XI

Then it is the end of summer. The forest is emptying. And with the first autumn wind, who is blown to him like a withered leaf? His aging mistress, the wife of the friend who sent him here. Clad in a summer frock she comes, a wide-brimmed straw hat on her head. Then she is clicking her high heels around his room, rummaging through his drawers, bending over the books, peering through the papers. She had gone for a brief vacation by herself somewhere in this neighborhood and had remembered him. How is it when a man sits solitary, facing the forest, night after night? She had wanted to surprise him. Well, and what has he come up with? A fresh Crusade perhaps? She is awfully curious. Her husband speaks well of him too. In this solitude, among the trees, says the husband, he may yet flower into greatness.

The fire-watcher is moved. Without a word, he points at the map on the wall. She trips over to look, does not understand. Actually she is interested in texts. What has he written? She is very tired. Such a time till she found this place and she's more dead than alive. The view is pretty, yes, but the place looks awfully neglected. Who lives downstairs? The Arab? Is that so! She met him on the way, tried to ask him something and suddenly—the shock! Dumb, his severed tongue. But the Afforestation Department—hats off to them. Who would have imagined such forests growing in this country! He has changed, though. Grown fatter? This new beard of his is just awful. Why doesn't he say something?

She sinks down on the bed.

Then he rises, approaches her with that quiet which is in his blood now. He removes her hat, crouches at her feet, unbuckles her shoes. He is trembling with desire, choking.

She is shocked. She draws back her bare tired feet at once with something of terror, perhaps with relief. But he has let go already, stands holding the binoculars and looks at the forest, looks long, peering through the trees, waiting for fire. Slowly he turns to her, the binoculars at his eyes, turns the lenses upon her mischievously, sees the tiny wrinkles whittled in her face, the sweat drops, her fatigue. She smiles at him as in an old photograph. But when the moment drags, her smile turns into protest. She draws herself together crossly, holds up a hand.

"Hey, you! Stop it!"

Only toward sunset does he finally manage to undress her. The binoculars are still on his chest, pressed between their bodies. From time to time he coolly interrupts his kisses and caresses, raises the binoculars to his eyes and inspects the forest.

"Duty," he whispers apologetically, smiling oddly to the naked, embarrassed woman. Everything mingles with the glory of the crimson sun—the distant blue of the sea, the still trees, the blood on his cracked lips, the despair, the futility, the loneliness of the act. Accidentally her hand touches the bald crown and flinches.

When the Arab returns, it is all over. She is lying in the tangle of her clothes, drowsy. A beautiful night has descended on the world.

He sits by his desk, what else should he do? The dark transforms her into a silhouette. The forest bewitches her. Suddenly she rouses herself. The soft voice of the little Arab girl sends a shiver through her. What is she doing here? She dresses rapidly, buttons, buckles. Her voice floats on the darkness.

Actually, she has come out of pity. No one had thought he would persist so long. When does he sleep anyway? She has been sent here to deliver him, deliver him from this solitude. His silence rouses suspicions. Her husband and his friends have suddenly begun to wonder, have become afraid, ha-ha, afraid that he may be nursing some secret, some novel idea, that he may outshine them all with some brilliant research.

A sudden dark breeze bursts into the room through the gap where there is no wall, whirls around for a little and dies out in the two corners. He is kindled. His eyes glow.

"Pity? No, unnecessary. When do I sleep? Always . . . though different from the city sleep. Leave here now, just like that? Too late. I haven't finished counting the trees yet. Novel ideas? Maybe, though not what they imagine . . . not exactly scientific . . . Rather, human . . ."

Does she wish him to accompany her on her way back through the forest, or perhaps would she go by herself?

She jumps up.

They cut diagonally across the hills. He walks in front, she drags behind, staggering over the rocks in her high heels, hurt and humiliated. Though thickset, his feet are light and he slips through the foliage swift as a snake, never turning his head. She struggles with the branches whipping back behind him. The moonlight reveals them on their silent trip. What do you say now, my autumn love? Have I gone completely out of my mind? But that was to be expected, wasn't it? Out of my round of pleasures, you have cast me into solitude. Trees have taken the place of words for me, forests the place of books. That is all. Eternal autumn, fall, needles falling endlessly on my eyes. I am still awaiting a conflagration.

Wordless they reach the black highway. Her heels click on the asphalt with a last fury. Now he looks at her. Her face is scratched, her arms bloodstained. How assertively the forest leaves its mark. She contains the thin cry rising in her. Her silence grants her dignity. After some minutes a sleek car driven by a lone gray-templed man halts at her waving hand. She joins him in the car without a parting word. She will yet crumble between his fingers on the long road.

He turns in his tracks. After a few paces, the Arab pops up in front of him. He is breathing heavily, his face is dull. And what do you have to say, mister? From where have you sprung now? The Arab holds out her forgotten hat, the straw hat. The fire-watcher smiles his thanks, spreads his arms in a gesture of nothing we can do, she's gone. But how amazing, this attention. Nothing will escape the man's eye. He takes the hat from the Arab and pitches it on top of his own head, gives him a slight bow and the other is immediately alarmed. His face is alert, watching. Together, in silence, they return to the forest, their empire, theirs alone. The fire-watcher strides ahead and the Arab tramples on his footsteps. A few clouds, a light breeze. Moonlight pours over the branches and makes them transparent. He leads the Arab over roads that are the same roads always. Barefoot he walks, the Arab, and so quietly. Round and round he is led, roundabout and to his hideout, amid chiseled stones and silence. The Arab's steps falter. His footfalls lag, die, and come alive again. A deathly cold grips the fire-watcher's heart, his hands freeze. He kneels on the rustling earth. Who will give him back all the empty hours? The forest is dark and empty. No one there. Not one campfire. Just now, when he would dip his hands in fire, warm them a little. He heaps up some brown needles, takes a match, lights it, and the match goes out at once. He takes another and cups his hands around it, strikes, and this one too flares up and dies. The air is damp and treacherous. He rises. The Arab watches him, a gleam of lunatic hope in his eyes. Softly the fire-watcher walks around the pile of stones to the sorry little hideout, picks up a tin of clear liquid and empties it over the heap of pine needles, tosses in a burning match and leaps up with the surging flame—singed, happy. At last he, too, is lit up a little. Stunned, the Arab goes down on his knees. The fire-watcher spreads his palms over the flame and the Arab does likewise. Their bodies press in on the fire, which has already reached its highest pitch. He might leave the flame now and go and bathe in the sea. Time, time wasting here among the trees, will do his work for him. He muses, his mind distracted. The fire shows signs of languishing, little by little it dies at his feet. The Arab's face takes on a look of bitter disappointment. The bonfire fades. Last sparks are stamped out meticulously. Thus far it was only a lesson. The wandering mind of the fire-watcher trembles between compromises. He rises wearily and leaves. The Arab slouches in his wake.

Who is sitting on the chair behind the book-laden desk? The child. Her eyes are wide open, drinking in the dark. The Arab has put her there to replace the roving fire-watcher. It's an idea.

XII

Strange days follow. We would say: autumn—but that means nothing yet. The needles seem to fall faster, the sun grows weaker, clouds come to stay, and a new wind. His mind is slipping, growing unhinged. The ceremonies are over. The donors have gone back to their countries, the hikers to their work, pupils to their study. His own books lie jumbled in a glow of dust. He is neglecting his duties, has left his chair, his desk, his faithful binoculars, and has begun roving endlessly about the forest, by day and by night; a broken twig in his hand, he slashes at the young tree trunks as he walks, as though marking them. Suddenly he slumps down, rests his head against a shining copper plaque, removes his glasses and peers through the blurring foliage, searches the gray sky. Something like a wail, suddenly. Foul fantasies. Then he collects himself once more, jumps up to wander through the wood, among the thistles and rocks. The idea has taken hold in his dim consciousness that he is being called insistently to an encounter at the edge of the forest, at its other end. But when he plunges out of the forest and arrives there, whether it be at night or at noon or in the early dawn, he finds nothing but a yellow waste, a strange valley, a kind of cursed dream. And he will stand there for a long time, facing the empty, treeless silence and feeling that the encounter is taking place, is being successful even though it happens wordlessly. He has spent a whole spring and a long summer never once properly sleeping, and what wonder is it if these last days should be like a trance.

He has lost all hope of fire. Fire has no hold over this forest. He can therefore afford to stay among the trees, not facing them. In order to soothe his conscience he sits the girl in his chair. It has taken less than a minute to teach her the Hebrew word for "fire." How she has grown during his stay here! She is like a noble mare now with marvelous eyes. Unexpectedly her limbs have ripened, her filth become a woman's smell. At first her old father had been forced to chain her to the chair, or she would have escaped. Yes, the old

Arab has grown very attached to the negligent fire-watcher, follows him wherever he goes. Ever since the night when the two of them hugged the little bonfire the Arab, too, has grown languid. He has abandoned his eternal hoe. The grass is turning yellow under his feet, the thistles multiply. The fire-watcher will be lying on the ground and see the dusky face thrusting at him through the branches. As a rule he ignores the Arab, continues lying with his eyes on the sky. But sometimes he calls him and the man comes and kneels by his side, his heavy eyes wild with terror and hope. Perhaps, he, too, will fail to convey anything and it will all remain dark.

The fire-watcher talks to him therefore, quietly, reasonably, in a positively didactic manner. He tells him about the Crusades, and the other bends his head and absorbs the hard, alien words as one absorbing a melody. He tells him about the fervor, about the cruelty, about Jews committing suicide, about the Children's Crusade; things he has picked up from the books, the unfounded theories he has framed himself. His voice is warm, alive with imagination. The Arab listens with mounting tension and is filled with hate. When they return at twilight, lit by a soft autumnal glow, the fire-watcher will lead the Arab to the tree-engulfed house and will linger a moment. Then the Arab explains something with hurried, confused gestures, wiggling his severed tongue, tossing his head. He wishes to say that this is his house and that there used to be a village here as well and that they have simply hidden it all, buried it in the big forest.

The fire-watcher looks on at this pantomime and his heart fills with joy. What is it that rouses such passion in the Arab? Apparently his wives have been murdered here as well. A dark affair, no doubt. Gradually he moves away, pretending not to understand. Did there used to be a village here? He sees nothing but trees.

More and more the Arab clings to him. They sit there, the three of them like a family, in the room on the second floor. The fire-watcher sprawling on the bed, the child chained to the chair, the Arab crouching on the floor. Together they wait for the fire that does not come. The forest is dark and strong, a slow-growing world. These are his last days. His contract is drawing to an end. From time to time he gets up and throws one of the books back into the suitcase, startling the old Arab.

The nights are growing longer. Hot desert winds and raindrops mingle, soft shimmers of lightning flash over the sea. The last day is come. Tomorrow he will leave this place. He has discharged his duty faithfully. It isn't his fault that no fires have broken out. All the books are packed in the suitcase, scraps of paper litter the floor. The Arab has disappeared, has been missing since yesterday. The child is miserable. From time to time she raises her voice in a thin, ancient lament. The fire-watcher is growing worried. At noon the Arab turns up suddenly. The child runs toward him but he takes no notice of her. He turns to the abdicating fire-watcher instead, grabs him between two powerful hands and—feeble and soft that he is and suffering from a slight cold—impels him toward the edge of the observation post and explains whatever he can explain to him with no tongue. Perhaps he wishes to throw the abdicating fire-watcher down two stories and into the forest. Perhaps he believes that only he, the fire-watcher, can understand him. His eyes are burning. But the fire-watcher is serene, unresponsive; he shades his eyes with his palm, shrugs his shoulders, gives a meaningless little smile. What else is left him?

He collects his clothes and bundles them into the other suitcase.

Toward evening the Arab disappears again. The child has gone to look for him and has come back empty-handed. Gently the hours drift by. A single drop of rain. The fire-watcher prepares supper and sets it before the child, but she cannot bring herself to eat. Like a little animal she scurries off once more into the forest to hunt for her father and returns in despair, by herself. Toward midnight she falls asleep at last. He undresses her and carries the shabby figure to the bed, covers it with the torn blanket. What a lonely woman she will grow up to be. He muses. Something is flowing between his fingers, something like compassion. He lingers awhile. Then he returns to his observation post, sits on his chair, sleepy. Where will he be tomorrow? How about saying good-bye to the Fire Brigade? He picks up the receiver. Silence. The line is dead. Not a purr, not a gurgle. The sacred hush has invaded the wire as well.

He smiles contentedly. In the dark forest spread out before him, the Arab is moving about like a silent dagger. He sits watching the world as one may watch a great play before the rising of the curtain. A little excitement, a little drowsing in one's seat. Midnight performance.

Then, suddenly—fire. Fire, unforeseen, leaping out of the corner. A long graceful flame. One tree is burning, a tree wrapped in prayer. For a long moment one tree is going through its hour of judgment and surrendering its spirit. He lifts the receiver. Yes, the line is dead. He is leaving here tomorrow.

The loneliness of a single flame in a big forest. He is beginning to worry whether the ground may not be too wet and the thistles too few, and the show be over after one flame. His eyes are closing. His drowsiness is greatest now, at this most wonderful of moments. He rises and starts pacing nervously through the room in order to walk off his fatigue. A short while passes and then a smile spreads over his face. He starts counting the flames. The Arab is setting the forest on fire at its four corners, then takes a firebrand and rushes through the trees like an evil spirit, setting fire to the rest. The thoroughness with which he goes about his task amazes the fire-watcher. He goes down to look at the child. She is asleep. Back to the observation post—the forest is burning. He ought to run and raise the alarm, call for help. But his movements are so tranquil, his limbs leaden. Downstairs again. He adjusts the blanket over the child, pushes a lock of hair out of her eyes, goes back up, and a blast of hot air blows in his face. A great light out there. Five whole hills ablaze. Flames surge as in a frenzy high over the trees, roar at the lighted sky. Pines split and crash. Wild excitement sweeps him, rapture. He is happy. Where is the Arab now? The Arab speaks to him out of the fire, wishes to say everything, everything and at once. Will he understand?

Suddenly he is aware of another presence in the room. Swiftly he turns his head and sees the girl, half-naked, eyes staring, the light of the fire playing over her face. He smiles and she weeps.

Intense heat wells up from the leisurely burning forest. The first excitement has passed. The fire is turning from a vision into a fact. Flames are mobilizing from all the four winds to come and visit the observation post. He ought to take his two suitcases and disappear. But he only takes the child. The lights of the neighboring settlements have become so pitiful, so plain. They are no doubt sure, over there, that the fight against the fire is in full swing here already. Who would imagine that the fire is still being nourished here, brooded over? Hours will go by before the village watchmen come to wake the sleepers. The nights are cold already and people not disposed to throw off their blankets. He seizes the trembling child by the hand, goes down and begins his retreat. The road is lit up far into the distance. Behind his back the fire, and in his face—a

red, mad, burning moon that floats in the sky as though it wished
to see the blaze as well. His head feels heavy, the road stretches
ahead. They drag along, dipping in light and in darkness. In the
lanes the trees whisper, agitated, waiting, A fearful rumor has
reached them.

The observation post can be seen from afar, entirely lit up.
The earth is casting off its shackles. After a long walk the trees start
thinning out at last, they grow smaller, then disappear. He arrives
at the yellow waste, the valley, his dream. A few dry, twisted trees,
desert trees, alien and salty; trees that have sprung up parched, over
which the fire has no hold. He sits the barefoot girl on the ground,
slumps beside her. His exhaustion erupts within him and covers
them both.

With sleeping eyes he sees the shining fire engines arrive at last,
summoned by another. They, too, know that all is lost. In a dream
the Arab appears—tired, disheveled, black with soot, his face ravaged—takes the child and vanishes. The fire-watcher falls asleep,
really asleep.

XIII

At dawn, shivering and damp, he emerges from the cover of the
rocks, polishes his glasses and once more he is the little scholar who
has some kind of future before him. Five, bare, black hills, and
slender wisps of blue-gray smoke rising from them. The observation
post juts out over the bare landscape like a great demon grinning
with white windows. For a moment it seems as though the forest had
never burned down but had simply pulled up its roots and gone off
on a journey, far off on a journey, far off to the sea, for instance,
which has suddenly come into view. The air is chilly. He adjusts
his rumpled clothes, does up the last surviving button, rubs his
hands to warm them, then treads softly among the smoking embers,
light of foot. The first rays of the sun hit his bald patch. There is a
sadness in this sudden nudity, the sadness of wars lost, blood shed
in vain. Stately clouds sail in the cold sky. Soon the first rain will
fall. He hears sounds of people everywhere. Utter destruction. Soot,
a tangle of charred timber, its wounds still smoldering, and a residue
of living branches unvisited by fire. Wherever he sets foot a thousand sparks fly. The commemorative plaques alone have survived;
more than that, they have gained luster after their baptism of fire.

There they lie, golden in the sun: Louis Schwartz of Chicago, the King of Burundi and his People.

He enters the burned building, climbs the singed stairs. Everything is still glowing hot. It is as though he were making his way through hell. He arrives at his room. The fire has visited it in his absence and held its riot of horror and glee. Shall we start with the books burned to ashes? Or the contorted telephone? Or perhaps the binoculars fused to a lump? The map of the area has miraculously survived, is only blackened a bit at the edges. Gay fire kittens are still frolicking in the pillow and blankets. He turns his gaze to the fire-smoking hills, frowns—there, out of the smoke and haze, the ruined village appears before his eyes; born anew in its basic outlines as an abstract drawing, as all things past and buried. He smiles to himself, a thin smile. Then abruptly it dies on his face. Directly under him, in the bluish abyss at the foot of the building, he sees the one in charge of forests who is edging his way to old age, wrapped in an old windbreaker, his face blue with cold. How has this one sprung up here, all of a sudden?

The old one throws his gray head back and sends up a look full of hatred. Looking down upon the man from his high post, his own eyes would be faintly contemptuous in any case. For a few seconds they stay thus, their eyes fixed on each other; at last the fire-watcher gives his employer a fatuous smile of recognition and slowly starts coming down to him. The old man approaches him with quick, mad steps. He would tear him to pieces if he could. He is near collapse with fury and pain. In a choking voice he demands the whole story, at once.

But there is no story, is there? There just isn't anything to tell. All there is, is: Suddenly the fire sprang up. I lifted the receiver—the line was dead. That's it. The child had to be saved.

The rest is obvious. Yes, the fire-watcher feels for the forest too. He has grown extremely attached to it during the spring, the summer, and half the autumn. So attached, in fact, that (to tell the truth, for once) he hasn't managed to learn a single line, actually.

He feels that the old man would like to sink to the ground and beat his head against some rock, would tear out the last of his white hair. The late fire-watcher is surprised. Because the forests are insured, aren't they (at least they ought to be, in his humble and practical opinion), and the fire won't be deducted from the budget of the old man's department, will it? Right now (this morning has found him amazingly clearheaded), he would very much like to be told about other forest fires. He is willing to bet that they were quite puny ones.

Except that now, ghostlike through the smoke, the firemen appear, accompanied by some fat and perspiring policemen. Soon he is surrounded by uniforms. Some of the men drop to the ground with exhaustion. Though the fire has not been completely tracked down as yet, they have already unearthed a startling piece of intelligence.

It has been arson.

Yes, arson. The smell of morning dew comes mingled with a smell of kerosene.

The old man is shattered.

"Arson?" he turns to the fire-watcher.

But the other smiles gently.

The investigation is launched at once. First the firemen, who are supposed to write a report. They draw the fire-watcher aside, take out large sheets of paper, ornate ballpoints, and then it appears that they have difficulty with the language, with phrasing and spelling. They are embarrassed. Tactfully he helps them, spells out words, formulates their sentences for them. They are very grateful.

"What have *you* lost in the fire?" they inquire sympathetically.

"Oh, nothing of importance. Some clothes and a few textbooks. Nothing to worry about."

By the time they are through, it is far into the morning. The Arab and the child appear from nowhere, led by two policemen. If he will be careful not to let his glance encounter those burning eyes, he may possibly sleep in peace in the nights to come. Two tough-looking sergeants improvise a kind of emergency interrogation cell among the rocks, place him on a stone and start cross-examining him. For hours they persist, and that surprises him—the plodding tenacity, the diligence, page upon written page. A veritable research is being compiled before his eyes. The sun climbs to its zenith. He is hungry, thirsty. His interrogators chew enormous sandwiches and do not offer him a crumb. His glasses mist with sweat. A queer autumn day. Inside the building, they are conducting a simultaneous interrogation of the Arab, in Arabic, eked out with gestures. Only the questions are audible.

The old forest manager dodges back and forth between the two interrogations, adding questions of his own, noting down replies.

The interrogators have their subject with his back against the rock, they repeat the same questions over and over. A foul stench rises from the burned forest, as though a huge carcass were rotting away all around them. The interrogation gains momentum. A big bore. What did he see? What did he hear? What did he do? It's insulting, this insistence upon the tangible—as though that were the main point, as though there weren't some idea involved here.

About noon his questioners change, two new ones appear and start the whole process over again. The subject is dripping with sweat. How humiliating, to be interrogated thus baldly on scorched earth, on rocks, after a sleepless night. The tedium of it. The fire-watcher spits, grows angry, loses his temper. He removes his glasses and his senses go numb. He starts contradicting himself. At three o'clock he breaks in their hands, is prepared to suggest the Arab as a possible clue.

This, of course, is what they have been waiting for. They suspected the Arab all along. Promptly they handcuff him, and then all at once everything is rapidly wound up. The police drivers start their cars. The Arab is bundled into one of them and there is a gratified expression in his eyes now, a sense of achievement. The child clings to him desperately. Autumn clouds, autumn sadness, everything is flat. Stupid. Suddenly he walks over to the forest manager and boldly demands that something be done for the child. The other makes no reply. His old eyes wander over the lost forest as though in parting. This old one is going mad as well, his senses are growing confused. He stares at the fire-watcher with vacant eyes as though he, too, had lost the words, as though he understood nothing. The fire-watcher repeats his demand in a loud voice. The old man steps nearer.

"What?" he mumbles in a feeble voice, his eyes watery. Suddenly he throws himself at the fire-watcher, attacks him with shriveled fists, hits out at him. With difficulty, the firemen pull him back. To be sure, he blames only this one here. Yes, this one with the books, with the dim glasses, with that smug cynicism of his.

The policemen extricate the fire-watcher and whisk him into one of their cars. They treat him roughly, something of the old man's hostility has stuck to them. Before he has time to say good-bye to the place where he has spent nearly six months he is being borne away at a mad pace toward town. They dump him on one of the side streets. He enters the first restaurant he comes to and gorges himself to bursting point. Afterward he paces the streets, bearded, dirty, sunburned—a savage. The first dusty rain has already smirched the pavements.

At night, in some shabby hotel room, he is free to have a proper sleep, to sleep free from obligations for the first time, just sleep without any further dimensions. Except that he will not fall asleep, will only go on drowsing. Green forests will spring up before his troubled eyes. He may yet smart with sorrow and yearning, may feel constricted because he is shut in by four walls, not three.

And so it will be the day after, and perhaps all the days to come. The solitude has proved a success. True, his notes have been burned along with the books, but if anyone thinks that he does not remember—he does.

Yet he has become a stranger now in his so-familiar town. He seems to have forgotten already. A new generation is breaking into the circles. His waggish friends meet him, slap him on the back, and with ugly grins say, "We hear your forest burned down!" As we said, he is still young. But his real friends have given him up in despair. He drops in on them, winter nights, shivering with cold— wet dog begging for fire and light—and they scowl and ask:

"Well, what now?"

Translated by Miriam Arad

SOURCES

Mendele Mocher Sforim. "Shem and Japheth on the Train," *Kol Kitvei Mendele Mocher Sforim* (Berlin: Moriah, 1922), vol. 5, pp. 55–70. Translated by Walter Lever, *Israel Argosy* 2 (Spring 1952), 7–32.

Y. L. Peretz. "Scenes from Limbo," *Kol Kitvei Y. L. Peretz* (Tel Aviv: Dvir, 1951), vol. 3, pp. 185–203. Translated by the editor for this volume.

M. Z. Feierberg. "In the Evening," *K'tavim* (Tel Aviv: Dvir, 1958), pp. 19–37. Translated by Hillel Halkin, *Whither? and Other Stories* (Philadelphia: Jewish Publication Society, 1972), pp. 81–105.

Ahad Ha-am. "Imitation and Assimilation," *Kol Kitvei Ahad Ha-am* (Tel Aviv: Dvir, 1956), pp. 88–89. Translated by Leon Simon, *Selected Essays of Ahad Ha-am* (Philadephia: Jewish Publication Society, 1912), pp. 107–124.

H. N. Bialik. "The Short Friday," *Kol Kitvei H. N. Bialik* (Tel Aviv: Dvir, 1953), pp. 140–144. Translated by I. M. Lask, *Aftergrowth and Other Stories* (Philadelphia: Jewish Publication Society, 1939), pp. 191–216.

―――. "Revealment and Concealment in Language," *Kol Kitvei H. N. Bialik* (Tel Aviv: Dvir, 1953), pp. 191–193. Translated by Jacob Sloan, *Commentary,* vol. 9–10 (February 1950), pp. 171–175.

Y. H. Brenner. "The Way Out," *K'tavim* (Tel Aviv: Am Oved, 1950), vol. 2, pp. 298–311. Translated by Yosef Schacter, *Hebrew Short Stories.* Edited by S. Y. Penueli and A. Ukhmani. (Tel Aviv: Institute for Translation of Hebrew Literature, 1965), vol. 1, pp. 121–133.

Asher Barash. "At Heaven's Gate," *Kitvei Asher Barash* (Tel Aviv: Masada, 1961), pp. 500–504. Translated by Yosef Schacter, *Hebrew Short Stories.* Edited by S. Y. Penueli and A. Ukhmani. (Tel Aviv: Institute for Translation of Hebrew Literature, 1965), vol. 1, pp. 200–211.

S. Y. Agnon. "Agunot," *Kol Sipurav shel S. Y. Agnon* (Tel Aviv: Schocken Books, 1953), vol. 2, pp. 405–416. Translated by Baruch Hochman in *Twenty-One Stories by S. Y. Agnon* (New York: Schocken Books, 1970), pp. 30–44.

————. "The Lady and the Peddler," *Kol Sipurav shel S. Y. Agnon* (Tel Aviv: Schocken Books, 1953), vol. 6, pp. 92–102. Translated by Robert Alter, *Commentary*, vol. 42, no. 6 (December 1966), pp. 37–42.

————. "At the Outset of the Day," *Kol Sipurav shel S. Y. Agnon* (Tel Aviv: Schocken Books, 1953); vol. 7, pp. 171–177. Translated by David Segal, *Twenty-One Stories by S. Y. Agnon* (New York: Schocken Books, 1970), pp. 252–260.

————. "Forevermore," *Kol Sipurav shel S. Y. Agnon* (Tel Aviv: Schocken Books, 1953), vol. 8, pp. 315–334. Translated by Joel Blocker, [revised for this volume by Robert Alter], *Israeli Stories*. Edited by Joel Blocker. (New York: Schocken Books, 1962), pp. 232–256.

Haim Hazaz. "Rahamim," *Avanim Rotkhot* (Tel Aviv: Am Oved, 1965), pp. 227–244. Translated by I. M. Lask, *The Jewish Caravan*. Edited by Leo W. Schwarz. (New York: Holt, Rinehart & Winston, 1935), pp. 785–791.

————. "The Sermon," *Reikhayim Shevurim* (Tel Aviv: Am Oved, 1968), pp. 210–217. Translated by I. M. Lask, *The Jewish Caravan*. Edited by Joel Blocker (New York: Schocken Books, 1961), pp. 66–86.

S. Yizhar. "The Prisoner," *Arba'ah Sipurim* (Tel Aviv: HaKibbutz Ha-Me'ukhad, 1959), pp. 115–138. Translated by V. C. Rycus, *Israeli Stories*. Edited by Joel Blocker. (New York: Schocken Books, 1962), pp. 152–174.

Yehuda Amichai. "The Times My Father Died," *BaRuakh HaNora'ah HaZot* (Jerusalem and Tel Aviv: Schocken Books, 1973), pp. 132–140. Translated by Yosef Schacter, *Hebrew Short Stories*. Edited by S. Y. Penueli and A. Ukhmani. (Tel Aviv: Institute for Translation of Hebrew Literature, 1965), vol. 2, pp. 270–279.

Amos Oz. "Before His Time," *Artzot HaTan* (Tel Aviv: Masada, 1965), pp. 59–74. Translated for this volume by Gavriel Moses.

A. B. Yehoshua: "Facing the Forests," *Mul HaYe-arot* (Tel Aviv: Ha-Kibbutz HaMe'ukhad, 1970), pp. 9–55. Translated by Miriam Arad, *Three Days and a Child* (New York: Doubleday & Company, 1970), pp. 131–174.

SUGGESTIONS FOR FURTHER READING (*in English*)

ORIGINAL WORKS

The following list is limited to books by the authors included in this anthology which are available in English translation. For other modern Hebrew writers available in English, and for translations appearing in periodicals or miscellaneous collections only, one should consult the exhaustive bibliography compiled by Yohai Goell, *Bibliography of Modern Hebrew Literature in English Translation,* Jerusalem: Israel Universities Press, 1968.

Mendele Mocher Sforim. *Fishke the Lame.* Translated by Gerald Stillman (New York: Thomas Yoseloff, Publisher, 1960).

———. *The Nag.* Translated by Moshe Spiegel (New York: Beechhurst, 1955).

———. *The Travels of Benjamin III.* Translated by Moshe Spiegel (New York: Schocken Books, 1949). All the Mendele translations were done from the Yiddish versions of books which the author himself recast into Hebrew.

Peretz, Y. L. *In This World and the Next.* Translated by Moshe Spiegel (New York: Thomas Yoseloff, Publisher, 1958).

———. *Prince of the Ghetto.* Translated and adapted by Maurice Samuel (New York: Alfred A. Knopf, 1948).

———. *Selected Stories.* Edited by E. Greenberg and Irving Howe (New York: Schocken Books, 1973). All the Peretz items are drawn from his Yiddish stories.

Feierberg, M. Z. *Whither? and Other Stories.* Translated by Hillel Halkin (Philadelphia: Jewish Publication Society, 1972).

Ahad Ha-am. *Selected Essays.* Translated by Leon Simon (Philadelphia: Jewish Publication Society, 1912).

Bialik, H. N. *Aftergrowth and Other Stories.* Translated by I. M. Lask (Philadelphia: Jewish Publication Society, 1939).

————. *Complete Poetic Works.* Translated by Israel Efros (New York: Histadruth Ivrith of America, 1948).

Brenner, Y. H. *Breakdown and Bereavement.* Translated by Hillel Halkin (Ithaca: Cornell University Press, 1971).

Barash, Asher. *Pictures from a Brewery.* Translated by Katie Kaplan (New York: Bobbs-Merrill Company, 1974).

Agnon, S. Y. *The Bridal Canopy.* Translated by I. M. Lask (New York: Schocken Books, 1967).

————. *A Guest for the Night.* Translated by Misha Louvish (New York: Schocken Books, 1968).

————. *In The Heart of the Seas.* Translated by I. M. Lask (New York: Schocken Books, 1948).

————. *Twenty-One Stories.* Edited by Nahum Glatzer (New York: Schocken Books, 1970).

————. *Two Tales.* Translated by Walter Lever (New York: Schocken Books, 1966).

Hazaz, Haim. *Gates of Bronze.* Translated by Gershon Levi (Philadelphia: Jewish Publication Society, 1975).

————. *Mori Sa'id.* Translated by Ben Halpern (New York: Abelard-Schuman, 1956).

Yizhar, S. *Midnight Convoy.* Translated by Miriam Arad, Misha Louvish, and Reuven Ben-Yosef (Jerusalem: Israel Universities Press, 1973).

Amichai, Yehuda. *Not of This Time, Not of This Place.* Translated by Shlomo Katz (New York: Harper & Row, Publishers, 1968).

————. *Selected Poems.* Translated by Asa Gutmann and Harold Schimmel (London: Penguin Books, 1971).

————. *Songs of Jerusalem and Myself.* Translated by Harold Schimmel (New York: Harper & Row, Publishers, 1973).

Oz, Amos. *Elsewhere Perhaps.* Translated by Nicholas de Lange (New York: Harcourt Brace Jovanovich, 1973).

————. *My Michael.* Translated by Nicholas de Lange (New York: Harcourt Brace Jovanovich, 1972).

————. *Touch the Water, Touch the Wind.* Translated by Nicholas de Lange (New York: Harcourt Brace Jovanovich, 1974).

Yehoshua, A. B. *Three Days and a Child.* Translated by Miriam Arad (New York: Doubleday & Company, 1970).

CRITICISM AND LITERARY HISTORY

The most balanced, informed, and precise survey of modern Hebrew literature is the entry under the heading by Ezra Spicehandler in the *Encyclopaedia Judaica* (New York: Macmillan Company, 1971), VIII, pp. 175–208, with bibliography on p. 215.

The following English books may also be useful to consult:

Alter, Robert. *After the Tradition* (New York: E. P. Dutton & Company, 1969). Includes discussions of Agnon, Amichai, Bialik, Yizhar, and a general essay on the Haskalah and its aftermath.

Bavli, Hillel. "The Modern Renaissance of Hebrew Literature" in *The Jews, Their History, Culture, and Religion*. Edited by Louis Finkelstein. (New York: Harper & Row, Publishers, 1949), II, pp. 567–601.

Halkin, Simon. *Modern Hebrew Literature: Trends and Values* (New York: Schocken Books, 1950). A perceptive thematic overview of modern Hebrew literature from its beginnings to the 1940s.

Rabinovich, Isaiah. *Major Trends in Modern Hebrew Fiction*. Translated by M. Roston. (Chicago: University of Chicago Press, 1968). Comprised of detailed discussions of important writers from Mendele to Agnon. Many of the critical discriminations are debatable, or couched in fuzzy terminology, but a general sense of patterns and generational change does emerge, and attempts at textual analysis are made.

Silberschlag, Eisig. *From Renaissance to Renaissance* (New York: Ktav Publishing House, 1971). This survey of Hebrew literature from the end of the medieval Spanish period through modern times suffers from the attempt to be encylopedic, the historical exposition overloaded with descriptive accounts of obscure and non-literary works; and the revisionist interpretative view of modern Hebrew literature is insufficiently argued. Nevertheless, the study makes available abundant factual details for the antecedents of modern Hebrew literature.

Spiegel, Shalom. *Hebrew Reborn* (New York: Macmillan Company, 1930; paperback reprint, New York: Schocken Books, 1962). Gracefully written and intelligent, it explains the nature of the revived language and provides useful biographical essays on important Haskalah writers, though the critical discussions of Bialik, Tchernichovsky, and Ahad Ha-am are rather dated.

Wallenrod, Reuben. *The Literature of Modern Israel* (New York: Abelard-Schuman, 1956). Tends to substitute lyric effusion for critical analysis, and is often imprecise, but it does provide a detailed survey of Hebrew literature in Palestine and Israel from the turn of the century to the 1950s, including minor writers.

Yudkin, Leon I. *Escape Into Siege: A Survey of Israeli Literature Today* (London and Boston: Routledge and Kegan Paul, 1974). This is the only descriptive overview in English of Hebrew prose and poetry from the 1940s through the early 1970s. Some of the characterizations of individual works are useful, but much of the book is taken up with mere plot-summary, and the critical vocabulary is often not adequate to the complexities of the issues it tries to engage.

Two book-length critical studies of S. Y. Agnon have appeared in English. Arnold Band's *Nostalgia and Nightmare: A Study in the Fiction of S. Y. Agnon* (Berkeley and Los Angeles: University of California Press, 1968) is an ambitious developmental survey of all the important stories and novels through the 1950s with elaborate bibliographical appendices. Baruch Hochman's *The Fiction of S. Y. Agnon* (Ithaca: Cornell University Press, 1970) is a briefer evaluation of Agnon's major phases with a sharp formulation of basic critical issues.